OUR PALESTINE QUESTION

GEOFFREY LEVIN

Our Palestine Question

ISRAEL AND AMERICAN JEWISH DISSENT, 1948–1978

Yale

UNIVERSITY PRESS

NEW HAVEN & LONDON

Published with assistance from the Mary Cady Tew Memorial Fund.

Yale University Press books may be purchased in quantity for
educational, business, or promotional use. For information, please email
sales.press@yale.edu (U.S. office) or sales@yaleup.co.uk (U.K. office).

Set in Scala type by IDS Infotech Ltd.
Printed in the United States of America.

Library of Congress Control Number: 2023935033
ISBN 978-0-300-26785-3 (hardcover : alk. paper)

A catalogue record for this book is available from the British Library.

This paper meets the requirements of ANSI/NISO Z39.48-1992
(Permanence of Paper).

10 9 8 7 6 5 4 3 2

To Jenny and Gabby

CONTENTS

List of Abbreviations   ix

Introduction: The Muddy Roads of Shatila   1

1   Zionism's Wayward Son   18

2   A Yiddishist's Dissent   56

3   An American Light unto the Jewish Nation   78

4   "Such Distinctions Cannot Be Maintained"   109

5   Anti-Zionists for Israel   152

6   Zionists for Palestine   186

Conclusion: Diaspora and Dissent   217

Notes   227

Acknowledgments   279

Index   287

ABBREVIATIONS

ADL	Anti-Defamation League
AFME	American Friends of the Middle East
AFSC	American Friends Service Committee
AIPAC	American Israel Public Affairs Committee
AJA	American Jewish Archives
AJAZ	American Jewish Alternatives to Zionism
AJC	American Jewish Committee
AJCAO	American Jewish Committee Archives Online
AJCongress	American Jewish Congress
API	Americans for Progressive Israel
AZC	American Zionist Council
the Center	The Arab League's Arab Information Center in New York City
CJP	Committee for Justice and Peace in the Holy Land
CONAME	Committee on New Alternatives in the Middle East
the Council	American Council for Judaism

IAAA	Institute for Arab American Affairs
ICIPP	Israeli Council for Israeli-Palestinian Peace
ISA	Israel State Archives
JCRC	Jewish Community Relations Council
JLP	Jewish Liberation Project
JTA	Jewish Telegraphic Agency
JUJ	Jews for Urban Justice
MERIP	Middle East Research and Information Project
NCRAC	National Communal Relations Advisory Council
OAS	Organization of Arab Students in the United States
YAPI	Young Americans for Progressive Israel

OUR PALESTINE QUESTION

Introduction: The Muddy Roads of Shatila

ON A COLD AND RAINY NOVEMBER DAY, a sixty-five-year-old American rabbi trudged down the muddy roads of Shatila, a Palestinian refugee camp on the outskirts of Beirut in Lebanon. When the rabbi and his colleagues stopped, refugees gathered around them in a scene of "disappointment, frustration, [and] despair." Gaunt men and "children, big-eyed and thin" walked up and clutched the rabbi's raincoat. Several began chanting in Arabic, "We want to go home!" Weary, broken women watched silently from their tents as rain and wind chilled their bare feet. Guilt overcame the rabbi. "In my deepest heart, I said the prayer of confession," the rabbi wrote, referring to a prayer recited on Yom Kippur, the fast of atonement. "*Anachnu Chatanu*." We have sinned.[1]

One could imagine this scene taking place recently, or at least some time after the 1982 massacre that made Shatila infamous. Yet it was 1953 when Rabbi Morris Lazaron walked through the Shatila refugee camp, witnessing firsthand the suffering of Palestinian families who had lost their homes during the war that accompanied Israel's creation in 1948. The "illimitable misery" of the refugees, to use Lazaron's words, had a decisive impact on the former head rabbi of the prestigious Baltimore Hebrew Congregation. After his trip, Rabbi Lazaron began calling on the Israeli government to recognize the right of Palestine's Arab refugees to return to their prewar homes and urged the Jewish state to admit 100,000 of them into the country immediately.[2]

Lazaron felt that the Jewish historical experience should compel all Jews to support the Palestinian refugees. As members of what he called "the tribe of the wandering feet," Lazaron pressed fellow American Jews to remember that they, too, were once "strangers in the land of Egypt." Jewish identity weighed heavily on the rabbi's mind as he considered how to respond to Palestinian suffering. Yet the hidden context of the rabbi's trip reveals that the stakes of his response extended far beyond the realm of Jewish ethics. Lazaron's visit to Lebanon had been organized and financed by a secretly CIA-funded advocacy organization called American Friends of the Middle East (AFME), a group created to give Americans a more sympathetic picture of the Arab side of the Israeli-Arab conflict. AFME published Lazaron's book about the trip in 1955, apparently as part of a broader public relations effort that aimed to make it easier for United States officials to pressure Israel to accept the return of 75,000 Palestinian refugees.[3]

The CIA was far from the only government body interested in American Jewish responses to the Palestinian refugee crisis. Lazaron articulated his lament on a playing field where various governmental actors—Israeli, American, and Arab—all jockeyed to shape U.S. public opinion surrounding the Palestinian refugee question. Just as AFME was organizing Lazaron's trip, Israeli diplomats were quietly working to undermine both the Jewish newspaper that Lazaron wrote for and the anti-Zionist Jewish group he represented, the American Council for Judaism, which in turn had begun fostering warm ties with Arab officials. The American Jewish debate over Palestinian rights involved a struggle over Jewish identity, as Lazaron's words reflect. But as his broader story shows, the debate also is, and always has been, part of a high-stakes political struggle between government officials and others over the future of Israel, the fate of the Palestinians, and the orientation of American foreign policy toward the Middle East.

There is a narrative about the trajectory of the American Jewish relationship with Israel that pervades all corners of the organized Jewish community today. "For millions of secular-minded American Jews, Israel was the glue. Israel was the cause," declared conservative commentator Bret Stephens at the American Jewish Committee's (AJC) 2022 Global Forum. "Zionism was an effective and powerful and emotionally satisfying substitute for religious observance," he continued, bemoaning that in contrast, "at the height of last year's war [the 2021 Gaza crisis], so many young American Jews were eagerly signing letters denouncing Israeli behavior."[4]

While young American Jewish letter-signers may not appreciate Stephens's tone, they probably would not dispute the gist of his historical observation, which is considered common knowledge both in Jewish political commentary and in scholarly works. For decades, American Jews had rallied around the Jewish state, with Israel uniting American Jewry in a way that nothing else could, including religion. But then at some point, according to this telling, young left-wing Jews began criticizing Israel over its policies toward the Palestinians, breaking with past generations to shatter this once-sacred consensus and imperil any semblance of Jewish unity.[5]

Despite its ubiquity, this narrative is flawed in its basic assumptions. Ever since an estimated 750,000 Palestinians lost their homes amidst Israel's birth in 1948, there have been American Jews deeply unsettled by Israeli policies toward both the Palestinian refugees and Arabs living under Israeli rule. These critics of old did not consist only of a few stray rabbis like Morris Lazaron, but in fact extended well into the American Jewish establishment—including leaders and staff members of the AJC. The collective amnesia with regard to this history has been complete: none of the over one thousand AJC members in Stephens's audience likely had any idea that in 1957 their organization's president confronted Prime Minister David Ben-Gurion, urging him to liberalize Israel's policies toward its Arab citizens. The audience would not have known that at an AJC gala sixty-six years before their own, the Jewish advocacy organization announced a plan to aid Palestinian refugees that it ultimately shelved in response to Israeli pressure. And unless they had sifted through faded yellow papers in their archives, they could not have known that the first Middle East expert on the AJC's staff, Don Peretz, lost his job because Israeli diplomats did not like his research on the Palestinian refugee issue.

Stephens and his audience cannot be faulted for being unaware of these past events because they are, more or less, unknown. Histories of American Jewish life make almost no mention of any communal concern for the Palestinians in the years after Israel's creation, implying that it emerged, at the earliest, in the 1970s. Even studies of Jewish anti-Zionism and non-Zionism during Israel's early years have tended to neglect the Palestinian question, focusing instead on debates over the role of nationalism in Jewish identity.[6]

Our Palestine Question reveals that Israel's policies toward the Palestinians did indeed create dilemmas for American Jewish individuals, organizations, and publications during the first three decades of the new country's history. These American Jews engaged in rhetoric and activities that aimed to help the Palestinians for a confluence of reasons that included anxieties about antisemitism, demands for consistency in values, and inspiration through direct contact with Arab and left-wing Israeli voices. These efforts arose in a context of "disconnect" between dominant forms of American Jewish liberalism and Israel's overall disposition toward the Palestinians. This disconnect emerged because Zionism, as implemented in Israel, contradicted some of the core values that American Jews had championed in their push for an inclusive America. Jewish advocacy organizations spent decades working to ensure that the United States would not simply be a country premised on advancing the interests of the white Christian majority, but rather a secular state with equality for all.[7]

As a self-declared Jewish state, Israel prioritized Jewish interests over the needs of non-Jews born in the lands that it controlled. This was clear in its immigration policy, which welcomed all Jews while preventing Palestinian refugees from returning to their homes. It also manifested itself domestically in that until 1966 Israel's Arab minority, despite receiving Israeli citizenship in 1952, faced many onerous military government restrictions that Jewish Israelis barely knew about. Israeli leaders justified policies that protected and privileged the ethno-national majority in part as a defensive response to centuries of anti-Jewish persecution, expulsions, and genocide in Europe and elsewhere. In contrast, for many American Jews, this same history led them to identify with other beleaguered minorities and dispossessed peoples. While Israel and Jewish refugees most often earned American Jewish sympathy, it should be no surprise that there was always some undercurrent of American Jewish empathy for the Palestinians.

The fact that this historical undercurrent is so unknown is, to some extent, the result of concerted campaigns. From the beginning, Israeli diplomats watched American Jewish interest in Palestinian rights issues with deep suspicion. Declassified Israeli foreign ministry files reveal that some of Israel's most celebrated diplomats secretly plotted to undermine American Jews who wrote about the sensitive question of Palestinian refugees, often succeeding in getting them removed from positions of influence. These diplomats persuaded reluctant employers to drop "troublesome" employees whom they had once trusted, quietly sidelining various American Jewish efforts to highlight or resolve Palestinian rights issues in the 1950s, 1960s, and 1970s.

These findings call for a rethinking of the very nature of the early Israel–American Jewish relationship. So much written about this era focuses on the emotional affinities that American Jews held for Israel, but far less has been written on Israel's views of American Jewry. Rather than acting from a place of emotional connection and intracommunal kinship, Israeli officials acted in pragmatic ways toward the American Jewish community in the context of a wider public relations battle that raged between them and pro-Arab voices, which included Arab diplomats and some in the U.S. government. Israel during its early years was in a precarious place as it faced an economic crisis, high security costs, and the expense of resettling hundreds of thousands of Jewish immigrants. To meet these budgetary needs, the Israeli government turned to American Jews, who between 1948 and 1956 sent Israel more than $700 million in charitable donations and over $270 million in cash from bond sales, a combined sum that would total over $10 billion in 2022 dollars. American supporters of Israel, including Jews, also lobbied elected officials on diplomatic issues and successfully urged the government to send economic aid to Israel, which totaled $450 million (around $5 billion today) in combined loans and grants during that same eight-year stretch. Since the young country was reliant on American Jewish support in so many ways, perhaps it should be expected that its officials acted to ensure that the question of Palestinian rights did not weaken American Jewry's commitment to Israel, harm Israel's public image, and damage the U.S.-Israel relationship more broadly. Israel was, in short, acting as any state might given the circumstances.[8]

To a certain extent, this book shows that Israeli leaders instrumentalized American Jewish organizations, which highlights the power of the young state and the political savvy of its diplomats. But to focus only on that would be an oversimplification. American Jewish organizations first had to yield some of their autonomy to the Jewish state. Doing so involved American Jews beginning to conceptualize their interests and ideals not as distinct from those of Israel but as identical to them—a process that blurred crucial differences between the community and the state. This required that these organizations turn away from a distinctive American Jewish identity as a historically dispossessed minority that has thrived in a liberal secular state and instead adopt the values of Israel, a country premised on meeting the needs of an ethno-national majority. To frame the question underlying this shift in biblical terms, as Rabbi Lazaron might have: Is the core of Jewish identity remembering that "we were once strangers in the land of Egypt"? Or is it all about maintaining a restored Kingdom of David?

American Jews of the 1940s, 1950s, and beyond often had remarkably deep conversations about the meaning of Israel's power over Palestinians. In recovering this history, *Our Palestine Question* serves not so much as a starting point for discussion but more precisely as a medium that will inform conversations that are already taking place today and engage them with lost voices from the past. From there, one can see how the path to the present involved not fate but crucial decisions made over the course of decades that have shaped the politics of today surrounding Israel, the Palestinians, and the nature of transnational Jewish politics.

In delving into this history, this book sheds light on political dynamics that at times feel very distant from those of the present. The American Jewish establishment did not always view anti-Zionism as inherently anti-semitic. Some Jewish community leaders considered themselves "non-Zionist" until years after Israel's founding. American Jewish institutions that had been established long before 1948 took time to accommodate themselves to the reality of Jewish statehood, a process that involved countless discussions about what Jewish sovereignty overseas meant for Jewish citizens of the United States. Jews had been a perpetual minority, so many American Jewish institutions had mobilized around liberal and left-leaning ideologies designed to protect minority groups and those seeking refuge. Suddenly, after 1948, there was a Jewish state that not only ruled over a non-Jewish minority group but also denied the right of refugees to return to their homes on the basis of their ethnicity and religion. Israel's birth created a sense of cognitive dissonance for these American Jewish organizations as they attempted to come to terms with Israel's power over the Palestinians without abandoning the ideologies that they regularly used to protect the rights of Jews outside the Jewish state.[9]

The mainstream organization that struggled most with these questions was the American Jewish Committee, which Israel considered the single most politically influential Jewish group in the United States during the 1950s. As political scientist Charles Liebman wrote, "There is no question that . . . for more than a decade [after 1948], the American Jewish Committee was the Jewish organization to whose views Israeli leaders were most sensitive," since they perceived the AJC "as the Jewish organization with the best access to American policymakers and as the most representative of wealthy American Jews." While in later decades Zionist groups like the American Israel Public Affairs Committee (AIPAC) and umbrella organizations like the Conference of Presidents of Major Jewish Organizations grew to hold greater political sway, at the start of the 1950s neither of these groups yet existed. While compared with the AJC, Zionist groups had far greater membership, they lacked unity, and no individual Zionist organization could match AJC leaders in terms of financial strength and political connections. So, for a pivotal period from the 1940s to the 1960s, one of Israel's most important links to Washington—and to American Jewish pocketbooks—lay with the American Jewish Committee.[10]

The AJC's leadership, however, was not exactly sure how it wished to relate to the Jewish state. Established in 1906 by an affluent and "Americanized" Reform Jewish elite to advocate for persecuted Jewish minorities throughout the world, with the passing of World War II, the AJC began to conceive of itself as a universalist human rights organization. With regard to Israel, the AJC stood apart from many other Jewish groups because of its reluctance to endorse Zionism, referring to itself as "non-Zionist" until 1967. The group's uneasiness about Jewish nationalism stemmed in part from its leadership's belief that Jews were solely a religious group, rather than a nationality. But it also came amidst fears that Zionism would potentially raise doubts about American Jews' loyalty to the United States, a "dual loyalty" anxiety stoked by both Zionist and anti-Zionist rhetoric. This concern prompted AJC president Jacob Blaustein to compel Israeli prime minister Ben-Gurion to "clarify" that Israel made no claims on the

AJC leaders meet with President John F. Kennedy in 1962.
From left to right: Jacob Blaustein, honorary AJC president; former U.S. senator
Herbert H. Lehman of New York, honorary AJC vice president; President Kennedy;
Irving M. Engel, honorary AJC president; Louis Caplan, AJC president; John Slawson,
AJC executive vice president. Photo Credit: Abbie Rowe. White House Photographs.
John F. Kennedy Presidential Library and Museum, Boston.

political loyalties of non-Israeli Jews in an agreement known as the 1950
Blaustein–Ben-Gurion "exchange of views."[11]

Much of this book centers on the AJC's internal struggles and the group's
interactions with various Israeli and Arab officials. In the aftermath of
1948, AJC officials viewed Israel as a potential source of problems for
American Jews, in part because of its policies toward the Palestinians, but
eventually they would come to see the fate of Israel and American Jewry as
inextricably linked. That newfound perception would lead the AJC to begin
including the task of defending Israel's image within its mission to combat
antisemitism, a shift made subtly despite its historic implications.[12]

Jewish anti-Zionism, which has a varied history in America that precedes
the creation of Israel by decades, factors into this story in a chapter focus-

ing on the American Council for Judaism (referred to here as "the Council"). Formed in 1942 by a group of Reform rabbis unsettled by their denomination's endorsement of Zionist aims, the Council's concerns about Zionism echoed those of the AJC, but it felt that the AJC's non-Zionism was too mild a response. Rather, Council leaders publicly campaigned against Zionism, viewing Jewish statehood as a potential catastrophe for American foreign policy, for their conception of Judaism, and for the position of Jews in the United States. The Council instead envisioned Palestine's future as a nonsectarian democracy for all its citizens and encouraged U.S. leaders to coordinate with the United Nations to settle displaced Holocaust survivors in countries throughout the world. After the Council failed to prevent Israel's creation in 1948, a schism slowly formed within the organization as some of its leaders began advocating for Palestinians while others, influenced in part by Israeli officials, urged for a much more subdued approach. The conflict between the Council's two factions would ultimately rip the group apart at its seams.[13]

In connection with the AJC and the Council, this book's first five chapters delve into the lives of an interconnected set of individuals who collectively could be termed the lost "first generation" of American Jews to advocate for Palestinians, given that they were active between 1948 and 1967. The Jews who made up this loose network included academic Don Peretz (1922–2017), journalist William Zukerman (1885–1961), attorney and philanthropist James Marshall (1896–1987) of the AJC, Rabbi Elmer Berger (1908–1994) of the Council, and their affiliates. Of these, the book's most central figure is Peretz, who was, without a doubt, more deeply involved with Palestinian affairs than any other American Jew of his generation. Born in Baltimore to an Ashkenazi American Jewish mother and a Sephardic Zionist father who had recently emigrated from Ottoman Palestine, Peretz covered the 1948 war as a journalist and in 1949 became the first American Jew to volunteer to aid displaced Palestinians. He then wrote the very first doctoral dissertation on the Palestinian refugee problem and became a leading academic expert on the topic. In 1956, the AJC hired Peretz to put together a Palestinian refugee aid initiative, which Israeli diplomats worked hard to oppose.

This book also excavates the story of a fascinating Palestinian who was Peretz's acquaintance and, in some ways, his mirror image. Born the same

year as Peretz to a Palestinian mother and a Syrian father, Fayez Sayegh
(1922–1980) was completing a PhD in philosophy at Georgetown University when the creation of Israel in 1948 prevented him from ever returning
to Tiberias, the city in Palestine/Israel where he had grown up. In the early
1950s, Sayegh began associating with AFME but was likely unaware of its
covert CIA funding. AFME sponsored his lectures about Palestine and other Arab causes, providing him a platform in Washington and elsewhere in
the country. When the Arab League opened a new public relations office in
the United States in 1955, Sayegh became its chief spokesman and served
as the office's director during the critical year of 1956 when the Suez Crisis
and ensuing Sinai War shook up international politics. Given that Sayegh
was the most active advocate for the Palestinian cause in 1950s America,
the ways in which Jewish groups from across the political spectrum responded to him reveal much about how they conceived of the connection
between anti-Zionism and antisemitism. Though some today remember
Sayegh for his crucial role in the 1975 United Nations vote declaring Zionism a "form of racism" and for founding the Palestine Liberation Organization (PLO) Research Center, this book is the first to recall in detail his
centrality in American discourse about the Middle East in the 1950s, which,
together with his later actions, makes him arguably the most important
Palestinian voice in America until Edward Said's emergence in the 1970s.
While only one chapter focuses on Sayegh, his presence looms throughout
much of this book.[14]

Our Palestine Question ends by moving past the stories of the "first generation" of American Jews concerned with Palestinian rights to those of the
"second generation," a cohort whose history has not been lost but has often
been mischaracterized. This larger, younger, and more diverse network became vocal only after 1967. Israel's occupation of the West Bank and Gaza
that began with the Six-Day War that year exacerbated the Palestinian
plight, provoking responses from an array of voices on the New Left, including some Black and Arab American groups, that vocalized solidarity
with the Palestinians more forcefully than ever before. Some American
Jews were among those voices, but within the realm of organized American
Jewish politics, a new group pushing for Palestinian statehood emerged
not just with a leftist but also with a Zionist pedigree. Founded in 1973,

Breira: A Project of Concern in Diaspora-Israel Relations became the first national Jewish organization in the United States to advocate for the creation of a Palestinian state alongside Israel, a proposal now widely referred to as the two-state solution. Breira, which means "alternative" in Hebrew, came to this position not out of disdain for Israel but because its members believed that achieving Palestinian national self-determination would help secure Israel's future. The group's stated support for Israel, however, would not protect it from getting caught in the political crossfire between Palestinian and Israeli officials who had very different visions for the region's future.[15]

The book's chronology, which begins in the 1940s with Israel's creation, concludes with Breira's collapse in 1977–1978. This end point also corresponds with two events in the Middle East that marked the beginning of a new era. One was the election of Menachem Begin of the right-wing Likud party in 1977, bringing an end to the twenty-nine-year-long rule of Israel's Labor Party, which many left-leaning American Jews had been inclined to trust. Prime Minister Begin, meanwhile, would expand Israeli settlements in the West Bank and also embark on a controversial war in Lebanon. His tenure, however, also saw Israel sign its first peace treaty with an Arab neighbor, the Camp David Accords with Egypt, in 1978, an event that complicated the Palestinian quest for sovereignty.

Reconstructing the stories that comprise this book was challenging, involving countless interviews and a meticulous examination of aging letters located across nine U.S. states, the West Bank, and Israel, including at the Israel State Archives in Jerusalem, in Salt Lake City (where Sayegh's long-forgotten archival collection is stored), and on the floor of Peretz's widow's retirement community bungalow in Bowie, Maryland. The process highlights not only the global nature of this book's subject but also how sidelined from history its cast of characters has been. When Israeli diplomats succeeded in undermining early advocates for Palestinian rights, they not only pushed them out of their positions at that moment; they seemingly succeeded in excising them from Jewish communal memory. If history is written by the winners, as the saying goes, it makes sense that Peretz and others were so often left out of the narratives that the mainstream American Jewish community has told itself. *Our Palestine Question* restores these figures to history, filling in major gaps in our understanding of the relationship between Israel and American Jews.

Some might say that the failure of these American Jews to raise awareness of the Palestinian plight was somehow inevitable. Israeli officials certainly did not feel that way. From 1948 onward, Israeli diplomats viewed American Jews who supported Palestinian rights as a threat to the consensus that they hoped would mobilize support for Israel's diplomatic priorities. Attempts by Peretz and others to highlight the plight of Palestinian refugees ran directly counter to Israeli efforts to downplay the issue with the aim of warding off international pressure to allow refugees to return. While Israel long denied its role in displacing hundreds of thousands of Palestinians in 1948, Israel's early leaders welcomed the development and quickly sought to consolidate what they viewed as gains. The mass displacement of Palestinians meant that Israel would have a much larger Jewish majority, roughly 80 percent, rather than the narrow majority of 55 percent that the 1947 United Nations Partition Plan had envisioned for a Jewish state. The refugees' permanent absence ensured that there would be more land in Israel on which to settle new Jewish immigrants and more material wealth available for the state and for Jews in terms of agricultural land and "abandoned" residential property. It also meant, in the eyes of many Israeli Jews, that there would be fewer Palestinians in the country who were inclined to be hostile to the very existence of the Jewish state.[16]

For all these reasons, Israelis felt that keeping Palestinian refugees from returning was essential. International opinion on this key issue differed, however, even in friendly foreign capitals such as Washington. At various times, the administrations of both President Harry Truman (1945–1953) and President Dwight Eisenhower (1953–1961) pressured Israel to permit a portion of the Palestinian refugees to return in hopes that it would help alleviate Arab-Israeli tensions. Much of the drama in this book takes place during a stretch from 1955 through 1957, which coincided with rising tensions in the Middle East, the opening of the Arab League's Arab Information Center in New York, and a secret Anglo-American peace effort called Operation Alpha, which involved pressing Israel and Egypt to make concessions. According to historian Hugh Wilford, in 1955–1956 CIA officials apparently encouraged AFME, the anti-Zionist American Council for Judaism, and friendly media sources to ramp up a pro-Arab public relations campaign to help make pressure on Israel more politically viable. This American effort came in the context of the Cold War, at a time when some American officials still hoped that they could forge alliances with Egypt and other Arab countries in order to keep the region out of the Soviet sphere of influence. Israeli leaders feared that any American push for Israel to accept thousands of Palestinian refugees would soon bring about broader international pressure that could overwhelm the country at a time when the young, overburdened state might not be able to handle it. In their effort to ensure that American pressure would never become too strong, Israeli diplomats relied on friends—the American Jewish community.[17]

American Jews, as Jews, always played an important role in the Israeli worldview. After all, Zionism understands all Jews to be part of one people and one nation, and the United States was the home of the world's largest Jewish population until Israel's Jewish population surpassed it around 2006. But during Israel's early years, the fledging state needed much from the wealthier and larger American Jewish community. This included funds, which came in the form of donations and government bonds, both of which facilitated the resettlement of Jewish immigrants into Israel and the basic upbuilding of the state. It also meant diplomatic and political support, which has endured through the present day.[18]

For many years, scholarship in the field of Israel–American Jewish relations focused on American Jews' vision of Israel and their contributions to the Zionist project. This one-sided approach tended to minimize the Israeli role in the relationship, lacking a true transnational perspective. Drawing from Israeli sources, *Our Palestine Question* highlights the role of Israeli government actors in crafting American Jews' relationship with Israel, showing their attempts to "manage" Israel's most powerful diasporic constituency. In doing so, the book adds to a growing wave of research on the topic that is redefining the field of Israel–American Jewish ties by drawing more from Hebrew sources to shed light on the Israeli side of the relationship. At the same time, this book's coverage of the 1948–1967 period has been shaped by various recent works in Jewish history and Palestinian history alike that offer a fresh take on that sometimes overlooked and oversimplified era.[19]

Alongside other recent literature, this book emphasizes the constructivist, contingent character of the U.S.-Israel relationship. In her study of Israel's role in American culture, the late Amy Kaplan sought to "recover the strangeness of an affinity that has come to be seen as self-evident" with regard to the broader U.S.-Israel link. In a way, this book similarly encourages readers to step back and, rather than view American Jewry's relationship with the Israeli-Palestinian conflict as "natural," consider it a culmination of decisions made by individuals during a pivotal period. When Israel first emerged and news of its various policy decisions made its way to American ears, American Jews had to decide how to respond. Their rabbis, organizational leaders, culture-makers, and others around them needed to choose which narratives to circulate. Nothing in this relationship was necessarily preordained.[20]

Our Palestine Question also builds on a growing scholarly conversation around Israel's hidden intervention in American discourse, painting a broader picture of the young state's long reach. Amy Weiss, scholar of Israel–American Christian relations, has shown, for example, how Israel, via the Jewish Agency–backed American Zionist Council (AZC), secretly funded the most influential pro-Israel Christian group of the late 1940s. Similarly, historian Natan Aridan's work has demonstrated the great extent to which early Israeli diplomats felt a need to manage and direct the state's American Jewish supporters. Meanwhile, several scholars have recently revealed just how active a role Israeli officials played in crafting positive images of their country in American books and films, including the blockbuster *Exodus*, which helped to "Americanize" the founding of the Jewish state for U.S. audiences.[21]

This book is divided into six chapters. While they are placed loosely in chronological order, each is primarily organized around an individual or an organization. Chapter 1 focuses on Don Peretz and his work with the AJC to draft an initiative to aid Palestinian refugees, revealing how Israeli diplomats, blindsided by the initiative, intervened and undermined the effort. Chapter 2 further documents Israeli efforts to steer American Jewish conversations away from the issue of Palestinian rights by uncovering the history of a publication called the *Jewish Newsletter*. Founded in 1948 by former Yiddish journalist William Zukerman (1885–1961), the *Jewish Newsletter* stood as the only Jewish newspaper in the United States that consistently and sympathetically covered the Palestinian refugee problem throughout the 1950s. Israeli archival sources show that future ambassador Avraham Harman and other Israeli diplomats pushed for a concerted campaign to isolate Zukerman, who they claimed was "confusing Zionists" through his nuanced journalism. Their effort succeeded in minimizing Zukerman's profile in the American Jewish press, depriving mainstream Jewish readers of any credible voice critiquing Israel's policies toward the Palestinians.

Chapter 3 returns to the story of the AJC. In 1957, the AJC sent a delegation of its leaders to Israel to investigate reports that Israel's Palestinian Arab minority faced discrimination and unfair treatment, as most Arabs in Israel then lived in areas of the country subject to military rule. Israeli documents show that AJC officials questioned Israeli prime minister David Ben-Gurion about these policies, pressing him to rethink Israel's entire approach to the Arab minority. Later, the AJC set up an office in Tel Aviv to advance liberal ideals in Israel, educate Israelis about democracy, and promote Arab-Jewish cooperation. The episode reveals the AJC's interest in shaping Israeli society to match its own liberal self-image, but the story also emphasizes the limits, and ultimately the failures, of these efforts.

Chapter 4 explores why exactly the AJC suddenly took such a heightened interest in Palestinian affairs in the mid-1950s. The organization was reacting to a major push to promote sympathy for Arab causes in the United States coordinated separately by the CIA-backed AFME and by the Arab League's new Arab Information Center in New York City. As acting director of the Arab Information Center and a close AFME affiliate, Fayez Sayegh emerges as the focal point of this chapter, which also casts light onto the history of the broader pro-Arab public relations effort that he helped lead. The AJC initially responded quite differently to these Arab advocacy efforts than did its peer organization, the Anti-Defamation League, but as the chapter shows, by the end of the 1950s, a new consensus formed regarding the threat of Arab anti-Zionism.

By the early 1960s, the anti-Zionist American Council for Judaism stood alone among Jewish organizations advocating for Palestine, but as chapter 5 shows, even the Council was a house divided on this issue. While the Council's executive director, Rabbi Elmer Berger, grew increasingly sympathetic to Palestinians through his ties to Sayegh and AFME, other Council leaders such as Council president Lessing Rosenwald responded to the active efforts of Israeli officials to court them to soften their positions. When Berger criticized Israel in the *New York Times* directly after the June 1967 war, the Rosenwald faction ejected him from the organization. The Council then halted its activism on behalf of the Palestinians, marking a temporary end to organized American Jewish efforts to advocate for Palestinian rights.

Focusing on the organization Breira, chapter 6 carries forward the story of Israel's reach into American Jewish communal politics, showing how political currents emanating from Israel brought about Breira's rise in 1973 and its fall four years later. Breira's young American Jewish founders had nearly all spent time in Israel, where encounters with Palestinians living under occupation and inspiration from Israeli peace activists led them to conclude that Palestinian self-determination served Israel's long-term interests. In the mid-1970s, Breira championed an Israeli group called the Israeli Council for Israeli-Palestinian Peace (ICIPP) that held talks with moderate figures in the Palestine Liberation Organization (PLO). Following the ICIPP's lead, two Breira members met with those same PLO moderates. Israeli officials leaked a report from that meeting to *Jerusalem Post* correspondent Wolf Blitzer, forcing Breira to defend itself against charges of consorting with terrorists. But backlash after the PLO meeting prompted a crisis from which the organization would never recover, contributing to Breira's financial collapse the next year. American Jewish communal leaders now took a clear stand on even self-identified Zionist support for Palestinian rights, claiming that it ran counter to Jewish safety and harmed the well-being of Jews in Israel and throughout the world.

Long before 1948, American Jews knew, in the most general sense, that Arabic-speaking non-Jews inhabited the land that became Israel. For those few who were really interested, and were willing to make the journey, seeing, encountering, and hearing from these Palestinian Arabs was a crucial part of understanding that they, too, constituted a people entitled to basic rights. Many of the American Jews featured in this book first encountered Palestinians during trips to Israel, or first began to understand the Palestinian plight through conversations with Israelis. These Jews thus often came to appreciate the importance of Palestinian rights through a journey that began not with hostility to or distance from Israel but rather through their feeling of attachment to the Jewish state. The title *Our Palestine Question*, with its ambiguous use of "our," harkens to those feelings of attachment as well as to related debates over Jewish collectivity that are central to the questions that this book raises.

For many Jewish advocates of Palestinian rights, being Jewish entailed both membership in an ethnic community and a commitment to ideals forged by the Jewish religious tradition and the historical experience of being a persecuted minority. Yet, while being focused on the particularities of Israel, Palestine, and American Jews, this study also touches on dilemmas that are universal—questions of identity, community, and maintaining loyalty to both ethical ideals and ethnic ties. It is my hope that the stories in this book not only resonate with Jews and Arabs but also feel relevant to people of all backgrounds who struggle to reconcile their urge to belong to a nonuniversal "people" with their urge to reject the tragic consequences that ethno-national particularism so often brings forth.

It is clear that in the decades since Israel's creation, the state has come to play a central role in American Jewish life. In that same period, however, so too has the impact of Israel's policies toward the Palestinians become harder to ignore, a fact that has led more American liberals, including many American Jews, to express growing sympathy with the Palestinians. Caught between the emotional attachment to Israel that has been instilled in them and the rising prominence of Palestinian rights issues worldwide, younger generations of American Jews have begun to ask how exactly so many questions crucial to their own identity and to Middle East politics were kept off of their community's agenda for so long. Among its many roles, *Our Palestine Question* provides at least part of the answer.[22]

1

Zionism's Wayward Son

ON JANUARY 5, 1949, WITH THE final battles of the first Arab-Israeli war still raging, a twenty-six-year-old named Don Peretz landed at Lod Airport in the recently established State of Israel. The young United States army veteran was on his way to deliver aid to recently displaced Palestinian Arabs as part of a mission led by the Quaker-affiliated American Friends Service Committee (AFSC). While the young Peretz had much in common with fellow AFSC volunteers, he differed from the rest in one important way: Peretz was Jewish.[1]

Throughout Peretz's eight months of distributing food and clothing to displaced Arabs in northern Israel, Jews and Arabs repeatedly asked him to stay in the country. Israeli Jews hoped Peretz would become a fellow citizen, while Arabs wished he would remain to continue aiding the internal refugees. Peretz ultimately decided to return home. The experience, however, marked not the end but the beginning of a remarkable trajectory that led Peretz to become one of the Americans most intimately involved with the Palestinian refugee question. Upon his return to New York later that year, Peretz enrolled in a graduate program at Columbia University. He decided to research the Palestinian refugee issue for his doctoral dissertation, which would be the first ever to cover the topic. By the mid-1950s, Peretz's research, which reportedly had "no near rival [in English] as the authoritative and scholarly work on the subjects covered," had become required reading for anyone interested in addressing the refugee problem, a category that included government officials and, perhaps surprisingly, leaders of the American Jewish Committee (AJC).[2]

In early 1956, the AJC, arguably the most politically well-connected American Jewish organization during the Eisenhower presidency, reached out to Peretz, offering him a position as the group's first Middle East consultant. Peretz's tenure at the organization coincided with a period of unprecedented AJC interest in Palestinian affairs. One of Peretz's primary tasks would be to put together an Arab refugee relief initiative with humanitarian aims. Despite the limited goals of the AJC's philanthropic initiative, which was not radical and might well be considered to be in Israel's interests, it—and Peretz—soon caught the attention of Israeli government officials. Israeli diplomats would initiate a quiet campaign to undermine the AJC refugee relief initiative and its creator, with the aim of ejecting Peretz from the organization.

The story of Don Peretz reveals much about the early American Jewish relationship with Israel/Palestine. It shows how one American Jew understood the Palestinian refugee issue, how the American Jewish community reacted to his attempts to study and address the question objectively, and how Israeli authorities, in turn, responded punitively to even limited American Jewish engagement with this controversial matter. Peretz and the AJC were by no means harsh critics of Israel. The AJC, despite its self-designation as non-Zionist, often advocated for Israel and always appeared far more sensitive to Israel's position than the strident anti-Zionists who dwelled at the margins of American Jewish politics. It was thus the mainstream nature of the AJC and its value as an asset to Israel that led Israeli officials to categorize any independent AJC action regarding the Palestinian question as a threat to the Jewish state. Don Peretz's intimate relationship with the Palestinian refugee issue and his role in encouraging American Jews to address the matter turned him into a vexing problem for Israel. Israeli diplomats felt compelled to act against him, not knowing, perhaps, that Peretz's ties to their country were, by some measures, even deeper than their own.

The Making of Don Peretz

Don Peretz's connection with Palestine came through his father, Haym, who was, in a way, a Palestinian refugee himself. Of Sephardic origin, the Peretz family first came to Palestine after being expelled from Spain in 1492, roughly four centuries before Haym's birth in 1894. Around that time, the Peretzes embraced the nascent Zionist movement, and Haym's father, Moshe, served as the *mukhtar*, or village leader, of the new Jewish settlements of Beer Tuvia and Gedera. During World War I, Haym worked for famed agronomist Aaron Aaronsohn, who spied on the Ottomans for the British. Ottoman authorities arrested Haym's father in 1915 because of his position, and Haym fled Palestine to Egypt en route to the United States.[3]

Settling in Baltimore, Haym quickly befriended Henrietta Szold, founder of Hadassah, an American women's Zionist organization dedicated to creating health and communal programs for Arabs and Jews in Palestine. Szold helped the young immigrant get settled in Baltimore, and they would remain in touch for decades. A few years after his arrival, Haym married Josephine Lasser of Trenton, New Jersey, and the couple gave birth to a son, Don Sholem Peretz, on October 31, 1922. After graduating from Johns Hopkins University in 1924, Haym became a Jewish community professional, a Zionist activist, and a Hebrew teacher, moving frequently before the family settled in Queens. Despite Haym's passion for Zionism, he never achieved prominence in the movement. He sometimes wrote ambitious proposals for American Zionist leaders, who dismissed his ideas as unrealistic and fanciful, leading Haym to partake in what Szold termed "excessive self-accusation and brooding." Writing to his son in 1943, Haym lamented that "life was meaningful up to when I left Palestine." In the United States, Haym "met challenges and suffered substantially because of principle . . . [and] defeats . . . made life bitter," but he felt good that, at the very least, he had stayed true to himself.[4]

Haym had high hopes for his only child, dreaming that Don would grow up to be a "loyal son of our people and a brother to all men," according to a letter that he penned to baby Don on the morning of his Brit Milah, the Jewish circumcision ceremony. Writing years later, Haym recalled present-

Haym Peretz with his son Don, age three or four,
in 1926. Courtesy of Deb Peretz.

ing a five-year-old Don to Zionist leader Rabbi Stephen Wise after religious services, using a biblical analogy. "Like Hannah who brought Samuel to Elie and consecrated him to the service of the Temple, mother and I brought you in the same manner to the 'universal Temple' with the hope that your service in the future will be consecrated to our people. Can you imagine," Haym wrote to Don, who then lived in Jerusalem, "my thinking of that [and what you now] hope to achieve on behalf of our people?" Haym hoped his son would follow in his footsteps by serving the Jewish community, ideally with more success than he had found in American Zionism. "Thinking of my youth," Haym wrote to Don, "of my dreams and hopes for the future which now, it seems, can only be fulfilled through you—my son—my son!"[5]

Although Don did not share his father's intense commitment to Zionism, he flirted with joining the Socialist-Zionist youth movement HaShomer HaTzair before gravitating toward Ihud, a party that Szold founded with Rabbi Judah Magnes, president of the Hebrew University of Jerusalem, which pushed for the creation of one binational Jewish-Arab state in Palestine. Influenced by both his neighbor, Rabbi Isidor Hoffman of the Jewish Peace Fellowship, and a Quaker teacher of his at Queens College, the young Peretz became pacifistic. Peretz's teacher introduced him to the American Friends Service Committee (AFSC), a Quaker-affiliated peace and social justice organization, and he spent summers volunteering on AFSC projects in upstate New York and in a small Mexican village. During the Second World War, Peretz registered as a conscientious objector; when drafted, he became a Japanese interpreter, studying Japanese at the University of Minnesota before being shipped out to Okinawa in 1945, where he served during the eponymous battle and subsequent military occupation of the island.[6]

Throughout his time there, the young soldier refused to carry a gun. Overall, the experience only increased Peretz's disgust with war. In Okinawa, Peretz witnessed soldiers in his medical unit mistreating native civilians. Peretz voiced his disapproval, which made him unpopular among fellow American soldiers. After returning home in 1946, Peretz used his G.I. Bill benefits to study at the Hebrew University of Jerusalem, in large part because Magnes and like-minded philosopher Martin Buber worked there. Magnes, who had faced derision as a rabbi in the United States for his pacifism during World War I, had by then become unpopular in some circles because of his binationalist beliefs. But for Peretz, Magnes's politics stood at the center of his appeal.[7]

Peretz grew impressed with Zionism during his first year in Palestine, then under British Mandatory rule. Writing to his American maternal grandmother, Peretz called his time in Jerusalem "one of the most interesting and valuable years of my life," having "learned more about our people, our history, customs, and our life than I had known heretofore." In Palestine, "one can come to appreciate more fully than anywhere in the world the positive Judaism which we hear so much about from the pulpits of our American rabbis," he wrote. "Here in Palestine," Peretz continued, "are hundreds of thousands of us who are living a completely Jewish life unfettered by the many pressures, diversions, and distractions [of the non-Jewish world]." After "seeing what the Jewish people have accomplished in the building of our ancient homeland," Peretz began feeling a close "attachment for this little troubled spot so many thousands of miles away," which he termed a "long lost parent-land."[8]

Writing to Haym, whom he called *Abba*, Hebrew for father, Don admitted that he could "now see how right you've always been" on Jewish issues, regretting that he had not understood Zionism earlier. "When one considers that the world seems little affected by the fact that one in every three of us [Jews] was murdered for no reason [and] . . . the great need of our people for this land, for the identification which it will bring us, one is drawn all the more toward it," Peretz stated. An American friend noted how Peretz's language shifted, observing that he had started using a collective "we" to refer to the Jewish people. "Back in the army," the friend wrote, "you never seemed to possess much Jewish conscience." In May of 1947, Peretz noted that "the more I see of Palestine, the more I learn about Judaism, the more I feel Zionism, the more I know that I want to be here, and that I probably would not be happy in America."[9]

Peretz's Zionist enchantment proved to be short-lived. Despite his budding admiration for Zionism, Peretz's politics still aligned with those of Magnes, whose binationalist vision of political equality for Arab and Jewish communities in Palestine only drifted further and further from the Zionist mainstream. While the November 1947 United Nations vote to partition Palestine and create a Jewish state led Peretz to reflect on the joy of his father, who "lived every day for this dream" and "lived every second of his life" for "this moment," the ensuing civil war in Palestine revealed a much darker facet of Zionism to the younger Peretz. While Zionists rejoiced at the United Nations' vote, the Arab majority in Palestine rejected the plan to divide the country into Jewish and Arab states, launching protests, strikes, and riots. Both Arabs and Jews, including some within the Labor-affiliated Haganah and the right-wing Irgun and Lehi, committed violence against innocent civilians, such as during the Haifa Oil Refinery massacre, the Balad al-Shaykh massacre, and other well-documented incidents. The killings hardened attitudes between communities, with both sides increasingly perceiving the other as an implacable foe.[10]

By February 1948, Peretz "[felt] very ill at ease," with "extreme" national-istic attitudes exemplified by the "almost hyper-thyroid hatred of Magnus [sic], in the attitude toward the Arabs with whom we shall be living the rest of our lives, and in the growing xeno-phobia [sic] within the Jewish com-munity. They think the world hates them, and they hate the world in re-turn." Peretz told his father that though he understood the reasons for this sentiment, "that does not obviate its danger of infecting the root of the Zi-onism you picture: a world force for creative endeavor, and a better life."[11]

In Palestine, "it seems there is no one to stop or slow this tide of extreme nationalism which threatens to engulf the constructive idealism of Zion-ism," Peretz wrote. "I feel very frustrated as a lone individual with these ideas. . . . They are not too popular; no more popular then [sic] were my expressions of non-hatred for the Japanese while I was in Okinawa. There, many were the verbal frays in which I engaged in expression of my 'traitor-ous sentiments.' " Don felt similarly in Jerusalem, longing for "something like the Quakers," to which he "could attach himself with a wholehearted enthusiasm and no qualms of conscience." He feared that his opinions could lead to physical threats from members of the right-wing Irgun. Yet despite all these feelings, Peretz, as a Jew "here now," felt unable to "aban-don commitment to constructive causes" in Palestine, perhaps because of his "oversensitivity to matters of pride, justice [and] injustice."[12]

In February 1948, amidst a Palestinian Arab blockade of the Jewish neighborhoods of Jerusalem, an unlikely series of events further compli-cated Peretz's relationships with the peoples of the region. After the war forced Hebrew University to cease regular operations, Peretz had become a "stringer" for NBC wartime correspondent John Donovan, then based out of the Jerusalem YMCA. As Peretz took a shortcut home from work on February 16, three armed members of an Arab militia "arrested" or ab-ducted Peretz and brought him to the militia's headquarters in Jerusalem's Old City. After Peretz acknowledged his Jewish identity, the militiamen in-terrogated Peretz and put him "on trial" for espionage. Though the militia-men pointed out that Peretz's address book indicated that he had no Arab friends, Peretz's support for Magnes made a favorable impression on his captors. After hours of detention, the Arab militiamen told Peretz that he would be escorted back on the condition he "never set foot in an Arab area again." But as the group's leader, a young officer whom Peretz referred to as Said Jundi, drove Peretz back toward his home, an Arab mob surrounded the car, demanding that the driver hand over the Jewish passenger. Jundi told Peretz that the mob had wanted to kill the young American Jew and that Jundi had only held them off by saying he was driving Peretz away to execute him quietly elsewhere. Jundi then released Peretz unharmed. That episode initiated an unlikely but limited friendship, with Peretz and Jundi meeting frequently at the YMCA over the next few months, during which time they talked about an array of topics ranging from politics to Jundi's Yemenite Jewish girlfriend.[13]

Peretz's dramatic abduction generated newspaper and radio coverage in both Jerusalem and New York. Ironically, while the experience could have led to Peretz's death at the hands of Palestinian Arabs, it instead fostered empathy and his first friendships with them. In Peretz's view, his new Arab acquaintances held more moderate political views than Palestine's Jews generally assumed. Jundi, for example, told Peretz that he disliked war but must "do my duty for my people, just as my Jewish friends in the Haganah must do what they have to do." Most Jews, Peretz complained, lack such sentiments, never spoke with Arabs, and looked on Arabs as "base creatures," noting that "there are many more Arabs who would accept Dr. Magnus's [sic] ideas than the Jewish Agency would like to admit there are."[14]

Peretz's abduction even came to the attention of Magnes himself, who fulfilled Peretz's longtime dream of meeting the rabbi by inviting the young American Jew to sit down with him. Peretz had hoped to solicit Magnes's support for a plan to bring the AFSC to Palestine to help with Arab-Jewish coexistence. In Magnes, Peretz saw a "soured and somewhat embittered man" beaten down after "many defeats and so very much maligning at the hands of the people whom he has served all his life." Yet, as Magnes was, in Peretz's opinion, the only Jew in Palestine trusted by Arabs, Peretz saw him as still "the one who comes closest" to knowing a way out of the "present maze of blood and violence."[15]

As war raged in the streets of Jerusalem, Peretz grew more and more despondent. He sat only blocks away when deadly explosions went off on popular Ben Yehuda Street and at the offices of the *Palestine Post*, a newspaper soon renamed the *Jerusalem Post*. He saw the violence and lack of

Arab-Jewish rapprochement as a "poison that is seeping into the whole structure of the Jewish endeavor in Palestine" as the "virus of hatred" infected more and more of both communities, preventing the emergence of any "healthy situation" free of the virus. Amidst the fighting, Peretz's belief in binationalism persisted. Despairing at the death on both sides, Peretz called plans to partition Palestine into two states "futile," a waste of energy and lives. He predicted a standstill after a bloody Arab invasion that would result in a United Nations–mediated compromise similar to Magnes's binational plan. These unpopular views increased Peretz's sense of isolation, bitterness, and rage. People "warned" him about his views, but Peretz reported that he "told all who seek to restrict" his speech or actions to "go to hell." He wrote to his parents that he would "not be coerced into a useless conformity when I can see a better way out. It may mean trouble for me but it would mean more trouble for my conscience than it has already, if I were to accede to threats from the goon squads of the Jewish Agency or Haganah."[16]

Peretz claimed that the Haganah, a mainstream Labor Zionist militia that would soon become the basis of the Israel Defense Forces (IDF), tried to intimidate him because of his political views and pressured him to enlist. Peretz, in turn, threatened to alert the American consulate after reportedly hearing that the militia had "blackmailed" American Jewish students into joining. Disgusted, Peretz wanted to go back to the United States, though he warily acknowledged that similar problems existed at home too, where he saw anti-communist hysteria gaining ground. "Oppression must be fought everywhere," whether in America, Russia, India, Czechoslovakia, or Palestine, Peretz declared.[17]

Peretz tired of debating his parents, particularly his Zionist father with his "pappa [sic] knows best" attitude. Zionism, in the younger Peretz's view, was "digging its own grave" and deluding itself by equating justice with victory over the supposedly unjust Arab cause. If he appeared unpatriotic, so be it. "Wasn't the prophet Jeremiah also branded a traitor?" Peretz queried rhetorically. Wartime nationalism and violence profoundly challenged his once warm feelings about Zionism. "What is happening here," Peretz wrote, "is like Okinawa and I'm afraid it is killing all my admiration for Palestine which was built in my first year here."[18]

Drifting, perhaps, into self-righteous paranoia, Peretz began feeling that even his family had turned away from him. A cousin in Tel Aviv informed Peretz that outrageous rumors circulated about him. When Peretz's father did not write, he feared abandonment: "Is he too involved in his conspiracy against me?" Peretz wrote to his mother, "If you too join in the sentiments of the rest of the family concerning my traitorous conduct, don't hesitate" to say it. "To me, peace is honor, and honor at any price. War is degradation and you may keep it." Magnes is vilified for his views, Peretz wrote. He observed, "The free man's body belongs in the gutter with the body of Dr. Magnes, Buddha, Gandhi and Christ. Death to the free man! Yells the crowd." There's no room in this world for a Gandhi, for a Magnes, for a Jesus—or for a Peretz, he implied.[19]

After months in besieged Jerusalem, Peretz decided to leave the new state of Israel via Tel Aviv, where he fled during the truce in June 1948 with help from his NBC employer, John Donovan. Freed from the pressures, chaos, and malnourishment of wartime Jerusalem and reunited with his father's family at their home a block from the beaches of Tel Aviv, Peretz calmed down. His local family, it turned out, had heard a rumor that Peretz had taken up fighting for the Arab Legion. As outrageous as the rumor sounded, some in his extended family had not dismissed it.[20]

Shortly before his departure from Israel, Peretz was present when Donovan interviewed Irgun leader Menachem Begin, whom Peretz characterized as a man "much like Hitler. He screams, cries, beats the table. . . . No one can tell him or [the Irgun] what to do. He's the leader, and that's that." Later that evening, Peretz witnessed a bloody encounter between the nascent IDF and the *Altalena*, a boat delivering weapons to Begin's Irgun in violation of the new state's aims to consolidate all militias into one national military. Peretz watched the beginning of the confrontation from the balcony of Tel Aviv's Dan Hotel but had to evacuate as bullets flew toward both the hotel and the Peretz family home across the street. The internal Jewish clash served as a fitting end to Peretz's conflicted sojourn in his father's homeland, especially considering that his stay in Jerusalem began on the same day that the Irgun bombed the city's King David Hotel in July 1946.[21]

Peretz left the country soon afterward. His two years in Palestine-turned-Israel left a lasting impact on his life. Among non-Israeli American Jews,

Peretz now already had uncommonly close contact with Palestinian Arabs. His letters home displayed an unusual and often antagonistic relationship with Zionism as well as a principled unwillingness to conform to Jewish communal standards. Yet Peretz felt intimately connected with the land where his family had dwelled for generations. These feelings and experiences complicated his relationship with the Jewish state but would ultimately lead him to return to it.

American Jew as Quaker Volunteer

During and after Peretz's stay in Palestine-turned-Israel, the country underwent vast demographic changes, which he himself noted as Palestinians gradually disappeared from western Jerusalem's Arab neighborhoods. By the time the dust settled, roughly 725,000 to 800,000 Palestinian Arabs lost their homes, including 15 to 25 percent of the Arabs who remained in the Jewish state. Hundreds of thousands of Palestinian Arabs fled the war's violence with the expectation of returning. The process began not long after the war started in late 1947 but accelerated after the Irgun and Lehi militias committed the infamous Deir Yassin massacre on April 9, 1948. In May, British forces withdrew, Zionist leaders proclaimed Israel's independence, and surrounding Arab states invaded the new state. Throughout 1948 and 1949, the Israeli army and the militias that preceded it forced hundreds of thousands of Palestinian Arabs from their homes, a fact that the Israeli government has long denied. While the Israeli military's role in expulsion is now largely a matter of scholarly consensus, a historical debate still rages over the government's overall strategy, a dispute that remains obscured by the government's unwillingness to release all pertinent documentation.[22]

What is clear is the state's policy to prevent, almost whenever possible, the return of displaced Palestinian Arabs. As Shira Robinson has demonstrated, the Israeli government waged an intense "war on return" in the years after 1948, pushing out returnees, deemed "infiltrators," as well as some undocumented residents who had never even left the country. In the diplomatic realm, Israel fought just as hard to counter international pressure and initiatives that would compel Israel to accept the refugees' return. Moshe Sharett, Israel's relatively dovish foreign minister, felt that displacement of Arabs constituted an excellent opportunity for ensuring a secure Jewish majority and viewed refugee return as "unthinkable." Meanwhile, United Nations (UN) mediator Count Folke Bernadotte began demanding in June 1948 that Israel recognize the rights of wartime refugees to return to their homes. By then, however, Israel's leaders had settled on a very clear story of what had transpired: Palestinian flight resulted from Arab orders and an Arab-initiated war, and Israel thus had no responsibility for the displacement whatsoever.[23]

As the crisis unfolded, the UN turned to international civil society to handle refugee relief. For an interim period that lasted until the creation of the United Nations Relief and Works Agency for Palestine Refugees in the Near East (UNRWA) in December 1949, the UN asked three well-established nongovernmental organizations to handle Palestine's refugees: the League of Red Cross Societies (LRCS), the International Committee of the Red Cross (ICRC), and the AFSC, which had recently received the 1947 Nobel Peace Prize for its work aiding World War II refugees, including Jewish victims of Nazi persecution. After the UN accepted the AFSC's conditions for undertaking the project, the organization began volunteer recruitment for a nonpartisan, humanitarian mission set to begin in the final week of 1948. The AFSC took charge of relief in Gaza and sent a small contingent of volunteers to aid internal refugees in northern Israel, headquartered in the city of Acre.[24]

Feeling personally invested in the Arab refugee crisis, Don Peretz volunteered for the AFSC mission and was assigned to the contingent in Acre, perhaps because of his Jewish background, Hebrew knowledge, and experience in the country. On January 5, 1949, Peretz and fellow volunteer Levinus Painter landed in Israel and moved into an old Arab house in Acre. Before long, the group began their task of distributing food and clothing to displaced Arabs who had taken refuge in Acre and towns scattered throughout the Galilee, an experience that brought Peretz into closer contact with Arabs than ever before.[25]

In the Arab villages, Peretz witnessed a side of the country that he had never seen before. He saw something "primeval and unchanging," an "agelessness" in their pattern of life that he suspected echoed back to biblical times. Despite his local familial roots and years in Jerusalem, Peretz

Peretz, second from left, sitting on the AFSC Jeep, which he
used to deliver provisions to displaced Arabs. In many Arab villages that
the AFSC aided, their Jeep was the only automobile around. Fellow AFSC
volunteers Levinus Painter to his left and Charles Freeman and Ruth Replogle
near Acre's sea wall, February 1949. Courtesy of Deb Peretz.

displayed an orientalist enchantment common to many Western observers
of the Middle East. Peretz also took note of the poverty among the newest
Jewish immigrants and heard how local Palestinian Arab villagers complained the new Jewish arrivals from Yemen were too primitive, even
though they got along fine.[26]

On his trip to survey local needs, Peretz noted that some villages seemed
unaffected by the war, while in others "life was thrown completely askew"
because of large influxes of refugees in some areas and labor depletion in
others. He also reported on how Israeli policies created even more challenges
for Arabs who remained in the state. In a letter to Simon Segal, the foreign
affairs director of the American Jewish Committee, Peretz wrote that the area
that he serviced was "under Jewish military government, in much the same
way that Japan or Okinawa was under American military government after
the conquest of that area." Warning Segal that "this may seem like a hyper-

bole," Peretz stated that "the actual fact is" that many Israelis, some military government officials, "have an attitude toward the Arabs which resembles that of American 'racists.' " Peretz noted that in some "unpleasant" instances, Israeli troops expelled refugees who tried to return home from Syria and Lebanon, but he suggested that rather than it reflecting state policy, it might be a case where orders were "misconstrued by a local commander."[27]

This and other realities of Palestinian life deeply disturbed Peretz. When he raised the subject of high Arab unemployment rates with Israeli officials, their discriminatory attitude of "we need to deal with our own people first" frustrated him. These Arabs were Israeli too, Peretz wrote to his father. Peretz also witnessed the Israeli army displacing residents of the village Tarshiha. According to a report that the AFSC sent to the American consulate, Peretz and a colleague, "who visited Tarshiha soon after [101 people were deported], believed that the 'concerted' Israeli campaign against infiltrators and those who harboured them seemed to be directed at making 'room for new Jewish immigrants.' " Months later, Peretz's friend at the American delegation to the Palestine Conciliation Commission, a UN body created to mediate in the conflict, told him that the commission had received the reports that the pair made on the Tarshiha incident and "implied that they saved the [remaining] original residents from being chucked out."[28]

In July 1949, Peretz traveled with fellow AFSC volunteer Rita Morgan to Beirut. There he witnessed another side of the refugee crisis—the conditions of Palestinian refugees in Lebanon, which he saw were "much worse than that of those who remained" in Israel. Walking in a Beirut park, Peretz and Morgan noted dozens of semi-tents and shelters. They met a man from Haifa who now lived in a six-foot-by-six-foot roofless shelter with his wife and two small children. A third, an infant, had died the week prior; one of those still alive, "perhaps two and a half years old," appeared very sick and "looked about ready to die." They gave the man money to go to the hospital but did not know what became of him. "Life is cheap" here, Peretz wrote, with the situation being so dire that "a dieing [sic] baby doesn't attract too much sympathy."[29]

Amidst the considerable need, Peretz felt pressure to extend his stay in Acre. But Peretz, who had already worked in Acre longer than any other AFSC volunteer, desired to return home to begin studying Middle East affairs. During his time in northern Israel, Peretz's work had ranged from

A photo taken by Don Peretz of women in a village where he distributed food
and clothes, somewhere in the Galilee, 1949. Courtesy of Deb Peretz.

surveying villages to distributing clothing, and ultimately to co-managing
monthly food distribution for seven thousand internal refugees spread
across twenty villages. Peretz's effectiveness led both Arabs and Jews to ask
him to stay beyond his planned departure date of August 29, 1949. One
Arab community member named Rushdie Sekaly told Peretz that he could
make a list of Arabs who wanted him to keep working. Though complimented, Peretz did not see himself as a relief worker in the long term, so
he declined. Instead, roughly five weeks after the signing of the last of the
Israeli-Arab armistice agreements, Peretz returned to New York to enroll in
a doctoral program at Columbia University.[30]

Aiming for "Objectivity": The First Dissertation
on Palestinian Refugees

At Columbia's Department of Public Law and Government, Peretz became a student of Professor J. C. Hurewitz, another American Jew who
researched the Middle East. When it came time to select a dissertation

topic, Peretz chose the issue that had already consumed months of his life: the plight of displaced Palestinian Arabs. In 1952, Peretz departed for a year and a half of research in Lebanon, Egypt, and Israel on a Ford Foundation fellowship. Peretz's wife since 1951, Heidy Mayer Peretz, a Jewish refugee from Germany who hosted a children's radio show in New York called *Here's Heidy*, remained behind. From there, she capably managed Peretz's fellowship applications and publication submissions, helping to ensure his professional success while he lived abroad.[31]

Peretz did not find his time in Cairo and Beirut particularly revelatory for his graduate work. He struggled to make connections in the Egyptian capital, but a member of the Muslim Brotherhood eventually befriended him, assuring Peretz that he did not judge people on the basis of their religion. This new friend introduced Peretz to leading figures in the Muslim Brotherhood as well as the former Grand Mufti of Jerusalem, Amin al-Husseini. He also met with members of the new revolutionary government, who impressed Peretz with their liberal thinking. In most of these discussions, Peretz's friend introduced him as "a Jewish scholar from America," except for during the visit with al-Husseini, who was known for spreading antisemitic propaganda when collaborating with the fascist powers during World War II. Nonetheless, Peretz found that during the visit, the exiled Mufti sounded much more hateful toward the British than toward the Jews or Israel.[32]

According to Peretz, his arrival at the American University of Beirut (AUB) "frightened" some American Christians there who worried that the presence of an American Jew researching the refugee issue would politically "contaminate" them in the eyes of the Lebanese. It is not clear what exactly they feared. "The AUB crowd convinced the local Ford Foundation representative to give me a 'hearing' before a group of 'concerned Americans' who found my presence in Beirut too compromising," Peretz later wrote. Even though local Arab faculty members maintained that they did not feel threatened by Peretz's presence, after the "hearing," Peretz's fellow Americans asked him to leave Lebanon for the good of the Foundation's other local grant recipients. He unhappily complied.[33]

In Israel, despite his lack of fluency in Hebrew and Arabic, Peretz had his most productive period. Unlike later scholarship on the Palestinian refugee question that made extensive use of declassified government documents, Peretz's research drew largely from material then publicly available in Israel or New York, including government publications, Knesset debate records, agricultural census reports and statistics, propaganda material from multiple sides, UN documents, and articles by an array of Middle Eastern news sources, particularly *Haaretz*. Peretz's work started appearing in scholarly journals beginning with a 1954 *Middle East Journal* article on Israel's Arab minority, the first academic article published in the United States to discuss the military government's rule over Arab areas of Israel. Given that there existed very few non-propagandistic and thorough accounts of the refugee question in English, Peretz's work found an eager audience in mid-1950s Middle East policy circles, requested by the U.S. Department of State, the United Nations, and the British government, which viewed resolving the refugee issue as essential for peace.[34]

Peretz completed his dissertation in 1955, and in 1958 the Middle East Institute published a revised version as a book titled *Israel and the Palestine Arabs*. The book, dedicated to Judah Magnes, aspired to be as "objective" as possible. To attest to that, Roger Baldwin, the founding executive director of the American Civil Liberties Union (ACLU) and chairman of the International League for the Rights of Man, wrote its foreword. "In this book, Dr. Peretz takes no sides nor does he offer a solution. . . . Both sides will charge prejudice . . . yet Dr. Peretz is as balanced and fair as any man could be," Baldwin attested.[35]

In contrast with the work of Israel's "New Historians" decades later, *Israel and the Palestine Arabs* did not focus on determining the cause of the refugee crisis, and even less so on assigning blame. If anything, Peretz downplayed the importance of those questions. He merely noted "Israel's explanation of the Arab flight" and the Arab claim "that the refugees were driven from their homes by the terrorism of Israeli military forces." For Peretz, the details were but "incidental" to contemporaneous policy questions. Despite the book's limitations, such as its lack of consultation with Arabic-language source material, it succeeded in outlining early Israeli, Arab, and UN public stances toward the refugee question and remains a useful scholarly resource on those matters.[36]

Peretz's research highlighted issues that leading Zionists would have preferred were not discussed publicly. He acknowledged local "Palestinian

Arab nationalism," detailed Israel's "inflexible" position on the refugees, used UN statistics rather than the lower Israeli figures regarding the number of refugees, and stated his belief that peace required addressing the refugee issue. Peretz reminded readers of past American pressure for partial resettlement and Israel's resistance to it, noting that Israelis feared that an influx of Arab refugees would threaten Israel's Jewish majority. His book also revealed many details about the restrictive military government over Arab areas of the country and Israel's confiscation of Arab property. While Peretz strove for a balanced account, and sometimes stressed the legitimacy of Israeli security concerns, Israeli officials disliked how his book revealed many unflattering Israeli policies to American scholars and policymakers in a credible, English-language monograph for the first time.[37]

Scholarship versus *Hasbara*—and Peretz versus Schechtman

Peretz's attempt to study the refugee problem in a neutral manner in hopes of advancing a solution ran counter to ongoing Israeli attempts to advance a narrative designed to sweep the problem under the rug. American opinion regarding the refugee issue mattered to Israel since international pressure to accept refugee return had been very high during and in the initial aftermath of the war. Israeli newspapers at the time argued that "American pressure was due largely to defective Israeli information services in the United States." Thus Israel sought to improve its *hasbara*—a Hebrew term that literally means "explanation" but is better translated as "public relations," "information services," or "propaganda," without the negative connotations.[38]

With this aim in mind, the Israeli government had already helped sponsor what it considered an ideal book on the refugee issue. The author of that 1952 book, *The Arab Refugee Problem*, was Odessa-born Joseph Schechtman (1891–1970), a longtime Revisionist Zionist activist who had immigrated to the United States in 1941. In America, Schechtman and another Revisionist immigrant, Eliahu Ben-Horin, became leading advocates of "population transfer"—the removal of Palestine's Arabs to a location outside Mandate Palestine. Despite its steep toll on the lives of ordinary

people, the idea of forced population transfer had found growing acceptance among the Allied powers during World War II, in the Eastern and
Central European context at least. Nazi Germany had recently used the pre-
text of minority German populations in neighboring countries as an excuse
for invading them, and some believed that ethnically homogeneous states
would facilitate a more peaceful future. In this context, Ben-Horin began
advocating for Palestinian Arab resettlement in Iraq in 1943. While employed by the American Zionist Emergency Council (AZEC), Ben-Horin
succeeded in gaining former president Herbert Hoover's support for the
transfer plan in 1945. Yet the idea never gained much traction among Jewish leadership in Palestine/Israel until 1948, when Zionism's Arab "demographic problem" became an Arab "refugee problem." In early 1949,
Israeli foreign minister Moshe Sharett, with AZEC approval, enlisted Ben-
Horin as a one-man lobby for the Iraqi resettlement idea. Ben-Horin then
wrote articles advocating the concept and lobbied officials in Washington.[39]

Schechtman published his first book on population transfer, in the European context, in 1946. For his research on population transfer, Schechtman
received a small Jewish Agency grant from Sharett—then still named
Moshe Shertok—at some point in the 1940s. When diplomatic pressure
surrounding the refugee question began to rise, Shertok "pressed his aides
in New York to arrange for the speedy publication of Schechtman's completed manuscript" on population transfer in Asia and the Middle East,
which "would contribute to an informational campaign Shertok was plan-
ning for the purpose of undercutting American pressure for return of the
refugees." In Israel, Schechtman received additional research funding
from Shertok's aides and, according to historian Nur Masalha, an invitation
to join the efforts of the Israeli government's Transfer Committee, which
aimed to solidify the country's demographic transformation. In March
1949, Sharett "instructed the American section of the Jewish agency to hire
Schechtman to direct 'research work pertaining to the problem of the Arab
refugees and their resettlement,' with Ambassadors Elath (formerly Epstein) and Eban as his supervisors." In this capacity, Schechtman began
authoring lengthy pamphlets for the Jewish Agency titled "Resettlement
Prospects for Arab Refugees" and "Arab Refugees: Facts and Figures,"
which, according to Rafael Medoff, "constituted [the Jewish Agency's] offi-

cial position for years." Schechtman soon became, in Nur Masalha's words, "the single most influential propagator of the Zionist myth of 'voluntary' exodus in 1948."[40]

An important claim of these pamphlets was that Palestinians fled from their homes on the basis of orders from their leaders. This myth, now viewed by most scholars as largely baseless, soon became an accepted fact in the United States and beyond. Writing in 1959, Palestinian scholar Walid Khalidi attributed that development to Schechtman's work. Drawing from the pamphlets that he created in 1948, Schechtman wrote *The Arab Refugee Problem* (1952), one of the first on the subject published in the United States. Schechtman's account differed considerably from Peretz's. Whereas Peretz tried to avoid advocating for a specific solution, Schechtman aimed to justify Arab displacement. Though Peretz felt that mass repatriation of refugees had too many practical impediments, displacement did not represent an ideal for him. Moreover, Peretz seemed uncertain about Schechtman's claim that Arab leaders called for Palestinian flight, expressing doubt regarding this "fact."[41]

While Peretz's work earned respect in certain policy circles, Schechtman's pamphlets outlined a narrative that quickly became orthodoxy within the American Jewish community. The Israeli government also issued booklets that blamed the refugee problem on Arab leaders for ordering evacuations, sanctioned the displacement in the context of contemporaneous population transfer, pushed for mass refugee resettlement, and argued for the injustice and impossibility of repatriation. The Israeli case against refugee return has remained virtually unchanged since 1949, including the argument that Middle Eastern Jewry's immigration to Israel constituted a de facto exchange of populations. The Israeli and Jewish Agency material flooded the American Jewish community. Meanwhile, Jewish groups such as the American Zionist Council printed their own pamphlets that parroted these talking points. Israeli diplomats also made their case in these terms directly to American Jewish leaders, including non-Zionists. When articles supporting the Israeli position appeared in the American Jewish press, Israeli consulates ensured their circulation.[42]

With help from Schechtman's pamphlets and related efforts, the mainstream American Jewish community—short of the anti-Zionists of the Jewish

Labor Bund, some Orthodox sects, and the American Council for Judaism—largely internalized and advanced the Israeli narrative. This included the AJC, the most prominent non-Zionist Jewish organization in America. For the AJC, not being Zionist did not mean that they were not supportive of Israel. Non-Zionism, for the AJC, simply meant that they did not believe that Jews necessarily constituted a nation and opposed efforts to convince Jews that they should feel obligated to move to the Jewish state. Thus, despite its non-Zionist designation, in the early years of Israel's existence the AJC proved to be one of the state's most effective friends in Washington.[43]

The AJC's non-Zionist label and the air of objectivity that it conveyed brought the organization additional credibility in official circles, as did the wealth of oil magnate Jacob Blaustein, the AJC's president from 1949 to 1954. Earlier in the 1940s, Blaustein and his predecessor Joseph Proskauer expressed great skepticism toward Zionism, with the latter even considered to be an anti-Zionist. As the years went on, both men warmed to Israel, if not to formal political Zionism. Much has been written on AJC-Israel relations under Blaustein, who had greater access to Truman in his second term and to Eisenhower in his first term than any other American Jewish leader. This White House access made Blaustein a major asset for Israel. He initially supported partial Arab refugee repatriation to Israel but refused a U.S. State Department request that he lobby Israeli leaders to accept 250,000 refugees. While the AJC did send the American leaders a letter urging aid for refugees, it also circulated Israeli government pamphlets advancing the Israeli narrative. Blaustein himself appears to have fallen into a more Israel-friendly position, supporting full resettlement. In the coming years, he showed no particular concern for the Arab refugee issue, though he did support peace initiatives that may have helped alleviate it. It was only after Blaustein departed from office that the AJC began taking Palestinian affairs more seriously.[44]

The AJC Takes on Peretz—and the Refugee Issue

In 1954, Irving Engel succeeded Blaustein as president of the AJC. Engel, born and raised in Alabama, had relocated to New York City as a young attorney after growing disgusted with the Ku Klux Klan's dominance of

Birmingham's court system. In New York, Engel found success as a lawyer and within the AJC, serving as chair of the AJC Executive Committee. An unsuccessful Democratic nominee for U.S. Congress, Engel never matched Blaustein in wealth or prestige. Moreover, he never obtained the close personal relationships with Israeli officials that Blaustein developed over the years. As AJC president, Engel traveled to Arab countries before visiting Israel amidst AJC efforts to aid North African Jewry; in Tunis, Engel "was admitted to the grand order of Nichan Iftikhar, the Tunisian Legion of Honor," for these efforts, a fact later noted in his obituary.[45]

During Engel's tenure, the AJC began to feel more acutely that the Arab refugee question not only burdened the Middle East but also created growing problems for Jews in the United States. The AJC perceived that both American Christians and Arab propagandists were increasingly discussing the Arab refugee problem. Minutes from a January 1956 AJC administrative board meeting noted that its Domestic Affairs Committee "had been mindful of the stepped-up Arab propaganda campaign. The Arab League's New York Information Office has spent at least $700,000 this year, and American Friends of the Middle East [a predominantly Christian pro-Arab group] are spending over $500,000." They viewed such a development as detrimental to Jewish-Christian relations and contextualized it within the fight against antisemitism. Israel-friendly AJC member Judge Simon Rifkind suggested that the AJC place "primary emphasis on combating Arab propaganda designed to foment antisemitism in the United States," while Judah Magnes's nephew, James Marshall, "recommended that AJC seek ways of solving the refugee problem, since this is the most formidable barrier to peace in the Middle East."[46]

The AJC did both, but only to a limited extent. During the 1950s, it pushed back against "Arab propaganda," but never to the degree that other Jewish advocacy groups like the Anti-Defamation League (ADL) did. The AJC explored Marshall's recommendation, creating a new subcommittee on the Arab refugee problem to be headed by former AJC vice president Colonel Harold Riegelman, a recent Republican nominee for mayor of New York who had served as the city's Acting Postmaster at Eisenhower's request. Riegelman's subcommittee would soon consider a proposal that the AJC recommend that the United Nations undertake a comprehensive

Don Peretz in the 1950s. Courtesy of Deb Peretz.

study of the Arab refugee problem, according to minutes from a June 1956 meeting.[47]

The AJC's growing interest in the Arab refugee problem led the organization to hire Don Peretz that year. Soon after completing his PhD in 1955, Peretz had given a presentation on the Arab refugee issue at an AJC executive board meeting. He must have made a good impression, since the AJC soon asked him to be the group's first Middle East consultant. In that position, Peretz advised AJC leaders on Middle East policy and wrote numerous reports for the group. Peretz's two-year tenure with the AJC, from early 1956 through early 1958, marked a period of heightened AJC interest in Palestinian affairs. During those years, some AJC leaders attempted to chart a more independent position on Arab affairs, for reasons both ethical and pragmatic.

As an AJC employee, Peretz composed several "Fact Sheets" of about twenty pages each, including "Steps to Middle East Peace" (July 1956), "The

Arab Refugee Dilemma" (September 1956), "The Plight of the Jews in Egypt" (March 1957), and "Christian Communities in Israel" (May 1957). "Christian Communities in Israel" discussed the rights of Christian religious institutions, missionary activities, rights of individual Christians, the protection of holy places, and Christian property in Israel. The effort to stress Christian freedoms and contextualize Israel's shortcomings clearly reflected AJC concerns about alienating American Christians. "Israel's impact on our lives as American Jews," according to one AJC source, "affects the way we are regarded by our Christian fellow Americans."[48]

As with Peretz's scholarly work, "The Arab Refugee Dilemma" likely pleased neither Israelis nor Palestinians. The pamphlet referred to Arab flight without mentioning expulsion, but also did not mention Schechtman's claim that Arab leaders ordered Palestinians to leave. While the pamphlet expressed sympathy for Arab refugees, it juxtaposed the issue with that of Jewish refugees from Arab countries, a reference common in pro-Israel discourse. What stands out most, however, was the AJC pamphlet's stance on a solution to the refugee problem—it offered none. While it seemed to favor resettlement as more viable, it did not rule out refugee return. This contrasted notably with pamphlets issued by Zionist groups. In place of offering a solution, it listed several proposals that involved resettlement, repatriation, or both, including a "compromise" proposal by Arab Knesset member Masad Kassis that would involve the return of roughly fifty thousand refugees for family reunification purposes. "At present, the greater emphasis is on resettlement, but none of the detailed plans thus far put forth provide a complete and overall solution," the pamphlet stated, concluding neutrally that "they are merely steps toward a settlement which must ultimately be based upon willingness of all concerned—the Arab states, Israel and other UN members—to consult, cooperate and, if necessary, compromise."[49]

AJC leaders and U.S. government officials took these pamphlets very seriously. The AJC's Mass Media Division had "The Arab Refugee Dilemma" distributed "to key people." Engel sent the Peretz-authored "Steps to Middle East Peace" to U.S. Secretary of State John Foster Dulles along with another pamphlet. During Engel's meeting with Dulles on August 9, 1956, he brought Dulles an updated version of "Steps" and summarized it briefly.

Dulles already had the pamphlets with him, noting that he had read them and complimented their "high quality." Dulles himself had, a year earlier, made a speech that addressed the refugee issue in which he said that the question should be resolved "through resettlement and—to such an extent as may be feasible—repatriation." Such rhetoric served as a reminder that, though no American leader would ever call for full refugee return, the prospect of American pressure for partial repatriation remained real. Since Israeli leaders opposed any level of repatriation, the willingness of a prominent American Jewish organization on which the Israelis often relied for support to publicly express any openness to partial repatriation no doubt caused Israel concern.[50]

Conspiring against a Friend: Israel and the AJC's Arab Refugee Initiative

Dulles's Israeli counterpart also learned of Peretz's work. She, however, did not consider it "high quality." A memo from October 11, 1956, stated that Foreign Minister Golda Meir had ordered mid-level diplomats to compose a response to Peretz's "Steps to Middle East Peace" that listed Israel's concerns with the document. The diplomats reached out to Judge Helmuth Lowenberg of Tel Aviv, who wrote monthly reports on Israeli affairs for the AJC, to get the inside story. In other words, Israeli officials used the AJC's local, part-time employee to gather inside intelligence on the organization. Drawing from the observations of Lowenberg and other "friends of Israel" within the AJC, Pinhas Eliav, deputy head of the Foreign Ministry's American division in Jerusalem, composed a confidential memorandum about the AJC. "For a while now, one senses that the committee's professional leadership desires to return to 'objectivity' on matters related to Israel," Eliav wrote. "There's a feeling that they went too far in identifying with Israel's position during the Blaustein period and that the pendulum must swing back. . . . [The AJC] is especially sensitive to accusations that it is neglecting American interests in the region," he continued, further noting AJC concern about Israel's "active defense" policies, which referred to retaliatory strikes that often resulted in Arab civilian casualties. Regarding the latter, Eliav speculated that this sensitivity stemmed from an AJC "fear of the possibility of a new blood libel that would present the Jews as murder-ers who kill the non-Jews."[51]

Eliav went on to claim that in the "Steps to Middle East Peace" pamphlet, "one sees this tendency toward neutrality that attempts to show both sides. This tendency is especially notable among members of the subcommittee on Israel and is being taken advantage of by Don Peretz, who wrote the document draft." Eliav's memo then listed ten critiques of the pamphlet, several of which argued that the viability of refugee resettlement in specific Arab countries was greater than Peretz had assessed. In general, however, the critiques basically asked the AJC to consider Israel's position more seri-ously, as well as to note the "Arab unwillingness to negotiate peace," which is "absolute" and "must be emphasized."[52]

Peretz's role in drafting the pamphlet led Israeli diplomats to discuss strategies on how to best persuade the AJC to fire him. One diplomat even suggested ruining Peretz's academic career. Esther Herlitz, an Israeli con-sul in New York City charged with managing Israel's relationship with the American Jewish community, wrote to her colleagues that she "learned from a credible source that, without a doubt, this program was written by Don Peretz. . . . It seems we should do more than we have previously to take this fellow out of the committee. We should talk to Blaustein, [Murray] Gurfein, Rifkind, and . . . [others] generally close to our views." Herlitz then reported that Peretz had received an appointment as a lecturer on Middle East affairs at Dropsie College, a small Jewish institution in Philadelphia. Peretz's "life goal is Princeton," Herlitz stated. "The embassy should con-sider digging him a grave at Dropsie."[53]

While the Israelis fumed about Peretz and his "Steps to Middle East Peace" pamphlet, Irving Engel blindsided them further during his presi-dential address at the AJC executive board dinner in New York on October 14, 1956. It had come time to unveil the initiative that Peretz and Riegel-man's subcommittee on Arab refugees had spent months formulating. "We in America must now bend our energies to the Arab refugee prob-lem," both for humanitarian reasons and for peace, Engel declared. Engel cited the Jewish experience as reason for Jewish involvement. "As Jews, we know what lies behind the word 'refugee'—the spiritual debasement, the resentment, the rebellion, the despair." As Jews and as Americans, Engel argued, American Jewry must act. Engel then outlined his proposal for an interfaith citizens' initiative. Jewish, Protestant, and Catholic groups would raise money to "help meet the educational needs of Arab refugees, especially for vocational training on the young." Jewish newspapers covered Engel's speech, noting his "interfaith, non-partisan, voluntary national citizens' council"—without criticizing it at all. "The project was included in a two-volume study on the Arab refugee situation that has been forwarded to President Eisenhower," *The American Israelite* stated, mentioning that the study had been undertaken by Dr. Don Peretz and had received positive comment from other religious groups and the United Nations.[54]

Crucially, Engel emphasized that the program did not assign blame or "responsibility for creation and continued existence of this problem." It would help alleviate the refugees' plight, "regardless of the ultimate political solution with respect to resettlement or repatriation." This attempt to take a middle road by not assigning blame or taking a side on the crucial resettlement versus return debate clearly aimed to shield the AJC from criticism. It did not.

The episode left the diplomats unsettled—and intrigued. In a memo titled "The AJC and the Arab refugees," Herlitz attempted to piece together what exactly was going on: "What is happening in the AJC is a story of *One Thousand and One Arabian Nights* that revolves around [Executive Vice President John] Slawson and Don Peretz, and a struggle within the committee to distinguish itself from the days of Blaustein." She reported that "insiders" speculated that Engel launched the refugee initiative for "publicity" and that Engel made his speech and released it to the press, "without anyone from the AJC knowing that he would throw such a bomb."

Herlitz wrote that during an AJC Administrative Council meeting after Engel's speech, Blaustein finally "intervened," arguing that "the resolution cannot be sent to the Resolution Committee without having passed through the Administrative Council first and should not have been included in a presidential address without prior consultation." Blaustein succeeded in getting the Administrative Council to block its approval, sending it to the Executive Council for further discussion. Herlitz continued, "Our friend in the AJC says that the trouble is that the prominent leaders [whom Israel trusts] on the committee like Rifkind, Gurfein, and their friends, are not dedicating enough time to Israeli matters."

Israeli diplomat Esther Herlitz with her longtime mentor, Foreign Minister (later Prime Minister) Moshe Sharett, 1949. Herlitz has been credited as a major figure in building Israel–American Jewish ties. David Eldan/Israeli Government Press Office.

Herlitz claimed that Peretz had written Engel's speech. She also noted that he had submitted a proposal to the Carnegie Endowment for Peace "on the possibility of assimilating the Arab refugees back into Israel." She noted that he expected to prove that "the refugees *CANNOT* return," as "Peretz does not believe in return, but in resettlement" and was thus, despite their differences, on the same side of Israel on this crucial question. Others allegedly shared this view of Peretz's plan, as Herlitz reported that Arab League official Fayez Sayegh harshly admonished Peretz over the AJC initiative, which Sayegh reportedly asserted "maneuvered public relations in a sophisticated way" in order to help Israel.[55]

The *National Jewish Post* publicly reported that Blaustein led the opposi-tion to Engel's proposal and that he expressed his fear that the initiative "might embarrass the Israeli government." It is unclear if Blaustein and Herlitz spoke before he moved to block the proposal. However, Blaustein did speak with Herlitz's superior, Israeli ambassador to the United States and United Nations Abba Eban, three weeks after Herlitz first proposed that Israeli officials raise Peretz's dismissal with Blaustein, so he perhaps understood their general feeling about this AJC "tendency" prior to Engel's speech.[56]

This tendency of some in the AJC to push for more objectivity regarding Israel during this period was no Israeli delusion. During a June 5, 1956, AJC administrative board meeting, a fascinating discussion on the topic took place.[57] At the previous meeting in April, board member and former AJC vice president Joseph Willen, who then served as executive vice presi-dent of the Federation of Jewish Philanthropies of New York, suggested a reevaluation of the "AJC's approach to matters pertaining to Israel," and in June that discussion took place. Willen's "thesis, which he offered as food for reflection, questioned whether AJC had at all times succeeded in main-taining an objective view of matters concerning Israel." He then cited in-stances of ethnic group influence on U.S. foreign policy and questioned whether they "were truly in the American interest." Willen noted that AJC leaders believed that they served American interests, but he warned that "emotional sympathy for Israel might on occasion result in [the AJC's] con-ception of the American interest taking a pro-Israel coloration." He then "suggested that AJC not only consider withdrawing from activity concern-ing Israel and desist from conversations with the State Department on this subject" but also take a formal stance opposing all ethnic group lobbying.[58]

An extensive discussion ensued. Some justified the AJC's concern for Israel, while others argued that it generally succeeded in maintaining ob-jectivity. Defenders of a pro-Israel orientation included Executive Vice Pres-ident John Slawson, contrasting with Herlitz's depiction of him. Peretz himself discussed the "tendency" that the Israelis associated with his pres-ence. When Slawson sent Peretz a memo criticizing the anti-Zionist Amer-ican Council for Judaism, Peretz used it as an opportunity to discuss his feelings about the push for objectivity. Peretz's letter, which he wrote mere

days after Blaustein and others "deferred" the Arab refugee initiative, tacitly addressed the episode.[59]

After assuring Slawson that he also disapproved of the anti-Zionist
Council and a newspaper critical of Israel called the *Jewish Newsletter* on account of their polemical tone, Peretz asked rhetorically, "Where can American Jews find a platform from which to voice not only eulogies of Israel, but
a *critical concern* about many of the problems in which the new state has
become involved . . . such as the Arab refugee problem, the condition of
Israel's Arab minority," and other such matters? "These questions are vital,"
Peretz continued, "not only to the future existence of Israel, but . . . if one is
farsighted, [they] can be seen to have an ultimate effect upon American
Jewry."[60]

Peretz lamented that apart from the Council and the *Jewish Newsletter*, no
American Jewish institution took up these crucial questions in a serious
manner. They "have been either neglected or considered from a transitory
propaganda point of view . . . or distorted so that American Jews have been
unable to face them realistically," Peretz wrote. "Even worse," he continued,
"individuals who would examine them realistically, have often been subject
to calumny and abuse by those who are most responsible for creating the
American Jew's image of Israel, as I myself can give evidence." Attesting
that the anti-Zionist Council was not too far off in characterizing "the ap-
paratus which shapes public opinion, especially Jewish public opinion, on
Israel" as "totalitarianism," Peretz lamented that "there is no open public
forum in the Jewish community [for] interpretation, and even facts, which
do not correspond to the accepted line." There is "need for an open platform," Peretz declared. "Frank and free discussion of these issues becomes
increasingly vital to the future welfare of both Israel and American Jews."

Peretz noted recent efforts "to create such a platform within the AJC" but
also acknowledged his awareness "of various pressures within and from
without the organization which slow up such a development." He seemed
to be urging Slawson not to give up. Using comparisons to the American
civil rights struggle with which the AJC had aligned itself, Peretz ended by
noting to the AJC's head staffer that the "emotional environment surrounding the issues of Zionism and the Palestine question" made it "perhaps as
difficult to create an atmosphere for free discussion as it is in the South

today, to discuss interracial relations." But, Peretz continued, "just as free discussion of the status of the Negro does not really constitute a threat to the White race, neither does discussion of the Arab minority or the refugee problem constitute a threat to Israel. Those who discuss desegregation do not love the white man any less," just as "many of those who discuss the plight of the Arabs do not have less affection for Israel by doing so." On the contrary, Peretz stated, "often those who discuss these issues are motivated by the realization that only through mutual concern for each other's problems, can these peoples prosper."[61]

Peretz's letter did not directly address the Arab refugee initiative, and it remains unclear whether Blaustein had succeeded in sinking it or had merely temporarily tabled it. In any case, the tabling soon became permanent. Mere days after the abovementioned events, Israel invaded the Sinai Peninsula, and all parties involved suddenly had more pressing concerns. No further mention of the initiative appeared publicly, neither in AJC material nor in the published histories of the organization. The initiative's very existence appears to have been forgotten.[62]

An epilogue to the tale of the AJC's Arab refugee initiative appears in the archives of a member who strongly supported the initiative—Professor Hans Kohn, a renowned scholar of nationalism who then taught at the City College of New York. In January 1957, Kohn, bemoaning how the Sinai invasion harmed the moral position of Jews everywhere, wrote to Engel telling him that if Engel's Arab refugee proposal had been adopted, it would have done Jews much good in the current crisis. Engel agreed and hoped he could push it forward someday, but said he did not believe this was the time. Engel's willingness to table the initiative left Kohn distraught. The "proposal to help the Arab refugees was the first light in a dark situation, dark not so much for the Arab refugees but for the moral standing of the Jews." Kohn wrote to a friend that "Engel apparently thinks . . . that this is no time to do anything for the Arab refugees. . . . Engel's point of view is understandable, but regrettable." The Prague-born Jewish academic continued, "Some people in Germany . . . of moral character hesitated to take certain steps because they thought the time was not [right]. . . . [Such steps] might have influenced the outcome" if these steps had not been tabled.[63]

Three months later, Kohn resigned from the AJC, citing its unwillingness to criticize Israel when it violated liberal standards. "I see no one of
sufficient standing in the community and sufficient courage to take the
initiative. It cannot be done by outsiders like me," he stated. Kohn implied
that the AJC should stand up for its principles on matters like the Arab
refugee crisis, and that he was leaving because it did not. The AJC, a "stal-
wart guardian of liberalism and humanitarianism," should criticize Israeli
actions that "were obviously violations of the standards of liberalism and
humanitarianism on which American Jews have insisted in other countries," Kohn maintained. "I am deeply convinced that the attitude of the
American Jewish Committee runs counter to the real interests of the Jews
in Israel and ultimately of the good conscience of American Jewry," Kohn
wrote in April 1957.[64]

Israel's "Peretz Problem" Gets Resolved

"We are all agreed you will try to hold a broad conversation with Engel.
One of the main goals will be to remove Don Peretz from his position,"
wrote Pinhas Eliav to fellow diplomats on October 24, 1956. Action against
Peretz had not simply been Herlitz's obsession; in the aftermath of Engel's
speech, it became a matter of consensus among all Israeli officials involved.
While Peretz's refugee initiative vanished from AJC history in October
1956, Peretz himself did not. The Suez War had contributed to wiping the
Arab refugee question off the AJC's agenda, yet it arguably increased the
AJC's need for someone like Peretz to work on other matters—namely, to
help Egyptian Jews who suffered from growing Egyptian state-sponsored
anti-Jewish persecution after the war. During the rest of Peretz's AJC tenure, he spent a greater proportion of his time dealing with Jewish affairs in
Arab countries. Meanwhile, the war no doubt kept Israel's diplomatic core
busy for the rest of 1956. Yet the disappearance of the refugee initiative and
Peretz's shifting portfolio did not bring an end to Israeli desires for his
dismissal. Nor did the December 1956 death of Peretz's sixty-one-year-old
father, Haym, whose obituaries in New York and Israel praised his Jewish
communal service, happen to catch the attention or bring forth the sympathy of the diplomats. But most notably, even diplomats' clear knowledge

that "Peretz does not believe in return, but in resettlement" did not halt their push for his removal.[65]

Israeli officials set up a meeting in January 1957 with John Slawson, during which they apparently planned to broach Peretz's firing. Writing afterward, the officials noted their surprise at seeing Don Peretz sitting next to Slawson. The AJC would not fire Peretz; rather, the group agreed that Israeli officials would review all of Peretz's work prior to publication. Decades later, Peretz expressed his frustration with this concession: "While I saw my role as educative, i.e., to keep the organization honestly informed about Israel and the Middle East, some of its officers believed that my function was to give a scholarly or credible overcast to AJC positions . . . on the region." These positions, Peretz continued, "tended to be uncritical if not defensive of Israel's government policies and highly critical of Arab, American, United Nations, or any other criticism of Israel." AJC leaders seemed "particularly sensitive about offending Israeli officials and nearly every item published concerning the Middle East [apparently only after the above-mentioned meeting] had to be checked with the Israeli embassy in Washington or the consulate general in New York." This led to "many hours" of internal debates with AJC staff, who "insisted on getting the official Israeli government view before publishing. Officials from the consulate would be invited to [the] AJC or to some 'neutral' meeting place like the Harmony [sic] Club to debate the wording and nuances of nearly every pronouncement or information bulletin" that dealt with the Middle East. Peretz's recollection is illuminating, but as documents show, the decision to have Israeli officials review his work emerged under specific circumstances and only after a year of employment.[66]

Peretz's account also confirms that after October 1956 his portfolio as the AJC's Middle East Consultant focused more on Jews in the Arab world. The AJC did not publish anything else by Peretz on Israel/Palestine except for "Christian Communities in Israel" (May 1957), which presumably is among the writings that underwent Israeli review. When, in mid-1957, AJC leaders went to investigate the status of Israel's Arab minority, Peretz, who had spent eight months in 1949 aiding that population, was not asked to be part of the delegation. Peretz instead spent summer 1957 back in the Middle East to investigate reports of the persecution of Jews in Syria. There he met with Syrian foreign minister Salah al-Din al-Bitar, a socialist politician who later became prime minister, and grew intrigued by the idea of a socialist-mediated peace between the socialist leaders of Israel and the Arab countries. Peretz, a socialist himself, then persuaded the AJC to send Norman Thomas, a Presbyterian minister and six-time Socialist Party of America presidential nominee, on a mission to the Middle East to investigate this prospect. The AJC consented but did not publicize its sponsorship of the peacemaking effort. Peretz joined in on the six-week trip in late 1957. The duo visited Egypt, Israel, Lebanon, Jordan, Syria, and Iraq. They spoke with Egyptian president Gamal Abdel Nasser, King Hussein of Jordan, Foreign Minister Golda Meir, and the foreign ministers of Iraq, Lebanon, and Syria about issues ranging from the prospects for peace to the protection of minorities and socialist politics.[67]

After returning to New York, Peretz turned his attention back to finishing his book. Unaware of how profoundly threatened Israeli diplomats felt by his work, Peretz sent his manuscript to the Israeli consulate at the consulate's request. He received an unhappy response from the consulate's Department of Research and Publications, written by Yaakov Morris, whose son Benny, ironically, would write a much more provocative study of the Palestinian refugee issue three decades later. "The overall picture you present, whether intended or not, is markedly biased toward the Arab position," the elder Morris wrote to Peretz in 1958. He continued, claiming that while Peretz "on one hand" attempted "to present both sides of the picture, the amount of space, detail, and material you devote to the critical aspects of your presentation about Israel practically renders the positive estimations irrelevant to the reader." Any "objective writer," Morris opined, should be able to tell that Arab social and economic progress in Israel is impressive considering Israel's security concerns. Morris noted that Peretz mentioned Israel's security situation but felt he did so in such a way that unintentionally made readers dismiss it. Morris concluded by stating that since Peretz seemed unwilling to revise his book to better express Israel's position, he saw no reason to read further.[68]

Sending his manuscript to the consulate may have harmed Peretz's career. Morris's colleague Adi Yafeh forwarded Morris's letter to AJC foreign affairs chief Simon Segal along with his own message. "You know that I like Don personally . . . yet all of us here [at Israel's Office of Information] feel that the book he is going to publish on the Arab refugees will bring more harm to Israel than lead to better understanding," Yafeh wrote. The problem, according to Yafeh, was Peretz's "whole approach, for unfortunately it is this aspect which worries me more than any of the details.' " Yafeh continued, "I just wanted to let you know what happened. I do not know whether there is anything that can be done now to prevent the harm which inevitably will be done when the book gets out."[69]

American Zionists also complained to the AJC about Peretz. Eliezer Whartman of the American Zionist Council (AZC) sent the AJC a copy of the *Jewish Newsletter*, a publication critical of Israel, that announced that Peretz would be writing a series on Arab refugees for it. "How the Committee can continue to keep Peretz on its roles [sic] is beyond me. You might want to call it to the attention of some of the executive staff. . . . The fact that he [writes for the newsletter] shows the length that he will go to earn a buck (or perhaps shows where his allegiance lies . . .)," Whartman wrote.[70]

At some point in early 1958, Peretz received word that his position at the AJC was being downgraded. Writing in 1993, Peretz recalled that several people in the organization were "not pleased" with his range of contacts in the Arab world, "which also seemed to disturb certain Israeli officials as well. The AJC was a mainstay of their 'information' efforts in the American Jewish community and in Washington; consequently, they did not want these contacts jeopardized by too friendly associations with Arab quarters." When his AJC employers offered Peretz the "downgraded status of a part-time job," he "got the message" and decided to leave.[71]

Peretz apparently heard that his having "Arab contacts" caused his demotion. This explanation seems odd considering that Peretz made many of his Arab contacts while on an AJC-sponsored mission, especially since these connections could have served as assets to the AJC in its quest to aid Middle Eastern Jewry. Given all the documentation revealed in this chapter, one wonders whether other factors may have been at play in Peretz's dismissal. Could the AJC have desired to distance itself from Peretz's forthcoming "pro-Arab" book? Did his willingness to write for the subversive *Jewish Newsletter* concern them? Perhaps the AJC had simply concluded that Don Peretz had become more trouble than he was worth.

It is unclear what "part-time" role the AJC desired for Peretz, but the organization quickly found a replacement for at least one of his tasks. While an AJC employee, Peretz had written the Middle East section in the AJC cosponsored publication *The American Jewish Yearbook*. After Peretz's departure, that role went to Professor Ben Halpern, a noted Zionist. While Halpern was a respected scholar, the shift from Peretz to Halpern is noteworthy considering the AJC's unwillingness to embrace the word "Zionist." The AJC's subcommittee on the Arab refugees continued functioning through 1958, when it considered but ultimately rejected endorsing a novel proposal to solve the refugee problem put forward by the Institute for Mediterranean Affairs. Only in the early 1960s did the AJC hire Peretz's full-time replacement as its Middle East staff member, Dr. George Gruen, a "traditionally observant Jew" with Zionist leanings who had written his dissertation on Turkey rather than on the thorny question of the Palestinians. Gruen's hiring, as one scholar has noted, marked yet another step in the AJC's broader shift toward further identifying with Israel.[72]

Yet the hidden controversy over Peretz's AJC Arab refugee initiative served as an even more noteworthy moment in this shift, one that is further emphasized by several key points. The first is the initiative's relative moderation. The initiative did nothing to advocate for refugee return. While claiming to be neutral on the repatriation versus resettlement debate, the AJC plan implicitly set the groundwork for resettlement by emphasizing training and education programs, which would have taken place in the Arab countries where they then resided. Engel's "neutrality" on the repatriation versus resettlement question likely served primarily as a tactic to ensure that liberal Protestants interested in the Arab refugee question would be willing to sign on to the interfaith initiative.[73]

Israeli diplomats knew this, and also knew that Peretz himself did not consider mass repatriation to be viable. Their knowledge of these points highlights how remarkably sensitive Israeli officials were to independent American Jewish engagement with the Palestinian refugee question. Despite their differences on the issue of Jewish nationalism, the AJC and Israel had a working relationship that advanced Israel's interests in Washington, which raised the stakes.

The sinking of the initiative also shows how Israeli diplomats effectively convinced even non-Zionist Jewish leaders in the 1950s that conforming to the Israeli government's Palestinian policies best served their interests. Israelis and Zionists succeeded in persuading them not to articulate an independent Palestinian policy agenda based on their own liberal impulses, their own research, and their own specific American Jewish interests. Though Engel had initially felt that the Arab refugee initiative served both American Jewish intercommunal interests and U.S. interests in the context of the Cold War, he relented. The Zionistic idea that among all Jews "we are one" had prevailed, blurring the lines between the interests of Israel and those of diaspora Jewry—and, just as crucially, showed who had the right to determine these monolithic "Jewish interests." As a result, organized American Jewry never adopted an independent stance on the Palestinian question, with the exception of a few small, outlying groups. This American Jewish deference to Israel's stance has deep roots. As Derek Penslar has shown, during spring and early summer of 1948, the American Jewish press featured expressions of compassion for Arab refugees, with many expecting that the refugees should and could return to their homes. But then Israel's position shifted, and American Jewish newspapers soon followed its lead.[74]

Israelis had reasons for opposing Arab refugee return relating to security, land and property ownership, the creation of space for future Jewish immigration, and demographic anxieties that emerged within the framework of ethnic nationalism. Peretz's own first book is a useful source outlining the widespread opposition within Israel regarding refugee return. The book cites various Israeli media reports showing the broad unpopularity of such a position across Israel's Jewish political spectrum. Israeli opposition to return is no new scholarly finding. However, it is now clear how far Israeli diplomats felt willing to go to subvert American Jewish activity and discussion related to the refugees. These diplomats felt that they could manage American Jewry and that they had a right to act against problematic figures. This included, essentially, conspiring against a friend—the AJC—which had done much to aid Israel.[75]

The episode did not deter Peretz from continuing to inform American Jews about the Palestinians' plight, nor did it mark Israeli diplomats' only foray into American Jewish politics in the 1950s. Soon after his departure from the AJC, Peretz's name began appearing on the masthead of a Jewish publication with which Israel had a less cordial relationship, the *Jewish Newsletter*. By the time Peretz joined the *Jewish Newsletter*'s editorial advisory board, the publication and its editor, former Yiddish journalist William Zukerman, had been marginalized from the mainstream political scene. That development, however, had not come about organically but rather involved Israeli intervention that foreshadowed Peretz's experience.

A Yiddishist's Dissent

The question of the Arab Refugees is a moral issue which rises above diplomacy. . . . The land now called Israel belongs to the Arab Refugees no less than to any Israeli. They have lived on that soil and worked on it . . . for twelve hundred years. . . . The fact that they fled in panic [during the 1948 war] is no excuse for depriving them of their homes.

—William Zukerman in the *Jewish Newsletter*,
September 22, 1950

Zukerman's anti-Israel writings . . . are growing now in volume. . . . From my sketchy following of the American Jewish press I have the impression that his pieces are getting fairly wide circulation. . . . Occasionally he is answered by a Zionist editor. . . . I do not think that is enough. His insidious propaganda is providing material not only for anti-Zionists but is confusing Zionists.

—Israeli diplomat Y. Harry Levin to future ambassador Abe
Harman, April 11, 1951

IN THE EYES OF ISRAELI OFFICIALS, the American Jewish Committee posed a threat to Israel's interests in Washington because of the AJC's access to American officials, its links with other prominent groups, and the affluence of the organization's membership. However, no one ever expressed concern that the mild-mannered AJC, often viewed as elitist and aloof from the majority of American Jews, would suddenly shift the tide of American Jewish popular opinion against Israel in any meaningful way. Similarly, no Israeli diplomat feared that Don Peretz's scholarly monograph would end up on synagogue bookshelves around the country.

Yet a figure with greater credibility and a more relatable Jewish background had in fact already once made Israeli officials worry that the broader Jewish community's faith in their project could be shaken. That figure was William Zukerman, a journalist who had written for the American Yiddish press for decades before creating his own English-language publication in 1948. The new publication, which Zukerman called the *Jewish Newsletter*, would discuss the Palestinian refugee issue more consistently throughout the 1950s than any other Jewish newspaper in the United States. In his newsletter and elsewhere, Zukerman vocally and frequently critiqued the Israeli government. Unlike other Jews who called attention to Palestinian rights issues during the 1950s, Zukerman seemed able to do so within the bounds of the core Jewish community, at least initially. His *Jewish Newsletter* reached both Zionist and anti-Zionist ears, with even many pro-Israel Jews at first perceiving him as an insider concerned about the Jewish community rather than an outsider whom they should ignore. Beyond his own publication, national Jewish news services in the early 1950s distributed Zukerman's columns to local Jewish newspapers throughout the country, with flagship Jewish community newspapers in Philadelphia, Boston, and elsewhere regularly publishing his work. He simultaneously served as a New York correspondent for British Jewry's newspaper of record, the London-based *Jewish Chronicle*, which only added to his credibility within the Jewish community.

This standing and audience made Zukerman a unique threat in the view of Israeli officials. According to declassified Israeli Foreign Ministry files from the early 1950s, Israeli diplomats repeatedly expressed alarm and frustration over the American Jewish community's willingness to tolerate Zukerman and his writings. Ultimately, these officials, including several future Israeli ambassadors, felt a need to push American Zionist leaders to initiate a campaign to remove Zukerman from various posts to prevent him from "confusing" Zionists about Israel and Palestinian rights.

From Teenage Immigrant to Transatlantic Journalist

One factor that made William Zukerman a particularly resonant voice for the average American Jewish reader was his relatively common background as a Yiddish-speaking immigrant from Russia. Zukerman was born in 1885 in the heart of the Pale of Settlement, part of the Russian Empire where 95 percent of its Jewish population lived owing to laws restricting their residence. Amidst a climate of poverty and the wave of antisemitic decrees that followed the 1881 assassination of Czar Alexander II, Jews emigrated in large numbers from the region in the decades surrounding the turn of the century, with their most frequent destination being the United States.[1]

The Zukermans were among these emigrants. William's father, Max, made the journey first, in 1900, settling in Chicago's Maxwell Street neighborhood, the epicenter of the Jewish immigrant community in the city. There he found work as a peddler selling rags. Later that year Max paid to have his eldest son William join him. During his journey across the Atlantic, a group of Orthodox Jewish passengers demanded to inspect the young William's food. Declaring it *treif*, or unkosher, they threw it overboard, leaving the teenager hungry, frightened, and reliant on the goodwill of other passengers for food to sustain him for the remaining sixteen days of the voyage. In the words of his son, this incident ignited in William "a flame of life-long hatred for orthodoxy" that would shape his politics for decades to come.[2]

When William arrived in Baltimore with no knowledge of how to get to his father in Chicago, another immigrant directed him to the Hebrew Immigrant Aid Society (HIAS), which fed him, gave him money, and put him on a train to Chicago. Max had high hopes for his son, so he enrolled him at the Lewis Institute (now the Illinois Institute of Technology), though William would eventually study at the University of Chicago. To help his father save money for the rest of the family's passage, William soon found a job as a paperboy, delivering the *Forverts* (later known as *The Jewish Daily Forward*), a Jewish socialist publication headquartered in New York, which later became not only the world's most read Yiddish newspaper but also the highest-circulating non-English daily paper in the United States. The job marked the beginning of what would be a lifelong career in journalism for

William Zukerman. Within a few years, he wrote his first article for the *Forverts* and gradually began working his way up the ranks of the Yiddish press in Chicago.[3]

World War I paused Zukerman's journalistic career and led him to Europe. During the war itself, Zukerman worked for the Jewish Welfare Board aiding American Jewish soldiers stationed in France. After returning to the United States, Zukerman, along with his father, grew concerned with the plight of their family and broader community in war-ravaged Eastern Europe. The elder Zukerman set up a society to raise money, and in 1919 the thirty-four-year-old William set off to Poland to transfer the funds out of his interest "in becoming acquainted with the big problems of the world, and especially of Jews," according to his father. In Europe, Zukerman was arrested and detained for an undetermined period; Max wrote that William was imprisoned in Warsaw owing to suspicions that he was a Communist spy, though other family sources claim otherwise. In any case, Zukerman succeeded in disbursing the funds, and over the next few years he lived in Danzig, Warsaw, Berlin, and Paris with his soon-to-be wife, Frieda Zeltzer, before moving to London in 1923, where they had two sons, future musicians Joseph and George.[4]

In London, Zukerman arranged to establish and run the European bureau of *Der Morgen Zshurnal* (*The Jewish Morning Journal*), one of the major American Yiddish daily newspapers at the time, which was published in New York. Ironically, given Zukerman's future political trajectory, *Der Morgen Zshurnal* was Zionist and historically the most conservative of the major American Yiddish daily newspapers, though it had taken a liberal turn before Zukerman's hiring. To make ends meet, Zukerman also sometimes wrote for the other major American Yiddish newspapers of the era, such as the socialist *Forverts*, the communist *Morgen Freiheit* (*Morning Freedom*), and the politically independent *Der Tog* (*The Day*).[5]

In London, the Zukermans were part of a circle of Jewish immigrant intellectuals with political views ranging from liberal to socialist to anarchist. The family socialized, for example, with renowned anarchist Emma Goldman, whom Zukerman admired, and one of Zukerman's closest friends was Max Mazower, a former leading figure in the General Jewish Labor Bund in Russia. The organization, known generally as "The Bund," was a

socialist, Yiddishist workers' party that fought for Jewish cultural autonomy in the Russian Empire around the turn of the century. Although, unlike
the AJC, the Bund accepted the notion of Jewish nationhood, it envisioned
Ashkenazi Jewry's future in Europe rather than in Palestine/Israel, bringing it into conflict with Zionists, who encouraged emigration and the use
of Hebrew instead of Yiddish. Though Zukerman himself never held membership in the Bund nor in any of its successor organizations, his links with
former Bundists reflected some of his own traits, such as his love of Yiddish, his secularism, his opposition to some aspects of Zionism, and his
belief that Jews constituted a secular people or nation rather than simply a
religious group. This worldview also explains Zukerman's stint in the 1930s
as an advocate for the Soviet Union's creation of a Jewish Autonomous
Oblast in Birobidzhan in the Russian Far East, near China, and for creating
Jewish semiautonomous settlements in the Crimea. This role fit with
Zukerman's overall political eclecticism. Though never a card-carrying
Communist, he lauded certain Soviet projects; though never a political Zi-
onist, he sometimes praised the socialistic aspirations of Labor Zionism.
By 1948, however, he would regret his past support for both.[6]

During the interwar period, Zukerman's main task involved not political
activism but rather simply reporting the news. As a journalist based in
London from the 1920s to 1940, Zukerman kept American Yiddish readers
informed of major events occurring throughout Europe amidst the rise of
fascism and the outbreak of World War II. In addition to his work in Yiddish, he wrote on occasion for American English-language magazines such
as *The Nation* and *Harper's Weekly*. His interwar writings on Zionism and
Palestine come off as neither anti-Zionist nor clearly pro-Zionist, and even
in the 1940s he occasionally wrote for Labor Zionist–affiliated publications. In these writings, one can detect warm feelings for certain early Zionist leaders and ideals. However, even in articles seemingly favorable
toward Zionism in the 1920s and 1930s, Zukerman's tone often indicated
that he viewed the project as moving away from its positive principles. During that period, he wrote a harsh condemnation of Revisionist Zionism in
a piece titled "The Menace of Jewish Fascism," published by *The Nation* in
April 1934. In it, he compared right-wing Revisionist Zionism to Nazism
and warned that this "Jewish fascism" was poised to take over the Zionist

movement. Using a class analysis, Zukerman predicted that the capitalistic and economically ruined Jewish middle class of Poland would immigrate in great enough numbers to overtake the idealistic Labor Zionists, upending the progress of the entire endeavor. Though Zukerman's pre-1948 writings occasionally mentioned Palestinian Arabs, it was extreme Jewish nationalism and other internal threats to Jews themselves that most concerned Zukerman about Zionism.[7]

"Independent Thinking on Jewish Problems"

Around 1940, Zukerman and his wife relocated to New York City. Despite his love for the Yiddish language, Zukerman knew that the circulation of Yiddish newspapers had been rapidly declining, and he had begun to feel that American Jewish journalism's future lay in English. In March 1948, he founded his own English-language publication, the *Jewish Newsletter*. Although Zukerman shifted to writing mostly in English, he stayed in dialogue with those who continued to write in Yiddish, and his publication served as a kind of bridge between these two linguistic communities. Zukerman's publication often quoted Yiddish writers and translated the quotations into English, enabling new audiences to hear their opinions. Despite his connections with the world of Bundism and socialism, he used the adjective "liberal" to describe his publication much more frequently than the term "socialist." Moreover, the designation that Zukerman valued most for the *Newsletter* was no doubt "independent," a word embedded in the motto above its masthead: "Independent Thinking on Jewish Problems."[8]

While the *Newsletter* published articles written by an array of authors, and Zukerman did sometimes employ assistants and correspondents, it was mostly a one-man operation with a modest circulation between three thousand and five thousand copies six years into its run. Perhaps to lend prestige to the paper, or to show that Zukerman was not an isolated voice despite his independence, the *Newsletter*'s masthead began featuring an "Editorial Advisory Board" in 1954. At one point or another, board members included prominent intellectuals such as Erich Fromm, David Riesman, Alfred Kazin, and Dwight MacDonald; socialist leaders J. B. S. Hardman, Judge Jacob Panken, Louis Nelson, and former presidential candidate Reverend Norman

William Zukerman, editor of the *Jewish Newsletter*,
in the 1940s. Photo courtesy of George Zukerman.

Thomas; American Civil Liberties Union (ACLU) founder Roger Baldwin; labor leader Louis Nelson; Rabbis Morris Lazaron, Richard Singer, and Abraham Cronbach of the American Council for Judaism; and eventually Don Peretz, after he parted ways with the AJC. Meanwhile, Hans Kohn served as "honorary chairman" of Friends of the Jewish Newsletter, the publication's fundraising body, with its list of "sponsors" including philosopher Horace Kallen, Jewish Labor Committee chairman Adolph Held, and Workman's Circle general director Nathan Chanin. Leading donors included Lessing Rosenwald of Sears-Roebuck, a leader of the anti-Zionist American Council for Judaism, and John Hertz of the Hertz car rental company.[9]

Upon Zukerman's death in 1961, the Jewish Telegraphic Agency referred to Zukerman as the editor of an "anti-Zionist publication," a designation that

Zukerman probably would not have contested by the 1960s. The few who have discussed Zukerman in recent years have also used the label "anti-Zionist" to describe the *Jewish Newsletter*. But it appears that in the publication's earliest years, Zukerman rejected the anti-Zionist label, and at least initially, the *Jewish Newsletter* did not sound anti-Zionist at all. In December 1948, the *Jewish Newsletter* called the "political formation of Israel" and the migration of European Jews to Israel "two historic miracles," the latter being a development that historians would consider "a marvel of the age." In March 1948, a lead article, "Disappointment at UN," expressed sympathy for Zionists, as did a January 1949 article that criticized Jewish communists for their "old vicious attacks on Zionism." Zukerman argued that the 1949 Israeli election results "showed that Israel wanted peace and is led by people who are statesmanlike, progressive, and humanitarian. . . . It was a great election, [making Israel] a moral victor." Zukerman praised Zionist leaders such as Rabbi Stephen Wise, Ambassador Abba Eban, and Foreign Minister Moshe Sharett. Rather than combating Zionism per se, the early *Newsletter* more often critiqued Israel over specific issues such as anti-Yiddish policies and "clericalism," a term that Zukerman used to refer to Orthodox Judaism's role in state affairs. Moreover, when he was accused of anti-Zionism in late 1949, Zukerman objected, calling himself "pro-Israeli."[10]

Though the *Jewish Newsletter* in its earliest form should not be termed anti-Zionist, even at that stage Zukerman did not hesitate to discuss Palestinian Arab affairs and other sensitive topics. An early reference to the refugee question appeared in June 1949 in an article titled "The Deeper Crisis." In it, Zukerman brought up issues of ongoing U.S.-Israel diplomatic dispute—America's insistence on the repatriation of some Palestinian refugees and the internationalization of Jerusalem, both of which Israel resisted. Zukerman discussed, without assessing whether either government was "right or wrong," how the U.S.-Israel disagreement created a dilemma for the American Jewish community, one that Jews could not simply wave away by claiming that Israeli and American interests always aligned. Well-known Zionist journalist Samuel Margoshes soon attacked the article in the Yiddish newspaper *Der Tog*, accusing Zukerman of implying that American Jews' siding with Israel against the U.S. State Department on the Arab refugee question was "more or less un-American." Zukerman responded in the *Newsletter*, claiming that Margoshes had clearly distorted his words, but noted that it was illogical to think that Israeli and American interests would never clash. Moreover, it was not only a non-Jewish clique in the State Department who wished for Israel to be generous in its treatment of Arab refugees, Zukerman wrote, since "a good many Jews" held the position as well.[11]

Margoshes's criticism did not deter Zukerman from writing on the Arab refugee issue, and perhaps even prompted him to look for opportunities to highlight a diversity of Jewish perspectives on the question. In October 1949, Zukerman re-reported in English a story by Zionist Yiddish author, playwright, and journalist David Pinski of *Der Tog*, who, after moving to Israel, reported on a conversation that he had with a Holocaust survivor living in a house formerly inhabited by an Arab family. The survivor, a young mother, "openly obsessed" about the morality of her position, especially after her children came across a closet full of toys that had belonged to the children of the exiled family. "The mother was suddenly struck by the thought that her children were playing with the toys of Arab children who were now exiled and homeless," Zukerman wrote. The woman began to brood, asking herself "what right she and her family [had] to occupy a house which does not belong to her. Is she not doing to the Arabs what the Nazis did to her and her family?" Zukerman ended that article by praising the fact that recent Jewish immigrants to Israel reportedly had reservations about the situation as they could serve as a moral anchor against unbridled nationalism in the state.[12]

Others in America's Yiddish-speaking community voiced sympathy for Palestinian refugees and Arabs in Israel as well. Writing in English, Benzion Hoffman, a prominent American Yiddish journalist who used the pen name Zivion, harshly criticized Israel's 1952 Nationality Law, which he viewed as discriminatory toward Arabs and bad for Jews everywhere. "Anti-Semites in many countries in favor of discrimination against Jews, have now received strong support of their own policies. They can point out now that the Jews, having attained the power to discriminate against others, avail themselves of it," Hoffman wrote. "I must admit it is a painful feeling to be accused of the very crime which we have always accused others of committing against us," he continued. "Jews have always protested against discrimination," but now "those who practice discrimination can reply to us: Are you Jews any better? Don't you do the same thing when you have the power? Don't you discriminate against members of another people living in your country?" Jews throughout the world have lost a lot by this law, Hoffman concluded sadly. "Morally the Jewish people has lost a great deal."[13]

The anti-Zionist International Jewish Labor Bund, a New York–based offshoot of the earlier Jewish Labor Bund of Eastern Europe, openly called for the return of Arab refugees to Israel from 1948 through at least the mid-1950s. The August/September 1948 issue of its English-language publication *The Jewish Labor Bund Bulletin* criticized Israeli leaders for entirely forgetting "two thousand years" of the "appalling plight of homelessness and exile" faced by Jews, including the deportations carried out by "Hitler's henchmen" a few years prior. "For the first time in two thousand years, the Jews themselves now have to handle the problem of displaced persons of the non-Jewish faith," the article stated, but "true to its Zionist self, the Jewish government of the State of Israel appears ready to forfeit [Jews'] moral rights . . . by refusing to permit the Arab refugees to return home to Palestine."[14]

The *Bund Bulletin*'s stance on the Palestinian refugee problem went far beyond that of its rival to the left, the Jewish communist publication *Jewish Life*, which fell in line with the Soviet stance opposing a United Nations resolution supportive of the refugee's return. The *Bund Bulletin*, for its part, reiterated its position in a 1952 article that sympathized with Palestinian resistance to resettlement outside Israel/Palestine since, naturally, "even poverty-stricken people reject vigorously efforts to treat them like cattle. . . . Human beings should not be forcibly removed and resettled elsewhere for the sake even of benevolent planners." That would be the second and final time that the *Bund Bulletin* mentioned the Arab refugees. Despite these bold critiques, Palestinian rights only receded on the shrinking organization's agenda over the years, as its struggle against Zionism became more focused on local debates surrounding Jewish communal organization.[15]

Though Zukerman's positions on the Palestinian refugees echoed those of the Bund, he himself did not affiliate with it. Rather, Zukerman associated with a more independently minded crowd of Yiddish speakers who organized in late 1949 as the Free Jewish Club. In the *Jewish Newsletter*, Zukerman defined the Club as a "loose association of people of different

views and ideas who have united for one fundamental purpose—to oppose
THE SPIRITUAL AND SOCIAL TOTALITARIANISM WHICH NOW
PREVAILS IN JEWISH LIFE IN THE UNITED STATES" in matters involving Israel. Though "not opposed to Israel, nor to aid for Israel," the Club
rejected "the morbid exaggeration of the significance of Israel for American Jews" and the redirection of so much American Jewish energy and
philanthropy toward the country. The Free Jewish Club claimed that it held
no overarching ideology or religious faith and merely focused on the breaking of consensus, according to Zukerman.[16]

The Free Jewish Club listed Zukerman among its fourteen founders in a
Yiddish flyer that outlined the group's principles. While recognizing Israel's important role, the Club emphasized the enduring importance of "the
Jewish masses in the Diaspora," where most Jews live. "We must ensure
their cultural freedom and creativity," the flyer continued, "we must stay in
close contact with the democratic movements of the non-Jewish peoples.
The Jewish people is a people belonging to universal humanity [literally, a
world-people] which must live in a free, united world." It went on to list its
purposes, which included opposing "totalitarian . . . narrowly nationalist
and militaristic tendencies" in Jewish politics, promoting free expression
in the Yiddish press, combating "the tendency to sacrifice all of Jewish life
and all of its institutions to the single goal of building Israel," and fighting
to protect Yiddish in the Jewish state and in American public life. According to a 1950 Club publication, most Yiddish newspapers responded negatively to the group, refusing to print the Club's press release while calling
its members "enemies of Zion." This is despite the fact that the Club never
termed itself anti-Zionist and did not mention Palestinians.[17]

Zukerman's views fostered criticism in the mainstream English-language
Jewish press as well. The *National Jewish Post*, which Zukerman openly
admired, labeled Zukerman an enemy of Zionism "worse than an anti-
Zionist because he parades as a friend of Zionism." In a letter published as
a reply, Zukerman wrote to clarify his position. He claimed that Israel's
creation made the terms "Zionist" and "anti-Zionist" obsolete. Zukerman
described himself as "pro-Israeli, but anti-nationalist" for Jews outside
Israel. Beneath the reprint of Zukerman's letter in the *Post*, the editor wrote
that, upon "careful analysis," the letter showed that there existed no differ-

ence between Zukerman and the "self-haters" of the anti-Zionist American Council for Judaism.[18]

Zukerman's response to the *National Jewish Post* sheds light on his reasons for covering Palestinian affairs. He opposed chauvinistic nationalism and felt that the Jewish diasporic experience warranted greater understanding for Arab refugees and minorities. Yet the Arab question did not function as Zukerman's entry point for criticizing Israel or Zionism. More importantly, Zukerman felt that his role as a journalist required him to be independent, to cover taboo issues, and to break uniformity. By 1950, Zukerman felt that "the question of the relationship of Israel to the Arabs in the new State and outside of it" was the most important matter facing Israel, labeling the Arab refugee problem as the "most crucial" moral issue. Starting in the mid-1950s, the *Newsletter* covered the Arab refugee issue and Israel's treatment of Palestinian citizens of Israel with growing frequency. This is in line with Zukerman's broader, gradual shift in the anti-Zionist direction. This involved both increased criticism of Israel and growing cooperation with the anti-Zionist American Council for Judaism ("the Council"). The latter came despite ideological differences between Zukerman and the Council about the nature of Jewish peoplehood and likely emerged out of Zukerman's need for more readers and donors; Council members served as an important source of both given the limited size of America's anti-Zionist Jewish audience.[19]

The Diplomat versus the Dissenter: Abe Harman's War on Zukerman

Despite the harsh Zionist critiques of Zukerman that began in 1949, Zukerman's journalistic writings continued to find audiences in the mainstream Jewish community. The Jewish student organization Hillel reportedly subscribed to the *Newsletter* for each of its campus chapters in 1950. Between December 1948 and September 1951, Boston's flagship Jewish newspaper, the *Jewish Advocate*, published fifty articles by Zukerman. Similarly, from December 1949 to June 1953, Philadelphia's *Jewish Exponent* published sixteen journalistic pieces and letters written by Zukerman. Neither the *Advocate* nor the *Exponent* could be considered marginal, serving as flagship newspapers in two cities that had among the largest Jewish populations in America. Sources from that era called the *Jewish Exponent* the "largest [English-language] Jewish daily in the United States," and the *Jewish Advocate* claimed to be America's oldest Jewish newspaper, having been founded at the request of Theodore Herzl in 1902. These newspapers could not have been unaware of Zukerman's reputation. In 1949, the *Exponent* published a letter by Zukerman responding to an accusation that he was being unfairly critical of Zionism. While Zukerman's pieces in the *Exponent* and the *Advocate* were softer on Israel than those that he published in the *Newsletter*, the mainstream press published articles by him mentioning Arab refugees and containing analysis critical of Israel and of Zionists. Though letters to the editor occasionally criticized Zukerman, his decades of writing in the Jewish press perhaps gave him the credibility to survive such attacks.[20]

A thick file on William Zukerman in Israel's Foreign Ministry archives reveals that the willingness of the mainstream Jewish press to publish his work alarmed Israeli diplomats, especially future ambassador Avraham "Abe" Harman, then head of Israel's Office of Information (Merkaz HaHasbara) in New York, and Yehuda Harry Levin, the embassy's press attaché. The file begins with letters from 1950 and ends with material written in 1954. Its contents include various pieces of information about Zukerman, his writings, and correspondence between Israeli officials. Within the latter, most surprising, perhaps, is their frustration with American Zionists, who they felt did too little to counter Zukerman. In a December 8, 1950, letter to Harman, Levin asked, "Don't you think it's time that someone started hitting back at this gentleman who appears to be conducting a many-fronted vendetta against Israel?" Lamenting that an article by Zukerman that reflected unfavorably on Israel had appeared in many Jewish newspapers, Levin suggested that they push the American Zionist Council (AZC) leaders Jerome Unger and Vic Bernstein to "do something, directly or indirectly" about Zukerman.[21]

Harman replied that he would press the Zukerman matter again, noting that he had already done so with Unger, but without success. A subsequent letter by Levin indicated that some sort of anti-Zukerman "initiative" was underway: "I received a copy of 'The Strange Case of William Zukerman,

Part II' issued by the Zionist Information Service. Is this the fruit of our initiative with Unger?" The Arab refugee issue arose in the Zukerman context as well. In early 1951, Harman personally helped several American Jews respond to Zukerman's claim that the Arab refugees totaled 800,000–900,000, an accurate number according to UN statistics. Harman's staff sent to the editor of *The Reconstructionist* Israel's official response claiming that the refugees numbered only 520,000.[22]

Meanwhile, months passed as Harman and Levin continued to fret about American Zionists' inaction on Zukerman. Levin warned that Zukerman's "anti-Israel writings" were growing in volume. "From my sketchy following of the American Jewish press I have the impression that his pieces are getting fairly wide circulation. . . . Occasionally he is answered by a Zionist editor. . . . I do not think that is enough. His insidious propaganda is providing material not only for anti-Zionists but is *confusing Zionists*," Levin wrote. To illustrate his point, Levin recalled his recent visit to a Zionist gathering in Richmond, Virginia, noting that he "was bombarded with questions about half of which . . . resulted from Zukerman's writings." Levin reported that this followed a similar experience in Milwaukee a few weeks earlier. No doubt, he wrote to Harman, "in lesser or greater measure your experience has been the same. I suggest you take the matter up again with Unger and/or others."[23]

Israeli concern with Zukerman spread to London, where an Israeli diplomat bemoaned Zukerman's "famous article in *Harper's Magazine* about the rule of theocracy in Israel," and to California, as seen in a letter from Eva Ballo of the Los Angeles consulate to Harman. "One of our loyal San Francisco friends," Ballo wrote, "seemed quite upset about the alleged fate of the Yiddish language in Israel" after reading the *Jewish Newsletter*. "We should also appreciate whatever 'dope' you may have on Mr. Zukerman himself," Ballo wrote.[24]

In the Israel State Archive file, there is a confidential dossier on Zukerman dated September 1951. The identity of its author is unclear. The dossier noted that the American Anglo-Jewish press republished Zukerman's articles; it claimed that Zukerman "conceals his cancerous enmity [for Israel] in 'goody-goody' support and advice. Thus in the name of liberalism he denounces Israel as theocratic [and] chauvinistic," citing his writings on

Arab refugees and several other matters. For the dossier's author, Zuker-man's danger stemmed from his projection of concern for Israel and for Jews, and the fact that his critique of Israel drew from liberal ideals, values that many American Jews shared. Whether AZC leaders had simply read this Israeli-written dossier or had compiled it themselves, it appeared that they finally felt ready to take action. That same month, the anti-Zionist American Council for Judaism reported "evidence of a Zionist write-in campaign" aimed at the *New York Herald Tribune* that attacked an article by Zukerman published in the paper. The Council asked select members to aid in a countereffort.[25]

A letter from Rita Grossman to Unger and former AZC leader Louis Lipsky, which was forwarded to Harman, implied the existence of this con-certed "Zionist write-in campaign" to the *Herald Tribune* but suggested a different path moving forward. Doubting whether they could succeed in convincing the *Herald Tribune* and other major newspapers not to print Zukerman's writings, the letter's author suggested undertaking "a planned campaign with the Anglo-Jewish press," where Zukerman's regular col-umns were "doing a lot of harm and creating doubts in many people's minds." This campaign would consist of circulating a memo in Jewish communities where Zukerman is published, "advising them to be on the lookout for his articles and urging them to react each time." They would then "supply suitable replies to local Zionists for submission to the pa-pers," with the author reasoning that "by encouraging a constant attack on Zukerman, we might be able to diminish his 'prestige' and persuade Anglo-Jewish editors to drop his material." Indicating the campaign's suc-cess, that month marked the last time Zukerman's writings appeared in Boston's *Jewish Advocate*. He had written roughly fifty articles for that pub-lication since the start of 1949 but none after September 1951.[26]

Zukerman's work continued to appear, albeit less frequently, in Jewish publications such as the *Exponent* until 1953. Yet despite the success of Is-raeli-initiated AZC campaigns against Zukerman in the Jewish press, Levin now increasingly worried about the general press, warning Harman that Zukerman's "poison is spreading further and further afield." The *Jewish Newsletter*, Levin wrote, "seems to be received by non-Jewish papers . . . and [Zukerman's] manner of writing succeeds in persuading uninformed readers of his apparent honesty and objectivity. . . . I urge you to take the matter up again with AZC." Levin mentioned attempts to convince general, non-Jewish papers not to publish Zukerman's work, but they appeared unsuccessful given that his anxiety over Zukerman continued into 1952: "Were you able to get Hal Lehrman [of *Commentary*] to undertake the Zukerman assignment? Failing him what about Marie Syrkin [editor of the Zionist journal *Jewish Frontier*] or Gerold Frank [who cowrote with Bartley Crum the pro-Zionist book *Behind the Silken Curtain*]?" Months later, Levin again wrote to Harman about Zukerman, "He is at it again . . . provid[ing] ammunition to our attackers. . . . I tell you once again, this man can't be overlooked. His influence may be limited, but he is going to cause us increasing trouble if we let him get away with it. We had better try to do something fundamental at this stage."[27]

Harman also sought to have Zukerman removed from his position as the New York correspondent of the London-based *Jewish Chronicle*. "This gentleman is causing us considerable harm," Harman stated, with his "weekly Newssheet which claims to be independent but which is actually a sustained attack on the policies of the Government of Israel." Though "we have no evidence," Harman wrote, of his expressing anti-Zionism in the *Chronicle*, his affiliation with it "adds considerably to his prestige," which itself threatened Israel. "Bring this matter to the attention of [former Israeli ambassador to the United States and then-ambassador to the United Kingdom Eliahu] Elath," Harman requested, so that he can let the *Chronicle*'s editors know of "Zukerman's activities."[28]

Zukerman lost the position the next month. The *Chronicle*'s publisher reportedly told Zukerman—off the record—that the true reason for his dismissal had nothing to do with his work for the *Chronicle* and instead stemmed from his writings in the *Newsletter*. In a private letter to a friend, Rabbi Elmer Berger of the American Council for Judaism, Zukerman wrote that the *Chronicle*'s publisher had recently met with Abba Eban, Israel's ambassador to the United States and United Nations, as well as with Abe Harman and officials from the Jewish Agency. All of them had told the publisher that Zukerman's connection with the *Chronicle* "prejudices the position of the paper" and hurts the publication. "This is the third and hardest knock that I have had in the last few years," Zukerman lamented to

Berger: "first, the *Morning Journal*; then the Jewish World News Service; and now the *Chronicle*," listing an American Yiddish newspaper, a major national American Jewish news agency that had syndicated out Zukerman's articles to local Jewish newspapers throughout the country, and the prestigious London Jewish publication that had all ceased publishing him.[29]

"A fine demonstration of Jewish MacCarthyism [*sic*] and of the 'freedom' of the press," "the forces against me are too strong and for the first time," he wrote sadly, "I feel beaten and sick at heart." In contrast, Israeli diplomats viewed their success in getting Zukerman fired as a source for celebration. "To have induced the *Jewish Chronicle* to dispense with the services of Mr. Zukerman is to have performed a real MITZVAH," Israeli consul general in New York Arthur Lourie wrote to a colleague who presumably aided in that task. "I wish all the Jewish journals, which publish material from his *Newsletter*, could be induced to do likewise," Lourie continued, noting that "some particularly violent quotations" from the *Newsletter* had been cited by an Arab delegate in recent discussion on the Palestinian refugees at the United Nations.[30]

Over the next two years, memos on Zukerman became less frequent in the Israeli government file, with the final letter dated May 13, 1954. It may be that Israel's diplomatic core simply ceased to obsess over Zukerman. The *Newsletter* continued for another seven years and grew increasingly critical of Israel. Articles on the Palestinian refugees, for example, appeared more often in the publication's later years when Peretz began contributing on the topic. Peretz's articles appeared regularly enough in the *Newsletter* that AZC leaders reported speculation in 1959 that he would eventually succeed Zukerman as its editor in chief. Zukerman himself began discussing the refugee issue with greater frequency. Writing in late 1958, he proudly termed the *Jewish Newsletter* the "only Jewish publication" in America that, since 1950, provided a "platform [for] . . . voices in the wilderness" to articulate clear Jewish "opposition" to the "official attitude" toward the Arab refugees, "a more humane and at the same time profounder and truer one than that of the Israelis."[31]

In underlined text, Zukerman wrote that "the opposition looked upon the Arab refugee issue as a basic humanitarian and moral problem, which rises above sectarian national interests and affects not only the Arabs and the Jews but the entire civilized world," while Israelis, on the other hand, "looked upon the Arab refugee as a political incidence in the building of their nation state for the sake of which all sacrifices of human beings and moral principles were permissible." Time has shown, Zukerman continued, that "the Israelis were wrong and their small opposition was right. Public opinion [everywhere else] is veering. . . . The Israeli government is wisely retreating from its previously uncompromising stance," but it must adopt "the fundamentals of the opposition program, namely the principle of repatriation of all Arab refugees who wish to return to their homes in Israel."[32]

That article may have been Zukerman's clearest public statement on the refugee question, highlighting his differences between him and the moderate AJC. But by that point Zukerman's writings had ceased to appear elsewhere in the Jewish press, a development that had likely resulted from the Harman-AZC collaboration against him. Zukerman's interest in Palestinian affairs increased, so much so that by the time of his death he had been working on a book titled *The Impact of Israel on American Jews*, which began with chapters on Israel's Arab minority and Palestinian refugees. Among other claims, the manuscript argued that the "displacement of the majority of the Palestinian Arabs was one of the fundamental aims" of Ben-Gurion after 1942. Along with Peretz's pieces, Zukerman published articles by dovish Israelis such as pacifist Natan Chofshi, an old acquaintance of Peretz's who wrote to rebut an American Zionist rabbi's claim that Arab leaders ordered Palestinian Arabs to evacuate in 1948. "We old Jewish settlers in Palestine who witnessed the fight could tell him how and in what manner we, Jews, forced the Arabs to leave cities and villages," Chofshi wrote. "Some of them were driven out by force of arms; others were made to leave by deceit, lying and false promises. It is enough to cite the cities of Jaffa, Lydda, Ramle, Beersheba, Acre from among numerous others," noted Chofshi in a February 1959 *Jewish Newsletter* piece. Thirty years before Israel's "New Historians" would raise a major debate within Israel and the Jewish world over the state's role in the Palestinian refugee exodus, the *Jewish Newsletter* acknowledged Israel's culpability quite clearly. But by this time, the once widely read William Zukerman no longer had the Jewish audience that he had once maintained, having been sidelined for refusing to cede his journalistic independence.[33]

The "Zukerman/Peretz Problem" in Jewish History

Zukerman's tale emphasizes one of this book's central arguments—that Israeli diplomats felt compelled to act against American Jewish dissenters. In the Zukerman context, the Palestinian refugee issue could be counted as only one among many critiques of Israel expressed in the *Jewish Newsletter*. But his case proves that the diplomatic discussions about Peretz were not isolated incidents but rather part of a pattern that actually preceded the Peretz affair and involved other high-ranking Israeli diplomats. Not only did Zukerman's relative moderation in the *Newsletter*'s early years fail to inoculate him against Israeli criticism, but the fact that parts of the mainstream American Jewish community accepted him made Israeli officials view Zukerman as particularly "dangerous" and inspired them to act against him.

Starting from almost the very beginning of Israel's existence, Israeli diplomats felt a need to "manage" the American Jewish community regarding sensitive issues, a finding in line with historian Natan Aridan's claim regarding the early Israel–American Jewish relationship overall. Aridan's book shows that Israeli diplomats often told American Zionists what they could and could not do in their pro-Israel activities directly after 1948. While they certainly celebrated Israel's creation, achieving that goal ultimately disempowered and disoriented American Zionists, who had enjoyed a more powerful role within the Zionist movement before 1948. This provided context for Harman's attitude toward the AZC; still, the AZC's initial reluctance to act against Zukerman stands in stark contrast with the later hypervigilance of American Zionists in drawing "red lines" for American Jewry.[34]

This hesitancy may reflect American Zionist leadership's difficulty in transitioning from coproducer of a movement to defender of a state over which it had little influence. A few years later, these feelings would be expressed by Louis Lipsky, a then eighty-year-old Zionist who had chaired the AZC in the 1950s, the Zionist Organization of America in the 1920s, and the American Zionist Committee for Public Affairs, now known as the

Abe Harman, Israeli ambassador to the United States, on left sitting
with Israeli prime minister Levi Eshkol and U.S. president Lyndon Johnson, 1964.
Moshe Pridan/Israeli Government Press Office.

American Israel Public Affairs Committee (AIPAC), when it was first
founded. "It is tragic that parties in Israel should control their counterpart
in the Diaspora," Lipsky declared in an address to the American Jewish
League for Israel in New York during May 1957. American Zionism, once a
creative and dynamic endeavor, had after 1948 "lost its initiative and com-
pass of direction." Now, in his words, American Zionism "knew only that
its primary duty was to serve the State." While it is doubtful that these remarks had any connection to the Zukerman affair, they do indicate a broader American Zionist discontent with Israeli attitudes toward American
Jewish organizations.[35]

The story of William Zukerman, like the experience of Don Peretz, also highlights an important trend in Israeli diplomatic history: the Israeli diplomats who sought to undermine Peretz and Zukerman are considered among the architects of Israel's relationship with American Jewry. After completing his role as head of Israel's Office of Information in America, Abe Harman became Israel's consul general in New York City and went on to serve as Israel's ambassador to the United States for a long, crucial period of 1959 to 1968. Esther Herlitz (1921–2016) was the diplomat charged with day-to-day management of Israel's relationship with American Jewish institutions in New York, where most were headquartered. She went on to become Israel's first female ambassador in 1966, representing Israel in Denmark, and later served in the Knesset.

When Herlitz received Israel's highest honor—the Israel Prize—in 2015, Prime Minister Benjamin Netanyahu lauded her as one of "the pioneers in establishing ties between Israel and US Jewry." Pinhas Eliav, deputy head of the Foreign Ministry's American division in Jerusalem, went on to become Israel's UN ambassador in Geneva. U.S.-based diplomats Yohanan Maroz, Shimson Arad, Michael Arnon, and Yehuda Harry Levin also later became ambassadors, to Switzerland, Mexico, Ghana, and Denmark, respectively. In at least one instance cited—writing a response to Peretz's AJC pamphlet—these diplomats followed direct instructions from Israeli foreign minister Golda Meir. While other officials also received many of the Herlitz-Eliav-Maroz correspondences, the exact role of higher-ranking Israeli officials in addressing the Peretz and Zukerman "problems" remains unclear. Meir's predecessor in the Foreign Ministry, future prime minister Moshe Sharett, certainly knew of Zukerman and followed his work, with some exasperation. "How can you possibly suggest that I may have forgotten you?" the foreign minister wrote in response to Zukerman in 1952 when the latter sent him a *Jewish Newsletter* article.[36]

William Zukerman passed away at age seventy-six in October of 1961. To commemorate his life, Hans Kohn put together an anthology of Zukerman's writings, and the publishers asked Don Peretz to help edit it. Zukerman's death marked the end of the *Jewish Newsletter*. Peretz continued his research on the Arab refugee problem independently and at the State University of New York at Binghamton, where he worked as a professor from

1966 to 1992 and director of the university's Southwest Asia and North Africa Program. The Palestinian refugee problem always stood at the center of his research agenda, and his work received considerable attention from American officials and major foreign policy think tanks. Beyond the Palestinian issue, Peretz found success in publishing a textbook called *The Middle East Today*, which became a fixture in Middle East studies courses for decades. But as far as the mainstream Jewish political map went, Peretz and his research now stood at the margins. With Zukerman dead, the AJC silent, and other voices alienated from the Jewish mainstream, independent American Jewish discussion of the Palestinian refugee question became even more negligible in the 1960s than it had been the decade prior. Peretz, for his part, continued writing books and articles on the topic for years but was never again employed by an American Jewish institution.[37]

3

An American Light unto
the Jewish Nation

ON JUNE 17, 1957, ELIAS KOUSSA, one of only a dozen Arab lawyers to remain in Israel after 1948, sat down in his Haifa office to compose a letter to an American civil rights attorney. Explaining that he had stayed in the country because of his belief that Israel would be a state "based on absolute equality of all citizens" as it promised to the United Nations, Koussa reported that Israel had fallen "painfully short" of this stated goal in its treatment of its Arab minority. "About 1,250,000 dunums [308,880 acres of land] . . . had been usurped from the Israeli Arabs rendering thousands . . . landless and jobless," Koussa wrote. "Some 35,000 displaced Arabs are scattered" in Israel, the lawyer continued, and "some of their villages were demolished to prevent the villagers' return, while others . . . stand intact but the villagers are forbidden to return." Koussa further noted that "the overwhelming majority of the Arabs in Israel live in three separate military areas governed by Army Officers where all sort of malpractice and humiliation are brought to play," and in which "freedom of Arab movement . . . is strictly forbidden except with permits often capriciously withheld."[1]

Koussa's letter accurately laid out the burdens shouldered by the approximately 156,000 Palestinian Arabs who remained in Israel after 1948. Despite receiving Israeli citizenship in 1952, most Arabs in Israel lived under military government rule until 1966, which meant that they faced ongoing surveillance, restrictions on their movement, land expropriation, curfews, and a corrupt patronage system that benefited Israel's ruling party. Koussa often wrote about these hardships, including for the Ihud publication *Ner*, but he had never before corresponded with the letter's recipient, attorney James Marshall. Marshall was not only a leading figure in the American Jewish Committee (AJC) but also the nephew of former Ihud leader Judah Magnes and the son of former AJC president Louis Marshall, widely regarded as American Jewry's most influential leader during the 1910s and 1920s. Koussa wrote to James Marshall, who also chaired American Friends of Hebrew University, upon hearing new reports of an AJC delegation coming to investigate the status of the Arabs in Israel. Worried that the delegation would receive a whitewashed image from Israeli government officials and from Arabs fearful of speaking the truth, Koussa urged Marshall to dig deeper to understand the real problems facing minorities in Israel.[2]

It is hard to know how Koussa's letter impacted Marshall, who had likely read Koussa's writing in *Ner* already, as he was among the publication's few major donors. But what is clear is that Marshall proceeded to investigate the situation with remarkable vigor, interviewing countless figures and compiling a lengthy report with policy reform suggestions that the AJC sent to Israeli leaders. Yet in any case, Marshall's personal motivations do little to explain why the AJC at large chose to investigate the issue at the moment that it did. As this chapter shows, for many within the AJC, including President Irving Engel, the reasons for addressing the minority question also had domestic roots. The chapter focuses on two periods of increased AJC interest in Israel's Palestinian Arab minority. The first came in June 1957, when a delegation of AJC leaders including Engel and Marshall visited Arab communities in Israel and heard their grievances. Breaking with the AJC's policy of non-interference in Israeli domestic affairs, Engel asked Israeli prime minister Ben-Gurion to rethink Israel's entire approach toward the Arab minority. Yet even though Israel did not fully address Marshall's or Engel's requests for a policy reappraisal, the AJC never publicly confronted the Israeli government. The AJC's gentle criticism of Israel soon faded, but in the early 1960s, the organization would make a second attempt to address the issue through its new office in Tel Aviv, which aimed not to influence policy but to educate the public about the AJC's liberal ideals.

Three intertangled motives shaped the AJC's approach to Israeli Arab rights, all of which connected in some way to the issue of the rights of minorities. For one, the AJC felt compelled to act because of its reputation as a liberal champion of human rights and defender of minority groups everywhere. According to the AJC's summary of the meeting between Engel and Ben-Gurion, the first reason for raising the issue was the AJC's interest "in human rights for everyone and therefore also the human rights of Arab minorities in Israel." Engel then noted a second reason, that "Arab propaganda is making a great point of the treatment of Arab minorities in Israel." This comment relates to the AJC's concern for Israel's welfare. Yet the AJC's anxieties about "Arab propaganda" also stemmed from a third concern, related to the AJC's central purpose—protecting America's Jewish minority.[3]

The American Jewish Committee: Liberal Integration before Zionism

Though similar to other American Jewish advocacy organizations, the AJC was historically distinct in terms of its constituency, goals, and relationship with Israel. In 1906, prominent American Jews, largely of Reform background and Central European origin, founded the group, adding a degree of institutional status to what had previously been the ad hoc efforts of a few wealthy, New York City–based Jews to defend the Jewish population against various forms of discrimination and defamation. Such discrimination had been growing in the United States since the 1880s because of the increased social snobbery of white Christian elites and the public's response to rising Jewish immigration from Eastern Europe.[4]

From the beginning, the AJC had a global scope and worked to oppose the persecution of Jews abroad—particularly in the Russian Empire—and in the period following World War I, it became increasingly involved in international discussions about Jewish rights in the postwar order. Despite this role, the AJC had a reputation as elitist, overly "Americanized" or assimilated, and out of touch with the larger recent wave of Jewish immigrants who tended to have little respect for Reform Judaism, often preferred Yiddish to English, and frequently affiliated with ideologies outside the American mainstream such as socialism, communism, anarchism, Bundism, and Zionism.[5]

One reason why the AJC appeared "out of touch" with many recent Jewish immigrants is that it distanced itself from Zionism, formally characterizing itself as "non-Zionist" for much of the mid-twentieth century. This decision stemmed in part from the organization's strong embrace of American identity and integration into American society, reflecting concern that Jewish nationalism was incompatible with Jews' American identity. To some extent, the AJC's long reluctance to embrace Zionism can be traced back to American Reform rabbis' Pittsburgh Platform of 1885, which declared that Jews were "no longer a nation, but a religious community." AJC members understood their national identity as "American," not "Jewish," as Zionism proscribed, though they proudly affiliated with Jewish religion.[6]

Yet for many in the AJC, the debate over Zionism mattered not for theological reasons but because it affected how the non-Jewish majority perceived them. From the 1920s to the early 1940s, there had been a worrying rise in antisemitism in the United States that the AJC worked hard to combat. One of its main responses involved emphasizing that American Jews were like white Christian Americans in almost every way except for religious faith. Drawing on approaches to group self-definition and political identity that had been worked out by generations of acculturated, mostly Reform Jewish leaders since the mid-nineteenth century, AJC material argued against generalizations about Jews' political views and denied that Jewishness was in any way a political or national identity, although it highlighted American Jews' loyalty to the United States. Overall, this message downplayed Jewish difference. For some in the AJC, Zionism appeared to argue the exact opposite: it was a particularist project that put the loyalty of American Jews into question, ascribed a non-American national identity to them, urged them to move to another country, and made demands on their political fealty and resources.[7]

Despite these deep ideological misgivings about Zionism, events of the 1940s—particularly the mass murder of European Jews and the postwar dilemma of where the displaced survivors should go—led the AJC to reassess its stance toward the movement. For "pragmatic" rather than "ideological" reasons, according to its own institutional telling, the AJC decided to support Israel's creation while formally retaining its "non-Zionist" designation, a term that it quietly ceased to use only after 1967. Though friendly to the new State of Israel, AJC leaders remained anxious about the implications of Jewish statehood, with AJC president Joseph Proskauer noting in an October 1948 speech that Israel's "existence creates new problems for us." He and his colleagues soon became alarmed by Israeli rhetoric that called for mass American Jewish immigration to Israel or implied that non-Israeli Jews naturally felt obligations to the Jewish state. One such statement of concern came from Prime Minister Ben-Gurion in 1949, when he reportedly stated, "Our next task . . . consists of bringing all Jews to Israel. . . . We appeal chiefly to the youth of the United States. . . . We appeal to parents to help us bring their children here. Even if they decline . . . we will bring the youth to Israel." Though Israeli officials claimed that the statement had been either "unauthorized" or misquoted, it would not be the last pronouncement by Israeli officials to elicit the AJC's ire.[8]

For the AJC, these Israeli statements represented a real threat to the status and security of American Jews. The great progress made in the fight against antisemitism could be imperiled, they felt, and questions being asked by prominent American Christians appeared to validate these concerns. To give one example, Rev. Henry Sloane Coffin, former president of the nondenominational Union Theological Seminary and one of the most famous Christian ministers in the United States, penned an article titled "Perils to America in the New Jewish State" for the prestigious liberal Protestant journal *Christianity and Crisis* in February 1949. As a result of Israel's creation, Coffin warned that American Jews would fall under "suspicion of being hyphenates . . . half Israeli and only half American. This undoubtedly will prove a source of prejudice and be an added difficulty for all Christians eager to end the hideously anti-Christian feelings against Jews." Continuing, Coffin cautioned that "no greater blunder could have been made by American Jewry than to espouse Zionism if they wished to do away with anti-Semitism in this country. . . . We can give our sane Jewish fellow citizens our hearty support in their effort to be members of our nation alone and to repudiate Jewish nationalism." Similarly, renowned journalist Dorothy Thompson in late 1949 declared that the idea that all Jews constituted a nation was an "alien concept" that conflicted with fundamental American principles and that Zionists jeopardized the equal civil status of American Jews.[9]

Neither Coffin nor Thompson could be dismissed as fringe figures, nor could their pronouncements be considered gaffes. Such statements were not rare among elite American Protestants in the late 1940s and into the 1950s. This period constituted a historical moment when American monoculture—an aspiration for conformity and an indivisible identity—persisted in much of the country. This cultural ideal had explicitly political components as well, especially for the Jews. In a period marked by McCarthyism, the Rosenberg trials, and House Un-American Activities Committee investigations, the question of whether accusations of divided Jewish loyalties threatened to roll back the gains made in the fight against anti-Jewish feelings was hardly theoretical. To help forestall these nascent tendencies, the AJC and Anti-Defamation League (ADL) engaged in positive anti-prejudice public relations campaigns, often partnering with liberal Christian groups. They also took staunch anti-communist stances to help head off dangerous associations between Jews and communists, a connection made frequently in the far-right antisemitic press. While antisemitism emanating from the Red Scare proved to be a more serious concern than antisemitism related to Zionism, the two issues overlapped in some ways. Antisemites on the far right often used the terms "Jew," "communist," and "Zionist" as interchangeable slurs. Moreover, some American Jews felt that the trial of Julius and Ethel Rosenberg had been motivated in part by antisemitic questions about Jewish loyalties. Others wondered, in the light of the Red Scare, if Jews would be blamed for "losing" the Arab world to communism if Arab states "went red" as China recently had.[10]

Concerns about how Israel affected Christian views of Jews were among the reasons why the AJC formed a subcommittee specifically to examine the "impact of Israel on American Jews." At its inaugural meeting in July 1949, AJC foreign affairs director Simon Segal declared that addressing the issue was "urgent, especially due to the anti-Israel campaign conducted by Catholic and Protestant circles here and abroad, the effect of which is very unfavorable on intercommunal relations here and abroad." Unlike in later decades, after Christian support for Israel solidified, a majority of U.S. Christians had been ambivalent during the 1948 war, according to AJC polls. Though support for the Jewish side was higher (34 percent for Protestants and 31 percent for Catholics) than support for the Arabs (12 percent for Protestants and 22 percent for Catholics), the numbers also indicated support for Zionism was far from a matter of consensus.[11]

In this context, ongoing statements by Israeli officials implying that American Jews had divided loyalties exacerbated AJC anxieties. These statements also empowered anti-Zionist voices within the AJC who urged President Jacob Blaustein to align with the anti-Zionist American Council for Judaism and distance the AJC from Israel. In hopes of disempowering anti-Zionists and alleviating concerns about antisemitism among AJC members, Blaustein set out to compel Ben-Gurion to publicly "clarify" his position regarding the problematic statements. Owing to the prominence, wealth, and influence of Blaustein—owner of what would soon be listed as one of the top ten most profitable corporations in the United States, AMOCO—and the AJC at large, Ben-Gurion complied. In August of 1950, the two issued an "exchange of views" in which Ben-Gurion stated unequivocally that American Jews "have only one political attachment and that is to the United States of America." The "exchange" involved Ben-Gurion making various statements about Jewish nationalism and immigration that flew in the face of his actual ideological views; Israeli newspapers expressed shock that a prime minister would bow to the pressure of an individual American, wealthy president of a Jewish organization or not.[12]

The AJC's Zionist critics at home went so far as to accuse the AJC of "blackmail against the State of Israel." Blaustein, however, viewed himself as a friend of Israel, feeling that his work in "clarifying" matters would remove obstacles to strengthening American Jewish ties with Israel and thus help Israel in the long run. The AJC's non-Zionism for Blaustein was thus not indifference or opposition to Israel but rather a unique way of helping Israel without accepting the core Zionist tenet that Jews constituted a nationality. While this distinction between being pro-Israel and being Zionist has melted away in decades since, it mattered much more in the context of the early 1950s, when conceptions of Zionism and American identity were both interpreted more strictly.[13]

"Non-Zionism" also fit into the organization's broader worldview regarding the question of minorities and national identity, Jewish or otherwise, as the AJC began thinking more about its role globally. Nathan Kurz has termed the AJC's prevailing ideology "liberal integrationist," which reflect-

Israeli prime minister David Ben-Gurion with AJC president Jacob Blaustein, owner of the major oil corporation AMOCO, seated next to Israeli labor minister Golda Meyerson (later Prime Minister Golda Meir). Israeli Government Press Office.

ed its members' faith that minorities could be happily and safely integrated into democratic societies through liberal institutions and reform. While the Zionist answer to the plight of Jewish minorities was *aliyah*, immigration to Israel, liberal integrationists believed that if a minority group faced discrimination, the preferred solution would be a process of liberalization and integration that would make Jews feel comfortable as citizens in their countries of birth.[14]

This non-Zionist understanding of Jewish identity fueled the AJC's embrace of civil rights at home and human rights abroad. After World War II, amidst both America's expanding global role and the destruction of European Jewry, the group had become a vocal champion of human rights worldwide. The AJC's embrace of this approach, Samuel Moyn notes, emerged from its postwar conclusion that "the cause of Jewish rights was best pursued through the larger cause of human rights," thus universalizing what might otherwise be dismissed as narrow Jewish concerns. The AJC's universalist human rights rhetoric meant supporting minorities everywhere—including, one might assume, Arabs in a Jewish state. Yet while the AJC felt compelled to raise Arab citizens' rights to Israeli leaders, they did so in a manner shaded by the nuances of Israel-Diaspora relations, contributing to a discreet approach that drew from their American experiences more so than the broader human rights agenda that they promoted elsewhere abroad.[15]

Arabs in Israel: The AJC's Increasing Awareness

The AJC's involvement in Arab affairs in Israel has a long history. In February of 1948, even before the state came into being, Blaustein maintained that in Israel "Arabs and Christians, representing minorities, must be assured equal and civil rights in fact and in theory." Months later, the group hired Israeli magistrate Helmuth Lowenberg of Tel Aviv to review Israeli media and to write a monthly "Report from Israel," which typically included a section on Arabs in Israel. Lowenberg, the same man who a few years later would relay internal information on his AJC employers to Israeli diplomats, usually provided relatively rosy depictions of Arab life in Israel. AJC leaders examined minority affairs only briefly during their first visit to Israel in 1949, and if any issue concerned them, it could be easily dismissed given that so much was in flux in the new state at the time. Over the next several years, the AJC supported American efforts to resolve the Israeli-Arab conflict, which aimed to settle Israel's disputes with Arab states as well as the Palestinian refugee issue. Blaustein, who served as the AJC's president from 1949 to 1954, did not conceptualize either the Arab minority issue or the refugee question as related to his broader concern with human rights. If anything, he believed that they were problems that would resolve themselves in the context of Arab-Israeli peacemaking. Despite their disagreements regarding Zionism, Blaustein and Israeli officials built a close relationship in the 1950s, and he, perhaps more than most other AJC figures, came to trust their judgment regarding the humane treatment of Arabs.[16]

Outside of Lowenberg's reports, which the AJC circulated only among a limited audience, AJC members could have heard about the Arab minority in publications like the *New York Times*. However, the *Times* usually contextualized obstacles facing Arabs by noting the developmental benefits that the Jewish state provided to them, and often emphasized Israeli security concerns. Other times, American newspapers framed articles about Israeli mistreatment of the Arab minority in a sort of "he-said, she-said" manner, with Israeli officials rebutting the claims of Arabs or Israeli communists, voices that likely appeared suspect to many American readers, especially Jewish ones. Moreover, the newspapers did not further investigate Arab claims beyond offering Israeli Jewish refutations.[17]

The more thorough articles published on the Arab minority in the early 1950s came, indirectly, from the AJC itself—in *Commentary*, a journal that the AJC owned but did not maintain editorial control over; at the time, Eliot Cohen, a friend of the late Judah Magnes, served as editor. "An oppressed (and depressed) minority in the midst of a Jewish state would be a historical irony and moral blunder too great to be tolerated," wrote *Commentary*'s Judd Teller in a seven-page December 1951 article titled "Israel Faces Its Arab Minority: The Native within the Gates." According to Teller, "Jewish minds and consciences both in Israel and abroad have been troubled by insistent rumors" of oppression. The article was longer and more nuanced than anything comparable in the rest of the American press. Though sympathetic to state security concerns, the article gave voice to critics of Israel's restrictive policies, citing Israeli media reports and specific legal cases. It quoted Elias Koussa's critiques of Israel's land expropriation and its prevention of Arab males above age fifteen from rejoining their families, though it devoted more space to critiques of Koussa than it did to quotes from Koussa himself. Teller furthermore quoted both Arabs who desired to be "good citizens" and those who argued that Israel is, in intent and practice, "racially exclusive." Above all else, the article emphasized "complexity," serving as a thoughtful exploration of what Teller terms the "ominous paradox" and the "uneasy compromise between what conscience dictates and what exigency seems to permit." On the whole, it gave *Commentary* readers an important window into many details and dilemmas not available elsewhere at the time.[18]

While falling far short of a moral indictment of Israel, Teller's article revealed many of the burdens faced by Israel's Arabs. Crucially, along with Don Peretz's 1954 *Middle East Journal* article, Teller's 1951 *Commentary* piece shows that the AJC did not lack basic information on the topic in these early years. Had the organization found the matter pressing enough, it could have investigated or raised the issue to the Israeli government in the early 1950s. It shows that the AJC's inherent traits—its liberalism, its non-Zionism, and its commitment to human rights—on their own did not spur the AJC to act. Doing so would require more American public attention to the issue, a development that came amidst ramped-up pro-Arab public relations efforts and bloody crises in the Middle East.[19]

Tensions in the region began heating up in 1956, reaching a new peak after President Gamal Abdel Nasser of Egypt nationalized the Suez Canal in July. Outraged, France and the United Kingdom conspired with Israel on a secret plan to depose Nasser, whom Israelis perceived as an existential threat. Essentially, Israel would invade the Sinai Peninsula while Britain and France then took the Canal Zone to "break up" the combatants. While the Franco-British side of the plot unraveled quickly, Israel succeeded in capturing the Sinai Peninsula after invading it on October 29, 1956. That same day, as Israeli troops entered Egyptian land, Israel placed a curfew over Arab-populated areas of the Jewish state that went into effect immediately, before Israeli Arabs were aware of it. As residents of Kafr Qasim, a town on the Israeli side of the border with the Jordanian-held West Bank, walked home after a day working the fields, Israeli border guards opened fire on them, killing forty-nine Arab citizens of Israel in an event that became known as the Kafr Qasim massacre. News of the massacre spread only in December after Israel lifted a gag order, and the tragedy soon became hard for the AJC to ignore.[20]

The event warranted the first extensive AJC report regarding the Arab minority, a December 1956 "Special Report" on "Israel and Her Arab Minority" written by Lowenberg. The report stated, "One of the greater tragedies in the young life of Israel has been the mutual attitude of the state and its Arab minority. . . . The first attempt to integrate the Arab minority into Israel has been a failure, and the situation cries out for . . . new solutions." Lowenberg divided Arab citizens into two groups: those "friendly" and those, mainly in the Galilee, who had "never been particularly friendly." Lowenberg regarded Israeli suspicions of the latter group as a "fifth column" as justified. The report detailed the eviction of Arabs from the village of Kafr Bir'im, now known as Kibbutz Bar'am, which, though dictated by security concerns, "rightly or wrongly . . . has poisoned the atmosphere among the Arabs in Israel." Isra-el's Absentees' Property Law of 1950 and Land Acquisition Law of 1953, which legalized Israel's mass appropriation of Arab-owned lands, had a sim-ilar effect on Arab attitudes toward the state. Grievances and political ten-sion, the report noted, "spread quickly from mouth to mouth, from Nargilah [hookah] to Nargilah," and before long "a general feeling of mistrust" emerged "between Israelis and her Arab minority." Lastly, it detailed the "Kafr Kassem outrage," explaining how border guards shot forty-nine "men, women, and children" who accidentally violated curfew. "This terrible car-nage . . . evoked a wave of horror. . . . Israelis should at once search for an answer to the problem of how to treat their minority," the AJC report stated.[21]

The fact that the massacre's victims were from Israel's Arab minority, rather than Arabs living in neighboring countries, seems to have struck a particular nerve for some American Jews. When, three years earlier, inter-national condemnation burst forth after Israeli forces killed sixty-nine Pal-estinian villagers, mostly women and children, during a reprisal raid in the Jordanian-controlled West Bank town of Qibya, many American Jews re-sponded defensively. Judd Teller, the same journalist who had written the informative 1951 *Commentary* exposé on Israel's Arab minority, persuaded U.S. newspapers to soften their critique of Israel over the massacre, earn-ing the praise of Israeli diplomat Abe Harman. Meanwhile, historian Doug Rossinow claims that the massacre prodded pro-Israel groups to mobilize for Israel like never before, creating new umbrella organizations. Though the AJC reportedly helped American Zionists perform damage control for Israel after the Qibya massacre behind the scenes, it resisted joining any formal umbrella efforts, reflecting the view of future AJC president Her-bert Ehrmann, who balked at the idea of issuing joint statements with Zi-onists or presenting a united Jewish front on the issue. After surveying newspapers and issuing polls to see how the massacre affected the public image of Israel and Jews in general, the AJC's main public response consisted of a vague resolution calling for the United States to intensify its efforts to bring about a lasting peace.[22]

While AJC leaders perhaps classified the Qibya massacre as an "off-limits" issue within the realm of Israel's security policies, it was hard to deny that the Kafr Qasim tragedy related to the treatment of minority groups, the AJC's professed focus. Writing to senior AJC staff members, Don Peretz spoke directly about the need for the AJC to address the Arab minority issue after the Kafr Qasim massacre. "Public silence," he wrote to his employers, "seemed somewhat inconsistent with the stated objectives of the AJC to advance civil and religious rights for all people of all religions and races." Peretz warned that others noticed the contrast between the AJC's vocal stance on the plight of Egyptian Jewry and its silence on Kafr Qasim. Similarly, U.S. State Department officials told the AJC in January 1957 that whenever America raised concern about the mistreatment of Jews in Arab countries, Arab diplomats brought up Israel's inhumane treatment of its Arab minority and implicitly accused Americans of hypocrisy. Yet the AJC still opted not to criticize Israel openly, instead resolving to look into the "treatment of minorities" in its upcoming Israel trip. An AJC memo regarding the trip stated that "one of the chief propaganda weapons against Israel is the treatment of its Arab minorities," particularly regarding "security restrictions, military government, and movement limitations" and "lack of equal opportunities in employment and confiscation of lands of Arab citizens." It noted that "clarification of the status of the Arab minority would assist us in our attempts to be helpful to Israel."[23]

The "Arab Propaganda Network" and America Jewry

Being "helpful to Israel" only partially explains AJC concerns. Even before the Kafr Qasim massacre, AJC leaders worried that "discrimination against the Arab minority could endanger our struggle against anti-Jewish discrimination all over the world." AJC officials specifically feared that Israel's treatment of the Arab minority would be used against American Jews amidst rising pro-Arab propaganda. A confidential AJC report titled "Arab Propaganda in the United States" outlined what it termed a transnational "Arab propaganda network that included the Arab League, the Egyptian embassy, business interests, anti-Zionist Jews, white Christian antisemites, American Friends of the Middle East (AFME), and various Arab states." The AJC worried that American "bigots" would publicize allegations against Israel to harm American Jewry, noting that right-wing Christian antisemites included Arab claims in their antisemitic periodicals to bolster their broader case against all Jews. According to the AJC, even groups and individuals who were not antisemitic created danger for American Jews when they highlighted questionable Israeli actions, because antisemites could use this material as evidence of Jewish moral deficiencies or American Jews' "divided loyalty."[24]

An example of the "propaganda" regarding Arabs in Israel that caused AJC leaders concern was a 1956 booklet by Dr. Fayez Sayegh, then acting director of the Arab League's Arab Information Center in New York City. The booklet referred to the Arab minority in Israel as "step children in their own homes . . . down-trodden, under-privileged," claiming that "their sad status belies the boastful claim that there is 'democracy' in Israel," and that "Arabs in Israel live under martial law in segregated ghettos—a painful anomaly of history, where yesterday's victims . . . impose that same abhorrent, degrading institution on [the Arabs]. . . . The martial law . . . ruthlessly restricts their movement and travel . . . [and] empowers . . . authorities to confiscate their property."[25]

Sayegh also penned a May 1955 article, "The Arab Plight in the Holy Land," for *The Moody Monthly*, a magazine published by the Chicago-based Moody Bible Institute, a central hub of Christian evangelical fundamentalist education, indicative of the fact that Zionism had yet to win over American evangelicals. The Arab Information Center also republished in May 1956 a pamphlet by Sayegh titled *Arab Property in Israeli-Controlled Territories*, which focused on Israeli confiscation of Arab lands, including those of its Arab citizens. More troubling than Sayegh's writing was a 1955 book published in Damascus called *Tension, Terror and Blood in the Holy Land*, distributed by the Syrian consulate in New York. While Sayegh focused on events in the Middle East, the Syrian book contained harsh, antisemitic critiques of American Jews as "aliens." Don Peretz felt particularly appalled to see that the book's chapter titled "The Arab Minority in 'Israel' " cited and distorted his own academic work on the topic, making the problem appear even worse than it was in reality. He distinguished this distortion with critical writing that appropriately cited his work, perhaps referring to articles by Sayegh and by Hal Draper, an American Jewish Trotskyite who excoriated Israel for its policies toward the Arab minority in a two-part exposé published in the socialist *New International* during the mid-1950s.[26]

The AJC began printing "fact sheets" to counter these Arab claims. Their intent was clearly to counteract any negative effect that these Arab accusations would have on American Christian opinions of Jews. In May 1956, the AJC published the fact sheet "The Middle East Ferment" as part of an effort to build a "community program for dealing with the domestic impact of the Middle East crisis." In 1957, the AJC issued a booklet related to Israel's Arabs, a twenty-four-page fact sheet titled "Christian Communities in Israel," discussing the rights of Christian communities, missionary activities, individual rights of Christians, the protection of holy places, and Christian property in Israel. Much of the pamphlet, likely written by Peretz but reviewed by Israeli diplomats, emphasized the religious freedom of Christians in Israel and state efforts to preserve Christian sites. It noted "some serious limitations of individual rights" but stated that "for the most part, these result from restrictive measures solely because of their Arab ties, not their religion." It noted that "security regulations . . . directly affect a majority of Israel's Arab population—both Christian and Muslim—living under military rule because of hostilities between Israel and Arab states," and that many "face lack of employment opportunities" and "must secure permits to travel." The booklet concluded by noting that "within the bounds of military necessity . . . Israel has attempted to preserve . . . Christian institutions. The picture is not always a happy one, but progress has been made. . . . Only with peace in the Holy Land will Israel's Christians enjoy the full measure of freedom . . . which is their due." The effort to stress Christian freedoms and contextualize Israel's shortcomings clearly reflected AJC concerns about alienating American Christians. "Israel's impact on our lives as American Jews affects the way we are regarded by our Christian fellow Americans," stated one AJC source. If not addressed, the Jewish state's mistreatment of Christians and other Arabs, the AJC feared, could harm Jewish-Christian relations in the United States.[27]

The AJC Goes to Nazareth

These concerns partially explain why the AJC chose to address Israeli Arab rights during its 1957 Israel trip. The delegation traveled to the Arab city of Nazareth and the demographically mixed city of Acre, among other places, meeting with local Arab leaders such as Bishop Isidorus of the Greek Orthodox Church, the mayor of Nazareth, Acre's deputy mayor, Arab students at Hebrew University in Jerusalem, and a Muslim religious judge. All had relatively positive things to say, perhaps because the AJC's Israeli government hosts apparently arranged the group's itinerary. Bishop of Acre George Hakim, who later became Patriarch Maximus V Hakim of the Melkite Greek Catholic Church, stood out as the most critical voice on the tour. Like the others, Hakim had no complaints about religious freedom. Instead, he discussed the many restrictions imposed on Arabs by the military government, arguing that in parts of the country far from the border, security could not justify such restrictions. Hakim asserted his belief that economics was the true motive for these restrictions as limitations on movement prevented some Arabs from competing in many labor markets with recent Jewish immigrants. He further complained about the Land Acquisition Law, which deprived many Arabs of their property and offered insufficient compensation. The delegation also heard a critical take from Arabs whom they met along with the American Friends Service Committee (AFSC) director at the Quaker house in Acre.[28]

AJC leaders took these complaints seriously. During a June 24 meeting between Ben-Gurion and AJC officials Irving Engel, James Marshall, John Slawson, Simon Segal, Herbert Ehrmann, and others, Engel broached the matter gently. "We have been careful not to bring up any points concerning internal administration, only points that are used against you," he said. This wording implied that propagandists' use of the Arab minority issue transformed it into an external and thus legitimate matter for discussion, rather than an internal Israeli issue beyond the AJC's purview. Lecturing Ben-Gurion on a purely internal affair would have undermined the spirit of the agreement that Engel's predecessor Blaustein had established and Engel himself asked Ben-Gurion to reaffirm. Engel then listed all the positive things that they heard regarding Arab welfare in Israel before turning to "the bad things"—the military government and the Land Acquisition Law that legitimated the mass confiscation of Arab property.[29]

Immediately after voicing the critique, Engel hedged by stating, "As an American, I have no right to point the finger at Israel." Ben-Gurion, attempting to draw Engel into the Zionist political collective, replied, "As a

Jew you have the right!" Engel then noted that "when we were at war with Japan, we did worse things than you have done to the Arabs," attempting to soften his critique of Israel by alluding to his own country's internment of American citizens of Japanese background. "I realize your security problem," Engel said. "Not fully," the prime minister interjected. "We have, however, the impression that if a good look were taken at the facts, it would be possible to change the whole situation [of the Arab minority] . . . and would decrease the ammunition of your enemies," Engel stated, again referring to Arab spokesmen who raised the issue in America.

Ben-Gurion replied that while Engel supported equality as an American, he himself supported equality not because he was an Israeli but because he was a Jew. "We were taught, some 3,000 years ago, if the foreigner shall live among you, you shall love him as yours because you were foreigners in Egypt," the prime minister recalled. He then claimed Arab citizens had equal rights, but went on to explain why the security situation warranted military rule and restrictions on movement. Ben-Gurion justified the restrictions by stressing that Israel's Arab enemies wanted to destroy Israel and kill Jews, blaming Palestinian Grand Mufti of Jerusalem Amin al-Husseini for the Holocaust. "When Hitler . . . exterminated 6,000,000 Jews, the Mufti perhaps gave him the idea," the prime minister stated. The suggestion expanded on a similar claim that Ben-Gurion made several days prior, when, after Engel mentioned the Arab refugee issue, he told the AJC leaders that "the Mufti actually took part in the extermination of the Jews in Germany." Despite the outrageousness of these accusations, they merited no particular response from Ben-Gurion's guests.[30]

With regard to the military government, Ben-Gurion then assured Engel that "the regime would be liberalized so as not to impose unnecessary hardships, especially economic, on the Arab population." The Israeli leader then shifted topics and began a long lecture on Zionism. Ben-Gurion emphasized that despite their differing views, he listened to them because he saw them primarily as Jews, not just as Americans. "Morally," Ben-Gurion declared, "we have nothing to learn from others," referring to non-Jews broadly and non-Jewish American leaders specifically. "Mr. Eisenhower is no authority for us. . . . We have nothing to learn from Mr. Dulles," referring dismissively to the U.S. president and secretary of state who had recently forced him to withdraw Israeli forces from the Sinai. Ben-Gurion went on to explain the messianic basis of his Zionist thought, and the conversation continued, covering a wide array of topics and ending on a positive note.

Underlying the whole conversation on Arab minority rights sat the question of what gave non-Zionist American Jews the right to speak on the matter. As a Zionist, Ben-Gurion felt certain of AJC leaders' right to express their views on Israeli affairs because of their Jewishness; meanwhile, the non-Zionist Engel felt a need to emphasize that Arab propaganda concerns made Arab rights an American issue and thus justified his right to speak as a non-Zionist American Jew.[31]

In public, Engel praised Israel and expressed gratification over an announcement of Israel's easing of security and travel restrictions for Arabs soon after the visit. The AJC attributed the reform to the meeting, but there is no evidence to support this claim. According to his diary entry, Ben-Gurion himself did not seem to think much of the AJC's "complaints about the treatment of minorities." According to an early book published on the topic, written by Sabri Jiryis, an Arab who himself had been subjected to military rule, the July 1957 reform was only "a slight alleviation in the system of travel permits," not a major change. In any case, it soon became clear that not everyone in the AJC felt satisfied with the July reforms.[32]

The Marshall Memorandum: An American Jewish Push for Arab Civil Rights

The AJC member most concerned with the question was, perhaps unsurprisingly, the one who had spent the most time in the country—James Marshall. While to Israelis Marshall may have looked no different than the other middle-aged Ashkenazi men who arrived with the delegation, his past experience in the country no doubt led him to view it with different eyes. Marshall had traveled to Palestine for the first time in 1927 to visit his uncle Judah Magnes and to report on the situation for his father, AJC president Louis Marshall, as the latter contemplated whether to cooperate with the Zionist cause. Not only had he met with a much younger Ben-Gurion during that 1927 visit, but he also developed a distinct appreciation for the Arab presence in the land. "The first thing that impresses one in Palestine today is that the land is Arab," wrote a thirty-one-year-old James Marshall for the *Menorah Journal* in 1928. "Essentially," he concluded, "modern Palestine is Moslem." The younger Marshall's impressions likely influenced the elder Marshall's pivotal 1929 decision to lead his fellow non-Zionists into a cooperative effort with the reconstructed Jewish Agency for Palestine, which rested on the assertion that they were "apolitical," philanthropic supporters of Palestine's Jewish settlements. But while Louis Marshall seemed uninterested in Arab-Jewish relations in Palestine during his negotiations with Zionist leader Chaim Weizmann in the late 1920s, the topic certainly mattered to James. "It is idle to talk of an Arab problem in Palestine," he wrote in 1928. "There is none; the problem in Palestine, as throughout the world, is for the Jew to . . . adjust himself to the existing civilization," which in this case was Arab or Islamic.[33]

While many American Jews could envision Palestine as a "land without a people for a people without a land," Marshall, who never considered himself a Zionist, certainly was not among them. At the time of his 1927 visit, Jews comprised only around 16 percent of the British Mandate's population, leading him to conclude in 1930 that a "completely Jewish Palestine" was an "adolescent fantasy." Instead, Marshall called for immediate self-rule for Palestine in the form of a government "representative of all groups living there." Just because Arabs comprised a large majority did not seem like a valid reason for indefinitely delaying democracy in the land, he implied. Despite these musings, Marshall did not consider himself a foe of Jewish settlement in Palestine, supporting the "safe-guarding [of] our cultural institutions, the Hebrew language and our religious freedom," as well as Jewish efforts at economic development, insofar as they promoted Jewish-Arab cooperation. Though the idea of a Jewish home being established within an Arab-majority Palestine later fell outside the bounds of Zionist thought, it was not so in 1930, a fact underlined by the decision of the Zionist Organization of America's *New Palestine* to publish Marshall's argument.[34]

Though Marshall never used the word "binationalism," it is clear that his perspective was informed by that of his uncle, Rabbi Judah Magnes, a prominent supporter of a joint Arab-Jewish state. Marshall had been close with Magnes both personally and ideologically, perhaps viewing him as a father figure after Louis Marshall's death in 1929. With Magnes's urging,

Marshall funded the first Arabic-Hebrew dictionary in hopes that it would increase mutual understanding between peoples. Published in mid-1947, the dictionary did not prevent war from erupting later that year, though Marshall felt proud enough of the effort that he told Magnes that he hoped his role in developing it would be inscribed on his tombstone someday.[35]

Both Marshall and Magnes expressed dismay at the AJC's decision to support the partition plan in November 1947. In August 1948, as war raged in Palestine-turned-Israel, Marshall wrote to Magnes to propose setting up a group of "Jewish intellectuals and people who more or less share your [Magnes's] viewpoint" to serve as an oppositional voice to the "official Zionist" line. Magnes proposed that philosopher Hannah Arendt serve as chair, though she declined taking up the role despite her strong interest in the group. However, Magnes died soon afterward, and instead, Marshall, Arendt, Hans Kohn, and others cofounded the Judah L. Magnes Foundation, which funded scholarships for Arab students at Hebrew University and supported Ihud's publication *Ner*. As leader of the foundation, Marshall received letters from Ihud leaders, who in 1952 told Marshall that they "consider the struggle for a change in the position of the Arab minority as our most important activity," which included "fight[ing] against the misdeeds of authorities" and "protest action against the new Citizenship-Law with its discriminating sections against the non-Jewish, particularly the Arab population of the state of Israel." As one of *Ner*'s few major donors, Marshall likely read its many English-language articles on the Arab minority's plight written by Elias Koussa and others.[36]

Marshall's own interest in Arab civil rights connected with his career. His primary concern as a lawyer was in the field of civil liberties, with a range of interests that included fighting the discriminatory employment practices of major corporations. He was involved with the National Association for the Advancement of Colored People (NAACP) in the 1930s and later lectured in public administration at New York University. A Republican, Marshall served as head of New York City's Board of Education, to which he was appointed after serving as Mayor Fiorello La Guardia's Manhattan campaign manager in 1934. Long active in international affairs, Marshall was involved in the United Nations Educational, Scientific and Cultural Organization (UNESCO) and, in the 1950s, headed the AJC's

Committee on International Organizations. By the end of the decade, he would become one of the AJC's vice presidents.[37]

The 1950s marked Marshall's return to what had become the State of Israel for the first time since his 1927 trip. In 1950, he took note of the empty Arab villages and visited a prisoner-of-war camp where Arab families lived behind barbed-wire fences. "Somehow, I have never been able to regard people with such animus that I could feel anything but horror at their containment in such camps," Marshall wrote later, calling them "cruel" and "inhumane." He returned to Israel in 1954, 1955, and 1956, when he visited the prime minister's residence and met with Ben-Gurion for the first time since his 1927 visit.[38]

All this is to say that Marshall came to Israel with the AJC in 1957 not as a newcomer to the question of Arabs' status in Israel but as someone who was particularly well informed—and well prepared. Throughout the AJC's many meetings in Israel, he carried around small notepads, jotting down nearly every detail of what he learned, and upon his return home, Marshall wrote a lengthy memorandum on Israeli Arabs for the organization. Throughout the delegation's trip, Marshall appeared so committed to the Arab minority issue that his colleagues felt as though he was "kind of acting as an independent mission."[39]

Marshall's 1957 memorandum not only detailed Israeli Arabs' many grievances about their government's policies; it also offered concrete and creative recommendations for mitigating or even resolving some of their complaints. The introduction of the twenty-seven-page memorandum noted Marshall's meetings with over thirty Arab individuals, which included "mayors, mukhtars, Arab civil servants, university students, professional men, refugees, a nurse, a politician, a teacher, farmers and keeper of a coffee house." Marshall met with them in six Arab villages and towns, in Haifa, in Nazareth, in Acre, in their homes, in schools, in offices, and in the temporary housing of internal refugees.[40]

Detailed and nuanced, the report presented the Israeli Arab plight in sympathetic terms. Marshall wrote that some Arabs felt like "virtual prisoners of the new state," and mentioned that one told him, "We are second class citizens. We feel we are not wanted here." He said their grievances were "sometimes justifiable," noting the issues of land seizure, inadequate compensation for land seized, the difficulty of litigation over land disputes, and the military travel permit system, which he termed "above all" a "humiliation, and one of the principal sources of the Arabs' feeling that they are not first-class citizens, and indeed in this respect they are not." Marshall expressed empathy, noting practical, moral, and religious reasons why Israel should grant equal rights to Arabs, and cited a Jewish official who said that though many Israeli Arabs might sympathize with Egyptian president Gamal Abdel Nasser, 95 percent of them pose no threat. Yet Marshall did not blame Israeli leaders, believing that Ben-Gurion and Moshe Sharett shared his concerns, nor did he fault Israel's right-wing opposition politicians. Instead, he faulted average Israelis, writing in one draft that "curiously, it is not Begin and Herut" who seek to deny Israeli Arabs their full rights "but rather many middle class Jews and Jewish laborers/farmers, who can now as conquerors project upon the Arab the attitudes which they experienced in other lands from the majority people there." Marshall recalled, "With American naiveté . . . I said that it seemed to me that the first important break in the situation . . . came when whites and blacks sat down to work out common problems, including the problem of Negro rights." He asked Israeli Jews, "Why . . . could not groups be set up in Israel in which Arabs and Jews would discuss their common problems?" One Israeli replied, "In America . . . the improvement in the condition of Negros is the result of the work of Jews, who felt themselves to be a minority. Here we Jews are not a minority." Marshall did not view that as a valid excuse.[41]

Marshall's reference to "whites and blacks [sitting] down" is striking. The emphasis on intercommunal communication instead of legislation characterized both the liberalism and the limits of the AJC's human relations agenda. Marshall's quote stands in contrast with Engel's reference to the internment of Japanese Americans during World War II. Both chose American cases to compare to the situation, notably not comparing the Arab minorities' plight with the mistreatment of Jewish minorities, despite the AJC's active involvement with such matters. Engel's choice harkened to a temporary measure tied directly to security concerns, while Marshall alluded to deeper issues at play in Israel, using terms such as "discrimination."[42]

Marshall noted many other issues plaguing Israel's Arabs, including economic problems, development limitations, and the plight of internal refugees. Some problems seemed to bother Marshall more than others, since he attributed some complaints not to discrimination but to Arab inabilities or the young state's bureaucratic limitations. He discussed the negative effects of Israeli policy, such as the restrictions keeping Arabs from returning to their homes, but noted that "it is not for us to pass judgment on the security phase of the case," deferring to Israel's military while still questioning the decision to some extent. Marshall also highlighted the positive aspects of the Israeli state for its Arab citizens—the freedom of religion, economic development, the courts, and the universities.[43]

Marshall then listed eleven recommendations that he felt would improve the circumstances facing Arabs in Israel. These suggestions included facilitating more contact between Arabs and Jews, expanding Arabs' local autonomy, increasing Arab integration into Israel's labor union, enlarging Arabic study in Jewish schools, legalizing more political parties, liberalizing the permit system, and more. Marshall's piece demonstrates a sense of optimism, a faith in creative solutions, and the belief that the Zionist project could be redeemed through moderate liberalization. His attitude typified a brand of liberalism that prevailed in predominantly white educated circles in mid-century America. His proposals blended human relations techniques with concrete policy proposals. Marshall accepted the reality of serious problems in Israeli Arab life, even though he hesitated to attribute moral failings to Israel's leaders. Ending on an uplifting note, Marshall reported "one great advantage at this time—that is the leverage that exists in the prophetic tradition while the present generation is in place of power in Israel; but such forces have a tendency to lessen as the generation of revolution is succeeded by another." It is "not safe to assume that time will cure the malady. Time is just as likely to harden positions and will probably lessen the moral drive," he declared. "The time to make use of prophetic morality to solve the Arab question is therefore now."[44]

The Next Step? The AJC in the Late 1950s

Juxtaposed with the urgent appeal at the end of the memorandum were three words underlined and capitalized at the top of the document: "<u>NOT FOR PUBLICATION</u>." Though Marshall circulated his memorandum among AJC leaders, the AJC did not want it distributed publicly. Don Peretz unsurprisingly disagreed, encouraging Marshall to publish an article based on it, and Marshall initially seemed to concur, as he asked at least one newspaper if it was interested. Though all AJC officials appeared sympathetic and interested, some suggested that the AJC urge Israel to implement Marshall's recommendations, while others suggested that Marshall send the memorandum to the Israeli government as his personal initiative, without official AJC endorsement. Owing to an office mishap, AJC staff sent Marshall's memorandum with a cover letter bearing AJC president Irving Engel's signature to Ben-Gurion, much to Engel's chagrin, adding to the memorandum's significance.[45]

In February 1958, Marshall finally received a response from Shmuel Divon, the prime minister's advisor on Arab affairs. Divon thanked Marshall but noted that Marshall's "relatively brief visits . . . did not allow for more extensive research into the complexities of the problems involved." Divon emphasized Arab economic development without noting the expropriation of land from Arab citizens or the restrictions on movement that deprived Arabs access to many economic opportunities. Though Divon's office replied to Marshall and made inquiries to other agencies, Divon showed little interest in altering state policy on the basis of Marshall's recommendations. An internal Israeli commentary on the memorandum began by stating that Marshall lacked balance in noting what Israel had done for its Arabs, but curtly conceded that Marshall had been correct on some points.[46]

Even prior to the ambivalent response from Israeli officials, writers in the Yiddish press had become aware of the AJC's meeting with Ben-Gurion. They perhaps learned of it from AJC press releases that briefly mentioned the topics discussed, or from a July 8, 1957, *Jewish Newsletter* article on the meeting titled "American Jews Criticize Israel." In a *Jewish Newsletter* article published later that month titled "Committee under Attack," William Zukerman, who defended the AJC, gave an overview of critiques in the press. The Labor-Zionist *Yiddisher Kempfer* called the committee "tactless": "Would anyone, for instance, dare to ask an Irish statesman if he speaks also in the name of Irish citizens of America? Or would anyone ask Chaing Kai-Shek if he speaks in the name of all Chinese in America?" Zukerman rebutted editorially to point out that no other country has naturalization laws like Israel's, dismissing as irrelevant the *Yiddisher Kempfer*'s query: "Is [Israel's nationality law] a reason for making the humanitarian national law into a constant source of suspicion and dual loyalty?"[47]

Zukerman also discussed a debate on the AJC's Ben-Gurion meeting in *Journal-Tog*. While editor S. Dingol and journalist B. Z. Goldberg concurred that the AJC should not have brought up Israel's nationality law, they disagreed about the Arab minority question. "It does not behoove a Jewish organization in America to come to Israel to speak about Arab minority rights and in this way help Arab propaganda to show that the Israeli government discriminates against its Arab citizens," Dingol wrote, adding that the AJC had made a weak case that Israeli violations of minority rights harmed Jewish minorities elsewhere. Goldberg disagreed, writing, "Jews have fought everywhere in all non-Jewish countries against discrimination on the basis of religion . . . and now comes a Jewish state which is still subsidized by the Jews of other countries and discriminates against non-Jews." Goldberg understood Irving Engel's cause for concern. These statements in the Yiddish press, Zukerman concluded, confirmed his view that the AJC's Ben-Gurion meeting marked the first notable criticism of Israel by American non-Zionist Jews. It helped clarify, in Zukerman's words, that "Israel is first and foremost a monolithic nationalistic state based on the undemocratic . . . principle of 'one nation and one religion' against which Jews of the Western world have always fought." The AJC "performed a great service, even if it angered the Zionists."[48]

For whatever reason, neither Marshall nor the AJC appeared to have pushed Marshall's agenda further. Was public criticism of even a brief summary of the AJC's critique enough to help make the group more subtle in its approach to the issue? Though Engel's speech to the executive board in October 1957 mentioned that minorities in Israel constituted an "issue of deep concern to AJC," at meetings from October 1957 to July 1958, the Israeli Arab issue was barely mentioned. Perhaps some AJC leaders felt satisfied enough with recent easing of restrictions. It may be that they simply became distracted by the many other issues under the AJC's purview.[49]

Minor changes did not, however, appease those whom the AJC viewed as "propagandists." In 1959, the Arab Information Center's Sami Hadawi published a new forty-page booklet, *Israel and the Arab Minority*. After detailing the restrictions on movement, the Land Acquisition Law, and the Kafr Qasim massacre, Hadawi concluded that "Israel's claim to be a democratic nation . . . is without foundation." Though dealing with similar facts as Marshall, who believed that Israel could be improved through liberal reforms, Hadawi asserted that the Zionist project was unredeemable. In light of this, the AJC's unwillingness to take a more public approach to dealing with Israeli Arab rights should be unsurprising, as the group's leaders had little interest in giving organizations like the Arab Information Center ammunition for their "propaganda weapon" against Zionists. Uninterested in a public confrontation and faced with the reality that limited private lobbying did not yield significant results, the AJC does not appear to have taken further action on behalf of Palestinians in Israel until the 1960s.[50]

A Committee on a Hill: The AJC's Israel Office

In 1960, the AJC announced that it would soon open an office in Israel with a mandate to advance liberal ideas within the Jewish state. AJC Israel Committee chairman Alan Stroock acknowledged that "some Israeli actions embarrassed the AJC" and insisted that countering "anti-democratic practices and attitudes" in Israel would make it easier for the organization "to invoke principles of human rights and practices in our country and abroad." Stroock specifically noted that the office would work for the rights of Israel's Arab minority. The AJC formally announced the opening of the office in 1961, after Ben-Gurion and Blaustein, then the AJC's honorary president, met to smooth out tensions that stemmed from the AJC's discontent with how Israel was handling the capture and trial of Nazi war criminal Adolf Eichmann. Israeli diplomats had mixed feelings about the AJC's proposed office, and some were weary of AJC meddling in Arab civil rights and other issues. The AJC appointed its former Latin America director, Maximo Yagupsky of Argentina, to head the new Tel Aviv office. On the very first page of his first report, Yagupsky noted that he had begun meeting with Israeli officials to discuss the Arab minority issue. He made plans to visit Arab areas of Israel and to meet with community leaders to discuss their problems. One Israeli official introduced Yagupsky to Arab Knesset members and promised to introduce him to military officials in charge of

Arab areas, after which Yagupsky could submit questions to the prime minister's assistant.[51]

During the years he spent heading the Tel Aviv office, Yagupsky dedicated effort to improving Arab minority affairs. But the AJC and Yagupsky
conceived their target audience not as the Israeli government but Israeli
Jews more broadly, who needed to be educated about the meaning and importance of pluralism and civil rights. This fit with the office's goals, which
included "develop[ing] greater understanding in Israel of the pluralistic nature of American society . . . [and] increas[ing] the knowledge of American
and Western Traditions of civic responsibility and civil liberties in order to
foster development of democratic institutions," as well as stimulating "ap-
plication of the insights of the social sciences to intergroup tensions in Israel and to help encourage respect for diversity of cultural and religious
expression."[52]

The office aimed to survey the Arab population regarding their well-
being, to promote integration, and to create a library to help educate Israelis
on how liberal democracy should function. Various reports from Yagupsky
mentioned the military government, and in 1962 AJC leaders further expressed to Ben-Gurion their opinion that military rule should be relaxed "in
order to permit Arab citizens to participate more fully in the democratic life
of the country." When the state eased some restrictions, AJC leaders expressed their gratitude to Israeli officials but said that their satisfaction
would increase "even more when the restrictions are completely eliminat-
ed," echoing Engel's 1957 statements. Yet the AJC's Israel office did more to
investigate and educate than it did to lobby, with Yagupsky sending reports
back to New York, opening a library, contemplating offering intergroup discussion sessions, and publishing a *Commentary*-like Hebrew journal, *Ammot*, to promote liberal thought and *Tfutsot Israel*, a bulletin meant to inform
Israelis about American Jewry and life in Western democracies.[53]

Yagupsky's views appeared in a 1966 *Trenton Times* article titled "American Jewish Group Teaches Israelis to Be Tolerant of Minority," which highlighted the fact that "young Israeli Jews, living in the only place on earth
where they are a majority, are being taught by an American organization to
be tolerant of their minority groups." The article, which centered on an interview with Yagupsky, emphasized that a main objective of the AJC's pro-

gram in Israel consisted of strengthening the democratic character of Israel's evolving society, because he and other AJC leaders "don't want the same errors of oppression that Jews have experienced among other majorities." The only path to peaceful coexistence, Yagupsky stated, came through education, which the AJC's experience in the United States had made it best suited to perform. "The AJC is doing a wide educational job in cooperation with the government, which has neither the means nor the time" to deal with it, he explained.[54]

Yagupsky's emphasis on education underscored the AJC's belief that the primary problems facing the Arab minority in Israel had sociological rather than governmental origins. Specifically, Jews from Middle Eastern countries allegedly expressed prejudice toward the Arabs, presenting a problem that the predominantly Ashkenazi AJC took upon itself to solve. "The young Israeli is a different type of Jew who is not familiar with the problems of discrimination," Yagupsky said. "We are studying their attitudes toward themselves and each other to see if they have to be oriented. About 53% of Israel's population is made up of Oriental Jews. Teaching them to avoid problems of discrimination is an educational job." Yagupsky's words reflect an orientalist assumption that Jews from Middle Eastern countries, known in Israel as *Mizrahim* (literally, "Easterners" or "Orientals"), were less likely than Jews of European origin to understand liberal democracy. According to this reasoning, rather than learning the value of tolerance from their experience as a minority, as American and Israeli Ashkenazi Jews ostensibly had, Mizrahi Jews despised Muslim Arabs because of discrimination they had experienced in their homelands, a claim seen in Israeli coverage of the Kafr Qasim massacre. It was up to the AJC and others to teach the "Oriental Jews," and Israelis more broadly, "how democracy works" and to help make Israel a liberal society in which minorities felt included. Otherwise, Yagupsky predicted, Israeli Arabs "will be exposed to becoming a fifth column inside the country," putting both Jews and Arabs at risk.[55]

While the specifics of Yagupsky's analysis of Israeli democracy, society, and minority relations may have been his own, his activities served as an extension of the AJC and its goals regarding the treatment of the Arab minority in Israel. He corresponded regularly with AJC leaders in New York, who determined his office's role, one shaded by a "human relations" approach mirroring that of the AJC's work in America. Yagupsky's views on the root of the problem threatening the Arab minority—society rather than government actions—also echoed certain sentiments that James Marshall had voiced years earlier. Marshall had similarly included integration programming among his proposed reforms; his wider emphasis on governmental reforms may have stemmed from the fact that the military government was more repressive in the 1950s than it was in the 1960s when Yagupsky worked in Tel Aviv, a city with a small Arab population, largely in Jaffa, which was not subject to military rule.[56]

Though both Yagupsky and the earlier AJC delegation viewed Israel as less democratic because of its treatment of the Arab minority, they diagnosed the situation differently. Yagupsky lived in Israel for years and had a daily working relationship with Israeli officials. He internalized their understanding of the roots of the "Arab problem" as well as that of the "Oriental Jewish" problem. Government officials were benevolent partners in education for Yagupsky, not obstacles. Israel's lack of investment in advancing Arab integration and educating the public stemmed from the state's limited means rather than Israeli leaders being opposed to that goal, in his view. For Yagupsky, the Israeli public did not understand what liberalism and democracy really meant, and they simply needed to be taught. Young Israeli Jews had forgotten what it was like to be a minority, whereas American Jews lived as one. The common thread between these episodes is that AJC officials believed it was up to them, as liberal Americans who specialized in protecting minorities, to educate Israelis, whether officials or citizens, on the importance of liberalism. Only then could Israel become the democracy they wished it to be—one devoid of the stain of discrimination, a sin the AJC did not take lightly, considering its own raison d'être.

Conclusion: The Limits of American Jewish Influence

The AJC's attempt to encourage Israel to shift its attitude toward the Arab minority was intimately linked to its earlier effort to aid Palestinian refugees, yet the dynamics differed in some fundamental ways. For Israel, the Palestinian refugee question was a high-stakes diplomatic issue, with Israel's fear of international pressure to permit the return of refugees being so great that its leaders felt the issue merited an intervention in American Jewish organizational life.

In contrast, the Israelis saw the Arab minority issue very differently. After giving its Arab population citizenship, the Israeli government had little concern about international pressure. Though military government rule of Arab areas violated the rights of many Arab citizens, Israeli leaders understood that this would ultimately be seen on the international stage as a domestic issue rather than a festering matter affecting the entire region like the Arab refugee question.

Instead, it was an American Jewish organization that felt compelled to "intervene" in Israeli governmental debates over its Arab minority policy. Hesitant to step beyond the organization's self-imposed bounds, the AJC's president framed the issue as a matter of public relations in America rather than as an ethical concern that drove him to critique Israel's actions. Yet there were those such as James Marshall who were clearly unsettled by Israeli policies and prevailing mentalities. How could he and others in the AJC who did so much to advocate for minority groups in the United States and elsewhere simply remain silent? After all, the AJC was not hesitant when weighing in publicly on internal human rights issues in Morocco and Egypt, where Jews were the beleaguered minority. For the AJC leadership, the question of the Arab minority struck too close to the heart of the organization's central concerns for them to ignore it. But ultimately, their efforts did little to change the outlook of Israeli leaders, who remained content to politely dismiss the AJC's concerns and to move toward any future policy reforms at their own slow pace.[57]

Just as the Arab minority issue was one of only a few major concerns raised by Engel to Ben-Gurion in 1957, the "liberalizing" of Israel through education, particularly in connection to attitudes toward minorities, was a major preoccupation of the AJC's Israel office in the 1960s. Rather than confront the government or publicize problems, the office focused on fostering intercommunal dialogue in hopes of eliminating discrimination against Arabs.

These AJC efforts to address the minority issue in the 1950s and 1960s, while similar in some ways, seem to have differed categorically; specifically, the 1957 efforts to press the Israeli government indicate a greater sense of urgency. Israel's loosening of military government restrictions between 1957 and 1962 only partially explains this difference.

The reason for this contrast came not from inside Israel or inside American Jewish politics but rather from the broader currents of U.S.–Middle East relations and the public discourse they inspired. It is no coincidence that the major dramas within the AJC described in this book—over the refugee issue in 1956 and the Arab minority question in 1957—came about in such a compact period of time. "Propaganda" about Israeli Arabs was among the AJC's major concerns, especially because it related in part to Israel's treatment of Christians and thus threatened to harm Christian perceptions of Jews in the United States. As the sources throughout the chapter described, these years were marked by elevated activity within what the AJC described as an "Arab propaganda network." Understanding what exactly led to this rise and subsequent fall requires looking outside the realm of Jewish politics and into the dynamics of the United States' relationship with the Arab world, American public discourse on Palestine, and the one talented, frustrated Palestinian at the center of it all—Fayez Sayegh.

4

"Such Distinctions Cannot Be Maintained"

Sayegh is one of the most competent polemicists that American Jewry has ever had to counteract. He is extremely astute and is all the more dangerous because a Jewish organization, the American Council for Judaism, propagates a line so closely resembling his. However, I really believe that Sayegh is trying to distinguish between the responsibilities of Zionist and non-Zionist Jews, between those who help Israel and those who don't. The difficulty is, however, that in the arena of public opinion, such distinctions cannot be maintained, and in the end, Zionists and Jews become identical in all but the most careful minds.

—AJC official S. Andhil Fineberg, 1956

As time goes on, it will be futile for any American Jews to be deluded by the proposition that Israel is "just another foreign state." Willingly or not, their destinies are closely linked to those of the people of Israel. . . . Realities caution against any other appraisal.

—Suppressed AJC "Fact Sheet" critical of Zionists, 1958

FOR FAYEZ SAYEGH, A PALESTINE Liberation Organization (PLO) executive committee member whose career had been punctuated by defeat, November 10, 1975, marked a major triumph. On that day, the United Nations General Assembly (UNGA) passed Resolution 3379, determining that "Zionism is a form of racism and racial discrimination," by a vote of seventy-two to thirty-five. Working as part of Kuwait's UN delegation, Sayegh had been the "principal author" of the resolution and "chief architect" of the successful vote. After the resolution's passage, Sayegh served as UNGA 3379's main defender in the body against denunciations by United States ambassador Daniel Patrick Moynihan and others.[1]

In condemning UNGA 3379, Moynihan echoed the organized American Jewish community, which viewed the resolution as a moral outrage. The many Jewish groups rallying against the measure included the American Jewish Committee (AJC), which in 1967 had tacitly ceased referring to itself as "non-Zionist." The AJC, along with nearly every other major American Jewish organization that raised its voice on the issue, condemned the resolution as antisemitic. Critics consider that labeling to be one episode in a long history of conflating anti-Zionism with antisemitism, an unfair tactic that they claim is used to silence criticism of Israel's infringement of Palestinian rights.[2]

While in a global context the origins of equating anti-Zionism with antisemitism may be impossible to determine, in the case of the AJC, its historical relationship with this notion can, in fact, be reconstructed. Until recently, scholars have tended to focus on the post-1967 years when discussing the proliferation of this conflation, sometimes linking it with the rise of the term "the new anti-Semitism" popularized by an eponymous 1974 book written by two leaders of the Anti-Defamation League (ADL). Yet consensus on conflating pro-Palestine anti-Zionism with antisemitism actually emerged among non-Zionist American Jewish groups not after 1967 but earlier, in the 1950s. This chapter demonstrates this finding with regard to the AJC, concurring with a similar conclusion reached by political scientist Matthew Berkman in his study of another major American Jewish group, the National Communal Relations Advisory Council (NCRAC). During the short period between 1956 and 1958, the AJC, then still the most adamantly non-Zionist player in the American Jewish establishment, prepared and then quickly abandoned efforts aimed to position itself as a neutral arbiter on anti-Zionism and antisemitism. Censoring its own material that criticized Zionists and softening its resistance to unity on Israel-related matters, the AJC soon joined broader communal efforts to combat "anti-Israel" activity on college campuses, having determined that countering pro-Palestine activism should be part of its campaign to combat anti-Jewish prejudice.[3]

At the beginning of this two-year period, however, amidst heightened tensions in the Middle East and rising tides of pro-Arab rhetoric in American public discourse, AJC officials not only debated the supposed link between anti-Zionism and antisemitism, but they even met with a much younger Fayez Sayegh, whom they deemed *not* antisemitic, to advise his Arab League office on how to express its anti-Zionist views in a tolerable manner. This quiet effort to hammer out an AJC–Arab League consensus took place at a time when the thirty-four-year-old Sayegh headed the Arab League's public diplomacy operation in the United States as acting director of its Arab Information Center ("the Center") in New York City. During that period, Sayegh served as the public face of the Arab cause in America and was reputedly its most talented public advocate in the country. On national television, CBS's *Face the Nation* called Sayegh the "principal spokesman in America for the Arab states" during one of his over 240 radio and television appearances that decade. Moreover, while Protestant leaders, Arab students, Lebanese Americans, and Jews of anti-Zionist, non-Zionist, and Zionist persuasions agreed on little, in the 1950s all considered Fayez Sayegh to be "the most effective Arab speaker in America."[4]

In meeting with Sayegh, the AJC parted ways not only with Zionist groups but also with its sole fundraising partner, the ADL. Reflecting an attitude toward pro-Arab rhetoric that it first adapted in the mid-1940s, the ADL led the charge in accusing the Arab Information Center of antisemitism. During a March 15, 1956, broadcast of the popular, nationally syndicated radio show *Tex and Jinx*, ADL leaders Arnold Forster and Benjamin Epstein called the Center a purveyor of antisemitism for menacingly accusing American Jews of "double-loyalty and double allegiance" for supporting Israel. As the Center's acting director, Sayegh later appeared for an interview on the same program to rebut the allegation. After categorically denying the charges of antisemitism, Sayegh had the radio host read a quote from Israeli prime minister David Ben-Gurion that Sayegh felt impugned the loyalty of American Jews. In highlighting Ben-Gurion's words, Sayegh maintained that it was primarily Zionists and Israelis—not anti-Zionists and Arabs—who put American Jews' loyalty into question.[5]

In response, rather than publicly attacking the Arab official, AJC leaders proceeded to admonish Israeli leaders for their rhetoric. In a stern letter to Ben-Gurion, AJC honorary president Jacob Blaustein noted how Sayegh had used the prime minister's quote on-air, and executive vice president John Slawson stated in a 1957 speech that "some propaganda, Zionist as well as anti-Zionist, does tend to make it *appear* as if American Jews harbor . . . dual loyalty." The group even drafted a pamphlet that accused Zionists of providing fodder to antisemites; had it been published, the pamphlet would have paralleled a similar "Fact Sheet" critiquing the anti-Zionist American Council for Judaism.[6]

The AJC's reaction to Sayegh reveals that, at least initially, it responded very differently from other Jewish groups to the dramatic rise in domestic pro-Arab advocacy brought about by the Center's opening in 1955 and the ramping up of public relations efforts by the CIA-funded American Friends of the Middle East (AFME). While other organizations like the ADL pushed back aggressively against pro-Arab advocates, the AJC sought to convince Israel to alter the policies and rhetoric that it viewed as the source of the problem. Moreover, while the non-Zionist AJC supported Israel and did not welcome pro-Arab activity, the group's expert on the topic did not view those who advocated for Palestinian rights as inherently antisemitic. Both Zionists and anti-Zionists, the AJC felt, could foment anti-Jewish feelings if they spoke recklessly, and it fell on the non-Zionist group to serve as an impartial referee.[7]

This remarkably wide gap between the AJC and its peer organizations, however, did not last, with the AJC's position undermined, in part, because of the actions of Arab officials. Though the AJC's key theoretician of prejudice, Rabbi Solomon Andhil Fineberg, maintained that chief Arab League spokesman Sayegh did not espouse antisemitism, Arab state diplomats over whom Sayegh had no authority frequently made antisemitic statements or collaborated with right-wing antisemites. Meanwhile, Sayegh's AFME allies sometimes invoked what Jewish groups viewed as threatening "dual loyalty" accusations that the AJC felt would foment antisemitism among American Christians.

Accordingly, both sets of allies inadvertently undermined Sayegh's goal of removing the taint of antisemitism from pro-Arab advocacy. In this context, the AJC became increasingly persuaded by those who labeled all pro-Arab rhetoric as threatening to American Jews. For even if Sayegh never uttered a single antisemitic word, his criticism of Israel was deemed to constitute "anti-Semitism by detour," in the words of a Jewish communal professional who argued that the entire American Jewish community had to unite to combat the skilled Arab spokesman. In early 1958, the AJC chose not to publish the "Fact Sheet" critical of Zionism that it had prepared, hesitantly moving toward consensus with Zionist groups in their efforts to counter Sayegh. Regardless of intent, the AJC concluded that public criticism of the Jewish state ran too great a risk of increasing anti-Jewish feelings in America, a decision that led the group to censor even its own critiques of Israeli and Zionist leaders.[8]

Opposition to Zionism and American Jewish Politics, 1937–1955

America's first major public debate over whether anti-Zionism constituted antisemitism came years before Sayegh entered the scene and more than a decade before Israel's emergence. Even though American Jews were never united on the question, leaders of major American Jewish organizations, remarkably, basically all held the same position—that Arab opposition to Zionism was certainly *not* antisemitic.

On June 5, 1937, WNYC radio broadcasted a town hall event hosted by an Arab American group in New York called the Arab National League. The program, which honored Lebanese American writer Ameen Rihani, opened with the reading of a cable by Grand Mufti of Jerusalem Amin al-Husseini and featured an array of speakers who criticized Zionism. In response, New York alderman Samson Inselbuch accused the radio station of "spreading anti-Semitism and racial hatred" and introduced a city council resolution denouncing WNYC's decision in what was likely the first legislative action taken against anti-Zionism in American history.

Yet the Arab National League and WNYC soon found defenders among American Jewish leadership—not only from the explicitly non-Zionist AJC but also from representatives of the National Council of Jewish Women, B'nai B'rith, the Orthodox movement's Rabbinical Council of America

(RCA), and the Zionist-affiliated American Jewish Congress (AJCongress). Defending the network, AJCongress leader Rabbi Stephen Wise, a leading Zionist who also headed the World Jewish Congress, wrote that "absurdly enough, it has been charged with anti-Semitism—as if Arabs and Jews alike were not Semites." Similarly, after listening to the speeches RCA president Rabbi Herman Goldstein stated that he heard "no anti-Semitic spirit" in them. Had Goldstein himself run WNYC, the Orthodox rabbi said that he, too, would have broadcasted the program. Sympathizing with Arab Americans as a fellow minority group, Goldstein told the *New York Times* that it "would be a sad day in America when minorities were throttled and were unable to express their viewpoints." Though Inselbuch and his supporters maintained that anti-Zionism was inherently "anti-Jewish," those at the top of American Jewry's institutional pyramid disagreed.[9]

Somewhere in the global upheaval of the 1940s, however, the attitudes of many American Jewish leaders changed. Reports of Nazi atrocities led many more American Jews to embrace Zionism, or at the very least view Palestine as a logical refuge for displaced Holocaust survivors. By 1945, 80 percent of American Jews thought that some form of Jewish state was necessary, a consensus that included virtually all Jewish political advocacy organizations short of the AJC and explicitly anti-Zionist groups. Meanwhile, exiled Mufti al-Husseini's collaboration with the Nazi regime, covered in depth by AJCongress publications, marred the Palestinian Arab cause and shaded the way some Jews viewed Arab spokesmen in America. Those feelings likely became even more negative after Eliahu Epstein, a future Israeli ambassador to the United States, baselessly alleged in a 1946 article for *The Nation* that al-Husseini had pushed Hitler to exterminate European Jewry.[10]

In this context, the national office of B'nai B'rith's Anti-Defamation League began vocally criticizing pro-Arab groups for the first time in 1946. Toward the end of World War II, Arabs in the United States had increasingly mobilized against Jewish statehood, mainly through an Arab American group called the Institute for Arab American Affairs (IAAA) and the Iraqi-sponsored Arab Office in Washington, DC. The ADL attacked both by publicizing links between them and right-wing antisemites and by arguing that Arab rhetoric provided fodder for the latter, although it stopped short of characterizing Arab opposition to Jewish statehood as inherently antisemitic. The ADL and others also emphasized al-Husseini's wartime alliance with the Axis powers. One ad by a group called the Non-Sectarian Anti-Nazi League literally "linked" the Arab Office and the IAAA with the "Nazi-Helping Ex-Mufti of Jerusalem," Adolf Hitler, and American fascists in an illustrated "chain" of antisemitism. The ADL repeated and expanded on these accusations, sometimes overstating tenuous connections. For their part, the AJC and most other Jewish groups largely refrained from publicly engaging with the controversy.[11]

Amidst these allegations and after their failure to prevent the United States from supporting the UN Partition Plan, the Arab Office closed in late 1947. The IAAA did not last much longer. As a result, before long, the most strident voices in the United States supporting strengthened U.S.-Arab relations—and opposing Jewish statehood—would be not Arabs but a cohort of American Protestants sometimes referred to as "Arabists." Some of these Protestants descended from early missionaries to the Middle East and maintained warm feelings toward the Arab world. Others worked for oil corporations that relied on the goodwill of governments in the region. All, however, felt strongly that American support for the creation of a Jewish state in Palestine would imperil the United States' standing in the Middle East and drive the Arab world—and its oil resources, which America's Western European allies desperately needed—into Soviet hands.

Personifying this perspective was Kermit "Kim" Roosevelt Jr., a grandson of President Theodore Roosevelt who had served in Cairo as an operative of the Office of Strategic Services (OSS), a forerunner of the CIA. To Roosevelt, Arabs looked like promising allies in the emerging Cold War, if only American leaders would refrain from alienating them by supporting Zionism. In February 1948, Roosevelt and roughly a hundred other Americans came together to form a group called the Committee for Justice and Peace in the Holy Land (CJP), with Roosevelt serving as its executive director. With the support of important Protestant clergymen, oil executives, academics, former diplomats, and anti-Zionist Jews including Rabbis Elmer Berger and Morris Lazaron, the CJP labored to counter Zionist efforts to create a Jewish state. The CJP lobbied against U.S. recognition of Israel, but when the group failed, it soon withered and folded. In 1950, CJP members regrouped to form a similar organization, the Holyland Emergency Liaison

Program, but that, too, fizzled out because of a lack of funds and public indifference.[12]

By 1951, Roosevelt found a solution to the Arabists' recurring financial problem. As head of the CIA Office of Policy Coordination's Near East desk, Roosevelt secured covert CIA funding for a new iteration of the group, soon to be named AFME. The amount totaled $1.5 million in AFME's first six years, equivalent to roughly $16 million in 2022. Though its members genuinely believed in the cause, AFME, as historian Hugh Wilford puts it, acted in many ways as a CIA "front" organization—or, perhaps better put, a "state-private network"—aimed at pushing American public discourse in a pro-Arab direction. If successful, this would give the government a freer hand in working with Arab states and pressure Israel to accept concessions that the administration deemed necessary.[13]

As for the problem of public indifference, Roosevelt hoped that recruiting celebrity journalist Dorothy Thompson to lead the group would provide the solution. Thompson, labeled by *Time* magazine as one of the two "most influential" woman in the United States alongside Eleanor Roosevelt, and by a *Fortune* poll as American's second-favorite news columnist, had been a staunch supporter of Zionism well into the 1940s, having forged warm ties with American Jews owing to her early critiques of Nazism. But a 1945 trip to Palestine made her reconsider her position, and within a few short years she became one of American Zionism's most prominent foes. Thompson's break with her Jewish friends would be further compounded when, beyond debating Middle East policy, she also questioned whether it was appropriate for American Jews to advocate for a foreign state at all, which her critics claimed cast aspersions on American Jewish loyalties.[14]

AFME had two agendas, one at home and one in the Middle East. Abroad, it ran student recruitment centers in Arab capitals and funded Arab students in America in hopes of influencing the next generation of Arab leaders to support America, countering parallel Soviet efforts. These AFME centers in Arab states also conveniently served as bases for CIA operations. On the domestic front, AFME ran its own propaganda campaign, which in its view aimed to counter that of the Zionists. This campaign, which peaked between 1953 and 1956, included setting up speaking tours, arranging conferences, sponsoring research, and publishing pamphlets and books.[15]

In addition to its own activities and rhetoric, AFME used its funds to help Arabs spread their message in the United States. In 1952, AFME invited Arab students from throughout the country to plan a national student convention in June at the University of Michigan. From it, a new organization, the Organization of Arab Students in the United States (OAS), would emerge. AFME provided the bulk of the budget—$5,000 ($55,000 in 2022 dollars) plus a dedicated staff member in its office and other noncash resources—for the first Arab student convention, which counted Dorothy Thompson and a young Arab United Nations bureaucrat named Fayez Sayegh among its speakers. AFME's involvement with Sayegh had begun earlier that year, when in February 1952 it helped publish a short book, or booklet, that the thirty-year-old had written. Titled *The Palestine Refugees*, it included a preface from Virginia Gildersleeve, who had chaired AFME's predecessor organization, CJP, and a foreword by Harvard philosophy professor William Ernest Hocking, another AFME member. *The Palestine Refugees* would be the first book published in America on Palestinian refugees to be written by one.[16]

AFME invited Sayegh to speak frequently as he represented precisely the type of Arab that they sought to present to the American public. He had been born in Syria in 1922 and grew up in his mother's native Palestine, attending elementary school in Tiberias and high school in Safed. Sayegh's Syrian father worked as a Presbyterian minister, which appealed to AFME members given that many of them affiliated with that denomination. The younger Sayegh had reportedly been quite religious in his youth. Later, as a student at the American University of Beirut, Sayegh became active in the anti-communist Syrian Social Nationalist Party, ultimately rising to become the party's publication editor and spokesman before being pushed out of the party in 1947 because of a dispute with its leader. Later that year, Sayegh enrolled in a PhD program in philosophy at Georgetown University in Washington, DC, which he completed in late 1949.[17]

Vast changes took place in the Middle East while Sayegh studied at Georgetown. The British Mandate of Palestine came to an end and the State of Israel emerged. Sayegh's entire family was displaced, though his brother Yusif only left the country after spending nearly a year in an Israeli prisoner of war camp. Like most other Arab citizens of Palestine who had fled, been expelled, or been abroad in 1948, Fayez Sayegh could not return. The United States offered him a residency visa, but even before finishing his doctorate, Sayegh began to work in the diplomatic realm as a research officer for the Legation of Lebanon in Washington (1949–1950) and advisor to Lebanon's delegation to the United Nations, both under the mantle of Ambassador Charles Malik, another Arab Christian whose religious affiliation helped him build ties with American Protestants. In 1951, Sayegh took up a job with the Middle East section of the radio division of the United Nations but soon moved to the UN's human rights division, where he worked until January 1955. Around this period, Sayegh developed a warm relationship with Rabbi Elmer Berger of the anti-Zionist American Council for Judaism, who did much to influence his thinking.[18]

After publishing his booklet on Palestinian refugees, AFME sponsored Sayegh's speaking engagements, often making sure to inform audiences of his Protestant affiliation and anti-communist credentials. Putting him on par with Israeli ambassador to the United States Abba Eban, known for his eloquence, Sayegh was introduced to audiences as the "Arab Eban" at AFME events. In 1954, the group even gave Sayegh a special research fellowship to write a book on a topic of his choosing. The resulting book, *Arab Unity: Hope and Fulfillment*, was published in 1958 by the conservative and staunchly anti-communist Devin-Adair Publishing Company and included an acknowledgment of AFME's support.[19]

Sayegh's future, however, involved advocating for Arab causes from a more resolutely "Arab" platform. Recognizing Sayegh's experience advocating for Arab causes in front of American audiences, in 1954 Arab League secretary general Abdul Khalek Hassouna asked him to draw up blueprints for a new Arab League office to direct Arab public relations in the United States. Hassouna reportedly told Sayegh that the plans would be sent out to all Arab foreign ministers for review. Less than a year later, on February 1, 1955, the Arab Information Center, also known as the Arab States Delegations Office, became a reality. Sayegh left his position at the United Nations to become the chief of research at the Center's headquarters in New York City.[20]

Despite Sayegh's role in drafting the blueprint for the office, the Arab League did not select Sayegh to run the office, likely because of his relative

Fayez Sayegh on the right with his older brother, economist Yusif Sayigh, in Baltimore, 1955. By permission of the family of Yusif Sayigh.

youth and lack of political connections. The directorship instead went to Kamil Abdul Rahim, a well-connected Egyptian who had previously served as his country's ambassador to the United States. Before the end of 1955, however, Sayegh would be named the Center's deputy and, six months later, acting director, when Abdul Rahim took leave for a year on account of illness.[21]

Sayegh's first few years with the Center witnessed an almost unbelievable amount of activity on his part, which took place as he also wrote books, pamphlets, and a weekly column for an Arab American newspaper. Within twelve months of starting his position, Sayegh gave nearly fifty lectures and appeared on television five times and on the radio four. This would be little compared with his April 1956 cross-country lecture tour; in only seventeen days, he made fifty-four appearances across nine states, traveling over eight thousand miles. During these lectures, Sayegh typically spoke extemporaneously. He debated Israeli diplomats, spoke at dozens of college campuses, and faced tough interviews on national television shows such as *Face the Nation* and *Night Beat* in these years. These feats were all the more impressive when one learns that he suffered from a severe heart condition, surviving multiple heart attacks when in his thirties. Undeniably, Sayegh was a workaholic; his staff, in contrast, did not appreciate when he pushed them to be as well. "It is unfortunate indeed that you do not distinguish in your mind between an office of civilians and a military camp," one coworker complained to Sayegh.[22]

Americans had never before seen on television an Arab spokesman with his level of persuasive power, and it was no exaggeration when one *New York Herald Tribune* journalist termed Sayegh "probably the most effective advocate for the Arab cause" in America, fighting "the propaganda battle of Palestine from coast to coast." One can see evidence of Sayegh's persuasive capacity in the musings of Mike Wallace, a hard-nosed journalist of American Jewish background who befriended Sayegh after interviewing him in 1957 on *Night Beat*. Sayegh "opened his eyes" and "left an enduring impression" on Wallace, according to several sources. "Back in the 50's, I met a man by the name of Fayez Sayegh who was a Palestinian, and he was really a Palestinian to his roots," Wallace himself recalled decades later, and "he helped to let the scales fall from my eyes about the relationship between Palestinians and Israelis. . . . You take on quite a chore when you go against your own religion . . . [and what you learn from your] folks growing up."[23]

No doubt the opening of the Arab Information Center and Sayegh's activity would have on their own caught the attention of Jewish groups. But compounding matters, 1955, the year of the Center's opening, also marked an expansion of AFME undertakings. This stemmed from developments in the Middle East; regional tensions were rising as border raids between Israel and its Arab neighbors increased in frequency, leading Israeli officials to believe that a larger future war was inevitable. The young, charismatic Gamal Abdel Nasser had recently emerged as Egypt's undisputed leader a few years after the "Free Officers" Revolt of 1952 deposed what some American officials saw as a lethargic monarch whose failure to develop the country left it vulnerable to Communist influence. Nasser, in contrast, made clear his ambitions to modernize Egypt, but also declared his hopes of securing greater armaments for the Egyptian military.

While for Israel Nasser looked like an existential threat, to some in the American foreign policy establishment, he looked like a perfect potential partner. The Truman administration, which had already cited Egypt as a pivotal Arab state in the Cold War context, owing to its vast population and strategic location linking the Red Sea and the Mediterranean through its Suez Canal, was enthusiastic about the regime that came to power in 1952. With regard to Nasser personally, AFME founder and CIA official Kermit Roosevelt had built a close personal relationship with him even before the revolution. Entering office in 1953, the new Eisenhower administration concurred that Nasser had potential. In a May 1953 conversation with Nasser, Secretary of State John Foster Dulles expressed "real enthusiasm for the new regime in Egypt," and noted that unlike Truman, Eisenhower owed no political debt to Jewish voters, implying that he saw no insurmountable domestic obstacle to strengthening U.S.-Arab ties. Despite American attempts to compel Nasser's Egypt to align fully with the West, Nasser preferred nonalignment, or "positive neutrality," which frustrated U.S. officials, who in turn refused to provide him with the arms and aid he desired without strings attached.[24]

Along with Nasser's neutralism, the other main impediment preventing a U.S.-Egyptian alliance was, in the minds of many in the Eisenhower administration, the State of Israel, or at least Israel's conflict with its neighbors. American officials cooperated with the British to launch a covert effort to alleviate tensions in the region. The plan, known as Operation Alpha, came to a head in early 1955, when the Americans and British proposed to Egypt and Israel an agreement that would have involved the resettlement of seventy-five thousand Palestinian refugees in Israel; Israel's ceding small parts of its Negev to Jordan and Egypt, creating a territorial link between them; and the institution of a state of nonbelligerence between Israel and its neighbors in lieu of a formal peace declaration.[25]

Getting Israel to make concessions could be challenging, however, if U.S. public opinion pushed too strongly against it. "The Administration had succeeded in deflating Israel in order to make a reasonable settlement possible," Dulles explained in early 1955. "As a result the Israeli position was now weaker than it ever had been, but by 1956 it was likely to gain new strength." AFME, according to historian Hugh Wilford, was apparently tasked with keeping Israel's position weak in the United States, a job that merited its heightened annual budget in 1955 as it waged a public campaign to strengthen U.S.-Egyptian ties in tandem with the diplomatic efforts. Dorothy Thompson, for example, penned a laudatory introduction to the English-language publication of Nasser's nationalist treatise, *Egypt's Liberation*, and her organization sponsored newspaper ads, speeches, and conferences at an even greater pace. This campaign came to a climax when AFME invited Arab League secretary general Abdul Khalek Hassouna to speak at the Waldorf Astoria in December 1955, which worried Israeli diplomats.[26]

Polls from 1955 to 1956 indicate that AFME efforts had some success, or may simply reflect the "weakness" of Israel's position at the time, to use Dulles's words. An October 1955 survey showed that Americans were only somewhat more likely to blame Egypt (19 percent) than Israel (11 percent) for the "present trouble" in the Middle East. Meanwhile, in April 1956, only 15 percent of the American public expressed sympathy with Israel (versus 4 percent for Egypt), and respondents opposed arming Israel by a fourteen-point margin. While support for Egypt was lower than support for Israel, these numbers make it hard to characterize the public at large as pro-Israel at the time.[27]

Antisemitism, Anti-Zionism, and the "Arab Propaganda Network"

For American Jewish organizations, the combination of these ramped-up AFME activities with the opening of the Arab Information Center caused great concern. The Organization of Arab Students, for its part, also continued to grow more politically active. Arab public advocacy had reached unprecedented levels. Something, it seemed, was in the air, as forces on both sides of the Egyptian-American relationship seemed to be longing for closer ties at Israel's expense.[28]

All of the "Big Three" American Jewish defense organizations—the AJC, the ADL, and AJCongress—took notice, interpreting the rising pro-Arab rhetoric as a threat to American Jews. In April 1955, the AJC's fact-finding division circulated a confidential memorandum titled "Arab Propaganda in the United States." It stated that "Arab propaganda in the United States, as it relates to Israel and American Jewry, is premised on a cardinal point of Arab propaganda strategy: The best way to weaken Israel is by undermining the status of the Jewish community in America." Arabs had settled on this strategy, its authors argued, because of "the obvious role the Jews of America have played in bringing about the establishment of Israel, its recognition as a state, and its sustenance through American Jewish aid in the many millions of dollars in the form of contributions and the purchase of Israel bonds." The report divided the network into categories such as "Anti-Semitism Inspired by the Arab League," "Anti-Semitism That Ties in with Pro-Arab Propaganda," "Business and Industrial Concerns," "Christian Religious Concerns," and "Other," under which it listed "American Friends of the Middle East" and "Arab students in the U.S. as propagandists."

The Arab League's Arab Information Center, the report noted, stood at the head of this network and devoted "most of its efforts in fomenting anti-Israel, anti-Jewish sentiment in this country. . . . After some initial impetus by the Arabs in the late '40s, a more potent and subtle type of propaganda is consciously or unconsciously waged by some of the most respectable elements in this country." The document further noted that there were really two Middle East issues that the American public cared about: "the plight of over 800 thousand displaced Arabs" and "alleged desecration of holy places and churches in Jerusalem, coupled with demands for internationalization of that city." It argued that the "distress of the Arab refugees" was "especially exploited among Protestant groups, where appeals are made on a humanitarian basis. Catholics are more receptive to the second point. Anti-Semitism, overt and identifiable, is generally not found in these appeals. Inhumanity or callousness is attributed to the 'Israelis,' seldom, if ever, to the Jews as Jews." However, it noted "references to U.S. policy," coupled with "hints of the importance of the Jewish vote, and not—too—obscure allusions to divided loyalty."

The report called AFME a "principal transmission belt of this type of propaganda," though noted that the organization never engaged in "patent anti-Semitism." It would be "hazardous openly to categorize this group or leadership as being anti-Semitic," it warned, referring to the power of AFME's clout and the thinness of the charges against it. Finally, it noted AFME's support for Arab students at American universities, who "appear to be well-oriented on their side of the problem, and in many cases are very voluble in presenting it."[29]

This analysis appeared not only in AJC research documents. Members of the AJC's executive board received a background memorandum titled "The Middle East Crisis and Its Impact on American Jews" that summarized the research memorandum's findings in advance of their May 1955 meeting. Another AJC memorandum from March 1956 stated that AFME and Arab governments arranged "anti-Israel" speakers with Arab students, and warned of a "heightening of attacks on 'Zionists' and 'Jews,' " threatening calls for "Moslem-Christian unity," and "slurs" made "against American Jews for alleged 'dual loyalty.' " AFME's executive vice president, Reverend Garland Evans Hopkins, did nothing to assuage these concerns when in October 1955 he publicly warned that American Zionist activities would lead to the "loss of the Middle East" to communism and raise questions that would provoke a "wave of anti-Semitism in this country," comments that some American Jews read as a threat.[30]

When compared with the reports of the AJC's peers, the ADL and AJ-Congress, one striking similarity and one striking difference instantly become clear. The similarity is that in content and in interpretation, the AJC Fact-Finding Division's memorandum essentially mirrors the findings of the two other organizations, so much so that it appears very likely that they shared information. The difference is that while the ADL and AJCongress moved quickly to publicly denounce pro-Arab voices, the AJC stayed mostly silent about its concerns with the Arab Information Center and AFME, leaving them largely confined to internal memoranda.[31]

The AJC's disinterest in publicly criticizing AFME and the Arab Information Center is clear when comparing drafts of a "Fact Sheet" that would ultimately be published as "The Middle East Ferment" in April 1956. While an early draft contained a section titled "The Arab Propaganda Network" detailing allegations against the Center and AFME, the final version retitled the section neutrally as "The Propaganda Battle in the United States." The earlier draft contained substantial material on AFME's collaboration with Arab propagandists and Arab students that was removed entirely from the printed version. The final version included no negative reference to OAS or the Center, merely noting that "the Arab Information Center and some 3,000 Arab students enrolled in American colleges are also advancing Arab positions."[32]

In contrast with the AJC, almost as soon as the Arab Information Center's doors opened, the ADL condemned it. In a February 1955 press release carried by the Associated Press, it accused the Center of "running a propaganda operation with the aid of anti-Semites." Center director Kamil Abdul Rahim denied the charge publicly. In response, the ADL's national director Benjamin Epstein and general counsel Arnold Forster dedicated a third of their 1956 book *Cross-Currents* to substantiating the allegations. The book also attacked AFME, coming months after Epstein and Forster met with Israeli diplomat Basil Herman to discuss "opening an offensive against [AFME executive] Garland Hopkins and AFME."[33]

Divided into three sections—"Cross-Currents in America," "Cross-Currents in Germany," and "Cross-Currents in the Middle East"—*Cross-Currents* mostly consists of internal memoranda on antisemitic activity said to come directly from ADL files. The first two sections focus on neo-Nazis and other far-right "professional anti-Semites." This category included Gerald L. K. Smith, a Protestant minister who edited *The Cross and the Flag* and ran as the America First Party's 1944 presidential nominee; James Madole, leader of the neofascist National Renaissance Party; Gerald Winrod, editor of the pro-Nazi newspaper *The Defender*; Merwin K. Hart of the National Economic Council; and Benjamin Freedman, an American Jew-turned-Catholic who espoused extreme antisemitic views. While these names may sound obscure today, the ADL and AJC took the threat that they posed very seriously. As former ADL staff member Sol Kolack stated years later, "Jews were seriously concerned about these anti-Semites. . . . I had some personal feeling that they were not consequential. But you must remember . . . this was immediately after . . . the Holocaust. So it may well be that they magnified the threat of the [Gerald L. K.] Smiths and other pipsqueak anti-Semites." Historian Stuart Svonkin notes that so soon after the Holocaust, those charged with protecting American Jews found it difficult to judge whether a "professional anti-Semite" should be considered a harmless "pipsqueak" or the next Hitler.[34]

The third section of *Cross-Currents*, which focused on the activities of the Arab League and other Arab officials, including their purported cooperation with the abovementioned "professional anti-Semites," paralleled the findings of the AJC and AJCongress but went into much greater depth.

"Since 1948, Arab propaganda in the United States has made use of two themes: the 'imperialistic' injustice to the Arabs in the reestablishment of Israel and the plight of the Arab refugees," the introduction to the section proclaimed. It continued, "But whatever the themes of Arab propaganda may be, one of its goals in this country is precisely similar to that of every dyed-in-the-wool American anti-Semite . . . the utter destruction of Jewish prestige in America." Despite their different motivations, *Cross-Currents* maintained, Arab propagandists allied with domestic antisemites because they believed that fomenting antisemitism was the best way to end U.S. support for Israel. "Dual allegiance" accusations against American Jews, after all, had been "something else the Arabs helped dream up," the authors alleged. The book continued by detailing many alleged acts of cooperation between Arab officials and "known Jew-baiters."[35]

Notably, the ADL leaders did not argue that anti-Zionism was inherently antisemitic, but instead asserted that anti-Zionist Arabs felt a need to foster antisemitism in order to weaken support for Israel. Yet most, if not all, of the memoranda in the book alleging cooperation between Arab officials and antisemites lacked any corroboration. For example, it stated that in 1952 Abdul Rahim had met for lunch with "professional anti-Semite" Gerald Winrod, who then reprinted a speech by Abdul Rahim in *The Defender*, and it reported alleged talks between far-right figure Allen Zoll and Egyptian officials about potential collaboration but did not note how the ADL knew of these meetings. It alleged, without providing evidence, that Frank Britton, editor of the antisemitic *American Nationalist*, had received Arab funds to publish an article that claimed that Israel mistreated its Arab minority and Arab refugees, that Jews gave their loyalty first to Israel, and that Israel was a perpetrator of atrocities. According to *Cross-Currents*, the Arab League's Omar Haliq paid for and drafted an article in the *American Nationalist* on the Qibya massacre that stated, "The parasitic state of Israel added another murderous chapter to its already blood-spattered record."[36]

While *Cross-Currents* discussed a few episodes from before 1955 and included some entries about antisemitism in the Arab world, the bulk of the section centered on the Arab Information Center. Chapter 3, titled "The New Director," focused on Sayegh's boss, Ambassador Kamil Abdul Rahim. Each entry in the book was formatted to reproduce original ADL documents, perhaps to convince readers that the material constituted tangible "proof." Here is one example:

> November 22, 1954
>   Research to AF [Arnold Forster]
>   Rahim made some interesting, off-the-record comments about American Jews to friends the day he arrived. If Arabs in the United States were to minimize their anti-Semitic agitation, said Rahim, many American Jews might lose interest in Zionism and Israel. But, added Rahim, this was not the solution; there is a better answer. Most Americans do not distinguish between Zionists and Jews. This, he added, is "something we have to exploit carefully." Understanding American opinion as well as he does, Rahim concluded, it won't be very difficult—although delicate.

The subsequent fifty pages of the book consist of similar purportedly reproduced internal memoranda that documented the Arab-domestic anti-semitic nexus without any external substantiation. The above memorandum served as the clearest "proof" of the Arab Information Center's intent to exploit antisemitism; by maligning Jews, Abdul Rahim allegedly hoped that it would weaken American Jews' ability to influence U.S. foreign policy and sour American Christians on Israel. In the book section, the name of nearly every major "professional anti-Semite" on the American far-right came up, ranging from the aforementioned Smith to California state senator Jack Tenney—all apparently interested in Arab funds, cooperation, or fresh anti-Jewish material for their publications. The relationship went both ways—if, of course, *Cross-Currents'* unsubstantiated accusations are to be believed.[37]

Documenting the Arab-Antisemite Nexus

While Forster and Epstein presented their findings as "indisputable evidence" of Arab representatives' intent to foment antisemitism and their cooperation with right-wing antisemites, their sources are highly questionable. Internal memoranda alone do little to prove what they allege. For example, how exactly did the ADL know that "Rahim made some interesting, off-the-record comments about American Jews to friends the day he arrived"? The reprinted memorandum authored by the ADL's research team is perhaps the most damning allegation of the Center's embrace of anti-semitism, but without any on-the-record source or primary document—or even the name of a credible informant—the book's claims can be dismissed as mere hearsay, if not defamation. Even if Forster and Epstein had indeed heard such allegations from "informants," it may well be that these informants simply earned money telling ADL officials what they wanted to hear.

Yet while most of the allegations in the book can neither be verified—especially with regard to the Center's intent—nor thoroughly disproven, the thrust of some of the Jewish organizations' claims can be easily corroborated. For one, some Arab diplomats, most notably Syrian ambassador Farid Zeineddine, are on the public record making statements that reeked of antisemitism. In November 1955, Zeineddine characterized Jews as "mongrelized Russians" who could not be integrated into host societies. In June 1956, during a speech at Illinois State Normal University, Zeineddine stated, "The American Jew is not an American emotionally or even ultimately. A Zionist cannot have real allegiance to the country in which he lives." Meanwhile, some Syrian and Egyptian consulates occasionally stocked pamphlets, printed in the Middle East, that criticized Israelis as Jews, crossing the line into overt antisemitism. In addition, it is true that antisemitic periodicals made use of Israeli actions in the Middle East to push their domestic anti-Jewish agenda, with articles by Arab representatives appearing in English-language antisemitic newspapers—though not always with the author's permission.[38]

Claims of Arab collaboration with known antisemites appear to have had a solid basis, despite Sayegh's best attempts to prevent it. The Center's own internal documents from 1956 note that antisemites often sought to work with them, so much so that the Center had to outline a clear policy for employees strictly forbidding any contact. Sayegh himself noted that he repeatedly turned away one neo-Nazi leader who appeared at his office five times. Yet while the American-educated Sayegh could easily discern potential "partnerships" that would be liable to undermine his cause, other Arab representatives in the United States lacked the will or sophistication to reject an invitation from "friendly" American antisemites.[39]

One of the most detailed accounts of Arab officials' collaboration with antisemites comes from a particularly credible source: an article written semi-anonymously by Don Peretz and published in the June 13, 1955, issue of William Zukerman's *Jewish Newsletter*. Written by "D.P." and titled "Arab Propaganda and Antisemitism," the article reported on a meeting the author had attended in New York in which Abdul H. Hassan, a member of the Egyptian delegation to the United Nations, "spoke for about fifteen minutes on Palestine and the Arab refugee issue." Hassan's talk, Peretz attested, "contained no anti-Semitic or anti-Jewish comment."

The problem, Peretz wrote, came not from the guest's words but from the organization hosting him: a neofascist group. Prior to introducing Hassan, the group's leader, James H. Madole of the National Renaissance Party (NRP), warned of the "Jewish International Bolshevik forces which run America." After Hassan finished, Madole took the stage again to express doubt that Hitler killed six million Jews, since so many "can now all be seen milling around the garment district any afternoon muttering in their foreign gibberish," and characterized "those who fought against segregation in schools as refugees from the Warsaw Ghetto who have noses so long you could hang your wash on them." Before concluding the meeting, Madole told attendees to take a look at the Egyptian embassy's pamphlets and invited everyone to return for the next meeting, during which a Syrian UN delegate would speak.[40]

The event would have fit right in as an entry in *Cross-Currents*, though it did not make the cut. The NRP was an unrepentant neo-Nazi organization. According to a U.S. House Committee on Un-American Activities report compiled a few months prior, NRP material "contains extensive rehashes of Hitler's speeches. Typical are National Renaissance Bulletin articles, 'Adolf Hitler Explains Nazi Anti-Semitism,' appearing in the February 1953 issue, and 'Adolf Hitler, the George Washington of Europe,' which appeared in the issue of May 1953."[41]

While the ADL's condemnation of Arab officials may have been motivated, at least in part, by a desire to defend Israel, to tar anti-Zionists as antisemites, and to sweep the Palestinian issue under the rug, the *Jewish Newsletter* article had no such goals. Peretz and Zukerman were among the American Jews most dedicated to making the public aware of the Palestinians' plight. Regardless of what solution they supported for the Palestinian refugee issue, the two clearly wanted American Jews to confront it as a serious moral question.

Convincing American Jewry of Israel's responsibility for the Palestinian refugee problem would never have been easy, and Arab officials' antisemitic ties
and pronouncements further complicated the task. The Hassan-Madole
lecture, Peretz wrote, did "much to corroborate the charge . . . that there is a
close nexus between Arab information services and anti-Jewish organizations." Commenting on the article, Zukerman bemoaned that the events
"confirm the Zionist equation of anti-Zionism and anti-Semitism," and that
led Arabs to "hurt their own cause by hob-nobbing [sic] with fascists and
hatemongers, and they make more difficult the lot of those liberal Jews
who seek justice for the Arab refugees and real peace between Arabs and
Jews."[42]

Arab officials' collaboration with local antisemites frustrated not only
Peretz and Zukerman but also the man charged with improving how Americans of all backgrounds viewed Arabs—Fayez Sayegh. Sayegh understood
acutely that any Arab flirtation with antisemites tarnished their cause. Even
as Sayegh fought back against the ADL and Zionist groups that attempted
to paint Arab officials as antisemites, he simultaneously challenged the
trends in Arab politics that made such antisemitic embarrassments inevitable. In Sayegh's struggle on the Arab side, the core of the challenge may
not have been antisemitism per se. Rather, Sayegh believed that counter-
productive activity like the Madole-Hassan event stemmed from the sheer
incompetence, nepotism, and corruption that led to Arab thoughtlessness
in appointing representatives abroad. The representatives sent by Arab governments to the United States often came primarily to enhance their résu-
més for Arab politics, according to Sayegh.[43]

AFME struggled to explain these same issues, but rather than blaming
them on corruption, its leadership attributed them to the diplomats' youth.
The Madole incident had led Rabbi Morris Lazaron to complain about it to
AFME's executive vice president, who replied that "the young diplomats
who took part in those disgraceful meetings have been called to task by
their superiors. Abdulrahim had nothing to do with the matter and has sent
around a list of the subversive agencies urging that the Arab diplomats do
not aligne [sic] themselves with." Abdul Hassan himself would only com-
pound the scandal in 1958. On Mike Wallace's television show *Night Beat*,
after Abdul Hassan denied to the host that he had spoken at the NRP meet-

ing, Wallace showed viewers a photo of the Egyptian diplomat with Madole as proof that his guest, still seated there, had lied.[44]

In any case, regardless of their underlying feelings about Jews, these diplomats lacked the experience and knowledge to avoid errors such as speaking at neo-Nazi events, not realizing that antisemitic pamphlets produced in the Middle East did not suit American audiences, and failing to distinguish between Jews and Israelis. To Sayegh, this all stemmed from a broader mismanagement of Arab public relations in the United States. Though Sayegh's conflicts with Jewish groups were most noteworthy, it was his critiques of fellow Arabs that would ultimately bring an end to his time at the Arab Information Center.

A Kosher Critique of Israel? Fayez Sayegh Meets with AJC Leaders

On March 21, 1956, following the publication of *Cross-Currents*, Don Peretz went to Sayegh to hear his response to the charges of antisemitism. Sayegh categorically denied the claims made against Abdul Rahim and all other Center staff, citing the Center's policy of refusing cooperation with antisemites. Sayegh asked for evidence of any antisemitic literature distributed by the Center or any connection between its staff and antisemites, aside from baseless ADL internal memoranda. When Peretz asked specifically about James Madole, Sayegh replied that Madole had come by his office five times to speak with him. On the fifth time, Sayegh relented, but he refused Madole the bulk copies of Center literature that he requested. Sayegh went on to clarify that he spoke only for his Center, not for Arab state diplomats, who operated independently. Regarding that matter, Sayegh told Peretz that after the Syrian UN delegation circulated antisemitic material, he wrote a strong letter to the Arab League secretary general, to Syria's foreign minister, to the Syrian ambassador, and to Abdul Rahim protesting the use of antisemitic publications. Reporting this conversation to the AJC, Peretz opined that "Dr. Sayegh is a reputable individual of high caliber whose statements on such a subject should not be dismissed lightly. . . . [He is] a man of a broad liberal and humanitarian point of view."[45]

Yet in reaction to the ADL's accusations, Sayegh soon made a move that alarmed the AJC. On April 27, 1956, he appeared on the popular radio show *Tex and Jinx* to respond to charges made against his office. During a March 15 broadcast of the same radio show, which reportedly had a listening audience of millions, Forster and Epstein had called the Center a purveyor of antisemitism for menacingly accusing American Jews of "double-loyalty and double allegiance" because of their support for Israel. Sayegh took to the airwaves to push back against the allegations of antisemitism. He challenged listeners to read all the Center's published material cover to cover and "find one document of ours which contains one paragraph or sentence or one phrase which—remotely, loosely, and in accordance with any definition of the term anti-Semitic—could be interpreted as anti-Semitic in letter or in spirit." The Center has "not published one single anti-Semitic word," Sayegh declared. Yet rather than stay on the defensive, Sayegh "took the offensive," as he put it. "I am anti-Israel. I am anti-Zionist also," Sayegh proclaimed, "but I am NOT anti-Jewish." Sayegh always distinguished between Jews and Zionists, he claimed, something he argued that Forster, Epstein, and Israeli leaders did not do.[46]

Sayegh then handed Tex, the show's host, a book, asking him to read a highlighted section on air. "When a Jew in America or South Africa speaks of 'our government,' to his fellow Jews, he usually means the government of Israel, while the Jewish public in various countries views Israeli Ambassadors as their own representatives," Tex read aloud. The quote, Sayegh pointed out, came not from an Arab official but from Israeli prime minister David Ben-Gurion. At Sayegh's prompting, Tex then read the book's title: the *Government Yearbook of Israel 1953–1954*. Sayegh said that he believed the statement to be a groundless insult to the loyalty of the innocent majority of American Jews, but what mattered was not what he thought but what American Jews felt. What, in fact, did the ADL think of Ben-Gurion's statement, Sayegh queried on air, and "why did they not take any action to urge Ben-Gurion to retract it"? Tex, a Christian and staunch Republican from Texas, then told Sayegh on air that he "recognize[d] that in logic and in law, you are probably right—why, you are definitely right—in your argument here" regarding the ADL, Ben-Gurion, and "dual loyalty."[47]

The AJC felt no less threatened than the ADL by the Center's rhetoric, but rather than attack publicly, it engaged directly. Soon after the broadcast, someone, likely Peretz, visited Sayegh bearing a surprising message from the AJC: its leaders wanted to meet with him. According to a letter from Sayegh to Ambassador Abdul Rahim marked "VERY, VERY CONFIDEN-TIAL," the AJC's messenger noted that Ben-Gurion's statement had indeed disturbed the AJC and that it had "decided to take some action as a result of [Sayegh's] challenge." Furthermore, the AJC wished to extend an invitation to Sayegh to speak with the group, privately, at greater length about the problem. Sayegh gave a tentative affirmative reply, receiving word that Don Peretz and an array of leading AJC figures, including Executive Vice President John Slawson, would be in attendance. Sayegh ended his note to Abdul Rahim by requesting permission to attend. "I personally urge very strongly that, unless there are serious reasons why I shouldn't, I be permitted to go," Sayegh wrote to the ambassador, his then absentee superior.[48]

The very fact that the AJC endeavored to meet with a man who, according to other Jewish leaders, operated a major hub of antisemitic activity says much about its politics and methods. This approach is reminiscent of the AJC's decisions to speak with Ben-Gurion directly about his Zionist rhetoric and the Arab minority question. Rather than engaging in apologetics or simply attacking those who criticized Israel, the AJC sought to deal with issues at their source. This preference for quiet intercession contrasted with AJCongress's embrace of mass politics, rallies, and legislation, and with the ADL's increasingly combative posture of investigating, exposing, and attacking those it viewed as foes from the 1940s onward.[49]

Politically, the AJC saw itself as an independent force within the American Jewish establishment, supportive of Jews everywhere while remaining objective on issues such as Zionism. While some Jewish critics of the AJC found the group's "above the fray" attitude to be patronizing and "more American than Jewish," the AJC saw value in its role as an umpire between Zionist and anti-Zionist politics. In its own words, written the same month as Sayegh's interview, the AJC stated that "although the American Jewish Committee supported the creation of Israel and is pro-Israel, it is not a Zionist organization. [It] is therefore in position to distinguish objectively between views which are anti-Semitic and views which, although critical of Israel, are not anti-Semitic."[50]

Sayegh received permission to attend the meeting with AJC officials from Arab League secretary general Abdul Khalek Hassouna. The meeting took place on June 26, 1956, at the Hotel Delmonico in Manhattan. In addition to Sayegh and Peretz, attendees included AJC executive vice president Dr. John Slawson, foreign affairs director Dr. Simon Segal, director of national affairs Edwin Lukas, vice president Alan Stroock, and Milton Weill, chair of the Committee on Israel. During the meeting, Sayegh explained that Arab views toward American Jewry stemmed not from antisemitism but rather from two changeable factors in the Israel–American Jewish relationship: one, American Jewry's seemingly uncritical support for Israel, and two, Zionism's claim that all Jews were an extension of the state. By not contesting the latter point, Sayegh said, American Jewry seemed to acquiesce to it. Arabs thus felt a need to defend themselves against this extension of Israel, he continued, despite the history of good relations between Jews and Arabs.

After the AJC leaders clarified that they had, in fact, made efforts on multiple occasions to distance themselves from Ben-Gurion's Zionistic pronouncements and to compel him to stop making such statements, Sayegh apologized for his ignorance. Had he known of the AJC's record, Sayegh claimed, he would not have made this point. Sayegh agreed to be much more careful in the future on the question of American Jewish loyalty, though he voiced enduring Arab concern about American Jewish financial support for Israel. In order to avoid future confusion, AJC said it would send him more of its material. Likewise, Sayegh gave the AJC some of his literature on the Arab world. Sayegh said that the Arabs could live with the State of Israel provided the fulfillment of "certain conditions," the AJC's minutes reported without elaboration. The AJC could help further by providing Arab governments with a "formula" to distinguish which American Jews were their foes and which were not, Sayegh stated. Both sides agreed that the meeting had been fruitful, and all hoped that it would arrest the "dangerous tensions which are now arising between Arab states and the American Jewish community." Sayegh expressed a desire to continue the productive dialogue in future meetings.[51]

It is unclear whether they met again, but Sayegh appeared to keep his side of the bargain. AJC files from the years that followed show no sign that Sayegh ever publicly raised the dual loyalty issue again. Meanwhile, in the immediate aftermath of the meeting, the AJC continued to refrain from openly attacking Sayegh. Instead, it decided to address the issue at its source—Ben-Gurion.

Even before the meeting, AJC leaders discussed the need to inform Israeli officials of the *Tex and Jinx* episode and to "find out how they plan to offset this and perhaps advise some statement on the part of Ben-Gurion to counteract it." Otherwise, Ben-Gurion's statement, which an AJC official noted was "not snatched out of context" by Sayegh, "will be a bonanza to the American Council for Judaism and to anti-Semites." Those involved asked former AJC president Blaustein, who had a warm relationship with Israeli officials, to forward the organization's complaints. In July, Blaustein told Abba Eban, Israel's ambassador to the United States and United Nations, to bring up the troubling Ben-Gurion quote with the prime minister himself. Eban did, reportedly telling Ben-Gurion that he, too, found "the statement in question very harmful" and requesting that the leader "reiterate positively his Statement to Mr. Blaustein in 1950" that had declared that Israel did not demand the loyalty of non-Israeli Jews. Though Eban assured Blaustein that he "press[ed] the Prime Minister hard for this and believ[ed] he [would] be successful," he did not ultimately secure the desired public reiteration from Ben-Gurion.[52]

Eventually, Blaustein—then the wealthiest Jewish person in the United States and owner of America's fourteenth-largest company—wrote to the prime minister directly. Blaustein began by noting that the two had not been in touch for some time, but that "a matter of grave concern to me and your other friends in this country" compelled him to write. He then repeated the line that Sayegh quoted from the *Government Yearbook of Israel 1953–1954* and a similar, more recent statement that Ben-Gurion had made. Blaustein wrote that such statements "obviously" contradicted the 1950 exchange, which he maintained did more than anything else "to win the good-will of American Jews to Israel; to free them . . . from the serious charge of dual-nationality; to thwart what otherwise would have been a far more effective thrust against your country by the Council for Judaism . . .

[and] to make possible the climate for the successful U.J.A. Campaigns in this country and the sale of Israel Bonds."[53]

The statement in the yearbook has again "opened up the furor that was existing at the time in 1950" that necessitated the exchange of views that year, Blaustein wrote. "My American Jewish Committee people are properly up in arms . . . [and] many others indeed are charging me with having been naïve in ever accepting the August 1950 statement as bonafide," he continued. "Your American Zionist friends here are alarmed. . . . Your Yearbook Statement . . . provides much ammunition to the Council for Judaism and Israel's other enemies here and to antisemites. Other governments are taking an alarming view of it. And the Arabs are using it," he noted, adding that "on one of our country's most important forums of the air . . . the April 27 nation-wide program of 'Tex and Jinx,' " the host asked "Dr. Sayegh" about the accusations of antisemitism that the book *Cross-Currents* made against the Arab League and its member states. Sayegh, Blaustein wrote, "replied by denying anti-Semitic activity on the part of the League and then requested that there be read your statement in the Yearbook. After that was done, he asked, 'If I said this would I not be considered anti-Semitic?' "

Months ago, Blaustein recalled, he had told Ambassador Eban that Ben-Gurion needed to clarify the matter. Eban had reportedly brought up the issue to the prime minister, but Ben-Gurion still did nothing. With a note of frustration and a hint of a threat, the American Jewish magnate continued, "I assure you that if you wish your country to retain its many friendships here—and at a time when you sorely need them—and wish to reduce the inroads of Arab propaganda . . . it is essential that you promptly correct the impression caused by your Statement in the Yearbook" and reaffirm the 1950 exchange.

Blaustein's letter also explicitly invoked potential foreign policy repercussions: "I felt the impact of this [*Tex and Jinx* episode] as a member of the United States Delegation to the United Nations and in my talks with the White House and State Department," noting that Eban and other Israeli diplomats also "must be frequently challenged and embarrassed by it." Despite Blaustein's pleas, Ben-Gurion did not offer a satisfactory response, leading AJC president Irving Engel to raise the issue again in his June 1957 meeting with the prime minister.[54]

The only reason why a line from a book published in 1954 made waves in 1956 was Sayegh's public citation of it. Yet rather than taking out their frustration on Sayegh, AJC higher-ups instead attacked Sayegh's "rabbi"— Elmer Berger of the American Council for Judaism. For years, the AJC struggled to convince the Council to be more careful in its criticism of Zionism and Israel, for they felt that Council propaganda raised "dual loyalty" concerns and risked fueling antisemitism. The AJC had long treaded carefully as several Council leaders had once been on the AJC's board and members of the two groups came from the same social milieu. But in 1956, the AJC lost its patience with the Council and issued a pamphlet criticizing the group as a source of fuel for antisemites. The AJC's "friends in the Council" then reproached the AJC angrily "for failing to subject the Zionists to the same analytical scalpel."[55]

AJC leaders, wishing to maintain their evenhandedness on the Zionist versus anti-Zionist debate, resolved to publish a similar pamphlet exploring how Israel and Zionists increased antisemitism. "A number of AJC members had proposed parallel treatment of this sort," as one account puts it. The Sayegh meeting also serves as important, if not crucial, context for this decision. A background memorandum for the fact sheet criticizing Zionists stated that "the most notorious" Zionist statement endangering American Jews was the exact same one that Sayegh cited on *Tex and Jinx*. The AJC's administrative board tasked three members with putting together a pamphlet on the ways in which Zionists inadvertently gave fodder to antisemites, drawing on a speech by John Slawson delivered in October 1957.[56]

While the AJC's top brass and foreign affairs staff looked toward Israel to resolve the questions raised by Sayegh, another AJC notable had to deal with Sayegh from a very different angle. Rabbi Dr. Solomon Andhil Fineberg for years (1939–1964) served as the AJC's national community relations director, one of the organization's most important domestic affairs staff positions. Fineberg, who wrote four books on antisemitism and prejudice more broadly, one of which won the 1950 Anisfield-Wolf Book Award alongside a book by Shirley Graham Du Bois, could be considered the AJC's foremost expert on the issue. Known as "the Dean of Jewish Community Relations," Fineberg served as president of the national Association of Jewish Community Relations Workers from 1950 to 1954, during which time he alienated some Jews on the left for arguing that Julius and Ethel Rosenburg had been guilty as charged of spying for the Soviets, contrary to those who portrayed their trial as an antisemitic witch hunt. Fineberg, in other words, expressed views typical of the AJC in his liberalism, his anti-communism, his Reform Judaism, and his non-Zionism. He was a bit more of a feminist than the average AJC staffer, however; born Solomon Anschel Fineberg, he signed his name "S. Andhil Fineberg" to acknowledge the help of his wife Hilda "Hil" Fineberg in all his professional endeavors.[57]

As national community relations director, Fineberg corresponded with local chapters more often than AJC foreign affairs staffers did. A few weeks after the AJC's meeting with Sayegh, Fineberg, who had not attended it, had to address local questions about how the AJC should deal with Sayegh's lecture tours. On July 3, 1956, a San Francisco AJC director sent Fineberg material regarding Sayegh's speech at the Commonwealth Club rebutting a lecture by Israeli consul general Avraham Biran. The AJC's local foreign affairs chair claimed that he had heard no antisemitism in Sayegh's speech, but the packet sent to Fineberg also included a lengthy analysis of the lecture by Earl Raab, director of San Francisco's Jewish Community Relations Council (JCRC). Raab's analysis, titled "Anti-Semitism by Detour," explained how Sayegh, without making a single antisemitic statement, tacitly instilled a "toxin" of Jew-hatred into listeners' ears for which an "anti-toxin had not yet been discovered by Israeli [Jonas] Salks." Raab warned that Arab speakers "possess a knowledge of American PR and thought processes, rhetorical dexterity, and psychological insight which Israeli speakers lack," adding that whereas "they know how the man in the street—the business man, the conservative—thinks, the Israeli knows only how to appeal to the intellectual; moreover they are heavy handed and lack subtlety in many cases." Given the missteps of various Arab state diplomats, one wonders if Raab's observation drew only from his impression of Sayegh, who reportedly "had acquired an amazing understanding of the American mind" and "knew what made Americans 'tick.' "[58]

"One of the central arts of the propagandist has always been the ability to make his point without ever being explicit," Raab wrote. "Ideally, the individual elements of his presentation are innocuous and unobjectionable, but when fitted together they provide the desired impact," he continued; "this is the algebra of propaganda where the X is never named, but the formula spells out its identity." One cannot be openly antisemitic today because of Nazism and the work of civil rights groups, Raab maintained, so Sayegh took a "detour." Sayegh kept on repeating the term "so-called Jewish state," claiming that he said "so-called" because he did not like the idea of a state based on a religion. Such a sentiment, Raab wrote, would both fit American sensibilities and tie "Jewishness" to Israel in the mind of listeners in a sneaky way. Additionally, it characterized Israel as a Jewish state rather than a state of refugees, the latter being a more sympathetic depiction, in Raab's view. Sayegh went on to say that Israel violated international law, inhumanely treated Arab refugees, and had "forcibly expelled" many Arabs in 1948, which Raab wrongly claimed was inaccurate.

Moreover, though Sayegh never mentioned "American Jews" as such, Raab felt that he hinted at dual loyalty by attacking uncritical support of Israel. Each piece of Sayegh's speech was not antisemitic, Raab acknowledged, but altogether he felt that Sayegh's talk had been "designed to bring into force the latent anti-Semitism of those who will reject the crude anti-Semitic statements of the Gerald L.K. Smiths but find this formula plausible." Most audience members, even Jews, Raab felt, would not realize the latent antisemitic message. "The Sayegh speech, radio broadcast several times over, was heard by perhaps 100,000 people in Northern California," Raab warned. "Its effect would raise anti-Semitic potential in that audience," Raab said, asking rhetorically, "How can we counteract it?" Raab noted that unlike Nazi propaganda, Sayegh's critique of Israel could not be met head-on as antisemitic and un-American. But if it is "anti-Semitism *in effect*," Raab emphasized, "then perhaps the community relations agencies have some responsibility to find some positive antidotes."[59]

After reading Sayegh's speech and Raab's analysis, Fineberg agreed that "Sayegh is one of the most competent polemicists that American Jewry has ever had to counteract. He is extremely astute and is all the more dangerous because a Jewish organization, the American Council for Judaism, propagates a line so closely resembling his." However, he continued, "I really believe that Sayegh is trying to distinguish between the responsibilities of

Zionist and non-Zionist Jews, between those who help Israel and those who don't." In Fineberg's view, despite that intention, there was still a major difficulty, given that "in the arena of public opinion, such distinctions cannot be maintained, and in the end, Zionists and Jews become identical in all but the most careful minds." Writing later that week in response to concerns about Sayegh's upcoming talk at The Ohio State University, Fineberg further added that Sayegh "has not resorted to anti-Semitism in public utterances," but instead "he is smooth, maintains dignity with impressive results. In all this there is considerable danger as he is able to in a subtle way to get his point across."[60]

Fineberg did not consider himself a Zionist. In addition, he felt a strong sense of sympathy with Arab refugees, naively hoping that he could go to the Middle East under AJC auspices to help solve the refugee issue. As a non-Zionist, Fineberg opined that the AJC should not join with other Jewish organizations to lobby for Israel as part of what became known as the Conference of Presidents of Major Jewish Organizations. But the Sayegh question pushed Fineberg into the arms of American Zionist leaders. As historian Douglas Rossinow has demonstrated, Zionist organizations such as the one later renamed the American Israel Public Affairs Committee (AIPAC) long desired the inclusion of non-Zionists within their tent, which they felt would increase their political sway by making it easier to claim they spoke for all American Jews. The AJC could be considered the biggest non-Zionist fish in the sea, and problems like Sayegh created an opportunity. While the AJC would not join up with the Zionists for a pro-Israel effort, they would, it turns out, join Zionists for an anti-antisemitism effort.[61]

In 1957, the American Zionist Council spearheaded a new "coordinating committee" on "anti-Israel agitation on campuses." The new organization included Zionist groups but also the National Council of Jewish Women, Hillel, B'nai Brith, NCRAC—and the AJC, which Fineberg would represent. "I made very clear at the meeting of this coordinating committee . . . that the AJC will not become involved in educational programs designed to win support for Israel," Fineberg maintained. However, "we have been involved in offsetting anti-Semitic propaganda *and* any propaganda that has a hurtful impact on American Jewry. . . . Therefore we are participating on a consultative basis" in what became known as the Campus Coordinating

Committee. Though in 1957 Fineberg saw himself as merely "participating on a consultative basis," the next year he considered himself a full member of the committee. Concern about campus politics on Israel/Palestine came in part from the activities of Sayegh, who reportedly spoke at more than 125 colleges and universities in the 1950s, as well as those of anti-Zionist Jews and the Organization for Arab Students. During the 1950s, the AJC quietly monitored Arab student activism on campuses while the ADL and Zionist groups attacked them, yet in the 1960s the AJC, too, joined the fray.[62]

Meanwhile, the AJC effort to "subject the Zionists to the same analytical scalpel" that it had recently used to dissect the anti-Zionist Council floundered just around the same time Fineberg joined the Campus Coordinating Committee. The AJC had charged the same three members who had written the "Fact Sheet" on the Council—Judge Charles Breitel and future AJC presidents Louis Caplan and Richard Maass—with writing a parallel booklet on Zionists. The trio was told to draw from an October 1957 speech by AJC executive vice president John Slawson on the topic. The three, who had not all heard Slawson's speech, were soon startled by the document that they produced. Regarding a section which noted that 10 percent of United Jewish Appeal (UJA) funds go to Zionist propaganda and educational efforts outside Israel, and that much of the rest "legally . . . has no direct relationship with a foreign government [but in practice] helps a foreign government absorb refugees and develop its resources," Maass commented, "WOW! We know it's true . . . but boy, are we giving fodder to the antis! Wasn't it the last session of Congress that a Southerner tried to . . . [take] away UJA's tax-exemption? Won't Council pick up this 'out of our mouths' and use it?"[63]

In presenting the draft "Fact Sheet" during a March 1958 AJC administrative board meeting, Breitel concurred. In converting Slawson's speech into a fact sheet, the trio took out all of the "talk"—the "shading of expression and inflection, overtones of sincerity [that] . . . make palatable even the most bitter truths"—and the result alarmed him. With all of Slawson's rhetorical "protective tissues . . . removed, we are left with nothing but the bare bones of truth," Breitel noted. He continued, "This of course is the purpose of a fact sheet—to uncover the truth. But what if these bare bones, in the eye of our enemies, are a skeleton in the American Jewish closet? Is it still our purpose to expose them?"[64]

Breitel continued, "We well know" that "Arab spokesmen and antisemites" will exploit "*any* assertion, whether Zionist or anti-Zionist, that makes
it appear as if American Jews might harbor a dual nationalistic outlook." He
went on, "How can we now, in all conscience, put forth a bill of particulars
on the misguided conduct of some American Jews—their Israel-centered,
instead of America-centered, public appeals; their overt political lobbying;
their thinly disguised maneuvers to erect a propaganda façade in the form of
an American Jewish 'Presidents' Club' "—referring to what is now the highly influential umbrella group, the Conference of Presidents of Major Jewish
Organizations—"their deployment, if not diversion, of tax-exempt American dollars to serve the ends of Zionism throughout the world," especially
given that the AJC just last year reprimanded the Council for airing similar
concerns? If the AJC did issue this fact sheet, even to only a handful of people, Breitel warned, it would "promptly [be] reproduced by every bigot press
in the United States." This was all true, future AJC president Maass replied,
noting cryptically that even within their own organization "only a handful of
AJC members really know what [the Presidents' Club] is all about."[65]

Others in the AJC concurred with Breitel that the pamphlet itself might
fuel the very antisemitism that it aimed to extinguish. One AJC member
noted that the pamphlet felt less necessary now than when the idea had
been conceived since Arab officials had stopped attacking Jews for dual
loyalty—perhaps in part because of the group's meeting with Sayegh. The
board voted unanimously to sink the whole idea of publicly criticizing
Zionist rhetoric on March 4, 1958.[66]

1958 and the American Jewish Consensus on Anti-Zionism

Within the AJC's narrative arc in this book, much of its drama begins in
the mid-1950s and ends in 1958. The AJC hired Peretz in 1956 and parted
ways with him in 1958. James Marshall's push to convince Israel to change
its policies ended in 1958. Fineberg started working with Zionist groups to
defend Israel's image, and the AJC board voted not to critique Zionism
publicly in 1958.

Each of these things are, in and of themselves, relatively minor incidents.
But altogether, they represent an end to what Israeli diplomat Pinhas Eliav

characterized in 1956 as the AJC's "desire to return to 'objectivity' on matters related to Israel" and as a "tendency toward neutrality that attempts to
show both sides."[67]

As this chapter has shown, this AJC "tendency toward neutrality" on Israel/
Palestine that came to the fore around 1955–1956 emerged in a very particular
domestic and foreign policy context. It came at a time of heightened Arab-
Israeli tensions, but also as actors such as AFME and the Arab Information
Center were promoting Palestinian claims to an extent never seen before, a
development that the AJC could not ignore. This pro-Arab advocacy could,
many Jewish groups feared, harm the public image of Jews in effect if not
in intent. The AJC was thus presented with a choice. It could try to resolve the
underlying problems that fueled critiques of Israel, Zionism, and Jews—
namely, the Palestinian refugee issue, Israel's Arab minority policies, and
"dual loyalty" rhetoric—perhaps while also disassociating American Jews
from Zionism. Or it could follow the path of its peer organizations—the ADL,
AJCongress, and some Zionist groups—in countering public criticism of the
Jewish state based on the presumption that it ultimately hurt American Jews,
who were increasingly identifying with Israel.

During much of the presidency of Irving Engel (1954–1958), the AJC
tried the former, but from 1958 onward, they gave up and increasingly drifted toward the latter. Despite the wealth and political influence of its leaders,
the AJC could not change Israeli policies or rhetoric, nor did it have the will
to make even symbolic gestures on the refugee question. Its grass roots,
moreover, often did not feel comfortable with anti-Israel rhetoric even
when it was not antisemitic. AJC leaders seemed caught between that
grassroots reality and the unclear meaning of their official non-Zionist yet
pro-Israel stance. One wonders if their encounters with Sayegh led them to
contemplate the contradictions inherent in this stance as well as their own
inability to maintain the distinction between Jews and the increasingly popular ideology of Zionism. After all, when Sayegh asked for guidance on
how Arabs could distinguish between Jews who were their foes for supporting Israel and Jews who were not, how could the AJC reply?

AJC officials could tell that American Jews were not associating with
Israel any less, particularly as the organization geared up to work with other
Jewish groups to celebrate Israel's tenth birthday. That endeavor prompted

an awkward verbal dance on the part of AJC officials, who wanted to take part in the festivities "to some extent" to indicate appreciation for Israel's absorption of "homeless Jews," while also warning local chapters that the celebrations held "dangers": Zionists might use them to enlist new supporters, make the events "jingoistic" by saying "Look how Israel surpasses every other country," or alienate non-Jews by pushing them to attend or take up too "much of their newspaper space" with it.[68]

Despite their misgivings about the Zionists, non-Zionists came around to working with them to counter anti-Zionism. This development marked a pivotal yet subtle moment in Jewish history, especially given that Zionists had long believed that showing a united Jewish front to politicians would make lobbying more effective. For the AJC, this meant ultimately expanding the group's purview from not only defending Jews to also defending Israel. This did not involve flipping a switch from saying anti-Zionism was not antisemitism to saying that it was. But it did involve accepting the notion that Israel's foes were also American Jewry's foes. A final drift toward conflating anti-Zionism with antisemitism, for the AJC, ADL, and others, would only come after the 1967 war.[69]

Much of the AJC's long-standing apprehension about Israel, anti-Zionism, and the Palestinians stemmed from their concern about "what the goyim [non-Jews] would think," yet developments in American culture were making this less of an issue. Books, movies, and other cultural products of the 1950s were making Israel appear more relatable and admirable to the American public, a process that historian Michelle Mart calls the "Americanization," "Christianization," and "masculinization" of Jews and Israel. Those same cultural works correspondingly depicted Arabs as "non-Western, undemocratic, racially darker" enemies. Arabs became even more foreign, Mart argues, as Israelis "became surrogate Americans." This came to a climax with the publication of Leon Uris's book *Exodus*, which was first published in the fateful year of 1958. The book, which dramatized Israel's founding through a story of a ship that brought Holocaust survivors to Palestine against the will of British authorities, was a record-breaking bestseller, offering readers a theatrical, Zionist-friendly tale that by all accounts led Americans to increasingly identify with Israel. A star-studded film version release in 1960 would further cement this effect.[70]

Finally, 1958 marked the completion of a major turnaround in U.S. foreign policy. During most of Eisenhower's first term, he had pursued efforts to court Nasser and other Arab nationalists, including by pressuring Israel to accept concessions with Operation Alpha. Yet Nasser rejected Operation Alpha anyway, diminishing the need to pressure Israel, leading the administration to pull the plug on the AFME's pro-Arab public relations campaign in mid-1956.

Even subsequent to this, and after Egypt accepted arms from the Soviet bloc, the Eisenhower administration forced Israel to withdraw from Egyptian lands captured in the Suez war, but "lost" major Arab states anyway. Rather than serving as a key ally, Nasser would, according to U.S. officials, pose a major threat to the pro-Western regimes of the region, as Nasserist fervor imperiled leaders in Jordan, Lebanon, Saudi Arabia, and Iraq. In form of the "Eisenhower Doctrine," the administration encouraged conservative Arab states to oppose Nasser. That policy fell flat on its face when a bloody 1958 coup replaced the Iraqi royal family with an Arab nationalist regime that appeared particularly friendly to the Soviet Union. Realizing the weakness of the remaining conservative regimes, Eisenhower began to look toward Israel for its strategic value. By 1958, Israel thus no longer appeared like an impediment to America's Middle East strategy but rather like a potentially integral part of it. This development, alongside growing American cultural identification with Israel, diluted the bases of the AJC's long-standing "dual loyalty" concerns.[71]

What became of Fayez Sayegh? He continued to work and lecture on Israel/Palestine, though a heart attack in late 1957 limited his activities, at least temporarily. By 1959, however, Sayegh was in better shape and traveled to the Middle East. In Beirut, he reportedly received a warm welcome from Lebanese officials and intellectuals, and in Cairo he met privately with President Nasser in June. In Lebanon that summer, Sayegh served as president of the Palestine Arab Congress and received a high honor from the Lebanese prime minister. Perhaps emboldened by these votes of confidence, Sayegh began publicly criticizing the way his superiors ran the Arab Information Center. Cronyism and inefficiency plagued the Center, Sayegh claimed, necessitating major reforms. With some extra money and serious work, Sayegh argued, it could be much more effective in swaying American opinion in the Arab direction. While some Arab onlookers believed that Sayegh's efforts to reform the office could succeed, Sayegh's public criticism of Center activities angered Ambassador Abdul Rahim, who used his political connections to have Sayegh demoted and sent to Cairo. Enraged, Sayegh quit the Arab League and returned to the United States, where he spent several months on a lecture tour supported by AFME. His departure was a major loss for the Center, at least according to the Brooklyn-based Arab American newspaper *The Caravan*, a pro-Sayegh source that documented the community's disappointment with the news. One Center employee wrote anonymously in *The Caravan* that Sayegh was among the only Arab League officials to appear on national television and that, in contrast, he had "neither heard nor seen Ambassador Rahim on radio or television in any capacity."[72]

Sayegh stayed in the United States after marrying Arlene Briem, an American with whom he had worked at the Center. Throughout the early 1960s, Sayegh made a living as an academic, based at Macalester College, Cambridge University, the American University of Beirut, and Stanford University, where AFME subsidized his salary for the 1960–1961 academic year. When Minnesota Jewish groups expressed alarm that Sayegh would be teaching at Macalester, optimists in the Jewish community simply felt relieved that now he would be stuck in one place. "I would not worry about Sayegh's coming to Macalester College," Fineberg wrote to a Minneapolis Jewish leader, carbon copying his new partners in the American Zionist Council. "The man is broken-hearted because he got a rough deal from the crowd at the Arab Information Center. He was their most competent speaker and propagandist, but internal politics kept him down. Now he is adrift with almost virtually no influence." But it would not be the last time that American Jewish leaders had to grapple with Fayez Sayegh.[73]

Conclusion: Losing the First World—and Winning the Third

In August 1967, an unprecedented crisis in Black-Jewish relations erupted in what would be the first of many controversies over Black radicals' support for Palestinians. A piece titled "Third World Round-Up—The Palestinian Problem" appeared in a summer issue of the *SNCC Newsletter*.

SNCC, a civil rights organization formerly known as the Student Nonviolent Coordinating Committee, had increasingly been moving in a radical, internationalist direction, but few—including those leading the group—had expected that the Palestine issue would catapult it into the headlines. Summarizing the controversy, historian Pamela Pennock recalls that the "Third World Round-Up" article "asked 'Do you know?' and listed thirty-two 'facts' about Israel and Zionism, such as '15. That the Zionists conquered the Arab homes and land through terror, force, and massacres?' "74

Alongside pictures of Palestinian victims of Israeli violence, the article featured "a striking drawing of a double lynching: two men, one Arab (resembling Nasser) and one black (resembling Muhammad Ali), wearing nooses around their necks were seized by a white hand bearing the Star of David. Primed to sever the men from the grip of their Jewish captor, a dark-skinned arm labeled 'Third World' clutched a scimitar engraved with the words 'Liberation Movement.' " It also contained a drawing of Israeli defense minister Moshe Dayan with dollar signs on his shirt, an image with overt antisemitic overtones. In addition, it claimed that Israel sought to exploit African economies, stated that the Rothschilds—who "control much of Africa's mineral wealth"—were at the center of the Zionist "conspiracy," and maintained that "Zionist terror gangs . . . deliberately slaughtered and mutilated" women and children.75

In the immediate aftermath of the *SNCC Newsletter*'s publication, at least five national Jewish organizations—the AJC, ADL, AZC, AJCongress, and the American Section of the Jewish Agency—strongly criticized the civil rights group that some of them had once cooperated with, "pointing out that 'Snick' now follows the line laid down by American racist organizations like [James Madole's] National Renaissance Party and the Ku Klux Klan," as one report put it. Many mainstream African American civil rights figures who saw Jews as allies also condemned SNCC for the article.76

AJC condemnation appeared indistinguishable from that of other Jewish groups. President Morris B. Abram of Atlanta released a statement saying that "it is tragic that 'Snick' has now adopted the oldest and most pernicious form of prejudice, namely anti-Semitism. Anti-Semitism has the historic quality of destroying whoever or whatever touches it, whether it be Nazi Germany or Czarist Russia." Abram continued, "It is also particularly devastating that 'Snick' should have adopted a program of extremist Arabs and Soviet anti-Semites who are at this time advancing the same arguments as 'Snick' did in its newsletter." By and large, American Jewish organizations considered this and other pro-Palestinian statements from the Black Power movement to be a product of urban Black-Jewish tensions, which Jewish groups found threatening. The AJC considered them a side effect of domestic antisemitism rather than a serious indictment of Israeli policy, with SNCC's clear use of antisemitic imagery overtaking any moral point the group aimed to make, in the view of most white Americans. Some Jewish groups termed it a case of Arab "exploitation" of "Black anti-Semitism."[77]

As if to make that point, the ADL noted that the *SNCC Newsletter* piece had drawn from Arab sources—namely, an article by Fayez Sayegh. The ADL's framing of the issue, historian Michael Fischbach points out, made it appear as though the article's Arab origin alone made it antisemitic, indicative of the view that antisemitism and pro-Arabism were inherently intertwined. In fact, Sayegh's original pamphlet from which SNCC drew contained none of the antisemitic imagery, embellishments, or phrases in the newsletter article. Sayegh made no comparison between Zionism and Black-Jewish relations in America. All of that had been added by SNCC staff. As had happened in the 1950s, Sayegh's attempts to put forward a pro-Arab platform untainted by antisemitism or by allegations of antisemitism had failed—except now because of Black Power's use of his pro-Arab material, rather than white supremacists' earlier appropriation of it.[78]

The AJC's brief outreach to Sayegh had occurred at a time when the group feared that a pro-Arab push might lead many white Christian Americans to develop anti-Israel views that would morph into anti-Jewish views. The group's attempts in the 1940s and 1950s to act as an evenhanded mediator on questions of anti-Zionism and antisemitism emerged in part out of the AJC's belief that its non-Zionist designation helped it make a credible case to the then Protestant-dominated American establishment. But with the decline of Protestant Arabist influence, American Jewish social ascent, and a broadening American consensus of support for Israel, the need for any sort of non-Zionist Jewish mediator fell. For a wide array of reasons, the AJC began engaging in public pro-Israel advocacy more than ever before. Rather than longing for credibility in non-Jewish circles, the

AJC increasingly sought credibility from Jews, a shift in priorities that also helped facilitate its dropping of the "non-Zionist" designation amidst the ethnic pride of the era.[79]

The Cold War's Middle Eastern fault lines began to settle in the late 1950s or early 1960s, with Israel more firmly in the American camp and secular nationalist Arab regimes in Egypt, Syria, and Iraq increasingly siding with the Soviet bloc. The efforts of Sayegh and AFME to foster a pro-Arab America and pro-America Arab world had failed. While Sayegh's early career had focused on making Palestine palatable to white Protestant Americans, the second half of his life aimed to build support for Palestine among the diverse, non-white populations of the Third World.

It was in this era that Sayegh left his most lasting impression on global politics, reshaping the way many in the world have viewed Israel in the decades since. Sayegh's writings in the 1960s and 1970s would be among the first to launch a new wave of critiques against Zionism, characterizing it as colonialist and akin to apartheid. Sayegh's first publication as founding director of the PLO Research Center, *Zionist Colonialism in Palestine* (1965), did just that, framing Israel as one example of the colonial powers that the peoples of Asia and Africa were fighting so hard against. Sayegh's pamphlet cited by SNCC had similar aims. While Sayegh's efforts to woo the Third World had likely not intended to impassion African American groups, they had that fascinating byproduct, as those in the Black Power movement understood themselves more and more as part of a global people of color. However, in framing its struggle as anti-Jewish rather than anti-white, SNCC's first publication dealing with Middle East politics had the effect of further associating anti-Zionism with antisemitism in American Jewish discourse.[80]

Though Sayegh returned to the United States in 1967, his activities thereafter had less to do with influencing the American domestic sphere and focused instead on the realm of United Nations diplomacy. In that role, as part of Kuwait's UN delegation, Sayegh served as the chief architect of UN General Assembly Resolution 3379. The resolution, passed in 1975, could be considered Sayegh's most notable achievement, bringing the Arab world, the Soviet bloc, and Africa together in a stunning denouncement of an ideology that had given Jews so much meaning and security. Most

Fayez Sayegh standing on the right between his sister and mother in Tiberias circa 1947, in what may have been the family's last full gathering before their displacement in 1948. By permission of the family of Yusif Sayigh.

American Jewish groups adamantly maintained that UNGA 3379 constituted antisemitism. Certainly, in a world full of exclusivist nationalisms, was it not an antisemitic double standard for these governments to single out one nationalism—Jewish nationalism—as racist?[81]

Reflecting the widespread American belief that UNGA 3379 constituted antisemitism, television shows such as *Saturday Night Live* ridiculed it as such. But when evaluating Sayegh himself, the equation might be considered differently. Was Sayegh's decision to call Zionism a form of racism motivated by the "toxin" of senseless antisemitism? Sayegh would never again be able to see Tiberias, where he grew up, his old high school in Safed, or his mother's hometown in the Galilee. He faced these restrictions not because of his actions or his character but because of his ethno-religious identity and the way in which Israel's dominant ideology and policies treated people like him.[82]

While many of the Communist and Arab state leaders who backed UNGA 3379 could easily be dismissed as antisemitic, it is less clear that

Sayegh's role in drafting and promoting the resolution would have led AJC's retired expert on prejudice, Rabbi Solomon Andhil Fineberg, to diagnose Sayegh with antisemitism even in 1975. While nearly the entire organized American Jewish community rallied against UNGA 3379, Sayegh had at least one rabbi in his camp reassuring him that his stance did not constitute antisemitism. That figure, Rabbi Elmer Berger, went so far as to publish an advertisement in the *New York Times* supportive of UNGA 3379. For Berger, the episode marked yet another step in his pro-Palestine trajectory, a journey of over fifty years with its own place in American Jewish history.[83]

5

Anti-Zionists for Israel

It would be wise . . . not to write off . . . individual Jews of which the Council is made up. It is entirely conceivable that some of them can be won over. . . . There are American Council Jews in a number of important high places. . . . [American Council for Judaism president] Lessing Rosenwald has never had an opportunity of hearing our point of view. . . . I believe that he is adopting his public positions on Zionism because he hates American Zionists, not because he hates Israel. . . . Might it not be worth considering getting one of our people to meet with him unobtrusively?

—Avraham Harman, Israel's consul general in New York, 1954

Dear Dr. Sayegh, I just had an opportunity to read your excellent pamphlet on "The Palestine Refugees." . . . I come to Washington with some frequency and, should you be interested in talking with me about the Council, I should count it as a great privilege.

—Rabbi Elmer Berger, 1952

FOR A QUARTER OF A CENTURY, the American Council for Judaism ("the Council") served as "the nation's leading anti-Zionist organization of Jews," embodying a voice of dissent against an ideology that increasingly won over fellow Jewish Americans. But in 1968, the organization, long subjected to external attack, fell victim to its own internal contradictions. Outwardly, the impetus for the Council's crippling schism of 1968 appeared to be the

Israeli-Arab war that had occurred the year prior. In July 1967, the *New York Times* quoted Rabbi Elmer Berger, longtime executive director (1943–1955) and executive vice president (1955–1968) of the Council, criticizing Israel for its "aggression" in the recent Six-Day War. While the war had started with Israel launching a surprise attack on Egypt and ended with Israel occupying the West Bank, the Gaza Strip, the Golan Heights, and the Sinai Peninsula, Berger's accusation outraged American Jews who felt that Israel's attack was a justified preemptive strike against a looming existential threat. In response to the controversy, the Council's board pushed Berger either to disavow the remarks or to resign, initiating a yearlong struggle that ended with Berger's ejection from the group. While the Council technically never folded, after the departure of Berger and his protégé, executive director Dr. Norton Mezvinsky, the Council soon became so inactive that, by the 1970s, its staff had to remind newspapers that it still existed.[1]

Yet the seeds of the schism had been planted long before 1967. In the years immediately after the Council's founding in 1942, Council leaders shared common motivations for their opposition to Zionism: they believed that Jews constituted a religion rather than a nation and that American Jews should have one indivisible loyalty, to the United States. Palestinian Arabs were of little concern to those founding the Council in the 1940s, including Berger. Yet in the 1950s and 1960s, the divergent experiences of leading Council figures led to a gradual parting of ways on issues related to the Israeli-Palestinian conflict. As Berger, inspired by his contact with Arabs, became closely aligned with the Palestinian cause, Israeli officials forged personal bonds with Council chairman Lessing Rosenwald, apparently designed to warm the latter's feelings toward the Jewish state. When faced with the wave of pro-Israel sentiment in the United States after Israel's victory in 1967, Rosenwald and his allies rebelled against Berger's pro-Arab advocacy, attempting to reframe the Council as "anti-Zionist" without being "pro-Arab" or "anti-Israel."

The Council's decline stemmed not only from the Berger dispute but also from transformations in the broader world that undermined the Council's raison d'être. The social and political forces that made an America-centric form of anti-Zionism attractive to a minority of American Jews melted away amidst ethnic revivalism, warming U.S.-Israel relations, and growing positive feelings toward Israel among Americans in general. Yet the late 1960s marked not an end to American Jewish critiques of Israel but rather a shift in their origins as Palestinians succeeded in raising greater awareness of their plight in left-wing circles worldwide. Surprisingly, the Council briefly attempted to open itself to these new critics during the short tenure of Council executive director Norton Mezvinsky, who held the role from 1967 to 1968. Mezvinsky's unsuccessful efforts to reorient the Council to win over New Left critics of Zionism and Jewish youth dissatisfied with American Judaism only further highlighted how anachronistic the Council's ideology had become. American Jewish critics of Israeli policies toward the Palestinians would gravitate toward other groups in subsequent years, including Berger and Mezvinsky's new organization called American Jewish Alternatives to Zionism (AJAZ), another new group initiated with the support of Noam Chomsky called the Committee on New Alternatives in the Middle East (CONAME), and other nonsectarian leftist organizations drawn in by the rising profile of Palestinian rights issues.

Reform Jewish Anti-Zionism and the Birth of the American Council for Judaism

Historians of American Jewry have largely ignored the sensitive question of Jewish anti-Zionism in the 1950s and 1960s. The American Council for Judaism, the first American Jewish group created specifically to oppose Zionism, has been the subject of only one major study, Thomas Kolsky's *Jews against Zionism* (1990). Those who remember the Council may recall that it opposed Zionism on the grounds of its beliefs that Jews did not constitute a nation and that Israel had no right to speak for Jews elsewhere. The fact that the Council of the 1940s did not rally around the Palestinian cause is perhaps why several recent anthologies on historical Jewish critiques of Zionism did not mention the Council. Moreover, Kolsky's book focused on the 1940s, perhaps inadvertently leading many historians to view the Council as static or defunct post-1948. However, in the 1960s, rather than having collapsed, the Council reported a membership of twenty-two thousand—a figure likely exaggerated by the inclusion of many lapsed members, but still plausible enough to be reported in a *Time* magazine article that profiled the anti-Zionist Berger alongside two prominent communal leaders, the non-Zionist Jacob Blaustein and Zionist Nahum Goldmann.[2]

Ideologically, the Council emerged from a long history of Reform Jewish rejection of Jewish nationalism, an attitude that originated in Germany and gained acceptance in the nineteenth-century United States. In 1885, leading Reform rabbis convening in Pittsburgh released a statement that, among other things, distanced themselves from the proto-Zionist movement emerging in Europe. The document, known as the Pittsburgh Platform, declared, "We consider ourselves no longer a nation, but a religious community, and therefore expect neither a return to Palestine, nor a sacrificial worship under the sons of Aaron, nor the restoration of any of the laws concerning the Jewish state." These Reform Jews, mostly of Central European stock, claimed to feel fully American and conceptualized Judaism as a religion, not as a nationality or race. While the Pittsburgh Platform carried resonance for decades, Reform Jews increasingly debated their relationship with Zionism as Jewish settlement in Palestine expanded, as more and more Zionist-friendly American Jews of Eastern European extraction joined the Reform movement, and as the situation in Europe became more dire in the 1930s and 1940s. The movement's Columbus Platform, issued in 1937 by its Central Conference of American Rabbis (CCAR), expressed Zionist-friendly views, attesting to the growing strength of a once-small Zionist faction of Reform rabbis. In 1941, the CCAR entered a new era with the election of its first avowedly Zionist leader, Rabbi James Heller.[3]

At the 1942 CCAR convention, the Zionist faction successfully put forth a resolution in support of a Jewish army in Palestine after most rabbis had already left the meeting. Outraged by the resolution, thirty-six dissident rabbis met in Atlantic City to formulate a response. They soon decided to create a formal organization, which they called the American Council for Judaism. The name reflected the rabbis' emphasis on "American" as their only national identity and as "Judaism" as solely a religious identity. The rabbis then selected one of their youngest and most enthusiastic members, thirty-four-year-old Rabbi Elmer Berger of Temple Beth-El in Flint, Michigan, to serve as the Council's executive director. Leaving the pulpit permanently, Berger moved to Philadelphia to set up Council headquarters.[4]

While the group succeeded in recruiting the prominent Lessing Rosenwald, former chairman of Sears, Roebuck and Company, to serve as Council president, most of the rabbis departed within the first year, making the Council primarily a lay organization. Compounding their challenges, reports of the Nazi genocide of European Jewry made headlines just two weeks before the Council's formal establishment. Further harming their image, the Council coincidentally and unfortunately chose to announce its formation on the same day that other Jewish groups designated as a day of mourning for Jews murdered in Europe.[5]

Jewish public interest in the anti-Zionist cause turned out to be far below what the Council founders had anticipated. American Jewry increasingly viewed Jewish statehood as a solution to Jewish problems, especially to the lingering question of where hundreds of thousands of displaced Holocaust survivors should settle. A September 1945 Roper poll of American Jews pegged support for the Council position at 10.5 percent, with only that proportion responding affirmatively to the statement "Jews are a religious group only and not a nation and it would be bad for the Jews to try to set up a Jewish state in Palestine or anywhere else." In contrast, 80.1 percent of those surveyed agreed that "a Jewish state in Palestine is a good thing for the Jews and every possible effort should be made to establish Palestine as a Jewish state, or commonwealth, for those who want to settle there." While the Council managed to stabilize its finances, in the wake of the Holocaust, and later Israel's birth, the Council shed moderate leaders, which strengthened the relative influence of its ideological executive director. At the helm of the group, Berger took it upon himself to develop American Jewish anti-Zionism intellectually, composing four books on the topic and serving as primary editor of the organization's written material. One can see from these writings that the Council's early critique of Zionism focused primarily on the threats it posed to American Judaism and to "Americans of the Jewish faith."[6]

Berger's early works expanded on Classical Reform arguments. His 1945 book, *The Jewish Dilemma*, exemplified the Council's core ideology. Divided into three parts, the book put forth a narrative of Jewish history that idealized "prophetic Judaism" and Jewish integration. Berger argued that Jews did not comprise a race or a people at all, but merely differed from others in terms of their religious creed. Rejecting any notion of Jewish "peoplehood," Berger contended that Zionism's emphasis on nonreligious traits of Jews diminished Judaism and provided fuel for antisemites, who, Berger claimed, had invented racialized conceptions of Jews. In a second book published in 1951, *A Partisan History of Judaism*, Berger expanded on this critique, bemoaning "the tragic acceptance of Hitler's racist twaddle" in America as playing into the hands of Zionists. Instead of responding to Nazism by further embracing democratic ideals, Berger accused Zionists of accepting "Hitler's decree of separatism and try[ing] to make of it a virtue and to use it as political capital to win a 'Jewish' state." In short, this pillar of Council ideology portrayed Zionism as a betrayal of Jewish history and religion, provincializing Judaism's universal message.[7]

On Zionism's threat to American Jewry, Berger explained in his 1951 book that "Israel is only an incident in the history of Zionism, the purpose of which is to nationalize the lives of all Jews. Having achieved this state now, [Zionists] are turning their attention to Jews in the United States." Berger further maintained that Zionists "hope to make American Jews members of a national minority group, a segregated bloc, marked out by a separate culture, with separate responsibilities to this so-called Jewish State." Unless "Americans of the Jewish faith" return to the fundamentals both of American life and of Judaism, Berger warned, "we are headed for something of a catastrophe."[8]

Berger ended the book by recommending that readers support the American Council for Judaism to counter the Zionist threat both to "the Judaism of the Prophets" and to the equality of American Jews as individual citizens of the United States. Another threat mentioned by Berger, but emphasized even more in a book by Alfred Lilienthal, former counsel of the Council's Washington chapter, was the one that Zionism posed to America's Cold War foreign policy interests in the Middle East, an issue they felt that Jews, as Americans, needed to put before concern for the Jewish state. Many of the Council's critics argued that raising such questions provided fodder for antisemites, but the Council strongly disagreed, maintaining that it was the Zionists who made American Jews vulnerable by publicly demanding that they should feel loyal to a foreign country.[9]

The Council Encounters Palestinian Rights

Neither Council literature of the era nor Berger's first two books dwelled on Zionism's impact on Palestine's Arabs, even though some American Jews had raised those concerns prior to 1948. Moreover, when setting new objectives for the Council after failing to prevent Israel's emergence, none of Berger's four goals had anything to do with Arabs. On the contrary, in the first five years after the creation of the Palestinian refugee issue, the Council prioritized combatting the spread of Zionism in the United States, only addressing Palestinian affairs in a few exceptional circumstances. Most notably, in 1949, Council president Lessing Rosenwald sent an open letter to American religious groups calling for Arab refugee "repatriation" and "resettlement," urging interfaith "cooperation in a program to cope with the 'desperate flight of some 750,000 refugees who have been rendered homeless by the recent hostilities in Palestine.' " He issued this call along with a letter to Secretary of State Dean Acheson urging greater aid for Arab refugees. Rosenwald's letter did not mark the beginning of any sustained pro-refugee action on behalf of the Council, however, or even much coverage of Palestinian affairs in Council publications. Yet the action stood out among those of Jewish organizations, and Rosenwald's willingness to take this unpopular stance in support of the Arab refugees indicates that his feelings toward Palestinians differed little from Berger's, at least in the initial aftermath of 1948. Berger wrote privately in 1949 that he supported the Council taking a stance on the Arab refugee question primarily because "intelligent and liberal Christians" expected such a statement from Jewish groups. American Christian leaders indeed praised Rosenwald's expression of support for the Arab refugees, with the Catholic Near East Welfare Association specifically welcoming Rosenwald's "reference to repatriation" of the refugees. "I rejoice that you share with us the same humanitarian sentiments," wrote the Catholic group's national secretary. Yet even Berger felt uncertain as to whether the Council should do anything beyond issuing the letter; to those inquiring whether the Council planned to act further, Berger replied that the Council did not take part in philanthropy, but that "if there were any widespread appeal made to raise money to assist [Arab refugees], I am confident that the Council would join."[10]

Two connections led Berger's interest in Palestinian Arab affairs to grow in the years to come. The first, his link with American Friends of the Middle East (AFME), had been made by George Levison, a Council vice president and former State Department employee who had once been roommates with AFME founder Kermit "Kim" Roosevelt. The second, Berger's friend-

Elmer Berger on the right with AFME president Dorothy Thompson.
Wisconsin State Historical Society.

ship with Fayez Sayegh, came in part from Sayegh's work with AFME. Le-
vision put Berger in touch with Roosevelt prior to 1948 and involved
Council figures in the Committee for Justice and Peace in the Holy Land
(CJP), a group that Roosevelt ran which lobbied the Truman administration
against partition on the basis of their view that it would harm U.S. foreign
policy interests. Berger then aided Roosevelt and other Protestant Arabists
as they regrouped to create AFME with covert CIA funding. As a central
player in AFME, well aware of the CIA link, Berger was on the CIA's payroll
for a period. Both Berger and the Council's honorary vice president, Morris
Lazaron, a former rabbi at the prestigious Baltimore Hebrew Congregation, joined AFME's board of directors. Around that same time, AFME
funded the publication of a booklet by Sayegh on the Palestinian refugee
issue. After reading it, Berger contacted Sayegh in March 1952 to praise the
booklet and to ask Sayegh if he would like to meet in person. Sayegh responded promptly and affirmatively.[11]

Berger later cited meeting Sayegh as a pivotal moment in the post-1948 reorientation of his anti-Zionism. A close personal and intellectual relationship soon emerged. Berger himself later reminisced, "We each had some things to learn from the other. And without ever saying so, we explored each other's thinking. The process made us life-time friends." Berger called it his first real friendship with an Arab, and it lasted. Sayegh's ideas and the many other Arab contacts he made for the rabbi "fundamentally changed my life," according to Berger. Berger encouraged Sayegh to write a lengthy piece on Zionism and Arab nationalism for an American Jewish audience, which Berger reviewed and the *Menorah Journal* accepted for publication. "I find it difficult to tell you how excited I am about the potential of this article," Berger wrote to Sayegh. "Although, as you know, we approach this problem from different directions, I am proud to find in the common ground we share, so able and articulate a champion of the Arab position. Reading your piece revives my sometimes lagging faith . . . [that] truth and justice will be done."[12]

On Sayegh's recommendation, Berger began lecturing to Arab student groups, perhaps finding fulfillment from crowds that welcomed him warmly in contrast to the chilly reception he received in most Jewish circles. Sayegh also made clear the mutuality of intellectual influence in their relationship. "With your permission, I shall draw not only from your books and other publications, but also on the address you recently made at the Third Arab Students Convention," Sayegh wrote to Berger. "I shall not fail to emphasize what I presume you would want me to—namely, that we approach this problem from different directions, but nevertheless find a very wide common ground between our positions," he continued. Years later, Berger wrote that because of his interactions with Sayegh and other Arabs, "my anti-Zionism was now being fleshed out. From some of the best minds and most responsible statesmen in the Arab world I gained my first, clear and long-lasting impression and specific details about what Zionism was doing to human beings other than Jews."[13]

In tandem with Berger's friendship with Sayegh came the rabbi's encounter with the Middle East more broadly. Berger nudged Roosevelt and Rosenwald to allow him to tour the region, and in 1955 they finally agreed, with Berger traveling on AFME's—that is, the CIA's—dime. Berger's time in Lebanon,

Syria, and Jordan and his discussions with Arab officials there deepened his understanding of the Palestinian refugee issue. He noted their numbers and the many difficulties they faced, citing his firsthand experience visiting Palestinian refugee camps in letters that he later made public. "Here human beings live like animals," wrote Berger about the worst of the refugee conditions, calling Arab refugee camps on par with or "worse" than the "camps in Germany where Jews lived," referring either to Nazi-run concentration camps or to postwar displaced person camps. He continued, "The squalor . . . the human degradation and above all, the eternal despair . . . I think I have never seen anything like it—and I hope never to have a look at anything similar again."[14]

Their conditions were "not the whole tragedy," wrote Berger while "suppress[ing] moral outrage" at former Israeli leader David Ben-Gurion for his mantra that "not a single refugee shall return" and at Israeli ambassador Abba Eban for his "glib advice" that refugees should resettle outside their homeland. Berger cringed with "hatred of the 'Jewish' racism that created a state" that would not permit these refugees to return. "The monstrous nature of this ideology [Zionism] is apparent everywhere here," reported Berger to Rosenwald and Clarence Coleman, outgoing and incoming Council presidents respectively, in a series of letters that the organization would soon publish as a book. The experience clearly had a powerful impact on Berger, deepening his ideological opposition to Zionism. Writing about Berger's 1955 trip, one early, unpublished biographical study of the rabbi, written by a rabbinical student who had extensively interviewed Berger, noted that "by this point he had become solidly critical of Israel and pro-Arab in his orientation," observing that Berger's general attitude during his time in Israel involved sentiments like "the beautiful houses and trees of Jerusalem were only beautiful because they had been built by the Arabs who inhabited them before 1948." Directly after returning from the Middle East, Berger wrote privately, "I am more convinced than ever of the absolute necessity for Jews outside of Israel to divorce themselves completely from . . . the moral degradation of which is apparent in the Arab refugee problem." Though Zionism's effect on Palestinians did not become Berger's only rallying cry, it certainly rose higher on his agenda.[15]

Berger's Middle East tour came after a similar trip by another Council rabbi, Morris Lazaron. Lazaron had also witnessed the Palestine refugee problem firsthand as a *Jewish Newsletter* correspondent on an AFME inter-faith journalists' trip to the region in late 1953. Earlier that year, Lazaron brought up the refugee issue at the Council's annual convention. The rabbi "hit out at the American rabbinate for failing to lift 'its voice' on behalf of the Palestine Arab refugees," according to a press report. "Where in the pronouncements of the [CCAR and] Synagogue Council of America is there any mention of the plight of the hapless Moslem and Arab sufferers? Does Jewish nationalism crowd out every feeling of sympathy for any other groups than Jews?" Lazaron inquired rhetorically.[16]

In *Olive Trees in Storm*, Lazaron's book about his 1953 Middle East trip published by AFME in 1955, the rabbi addressed the refugee question in greater detail than any Council member had before. Lazaron spent much of his chapter on Lebanon detailing the miseries faced by the refugees there. Recalling the suffering he saw in the Shatila refugee camp and comparing it with the sad Jewish faces he witnessed in 1930s Germany, Lazaron wrote that he wished to call out to fellow Jews, "Oh tribe of the wandering feet and weary breast, oh heavy laden and burdened, you must know that longing to go home. Have you forgotten the injunction, 'Remember ye were strangers in the land of Egypt!' " From his time in Israel, Lazaron also reported the hardships and civil rights violations faced by Arabs citizens there. He recommended that Israel end discrimination against the Arab minority, "grant the principle of repatriation," and "take immediate steps" to absorb 100,000 Palestinian Arab refugees. Similarly, former Council official Al-fred Lilienthal also discussed the Arab refugee issue more in his 1957 book, also the product of extensive Middle East travel, than he had in previous writings. Lilienthal, too, received funds from AFME for his Middle East travels; the total amount that AFME gave him would exceed $27,000 in today's currency.[17]

Israeli Officials, Lessing Rosenwald, and the AFME-Council Threat

AFME's decision to sponsor Berger's trip and Lazaron's book in 1955 ap-pears not to have been a coincidence. As Hugh Wilford has noted, the ramped-up activity of the AFME-Council network during this period suggests that the network was engaged in a campaign to mobilize American public support for Operation Alpha, a secret Anglo-American peace initiative that would have compelled Israel to accept at least seventy-five thousand refugees and cede some amount of land to neighboring Arab states. While the Council always represented a minority voice within American Jewish politics, its efforts to work with and serve as a "Jewish friend" to Christian groups like AFME threatened to shift the opinions of non-Jewish Americans and to affect U.S policy.[18]

The Council's marginality in American Jewish politics had no bearing on its standing within American politics more broadly, where it punched above its numerical weight. This was on account of both its AFME connections and the prominence of figures such as Rosenwald, who met with President Harry Truman to present the Council's case on at least one occasion. Even after 1948, the Council received warm letters at its conferences from Truman, a Democrat, and from Republican Senate minority leader Robert Taft, both considered friends of Israel. President Truman's 1951 message to the Council's conference stated that "the Council deserves high credit for its program dedicated to the increasing national, civic, cultural and social integration of Americans of Jewish faith and for its belief that nationality and religion are separate and distinct," expressing hope that "the success which so far has crowned the efforts of the Council will continue and grow with the years in the interest of your coreligionists and of Americans of all faiths as well."[19]

The ascent to the presidency of Dwight Eisenhower, known to be closer to the AFME-Council network—so much so that the pastor of the president's church, who baptized him in 1953, even served on AFME's five-member board—posed a problem for Israel of which the country's leaders were profoundly aware, increasing the urgency of a pro-Zionist public relations push. "Until now, there was only one conduit to the White House—the Israeli. From now on, there will be an Arab one as well," wrote Israeli prime minister David Ben-Gurion after Eisenhower's election. The Israeli leader specifically noted the specter of AFME influence, asserting that "Eisenhower adores his younger brother Milton who is close with the pro-Arab group of Dorothy Thompson [AFME]. Efforts must be made to influence Milton in our direction." Meanwhile, an Israeli diplomatic report

Secretary of State John Foster Dulles on the
left with Lessing Rosenwald, president of the
anti-Zionist American Council for Judaism.
Wisconsin State Historical Society.

claimed that Secretary of State John Foster Dulles told his staff that "we shall not be prisoners of Israel any longer" in February 1953. The comment reflected Dulles's broader critique of the outgoing Truman administration for being too willing to yield to Zionist pressure at the expense of America's relationship with the Arab world. Given that America's Western European allies relied on Middle Eastern oil, Dulles and Eisenhower feared that becoming too close to Israel would drive the Arabs into the Soviet orbit, which would be a critical loss in the context of the Cold War. This meant that the new administration would either have to distance itself from Israel or push for a resolution to the Jewish state's underlying conflict with the Arab world.[20]

Despite this dynamic, the Eisenhower administration was not entirely unfriendly to the State of Israel. Shortly after entering office, Eisenhower himself told Dulles that he felt "extremely hopeful that we can improve the political and economic position of Israel." With regard to Israel's economy, which struggled to absorb masses of immigrants in the early 1950s, Eisenhower certainly did work to strengthen Israel's position. As historian David Tal has shown, Eisenhower's administration ultimately supplied Israel with a more generous economic aid package than had the Truman administration and provided it primarily in the form of grants, rather than loans as Truman did. Financial generosity, however, did not mean that the administration would follow Israel's lead on political matters. The Eisenhower administration would chart its own course on Middle East policy, which sometimes involved direct pressure on Israel, putting it at odds with many in Congress whose views often reflected those of their pro-Israel constituents and various American Zionist groups. As for the White House, in place of Zionists, it would be the non-Zionists of the AJC and anti-Zionists of the Council who more frequently had the administration's ear.[21]

Eisenhower's first term marked the pinnacle of Council influence in Washington, aided by the administration's hopes of forging a partnership with Egypt, which it presumed required pressuring Israel to make concessions. In April 1953, Council president Lessing Rosenwald met with an "extremely attentive" President Eisenhower, who gave "the impression that what he heard was in general agreement with his views." The meeting may have contributed to the sentiments behind Eisenhower's October 1953 observation that "the political pressure from the Zionists in the Arab-Israeli controversy is a minority pressure. My Jewish friends tell me that except for the Bronx and Brooklyn the great majority of the nation's Jewish population is anti-Zion." Secretary of State Dulles, on his first tour of the Middle East, reportedly took with him Council material that Rosenwald had given Eisenhower. Upon his return, Dulles's speech calling for a more evenhanded U.S. policy toward the region "contained passages that bore a striking resemblance" to Council proclamations.[22]

More frequent than direct Council contact with Eisenhower and Dulles was the group's communication with Henry Byroade, then the U.S. assistant secretary of state for Near Eastern, South Asian, and African affairs. Berger and Byroade quickly developed a warm friendship, coming to refer to each other affectionately as "Hank" and "the mad rabbi." Byroade had no qualms with making their personal relationship public. In late 1953, when confronted by Jewish Telegraphic Agency (JTA) journalists reporting that a "secret luncheon meeting" had taken place involving Rosenwald, Berger, and the assistant secretary, Byroade told prying reporters that "I merely met with some old friends whom I have known for a number of years." Rosenwald remained tight-lipped about the luncheon, reporting that there was "absolutely nothing for publication about the meeting today."[23]

Yet as the reporters suspected, Byroade's relationship with Council leaders went beyond mere personal ties. Berger had a hand in two of Byroade's speeches on the Middle East in 1954, one delivered in Dayton and the other for an American Council for Judaism conference in Philadelphia. In the Dayton speech, the assistant secretary called on Arabs to accept Israel's existence and on Israelis to "drop your conqueror attitude and see your future as a Middle Eastern state and not as a headquarters of worldwide groupings of people of a particular religious faith who must have special rights within and obligations to the Israeli state," sentiments that echoed typical Council rhetoric. In an article titled "Byroade Inferentially Blames Israel for Middle East Tension," JTA termed the speech "a major policy declaration by the United States Government on the Palestine question." Underneath a section heading titled "Assistant Secretary Presents Purported Arab Views," the article noted Byroade's statement that "although Israel talks of peace, the Arabs see it as bent only on aggression and that the Kibya and Nahalin incidents were deliberately planned by the Israel Government," referring to two Israeli reprisal raids that resulted in Palestinian civilian casualties. Byroade reportedly continued, "The Arabs fear that further Jewish immigration into Israel will inevitably result in territorial expansion by Israel." He went on to state that the Arab refugees are viewed as "end products of Israeli terrorism driven from their homes by cold-blooded massacres such as that at Deir Yassin." In his subsequent speech to the Council, Byroade elaborated on how the Zionist call for Jewish immigration stoked Arab fears of Israeli expansionism and frustration over the state's unwillingness to allow the Palestinian refugees to return. The high-ranking official then added that Israel should compensate the Arab refugees for the property that they had lost.[24]

Byroade's speeches caused a furor in Israel in newspapers and in the Knesset. The text of his Council speech circulated among members of the government. An Israeli foreign ministry spokesman criticized much of what Byroade had said. Prime Minister Moshe Sharett even denounced the speech on the floor of the Knesset, leading Berger to rejoice that "the Israeli Prime Minister . . . [has] properly evaluated as high policy pronouncements two recent addresses of Assistant Secretary of State Henry Byroade. Such proper recognition of the importance of these statements . . . is a first, constructive step." Rosenwald publicly hailed Byroade's statements. The Council had proved itself a menace to the Israeli government, not because of its place in the American Jewish community, which could always be considered marginal, but rather because of the powerful friends that had in Washington.[25]

In contrast with William Zukerman, who Israeli diplomats felt had "confused" American Zionists through his nuanced critiques of Israel and his unclear position on the Jewish political spectrum, Zionist groups in the United States always identified the Council as a dangerous political foe and worked to combat the group from its early days. There was no need for the Israeli government to prompt its American supporters to take action against the Council; on the contrary, Israeli officials wondered if American Zionists' tone had contributed to the problem. Rather than simply criticize the Council, Israeli diplomats pondered whether the best way to undermine the troublesome organization might be to co-opt its more moderate leaders, who they suspected felt more irritated by American Zionists than by the State of Israel.[26]

Prior to Rabbi Morris Lazaron's AFME-sponsored trip to the Middle East, the rabbi met with Israel's counsel general Avraham Harman at the consulate in New York City. Sensing Lazaron's moderation relative to other Council leaders, Harman put the rabbi in touch with foreign ministry officials Yaakov Herzog (whose brother and nephew would both later become presidents of Israel), S. Bendor, and Leo Kohn, whom he asked to aid Lazaron with anything he needed. "Lazaron came to see me to ask whether he would be received in Israel," wrote Harman to his colleagues, adding, "I assured him that he would be and that we would not regard him as being a lost soul. I added that I hoped he would go in with an open mind and would not allow his anti-Zionism to lead him to look at Israel in a prejudiced way. . . . He accepted this view." In January 1954, the pair met again after Lazaron's return from the Middle East. Harman wrote, "Lazaron expressed great satisfaction with the way in which he had been received in Israel. There was only one aspect of his visit which should give us some cause for consideration." Lazaron had told Harman that in all the Middle Eastern countries that his delegation had visited, he had met with members of minority groups. In some instances, the meetings took place without the presence of state officials; in others, meetings occurred with state officials in the room. In Israel, a state official accompanied him when he met with Arabs, which made the rabbi suspicious. Harman suggested a change to that practice: "I am sure we have nothing to fear very much from visitors meeting Arabs unaccompanied. . . . [We don't want] to create the impression that we are afraid to leave our Arabs alone with foreigners."[27]

Lazaron showed the Israeli diplomat his written reflections on the trip, a paper that Harman termed "an astonishing document" because of Lazaron's "fairly objective account." Harman considered it "clearly the work of a sincere man who has not sought to distort anyone's views" and had "no solutions in his pocket." When Harman prodded Lazaron about his views regarding Jewish peoplehood, the anti-Zionist rabbi conceded that he felt a "brotherly solidarity" with Jews everywhere. Writing to colleagues, Harman emphasized this point, contending that "the essential conflict between the American Council for Judaism and the Zionist movement is to be defined only in terms of assimilation," and assessed that "Lazaron is not an assimilationist." Lazaron had long served as the head rabbi of a prestigious congregation, Harman noted. "I am quite convinced that his brand of Judaism is not assimilationist in intention," though it may be in effect, he felt. Harman noted that by virtue of Lazaron's first marriage, he formerly had been a brother-in-law of Zionist leader Rabbi Abba Hillel Silver. He thus suggested that familial estrangement rather than ideology fueled Lazaron's anti-Zionism—meaning that the rabbi's attitude toward Israel could be subject to change.[28]

Harman continued his letter by outlining what he thought Israel's policies toward leading Council figures should be—direct engagement. "I do believe that it is possible to deprive the American Council" of those who are not assimilationist in intent, the diplomat maintained. The American Zionists can fight the Council all they want, Harman wrote, but Israel should not write off all Council members—some may only affiliate with the Council on account of their opposition to American Zionist tactics. He remarked, "It is entirely conceivable that some of them can be won over to identify themselves with certain phases of the work for Israel, such as the United Jewish Appeal"—a philanthropy that Harman did not mention had been co-chaired by William Rosenwald, Lessing's younger brother. "There are American Council Jews in a number of high places," Harman noted. In the past Israel had hoped to "tackle them through the instrumentality of other American Jews," though a direct Israeli approach may be required. "For example, Lessing Rosenwald has never had an opportunity of hearing our point of view as we would like our point of view expressed," Harman stated. "I believe that he is adopting his public positions on Zionism because he hates American Zionists, not because he hates Israel," Harman continued, mentioning that Rosenwald claims that his policy views are guided by American interests alone. "We [Israeli officials] believe that a pro-Israel policy is an American interest—we therefore ought to be able to sell that policy even to an American like Lessing Rosenwald," wrote Harman. This would place before Rosenwald a "new dilemma," he noted, "namely that as an American he ought to be pro-Israel even if as a Jew he is anti-Zionist. Might it not be worth considering getting one of our people to meet with him unobtrusively?"[29]

While that Israeli foreign ministry file contains no response to Harman and outlines no clear plan for engaging Lessing Rosenwald, it does appear that Israeli officials made an effort to win over the Sears, Roebuck heir. In January 1957, Prime Minister Ben-Gurion invited Rosenwald to Israel to see the country for himself. Rosenwald, former Council president and then chairman of the Council's board of directors, accepted. While the trip did not convert Rosenwald to the Zionist cause, it was largely a success for the Israelis. According to a memo circulated internally by the Council's non-Zionist rival, the American Jewish Committee (AJC), upon his return to the United States, Rosenwald gave a mostly positive report on his time in Israel to about two hundred people at a meeting of the Council's New York chapter, a crowd that included "a sizable number of observers from Jewish organizations, reporters from the Jewish press, and two Arabs."[30]

The memo reported that Rosenwald "highly praised Israel as a haven for refugees, the warmth and friendliness of the Israelis, their dedication and zeal in building the country, the high standard of living despite adverse conditions," singling out three universities for their "superior contributions to education and science." Rosenwald further "praised the Israeli army as a force for uniting and educating the Israelis and described the spirit of comradeship between officers and enlisted men, despite difference in rank." He even explained why Israel insisted on holding on to occupied Egyptian territory, describing Israel's need for access to the Red Sea through the Gulf of Aqaba and the state's concern that Gaza would be used for further "Arab guerrilla raids." Rosenwald met with many Israeli officials, including Ben-Gurion, on five separate occasions and "once for the entire day"—"I had a very interesting talk with Ben-Gurion, or rather I should say he talked with me," Rosenwald stated. When asked as to whether he would contribute funds to resettling Jewish refugees in Israel, Rosenwald responded affirmatively in the abstract, but only given certain conditions that he felt Israel would be unlikely to agree to, though he was willing to discuss the matter with Ambassador Eban.[31]

Rosenwald's report included some critiques. He felt, for instance, that the national trade union, the Histadrut, had an outsized role in the Israeli economy, and he opined that there was a lack of true Jewish religious feelings in Israel, which had been replaced by "nationalist and chauvinist feeling." Most Israelis, Rosenwald said, "were indifferent to the suffering of the Arab refugees." He stated that he "would be curious to see whether the Israelis would provide the refugees with compensation similar to German reparations to Israel." Rosenwald also maintained that "Arabs in Israel were not treated as first-class citizens." When it came to the question of peace, he noted an Israeli willingness to discuss it, though "he did not have the impression that they approached this subject with the same zeal and enthusiasm that they apply to other seemingly insoluble problems."[32]

Though Rosenwald ended his talk by confirming his commitment to the Council's principles, the AJC and Jewish newspapers covering the event all concluded that his statements had, on the whole, been surprisingly laudatory of the Jewish state. One observer, Moshe Kohn, a former managing editor of the *National Jewish Post* who had been unfamiliar with Rosenwald's politics prior to attending the meeting, said that Rosenwald and his wife discussed Israel in the same critical, nuanced manner that any Israeli would: "He speaks like an honest, loyal, knowledgeable citizen of Israel, and she speaks like a veteran kibbutznik who has some criticism." The AJC's Lucy Dawidowicz termed Rosenwald's position one of "friendly criticism, not unlike the view held by many members of the American Jewish Committee." But, Dawidowicz continued, "this position is completely at variance with the views of Rabbi Elmer Berger . . . [who] never looked upon Israel as a genuine haven for homeless people [and] had repeatedly attacked non-Zionists [including AJC members] for taking this view."[33]

Dawidowicz noted that Berger had not been present at the event, which may have had a simple explanation or may have been a product of "the fact that Mr. Rosenwald's report was in essence a repudiation of all of Rabbi Berger's views about Israel." She pointed out that Berger attacked non-Zionists for "their support of and interest in the Israeli institutions of higher learning that Mr. Rosenwald lavishly praised." Israeli universities, incidentally, represented the sort of philanthropy that Harman hoped that Rosenwald might support; universities had been long-standing recipients of contributions during the British Mandate period by American non-Zionists aiming to contribute only "philanthropic" but not "political" aid. Dawidowicz also noted that the Rosenwalds spoke warmly of the people of Israel, whom Berger "did not like." More importantly, Rosenwald "clearly showed Israel surrounded by a wall of Arab hostility," in contrast with Berger, who questioned Israel's sense of insecurity. Though Dawidowicz did not mention it explicitly, as a reader and occasional critic of Berger's books, she, too, would have likely been surprised that Rosenwald chatted for hours with Ben-Gurion and Eban, men toward whom Berger could barely "suppress moral outrage" because of their unwillingness to consider allowing for the return of Arab refugees.[34]

Theodor "Teddy" Kollek, director of the Prime Minister's Office, appears to have been tasked with building a relationship with Rosenwald or perhaps did so of his own volition. An Israel State Archive file on Lessing Rosenwald consists primarily of warm correspondence between Rosenwald and Kollek from the years 1961 through 1965. If Israeli officials were to have chosen one among themselves as a formal liaison to reach out to the anti-Zionist Jewish elite, Kollek would likely have been the man for the job. In 1949 and 1950, Kollek had helped mediate the disagreement between Ben-Gurion and AJC president Jacob Blaustein regarding the latter's objections to Ben-Gurion's overly Zionistic statements, indicating that Kollek had experience winning over wealthy American Jewish skeptics of Zionism.[35]

Correspondence from the 1960s indicates that Kollek and Rosenwald had likely met during their 1957 trip, having forged a "pleasant relationship" some "years ago," particularly when Kollek had hosted Mr. and Mrs. Rosenwald in Israel. "We often speak of the enjoyable visit we had with you during our visit to Israel and we would be delighted to have this association renewed at some time in the future," the anti-Zionist couple wrote to the man who would soon be elected mayor of Israel's capital city. The Rosenwalds even invited Kollek and his wife to their golden wedding anniversary; Kollek apologized profusely when he could not make it. "It would indeed have given us a great pleasure if you and Mrs. Kollek could have attended our celebration," wrote Rosenwald, further thanking Kollek for sending an ancient Tyrian shekel as an anniversary gift.[36]

Ben-Gurion also stayed in touch with Rosenwald, meeting with him during a May 1961 visit to New York City, a day after the prime minister conferred with President John F. Kennedy. While their encounter appeared to have been cordial—"we thoroughly enjoyed seeing you in New York and Mrs. Rosenwald joins me in sending our very kindest regard to you and to Mrs. Ben Gurion"—each privately voiced concern. Ben-Gurion told Rosenwald that Berger's alleged comparison of Israel with Nazi Germany had troubled him, prompting Berger to pen a polite letter to his "Excellency" Ben-Gurion denying that he had done so. Rosenwald, for his part, told Ben-Gurion of "the great difficulty he had in reconciling the conflicting statements of the State of Israel and the United Arab Republic on the basic cause of the great evacuation of Arabs from what is now the State of Israel." The Israeli leader reportedly had given his "very sincere and firm opinion of the situation" during their meeting, but in a follow-up letter to the prime minister, Rosenwald asked for Ben-Gurion's thoughts on a serious journalistic piece by Erskine B. Childers, a reporter "struck by the fact that no primary evidence of evacuation orders [from Arab leaders] was ever produced." The article, published in May 1961 by *The Spectator* of London, anticipated some of the findings of the Israeli "New Historians" decades later. On Ben-Gurion's behalf, Kollek replied by offering two quotations from Arab leaders allegedly acknowledging that their side had started the war, although he did not mention anything about evacuation orders and downplayed the importance of the matter. Rosenwald appeared not to have raised the issue further.[37]

Becoming "the PLO's Rabbi"—Elmer Berger and the Palestinians

While the Council's founding president became friendlier with Israelis, Berger continued to work with Arab officials, both in the Arab League and in the fledgling Palestine Liberation Organization (PLO). Their cooperation included Council support in raising awareness of the "Arab narrative" of the birth of the Palestinian refugee problem. In addition to the rabbi's long-standing friendship with Fayez Sayegh, who worked for both the Arab League and the PLO at various points in his career, Berger also met with Egyptian president Gamal Abdel Nasser in 1959, with Jordan's King Hussein in 1964, and with PLO chairman Yasser Arafat on several brief occasions. Though the primary thrust of Berger's argument still revolved around the nature of Jewish identity, the Palestinian question became increasingly conspicuous in his rhetoric as time went on, no doubt fueled in part by his contact with Arabs abroad and at home. Indicative of Berger's growing interest in Palestinian rights, in 1961 Council publicity director Bill Gottlieb, likely at Berger's urging, asked a television show to host the rabbi specifically to discuss the Arab refugee issue, a topic on which Berger was an "outstanding authority" on account of his travels. "The United Nations debate on the Arab refugee problem comes up again this week. It should be a humdinger. . . . I would like to suggest that you invite Rabbi Elmer Berger as a guest to discuss . . . this tough problem," wrote Gottlieb, suggesting that they call the segment "The Arab Refugees Still Wait." Berger, stated Gottlieb, stood ready—and seemingly eager—to answer questions such as "Did the Arab refugees leave Palestine or were they driven out in 1947–48?" and "What right do the Arab refugees now have to their former land in Israel?"[38]

While some Council publications mentioned Israel's treatment of Palestinian Arabs, it never became a particularly prominent subject of discussion. Berger represented a minority within the organization passionately

opposed to Israeli policies toward Palestinians and other Arabs; Berger himself recognized that he was one of the few in the Council who wanted to
"destroy" Zionism. A view apparently more representative of the Council's
rank and file comes across in an op-ed written by a Chicago regional vice
president who, when criticizing Abba Eban's rhetoric about the Diaspora,
hedged his critique by stating, "All Americans admire many of Israel's accomplishments." The most that the average Council member did for the
Palestinians was donate to the American Council for Judaism Philanthropic
Fund, which in some years allocated nominal sums to Arab refugee relief
efforts, an activity that required no critique of Israel. Moreover, it is possible
that many donors to the fund had little awareness that part of their donations went to Palestinians, with a much larger portion going to Jewish refugees who wished to settle outside Israel. Some Council Philanthropic Fund
money even went to an Israeli hospital, Shaare Tzedek, in Jerusalem. In any
case, Berger's harsh criticism of Israeli policies increasingly veered away
from the broader Council's focus on opposing Zionism's effects on Jews. If
Council members had a problem with Berger's growing embrace of Arabs,
they were free to resign or complain, but it did not affect Berger, who noted
that these internal critics never really confronted him directly. That all shifted after the 1967 war, a moment when nearly the entire American Jewish
community celebrated Israel's dramatic victory.[39]

Elmer Berger's July 1967 interview with the *New York Times* had, ironically, been set up by Council president Richard Korn, a member of the
same clique of affluent Council leaders who would be so outraged at its
consequences. In encouraging his friend, *New York Times* publisher Arthur
Ochs Sulzberger, to commission the article, Korn had hoped, perhaps naively, that a piece on the Council featuring an interview with Berger would
help the embattled group's image. Besides noting the Council's—that is,
Berger's—critique of Israel's "aggression," and reporting Berger's attacks
on other Jewish groups, the article listed the names of six of the Council's
most prominent supporters. The article elicited angry reactions from five of
the six men whom it mentioned, who were unhappy to be linked with Berger's statements; these included Neiman-Marcus president Stanley Marcus,
Random House vice chairman Donald Klopfer, president of Abraham &
Straus department stores Walter N. Rothschild Jr., New York state official

Joseph Louchheim, and John Mosler, head of the world's largest manufac-
turer of safes. "In assailing the position of the anti-Zionist group," a Jewish
Telegraphic Agency article reported, "the five leaders stressed their sympathy for Israel and declared they had made substantial contributions to Israeli causes during and right after the June war."[40]

Outside of their relative prominence and connection to the Council, the
five had no particular link to one another, nor did they constitute any sort of
"counter-establishment" within the Council or in American Jewish politics
more broadly. None personally held major roles in national Jewish politics,
though Rothschild's wife's grandfather, Jacob Schiff, had cofounded the
American Jewish Committee, and her father, Felix Warburg, had founded
American Friends of Hebrew University. Marcus, the best known of the five,
had been publicly noted as a Council member in a 1957 *Commentary* profile of
his Dallas-based business, but it did not portray him as an anti-Zionist ideo-
logue. "Though he is a member of the American Council for Judaism," the
article stated, "Marcus also works with the Dallas representatives of the American Jewish Committee. (No fanatic, Marcus said ironically, when I asked him
whether he had visited Israel, that he was afraid to because he might be con-
verted)." In the realm of national politics, Marcus had close ties to President
Kennedy and President Johnson, and many considered him to be one of the
most important business innovators in Texas and in his industry at large.[41]

Despite his renown, or perhaps because of it, Marcus was the mildest in
his critique of Berger's statement. Louchheim and Klopfer resigned from
the Council, with the latter stating that the Council had "completely mis-
represented my views about Israel." Mosler said he did not realize that his
office still sporadically paid Council dues and noted publicly that "I do not
want to be associated in any way with this movement any more than I
would want to belong to the John Birch Society," complaining that the
Council's use of his name without his permission was "highly improper."
Rothschild's colleague said that Rothschild himself would have repudiated
the Council's views were he not overseas, noting that the alleged Council
backer had "contributed to the Israel Emergency Fund."

Capitalizing on the outrage, the chairman of the American Zionist Council told reporters that the criticism "was proof that American Jewry was
100 percent behind the present position of Israel," implicitly refuting the

New York Times article's title: "U.S. Jews Split on Mideast War: Some See Response in Nation as 'Hysteria.' " The only one of the six named in the *New York Times* article to not denounce the Council, John Loeb of Loeb, Rhoades & Co., would eventually shift toward Israel as well. "In his later years," his obituary noted, "Mr. Loeb became a friend of Mayor Teddy Kollek of Jerusalem and became deeply interested in Israel, where his philanthropic activities included the founding of a community center in East Jerusalem."[42]

In his memoirs, Berger claimed that he meant to characterize Israel as the aggressor in the overarching conflict over Palestine rather than in the recent war. In any case, he refused to retract his statement despite pressure from Council board members. Within the Council, the question moved from that specific statement to Berger's overall "pro-Arab" orientation, with many members hoping to diminish any focus on Arab rights in Council rhetoric. "I know that our members, by and large, want to be assured that their continued support for the Council does not mean their undying hatred of the State of Israel," wrote former Council president Clarence Coleman, "or, of even greater importance, their endorsement of the position and tactics of the Arabs. They are Jews, and share and delight in the accomplishments of their fellow Jews." In a back-and-forth struggle that lasted over a year, Council board members attempted to pressure Berger either to promise to not make pro-Arab statements or to resign. Berger refused, and the Council finally voted to let him go in 1968.[43]

The anti-Berger push was led by former Council presidents Rosenwald and Coleman, the latter of whom had previously clashed with Berger after accusing him of squandering Council resources on pet projects of little interest to other members and for advancing initiatives in Washington without consulting the board. The board came to a consensus to accept Berger's 1967 letter of resignation when it met at Rosenwald's home on June 5, 1968, with the national executive committee voting to support the motion by a wide margin several weeks later. The decision was based "mainly on Elmer's . . . militant involvement in the Arab-Israel confrontation." While the Council had no formal policy vis-à-vis the conflict, a memo stated, "Elmer's policy is divergent and gives the unfortunate impression that Israel is always wrong and the Arabs right," an impression that he had again recently advanced when "championing the Arab cause" on a recent BBC panel.[44]

Lessing Rosenwald's central role in the ousting of Berger resulted from transformative events of 1967, but his stance on the issue likely developed in part from his own experiences in Israel and through conversations with Middle Easterners, which differed drastically from Berger's experience. Yet it also likely emerged as a consequence of the warming American relationship with Israel. In the years directly after Israel's founding, many on the Council doubted that support for socialist Israel generally served U.S. foreign policy interests, a concern fueled in part by U.S. government officials who shared those concerns and spurned Zionist pressure. By the mid-1960s, positive feelings about Israel had spread among Christian Americans, including President Lyndon Johnson, both because of developments in American culture and because of the drift of several key Arab states into the Soviet orbit. In 1954, Avraham Harman speculated that Rosenwald would be hard pressed to oppose Israel if he could be convinced that supporting Israel served American interests. By 1968, the latter position had become a matter of near consensus in American elite circles, and Rosenwald indeed opposed Berger's efforts to make the group an "anti-Israel" organization.[45]

The Mezvinsky Experiment: The Council Tries a New Direction

In the middle of the Berger controversy, the Council lost another dynamic figure—one who felt that, in his own way, he was trying to save the organization from itself. Professor Norton Mezvinsky became executive director of the American Council for Judaism only a few months prior to the June 1967 war. In contrast to the Reform, German-Jewish origins of most Council members, Mezvinsky, born in Iowa in 1932, came from a family that was Orthodox, Zionist, and of Eastern European origin. In addition, many members of his extended family had settled in Israel. Perhaps unsurprisingly, given his background, Norton Mezvinsky's connection with the Council originated with opposition to it. As an undergraduate who planned to move to Israel after graduation, Mezvinsky first contacted Berger for research purposes while writing his senior thesis on anti-Zionist propaganda in the United States. Though his thesis criticized the Council, as a result of their correspondence and subsequent meetings, Mezvinsky ultimately came to appreciate many aspects of Berger's critique of Zionism. Religious arguments against Zionism helped convince Mezvinsky to turn against the ideology, though Mezvinsky felt even more affected by the Palestinian question. He soon began to oppose the concept of a Jewish state on these bases. A few years after finishing his PhD in history at the University of Wisconsin in 1959, Mezvinsky moved to New York City to accept an academic position at the City College of New York, though he went on to spend most of his career at Central Connecticut State University. He became closer with Berger, so much so that when the Council needed a new executive director in early 1967 after longtime staff member Leonard Sussman departed to head Freedom House, it hired Mezvinsky at Berger's urging.[46]

Mezvinsky's brief tenure as Council executive director foreshadowed the future of American Jewish anti-Zionism and highlighted the Council's inability to reinvent itself. From the start, Mezvinsky and the Council made an odd pairing. Mezvinsky, the young leftist academic of Orthodox Jewish heritage, meshed poorly with the stodgy, older Reform Jewish businessmen who dominated the Council. Though an anti-Zionist, Mezvinsky did not reject the notion of Jewish peoplehood as the Council did. Mezvinsky had different concerns, which he voiced at a dramatic press conference announcing his resignation after only sixteen months as executive director.[47]

According to a statement released to accompany that May 1968 press conference, Mezvinsky wanted to work with African Americans, but Council board members resisted for racist reasons. He wanted the Council to join the Soviet Jewry movement, but it remained paralyzed on that question. Mezvinsky desired to bring in younger Jews of various backgrounds, but a Council leader reportedly told him, "I'm not sure that we want such Jews." Mezvinsky expressed a broad frustration with the Council's relationship with Judaism. He declared a need for an "authentic" Jewish alternative to Zionism, but the Council and its aging leadership appeared uninterested in providing it. Though he applauded Berger's "knowledgeable and sincere . . . advocacy of Arab interests," he called Berger biased, narrow, and overly preoccupied with the Middle East conflict. Yet he also critiqued the shallowness of Berger's Council critics, who merely opposed Berger because they felt that his "ideas and advocacy of the Arab cause are somehow bad for the Council's image." All in all, Mezvinsky portrayed the Council less as a po-

litical advocacy group and more as a stuffy social club uninterested in finding new members or trying new ideas.[48]

Whether realistic or not, Mezvinsky's vision would have reoriented the
Council toward trying to attract the new wave of leftist critics of Israel who
emerged after the 1967 war. It would have opened the Council up to Jews
who felt upset with Israel's occupation of Arab lands, as well as those grap-
pling for a new sort of authentic Jewishness outside the bounds of an increasingly Israel-focused American Jewish mainstream. Though unlikely,
this might have tied the budding political currents of 1968 to the ailing
though not insignificant infrastructure of the Council. Yet such success appears to have been impossible. The Council's board had little interest in
attracting young radical Jews. Instead of expanding after 1967, the Council
chose to contract. It fell back on its core mission of defending American
Judaism from Zionization and decided to cut loose from its reputation as
being "anti-Israel" and "pro-Arab," which Berger had fostered. That urge
led to his dismissal—an attempt to rebrand, or perhaps unbrand, at a time
when American Jewish support for Israel reached an all-time high. During
his tenure as executive director from February 1967 through May 1968,
Mezvinsky saw Zionism's crest, and any new initiative of the kind he envisioned would likely have been too early to capture the wave of Jewish criticism of Israel that emerged only later. Along with Berger and Mezvinsky,
the Council lost other key staff members around 1967–1968, and many
pro-Berger members resigned. With aging leadership, meager funds, and
an unclear platform, the Council itself sank into obscurity and by the 1970s
lacked the funds to even hold national conferences. Jews interested in Palestinian rights would have to wait for a new organization to emerge.[49]

AJAZ, CONAME, and American Jewish
Critiques of Zionism, 1969–1973

"Rabbi Berger knows that as of late his point of view enjoys a great sympathy from the 'new left' groups in America and Europe, who at least see a
vague similarity between the situation in Vietnam and the Near East," a
Dutch newspaper noted in March 1968, having interviewed Berger a few
months prior to his final split with the Council. The line served as Berger's

acknowledgment that the locus of anti-Zionism in America had moved far from the respectable milieu of AFME and Reform Jewish businessmen. No doubt Berger had heard of the pro-Palestine statements coming out of the Black Power movement in the late 1960s, as well as from others on the emergent New Left. While Berger had, from the 1940s through the 1960s, arguably been America's single most recognizable Jewish critic of Israel, that title would soon pass to others. Yet Berger did not retire from his struggle and in fact became only more deeply aligned with the Palestinian cause, putting him into a transnational orbit of Palestinian, American, and Israeli radicals who might appear to be odd bedfellows for an aging, Midwestern rabbi.[50]

The years 1969–1970 marked the emergence of two small organizations run by American Jews which each, in their own way, sought to foster a transnational, critical discourse on Israel/Palestine. Berger founded one of the two, which he ultimately named American Jewish Alternatives to Zionism (AJAZ), at the urging of his supporters in 1969. AJAZ served as a platform for Berger's views rather than as a mass membership organization, though it did have officers, members, a secretary, and an office, which Mezvinsky ran when Berger spent winters in Florida. AJAZ quickly became more focused on Palestinian rights than the Council had ever been. Reasons for that included Israel's post-1967 occupation of the West Bank, Gaza, and other territories, along with Palestinian militants' success in bringing their cause to the world's attention—but those developments are only one part of AJAZ's story. While Jewish Council members had ostensibly been Berger's constituency while at Council, Berger's constituency at AJAZ comprised whoever wanted to hear from him and Mezvinsky, regardless of their religion or nationality. Increasingly, those who wished to hear from Berger included Arabs and New Leftists; the aging rabbi even shared a stage with the Black radical leader Stokely Carmichael at a Palestine Week rally at George Washington University.[51]

But the most prominent Jewish critic of Israel on the New Left would soon emerge from a very different political pedigree. In contrast with the lifelong anti-Zionist Elmer Berger, Professor Noam Chomsky, born in 1928 to prominent Hebrew-language scholar William Chomsky and his wife, Elsie, grew up in what he termed the "cultural ghetto" of the 1930s Philadelphia Jewish community, an insular setting surrounded with people dedicated to the revival of Hebrew culture, various shades of pre-state Zionism, and left-wing politics. "I was an organizer of what were then called Zionist youth groups, which I suppose would now be called anti-Zionist, because they were mostly opposed to a Jewish state" and supported a binationalist solution, Chomsky recalled. Like a young Don Peretz, Chomsky gravitated toward the Labor Zionist youth group HaShomer HaTzair, which at the time envisioned a socialist binational state in Palestine, and the people he connected with "were committed to Arab-Jewish working-class cooperation" in a socialist context.[52]

He had considered "making *Aliyah*" to Israel in the 1940s, though as a binationalist Zionist he became disillusioned by the 1948 war. Nonetheless, Chomsky and his wife volunteered at a HaShomer HaTzair kibbutz in 1953, an experience that he "loved" despite being disturbed by the ruins of an abandoned Arab village nearby and by the attitudes many Israelis held toward Arabs and Moroccan immigrants. For the next decade and a half, however, Chomsky said little publicly about Israel or the Palestinians, a development that changed around 1969.[53]

That year, "a friend who was a grad student in math at MIT, Assaf Kfoury, suggested to me that I add a talk about Israel-Palestine to the dozens I was giving about the Vietnam war, foreign policy, and a host of other issues. I agreed," Chomsky recalled. The speech titled "Nationalism and Conflict in Palestine" would in essence be repeated later in Chomsky's 1974 book *Peace in the Middle East*. "It aroused a firestorm. At the time, worship of Israel was intense and virtually unanimous," Chomsky reminisced over fifty years later. From then, Chomsky's involvement in the issue "was constant."[54]

In the spring of 1970, by then a well-known critic of America's involvement in Vietnam associated with the New Left, Chomsky circulated a letter asking fellow leftist intellectuals why their concerns about America's Indochina policy did not extend to the Middle East. From that letter, a new organization called the Committee on New Alternatives in the Middle East (CONAME) emerged. A left-wing activist named Berta Langston volunteered to serve as CONAME's secretary to help organize the group's first initiative, a lecture tour for activist Arie Bober of the Israeli revolutionary socialist and anti-Zionist group Matzpen. Langston soon resigned from the organization because she was unwilling to work with any speakers who did not explicitly oppose Zionism, while Chomsky and others wanted CO-NAME to highlight a spectrum of views. With a small grant from his former employer, the American Friends Service Committee, Jewish peace activist Allan Solomonow relaunched CONAME as an organization more ambivalent about Zionism. While Chomsky remained involved, it would be Solomonow who led the organization. Along with Solomonow and Chomsky, the group's steering committee included Rabbi Everett Gendler, journalist Paul Jacobs, and academics Irene Gendzier, Don Peretz, Stanley Diamond, and Seymour Melman, as well as a graduate student named John Ruskay. Though most of those involved with the group were Jewish, CONAME's leaders decided that it would be nonsectarian. Two young CO-NAME figures, Ruskay and Solomonow's assistant Robert Loeb, however, would soon desire to be part of an explicitly "Jewish" platform for Middle East engagement, leading them both to play central roles in a new group, Breira, which would have that Jewish communal orientation. While their time with CONAME no doubt deepened their understanding of the region, Loeb's and Ruskay's past ties with the group would later be used to discredit Breira.[55]

AJAZ and CONAME both hosted Israeli and Arab speakers, and leaders of both groups would sometimes visit the region. Berger and Mezvinsky toured the Arab Middle East in 1971. Berger soon became close with the new Institute for Palestine Studies, founded that year in Beirut; the Institute happily published his books when the Council no longer would. Mezvinsky often traveled to Israel, the Palestinian territories, and Lebanon, where he built close personal relationships with Palestinian and Israeli activists such as Israel Shahak, Uri Davis, Fouzi El-Asmar, and PLO official Sabri Jiryis.

These four had all, in important yet different ways, done much to promote the Palestinian cause within the Middle East, but their links to Mezvinsky, Berger, and Chomsky would extend their voices into the United States for the first time. Mezvinsky in particular forged close friendships with all four of them. Though Chomsky and Jiryis never met, Chomsky wrote the foreword for the 1976 edition of Jiryis's *The Arabs in Israel*, a book that exposed many international readers to the problem faced by Palestinian citizens of

Israel. Shahak, a Polish-Israeli Holocaust survivor and Hebrew University chemistry professor, chaired the Israeli League for Human and Civil Rights, while Davis—a onetime pacificist civil rights activist who drifted toward radical, and later militant, anti-Zionism—served as his vice chair. Both later became Mezvinsky's coauthors, starting in 1975 when he and Davis coedited *Documents from Israel, 1967–73: Readings for a Critique of Zionism.* AJAZ sponsored national lecture tours for Davis, Shahak, and El-Asmar, a Palestinian activist in Israel whom the state had preventatively detained for political reasons. After El-Asmar's lecture tour in the early 1970s, Mezvinsky helped him enroll at Central Connecticut State and offered him housing, leading to a lifelong bond.[56]

Noam Chomsky attested to the role of this transnational network, especially Shahak, in developing his views: "From about 1970, I began what became a very intensive correspondence with Israel Shahak. . . . We exchanged massive amounts of documentary materials . . . along with extensive discussion of many issues. For me, as for many others, Shahak became an indispensable source of information and ideas, particularly, for me, in personal correspondence and several meetings." Chomsky noted how much he learned from Jiryis's "path-breaking book" and from his friendships with El-Asmar and Davis, who gave him tours of Bedouin areas and West Bank settlements.[57]

Whether discussing Elmer Berger or Noam Chomsky, one cannot understand the growing focus of Jewish critics of Zionism on Palestinian rights without taking into consideration the impact of their deepening contacts with Arabs and Israelis. This consists of a transference of both ideas and of basic knowledge. Chomsky's dissent on Israel began privately in the 1940s, but only through contact with Palestinian and Israeli radicals, as well as trips to the region, did he more thoroughly refine his view of Israel's impact on the Palestinians. Sayegh played a role for Berger in the 1950s that Shahak, Jiryis, and Edward Said later did for Chomsky, Mezvinsky, and others.

As to whether the Israeli government ever asked American Jewish organizations to act against Chomsky, it is hard to give a definitive answer, as no Israeli file bearing his name can be requested from the Israel State Archives. But given what files are available, it appears that American Jewish groups did so without any external prompting. The Boston office of the

Anti-Defamation League (ADL) began compiling a dossier on Chomsky in 1970, which includes notes taken by ADL employees who attended his lectures. Correspondence between the ADL and Israel's consul general appears in the dossier, but instead of Israel asking the American group to keep an eye on Chomsky, the ADL simply kept the diplomat updated on its own monitoring. While only a single data point, the episode perhaps hints at just how far political dynamics had shifted since Israeli diplomats had to push the American Zionist Council to do more to undermine William Zukerman two decades prior.[58]

Conclusion: From the Pittsburgh Platform to a Palestinian Platform

Anti-Zionism emerged among American Jews long before the creation of the State of Israel and the mass displacement of the Palestinians in 1948. Considering that American Jewry had relatively little contact with Middle Easterners outside of Zionist Jews before 1948, it should not be surprising that Palestinian Arabs did not animate early American Jewish anti-Zionism. Rather, pre-1948 Jewish anti-Zionism as embodied by the Council emerged as a response to local concerns, feelings, and ideologies. On the basis of the dichotomy between religion and nationality that they perceived in the United States at the time, some Reform Jews understood Judaism purely as a religion. They considered America their home and felt troubled by suggestions to the contrary. They responded negatively to changes made by other American Jews who adopted symbols, rituals, and customs from Zionism or Israeli culture, which they viewed as foreign. The 1940s and 1950s American context appeared relatively less open to "hyphenated Americanism"; meanwhile, the Cold War backdrop of the House Un-American Activities Committee, McCarthyism, and the Rosenberg trial served as a reminder of the importance of undivided loyalty during that period.

The Council began as a decidedly non-transnational organization. There is no particular reason to expect that the group would suddenly reorient its ideologies and agenda around Palestinians after 1948. While the group did take up the issue eventually, the interest was mostly limited to the leaders with direct exposure to Palestinian concerns. Berger and those in his faction openly propagandized about Israel's treatment of the Palestinians from the 1950s onward, though it should be emphasized that Berger never dropped his earlier concerns about Zionism's impact on Americans of the Jewish faith. The Council board tolerated Berger's pro-Arabism for years, until 1967, when the position became too untenable even for Council leaders.

By 1968, the Council could be characterized as an aging, waning organization with a diminishing commitment to opposing Israel in light of the state's many successes and broad popularity among American Jews. The conditions under which the group emerged two and a half decades earlier had fundamentally changed. As the 1960s went on, fewer and fewer Jews feared "hyphenated Americanism" and associated "dual loyalty" accusations. The trend known as "white ethnic revival" had begun. Meanwhile, during the largely pro-Israel presidencies of Lyndon Johnson and Richard Nixon, American Jews did not feel stuck between conflicting American and Israeli interests, as they sometimes had during prior administrations. Other white Americans seemed to support Israel too, particularly after 1967. The old distinctions between elite "German" Jews and the Eastern European Jewish majority mattered much less than they had in the past. The Council was clearly antiquated.[59]

Unlike the Council, post-1967 American Jewish critics of Israel often did not dispute Jewish peoplehood, or at least did not see Jewishness as solely a religious identity. Many of them, like Chomsky, grew up in American Eastern European Jewish circles that had embraced Jewish nationalism, which took various forms outside of statist Zionism. These critics had little in common with the Classical Reform, integrationist, and America-focused Council, even if they appreciated Berger's later work. What bothered them more about Zionism was its impact on the Palestinians, which became increasingly apparent after an independent Palestinian national movement won growing international recognition and support in the late 1960s and 1970s. While the Council's decline led aging anti-Zionists to soften their opposition to Israel, another story involves the exact opposite trend: young Zionists advocating for the creation of a Palestinian state.

6

Zionists for Palestine

ON NOVEMBER 15, 1976, five American Jews and two Palestine Liberation Organization (PLO) officials gathered at the home of an American Friends Service Committee staff member in Washington, DC, for a secret meeting. Their conversation was not particularly fruitful, leading one attendee to call it a meeting of only "modest significance." Yet when the names of the five American Jews were leaked to the media—apparently by Israeli officials— the ensuing controversy marked an important moment in Jewish history.[1]

Newspapers identified two of the five, Arthur Waskow and Rabbi Max Ticktin, as members of the executive committee of Breira: A Project of Concern in Diaspora-Israel Relations, while the other three, Olya Margolin, Herman Edelsberg, and David Gorin, worked or had previously worked for the National Council of Jewish Women, B'nai B'rith, and the American Jewish Congress (AJCongress), respectively. While the latter three organizations immediately condemned the meeting, Breira did the opposite, publicly defending the legitimacy and wisdom of meeting with the two PLO moderates, Issam Sartawi and Sabri Jiryis. Weeks later, an obscure group called Americans for a Safe Israel aggressively circulated a pamphlet in all corners of the Jewish community attacking Breira, all its members, and the meeting. The negative response was overwhelming; to Breira members, it felt like a coordinated campaign had suddenly struck. While Breira did not immediately collapse, the episode marked the beginning of the end of the group, as members, donors, and affiliated rabbis faced increased scrutiny from the rest of the American Jewish community, including unfounded accusations that the organization was a PLO "front."[2]

As the first national American Jewish organization to advocate for the creation of a Palestinian state alongside Israel, Breira, in a way, had succeeded in becoming the type of platform that an earlier generation of Jews supportive of Palestinian rights had wished for in the 1950s. Echoing sentiments expressed by William Zukerman and Don Peretz decades earlier about the need for more open conversation in the American Jewish community about sensitive Israel-related topics, Breira's founding statement emphasized that its mission was in part to oppose "pressures in American Jewish life which make open discussion of these and other vital issues virtually synonymous with heresy." Unlike the reserved and cautious AJC, Breira spoke openly about the needs of the Palestinians while attempting to maintain legitimacy in the broader Jewish community by arguing that Palestinian statehood served Israeli interests. With a very active fifteen hundred members, including over a hundred rabbis, and chapters in cities throughout the country, the group had some success. But as Breira's image increasingly became identified with the Palestinian question, it faced growing pushback that would ultimately overwhelm it.[3]

In contrast to earlier parts of this book, this chapter tells a story that scholars have examined before. Yet until now, historians have written about Breira as an American phenomenon. Published works on Breira situate the group in American Jewish history, emphasizing its origins in Vietnam War–era protest culture. Existing publications on Breira have something else in common: none draw from Breira's archives. These secondary works draw from each other, as well as from press releases, news reports, and contemporary critiques. As a result, even book chapters written by academic historians tend to echo external views of Breira from when it was active. Jack Wertheimer, for example, understands Breira primarily as a domestic "sixties generation" countercultural rebellion against American Jewish leaders, downplaying the group's emphasis on Israel. While Michael Staub's work takes Breira's stance on Israel more seriously, it focuses on the broader debate over Breira and lacks the archival footing needed to understand why the group adopted the views that it did. This portrayal of Breira is not wrong, but in forgoing the transnational dynamics at play, it is incomplete in a way that makes the group's thoughtful engagement with Middle East politics easier to dismiss.[4]

Though Breira framed itself as an alternative to the American Jewish "establishment," it seems that Breira's young leaders courted mainstream Jewish elders no less frequently than they criticized them. Breira's letterhead and the masthead of its journal, *Interchange: A Monthly Review of Issues Facing Israel and the Diaspora*, were peppered with the names of establishment figures such as Rabbi Joachim Prinz, former head of both AJCongress and the Conference of Presidents of Major American Jewish Organizations; prolific Jewish studies scholar Jacob Neusner; Rabbi Robert Gordis, former head of the Synagogue Council of America; *Sh'ma* editor Rabbi Eugene Borowitz; and *Hadassah Magazine* editor Jesse Zel Lurie. No doubt, Breira sought out these senior figures as sources of communal legitimacy.[5]

But in terms of latching onto others to gain Jewish credibility, another set of names recurs even more frequently in Breira's files—those of Israeli left-wing figures: retired Israel Defense Forces (IDF) general Mattityahu Peled; Knesset members Lova Eliav, Shulamit Aloni, Uri Avnery, Marcia Freedman, and former IDF colonel Meir Pa'il; and journalists Amos Kenan, Simcha Flapan, and David Shaham. In the eyes of these Israelis, their country's 1967 territorial gains had created an opportunity to resolve the Israeli-Palestinian conflict by establishing a Palestinian state in those lands. Concurring with this assessment, Breira hoped that hosting like-minded Israelis in person and in print would add to their organization's credibility. Just as Breira, according to one scholar, "consistently asserted its own loyalty to Zionism," it also emphasized that its platform reflected that of many respectable Israelis. Accordingly, more so than 1960s American counterculture, one sees 1970s Israeli left-wing politics in the archives of Breira.[6]

Along with Breira's archival material, another set of sources—oral histories of the founders of Breira and affiliated groups—also help shift its story toward the Middle East. A review of transcripts of dozens of interviews with Breira's founders and core activists reveals that the cohort had remarkably similar formative experiences. Most had spent months or years in Israel, often at Israeli universities or on kibbutzim, during which time their connections with Israeli leftists or firsthand encounters in the occupied territories forged their views on the Palestine question.[7]

Drawing from these sources, this chapter argues that the rise of Breira and the broader "second generation" of American Jewish supporters of Palestinian rights is as much a part of the history of Israel/Palestine as it is of American Jewish history. By weaving these episodes into a broader transnational narrative, the chapter argues for a rethinking of the motives of various actors—and even the question of *who* constitutes the major actors in this history. In doing so, it responds to Markus Krah and other scholars who call for greater focus on the entanglements between American Jews and other Jewish communities, highlighting what is gained by writing a more multidirectional history of Israel–American Jewish relations. While Breira's methods and tone may have been inspired by domestic American trends, political currents emanating from the Israeli left shaped its content. Breira consistently invoked dovish Israeli voices and invited them to speak to American Jewish audiences. Ultimately, Breira's strong embrace of Israeli doves is what led to its fateful decision to defend the controversial PLO meeting, adding fuel to the delegitimization campaign against it.[8]

Before Breira: The Young Jewish Left and Palestinian Rights, 1967–1973

The mid- to late 1960s and early 1970s witnessed a proliferation of left-wing Jewish organizations and publications, reflecting a broader activist trend in American society. These Jewish groups were small, mainly consisted of young members, and operated on a local scale. Their names were often creative (*Brooklyn Bridge*), evoked Hebrew, Yiddish, or Judaism (Yavneh, Chutzpah, Fabrangen, *Genesis 2, Hayom, Bagolah, Achdut, Hakahal*), or emphasized their radical nature (the Radical Jewish Union, the Jewish Liberation Coalition, *Jewish Radicalism*). Some affiliated with the emerging Havurah movement, which emphasized small, egalitarian Jewish community experiences. They tended to critique American Judaism and established community organizations as "superficial or inauthentic," but beyond that and a general inclination to embrace "radicalism," no consensus issue united them.[9]

In this context, a "second generation" of American Jews concerned with Palestinian rights arose. The impetus came both from Israel's occupation of territory seized during the 1967 war and from left-wing reactions to it. Following the lead of SNCC, many groups that comprised the New Left began championing the Palestinian cause like never before, harshly critiquing Israel and Zionism. Alienated, some young Jews turned away from the left entirely. However, among those who still considered themselves "radical," a choice now had to be made: embrace the Palestinian cause wholeheartedly, or try to reconcile Zionist and leftist commitments, including, perhaps, by recognizing the legitimacy of Palestinian calls for self-determination.[10]

This range of responses is illustrated through the lives of two radical Jewish women, who despite having much in common—including support for Palestinian national aspirations—held drastically different positions on Israel. Sharon Rose and Aviva Cantor (known for a period as Aviva Zuckoff) were both born in early 1940s New York. They both went to Israel as young adults—Cantor for her first two years of college at Hebrew University in the late 1950s, and Rose right after college in 1963. Each of them became involved in radical Jewish circles while in their twenties, expressing similar left-wing critiques of "Amerika" and of the American Jewish establishment, viewing suburbanizing Jewish communities as vapid, devoid of deeper meaning that once existed within Jewish identity.[11]

Both worked for Jewish organizations in the 1960s, Cantor for the Americans for Progressive Israel (API) publication *Israel Horizons* and Rose as the executive director of Jews for Urban Justice (JUJ) in Washington, DC. From there, their paths diverged. Cantor's affiliation with *Israel Horizons* grew out of her lifelong affinity for Zionism. Rose, in contrast, did not see herself as a Zionist. Here one sees a dichotomy between "Radical Zionists," who congregated around groups like the Jewish Liberation Project (JLP), which Cantor later cofounded, and "Radical Jews," which included pro-, anti-, and non-Zionist activists who collaborated on domestic justice issues in organizations like JUJ. For both women, the path toward a deepened understanding of the Palestinians came via their experiences in the Jewish state. While for Cantor this emerged through the bonds that she had built with the Israeli left during her time there, for Rose, her 1963 trip to Israel raised difficult questions that would only become more urgent after 1967.[12]

Rose discussed her political trajectory in a piece published in the alternative newspaper *Win* in June 1970. "Once, in another life" as "a nice Jewish girl from New York, just graduated from college . . . I stayed on a Kibbutz and picked grapes and peaches and dug the whole scene; the communal dining hall" and so forth, Rose wrote. But she soon saw "things which conflicted with her liberal outlook . . . and [she] asked embarrassing questions: Why are all the dock workers and other laborers dark-skinned Moroccan Jews and Arabs [and] all the ditch-diggers . . . dark-skinned Yemenite Jews and Arabs? Why do the Arab villages live under military rule? Why are crucial civil rights denied Palestinian Arabs under Israeli rule?" Receiving no satisfactory answer from her Israeli friends, "I saw that I am not a Zionist," Rose wrote, noting how the marches of Martin Luther King Jr. that she supported seemed directly at odds with prevailing Israeli mentalities.[13]

"For me," Rose continued, "my own liberation, and that of all people who are Jewish, is inexorably tied to the liberation of all man and woman-kind." Declaring that the "revolution will come to Israel" and that "the Palestinian Arabs will gain self-determination," Rose stated her belief that "a bi-national, democratic, and secular state will provide the best environment to carry out such revolutions, to create a truly just economic system for the people of the region." Even though her opinions clashed with those of most Jews, Rose still chose to "organize in the community I think I can still talk to best: the Jewish community."[14]

Yet Rose soon became increasingly active outside the realm of Jewish politics. In August 1970, she embarked with sixteen other Americans on a trip to Lebanon, Jordan, and Syria that had been organized by a group of left-wing former Peace Corps volunteers. There Rose toured Palestinian refugee camps and attended the Second World Conference on Palestine. The trip clearly made an impression. From the conference, held in Amman, Rose and two other American Jews issued a statement declaring that "as revolutionaries of Jewish heritage . . . we cast our lot with the Palestinian Liberation movement . . . [and] will attempt to combat the Zionist propaganda machine." The trio concluded by stating that "our struggle is to get the Zionists . . . out of Palestine. . . . We thank our Palestinian sisters and brothers for welcoming us here . . . to see for ourselves the fascist nature of Zionism." Days later, the group's time in Jordan ended dramatically as they fled to Syria amidst a government crackdown on the PLO that marked the start of the Jordanian Civil War, also known as Black September.[15]

The bonds forged among those on the trip proved pivotal; in early 1971, Rose joined with five of them and a few others to form a new organization known as the Middle East Research and Information Project (MERIP). Though not focused exclusively on Palestine, MERIP, which considered itself part of the New Left, published material on various Middle East conflicts, including many articles highly critical of Israel. In April 1971, Rose left JUJ to work at MERIP. From then on, she would be one of a small but growing number of young left-wing American Jews to advocate for Palestinian rights outside of Jewish auspices. Of particular note, Rose cowrote one of the first pro-Palestinian articles to appear in an American feminist journal, foreshadowing debates over Israel/Palestine that would soon become more prominent in the women's movement.[16]

In the eyes of Cantor—a feminist herself, who later initiated and cofounded the Jewish feminist magazine *Lilith*—Rose and others like her in New Left groups that criticized Israel were deeply misguided. Cantor identified as both a leftist and a Zionist, challenging the notion that the two labels conflicted, and she would soon help form a group dedicated to defending that synthesis. In connection with her job at *Israel Horizons*, Cantor also helped run the youth wing of API, Young Americans for Progressive Israel, known as YAPI. After the 1967 war and subsequent left-wing condemnation of Israel, Cantor recalls that "all of a sudden these [young American Jewish] refugees from all of these [New Left] organizations" started coming to YAPI meetings, "all very upset because they suddenly discovered that they cared about Israel and they suddenly discovered that their comrades didn't." This blend of preexisting YAPI members and "refugees" from New Left organizations like Students for a Democratic Society (SDS) began referring to themselves as "Radical Zionists" and in 1969 decided to call their group the Jewish Liberation Project (JLP). Based in New York City, JLP described itself as "a small group of young, 25–40, Jewish radicals who have a strong commitment to Jewish values, Israel, and [positive] social change." Cantor would serve as editor of its publication, the *Jewish Liberation Journal*, which soon became one of the most influential radical Jewish newspapers.[17]

Similar groups and publications popped up across North America, attracting supporters from various camps. From one side, many Jews who had been active in New Left causes began feeling alienated from them when these circles embraced anti-Zionism. From the other side, some Zionists like Cantor had grown attracted to radical politics. JLP and its counterparts in other locales critiqued not only the New Left but also established American Jewish organizations and whoever else they felt impeded justice or obscured what they felt reflected authentic Jewishness.[18]

All such groups had to grapple with the growing predominance of support for the Palestinian cause on the New Left. The JLP's founding statement in 1969 made no mention of Arabs or Palestine. But in 1970, Times Change Press asked the young radical group to elucidate the Radical Zionist position for a booklet titled *Arab-Israeli Debate: Toward a Socialist Solution*, which was essentially a printed debate between the JLP and the pro-Palestine Committee to Support Middle East Liberation. Though not central to the group's mission, on page eight of the ten-page JLP statement, it noted its support for a "state of Palestine" alongside Israel that would "more or less include the area occupied by Israel in '67" plus parts of neighboring Arab states. Similarly, the *Jewish Liberation Journal* occasionally indicated support for Palestinian self-determination, but critiques of Palestinians appeared more frequently. Fatah, the largest faction within the PLO, provoked considerable ire. One example, a June 1969 article by left-wing Israeli writer Amos Kenan titled "New Left Go Home," stated its "advice to Fatah": "If you are struggling for recognition of Palestinian rights, you will find allies among us. The Land of Israel has room for two nations," but while "we [Israelis] are prepared to do with half . . . you want everything." While the *Jewish Liberation Journal* maintained that individual articles did not speak for the JLP, Kenan's attitude toward the Palestinians mirrored that of most other pieces in the journal on the topic.[19]

Other Jewish leftist groups shared the JLP's stance toward the Palestinians—anti-Fatah/PLO, but supportive, at least in abstract, of the Palestinians' right to self-determination. In February 1970, JLP joined a dozen like-minded organizations, including Boston Area New Zionists, the Jewish Liberation Coalition of Providence, and groups with similar names from Ohio, Michigan, Saskatoon, Montreal, St. Louis, and Washington, DC, to form a loose umbrella group called the Radical Zionist Alliance, which in its founding statement noted that its members looked "toward mutual recognition of the national rights of the Jews and Palestinian Arabs." In a March

1971 platform, the Alliance, in slightly less vague terms, elaborated, "We believe that no just and lasting solution to the Arab-Israeli conflict can occur without the mutual recognition of the right to self-determination of the Jewish people and of the Palestinian-Arab people."[20]

Accepting the need for Palestinian self-determination was in itself a provocative step for the Radical Zionist Alliance to take given prevailing American Jewish attitudes at the time. But it differed from forcefully calling, as Jews, for Israel and the American Jewish establishment to support the creation of a sovereign Palestinian state. The Alliance also contrasted with MERIP and other nonsectarian groups that advocated for Palestinians outside the realm of Jewish politics. Instead, it fell to the next wave of organizations to push for Palestinian statehood in the Jewish sphere, a constellation of groups that ultimately came together after the formation of Breira in 1973. In the interim, JLP dissolved in 1972, a fate that perhaps befell some of its counterparts in other cities, as many of its leaders moved to Israel or moved on in life as the vigor of the activist left faded.[21]

A Movement Born in Israel

Breira emerged in this context. While in a literal sense the organization grew out of a series of meetings at Rutgers University in 1973, in deeper ways the seeds of Breira were planted in 1960s Israel. The 1967 war marked the start of Israel's occupation of the West Bank and Gaza Strip, which would complicate America Jews' feelings about Israel in the decades to come. But in the shorter term, Israel's dramatic military victory gave rise to years of heightened American Jewish excitement for Zionism. More and more energetic young American Jews traveled to Israel to study, to volunteer, or to work, often for months or even years. Among them were many future leaders of Breira and related groups, who, during their time in Israel between 1967 and 1973, met with Israeli leftists, visited the occupied territories, and came to recognize the centrality of Palestinian national aspirations in the Israeli-Arab conflict. Their political views generally fell somewhere between those of the ardently Zionist Cantor and the anti-Zionist Rose, but in any case, their experiences in Israel would ultimately direct them to a similar issue—the question of Palestinian rights.

At its peak, Breira consisted of several layers: its members, which numbered fifteen hundred throughout the country and included many from the ranks of the Havurah movement, API, and the socialist Zionist Hashomer Hatzair; its older executive board members, which included rabbis, Hillel directors, Jewish community professionals, and academics, including Don Peretz, to add to the credibility of the youthful organization; and, finally, what might be termed the "founding cohort" of the group and the organizations that merged into it. First were Breira's cofounders, which included political science graduate student John Ruskay and rabbinical student Gerold Serotta, and its staff—Ruskay, who briefly served as codirector; executive director Robert Loeb; publications editor Arthur Samuelson; and national coordinator Faye Ginsburg. Though Breira became a national organization, it was initially only the New York version of the many local groups that comprised the emerging American Jewish peace camp. Other local initiatives that ultimately merged, formally or informally, into Breira included Yaish Breira (There Is an Alternative), an initiative based in Berkeley; Yozma (Initiative), a small group based in Los Angeles; and Tzedek Tzedek (Justice, Justice), which operated in Washington, DC. Leading members of these groups included Berkeley graduate student Ian Lustick of Yaish Breira, UCLA graduate students Yoav Peled and Steven Zipperstein of Yozma, and Institute for Policy Studies fellow Arthur Waskow of Tzedek Tzedek. While board members exercised varying degrees of control over Breira, this chapter focuses mostly on this young "founding cohort" of grassroots group organizers and staff, who provided the dynamism of 1970s activism.[22]

Focusing on several individuals illustrates how this cohort of the American Jewish peace camp acquired their views, offering a collective biography of sorts. Take, for instance, the case of Yaish Breira and its founder, Ian Lustick. In late 1972, the twenty-two-year-old political science graduate student at University of California, Berkeley, launched a petition that garnered over four hundred signatures worldwide. Addressed to the Israeli government, it stated, "As Jews deeply committed to the welfare of Israel . . . we call upon the Israeli Government to pursue a policy of peace which will encourage the emergence of a non-belligerent Palestinian state on the West Bank and Gaza Strip." In a December 1972 JTA article, Lustick called the petition campaign "a grassroots attempt to develop a consciousness-raising effort with respect to the entire Palestinian national question, the policies of de facto annexation that are seemingly being pursued, and the dangers involved with regard to the future health and harmony of Israel." Lustick continued, "By allowing Jewish civilians to settle in these areas, the Israeli government is locking the Jewish State into a political dungeon from which there will be, in five to ten years' time, no escape."[23]

What led Lustick to embrace such views? His experience in Israel/Palestine. During a six-month Brandeis study abroad program in Jerusalem in 1969, "I had my first encounter with Palestinians in a refugee camp," Lustick reported, and then "wrote my political science paper there at [Brandeis's] Hiatt Institute on 'What West Bank Arabs Really Want.' And my argument was, even though the PLO wasn't saying it yet, eventually they would come out for a two-state solution, and that already the West Bank Arabs wanted that." According to Lustick, the paper "was based on widespread interviews I did in the West Bank and Gaza in 1969. . . . I published it in *Jewish Frontier* [a Labor Zionist magazine] . . . [in] June 1970."[24]

Arthur Waskow, another Jewish activist who called for Palestinian self-determination before Breira's founding, also went to Israel in 1969. Then a fellow at the Institute for Policy Studies, a progressive think tank in Washington, Waskow rose to prominence as a radical activist who blended his activism with newfound religious ideals. During Waskow's Middle East trip, Israeli leftist Dan Leon took him to meet Palestinians for the first time, a visit that helped him understand the Palestinian desire for independence. Two years later, Waskow wrote, "the more seriously I took the existence of an Israeli people, the more seriously I took the reports . . . by some Israelis that there was a Palestinian people: not 'Arab refugees,' but a *Palestinian people*. With help from left-wing Israelis, I was able to arrange a brief visit to . . . Palestinian political figures on the Israeli-occupied West Bank." The experience led Waskow to organize a historic 1971 ad in the *New York Review of Books* with journalist Paul Jacobs titled "The Liberation of Palestine and Israel," which called on Israel to negotiate with Palestinian leadership on "how to withdraw Israeli troops from the West Bank and Gaza." Bearing the signatures of Breira's future chair Arnold Wolf and future cofounder John Ruskay, as well as Noam Chomsky and Sharon Rose, whom Waskow then worked with at JUJ, the ad, like Breira soon after it, involved the cooperation of Americans who held a wide range of perspectives on Zionism.[25]

Other activists similarly cited the importance of their exposure to Israeli left-wing views. Robert Skeist of the Breira-like group Chutzpah in Chicago published a 1971 ad in local alternative newspaper *The Seed* declaring that radical Jews have a "responsibility in developing a position on Israel that takes into account the needs of two oppressed and manipulated peoples, the Jews and the Palestinian Arabs. . . . One possibility for a solution to this problem would be the creation of a separate state for the Palestinian Arabs." Skeist, who had attempted to volunteer at a kibbutz in 1967, noted that he "was very impressed, very moved by an [Israeli-Arab dialogue] publication called *New Outlook*," and brought its deputy editor David Shaham to speak at a Chutzpah event in 1973.[26]

Steven Zipperstein, a steering committee member of the Los Angeles group Yozma who later became a prominent historian based at Stanford University, cited as influential his contact with the Israeli New Left group Siach (an acronym for the "Israeli New Left" that could also be translated as "Conversation") as an undergraduate at the Hebrew University in 1970. Zipperstein had been recruited by Reuven Kaminer, an activist and Hebrew University study abroad administrator who has been called "the godfather of Israel's radical left" by Stanford historian Joel Beinin, another American Jew whose political trajectory Kaminer helped shape. Zipperstein recounted that he "was introduced to the inner workings of Israel's left-leaning politics and probably there [in Israel] was where I first heard the word 'Palestinian.' Returning from Israel in 1972, I was among the founders, at least the first members of Yozma, always a small group." Yozma's most active figure was himself an Israeli leftist—Yoav Peled, son of General Matti Peled. Though Yozma, like Chutzpah, considered itself radical in comparison to Breira, after Yozma merged into Breira, the younger Peled became Breira's "West Coast Organizer."[27]

For Breira cofounder and board member Gerry Serotta, the pivotal moment came while he worked in Israel as a journalist for the Jewish Student Press Service from 1970 to 1971. "The most interesting experience I had was traveling with Joseph Abileah . . . a war resister . . . somebody who spoke to Palestinians, knew Palestinians," recalled Serotta. Traveling through the West Bank, "it seemed obvious" to him "that there should be two peoples and some expression of Palestinian self-determination. . . . That was clear to anybody with their eyes open in 1970." Breira's other co-founder, John Ruskay, had spent time in Israel during the mid-1960s, and in the early 1970s he was on the steering group of the Committee on New Alternatives for the Middle East (CONAME). CONAME facilitated cross-country tours of leftist Israeli and Arab speakers, but it was not an explic-itly Jewish group, though it was run by Allan Solomonow, an American Jewish pacifist, and had a board composed primarily of Jews, including Noam Chomsky, Irene Gendzier, and Don Peretz. Most of these Jews did not consider themselves Zionists at the time, though Ruskay later would.[28]

Future Breira executive director Robert Loeb served as Solomonow's as-sistant at CONAME in the early 1970s after studying at Hebrew University from 1968 to 1969. The experience disoriented Loeb, who found Israeli attitudes toward Palestinians to be "in direct contradiction to everything that I had been struggling for in the States in terms of civil rights. It just didn't make any sense." Loeb and Ruskay encountered many more Israeli and Palestinian voices through their link with CONAME, a connection that would later be used against Breira.[29]

Breira's other staff members, including publications editor Arthur Sam-uelson and national coordinator Faye Ginsburg, had also spent time in Israel, while associate director Dan Gillon was an Israeli citizen. Samuel-son, who lived in Israel in 1969 and 1971–1973, ran Breira's newsletter, *Interchange*. He later viewed his time in Israel as a formative experience. "I'd hitchhike through the West Bank. . . . I went to Tel Aviv University for a year. . . . [I] read *Haaretz*. . . . I went to a kibbutz . . . and worked at *New Outlook*, and I worked there for almost three years. I was like an assistant editor. That's how I knew Don Peretz," Samuelson recalled. He became involved in Israeli politics, joining a left-wing political party called Moked, led by Colonel Meir Pa'il, and wrote a senior thesis titled "Development of Israeli Left Attitudes Towards the Palestinian Question," which led to him meeting PLO members in Beirut.[30]

Collectively, these oral histories highlight that those who founded and led Breira and its forerunners were by no means uninformed, and certainly not anti-Zionist. On the contrary, many felt so enthused by Israel and Zionism that they spent even more time in Israel than did their less critical Jewish peers. These intimate encounters with Israel are precisely what led them to adopt bold, often controversial stances regarding the conflict. They often came to these opinions after witnessing Arab life under Israeli rule or, alternatively, when they heard the views of Israeli leftists, who themselves were becoming more convinced of the wisdom and morality of Palestinian self-determination. As an organization, Breira would seek to introduce these Israeli views to American Jewish audiences.

Breira leaders hoped that by amplifying certain Israeli voices, they could convince American Jews to consider an "alternative" to supporting a permanent occupation. But following Israeli doves ultimately led the group to make decisions that provided ammunition to their critics. As a result, Breira would be publicly defined more by a brief meeting involving only two of its members than by the time its leaders had spent in Israel and the conclusions that they had come to when there.

Embracing the Israeli Alternative

Founded in 1973, Breira—formally known as Breira: A Project of Concern in Diaspora-Israel Relations—was initially headquartered in Ruskay and Serotta's New York apartment. The Hebrew word *Breira* literally means "choice" or "alternative," a reference and response to the slogan *"ein breira"* that some Israelis invoked when claiming that there was "no alternative" to the continued conflict with the Arabs. The organization's use of Hebrew also underlined its commitment to Hebrew culture. This in part reflected the membership's links to Israel and the fact that its members "had been involved all their lives with Jewish schools, Jewish youth groups, seminaries, summer camps, programs in Israel, Jewish publications and the like," according to Breira member William Novak. The organization quickly gained steam, winning the support of many rabbis and other Jewish communal professionals, including former AJCongress president Rabbi Joachim Prinz, a co-organizer of Martin Luther King's 1963 March on Washington, who agreed to join the group's board; David Tulin, head of the Philadelphia Zionist Federation, who served as Breira's vice president; Rabbi Balfour Brickner of the Union of American Hebrew Congregations;

and Rabbi Arnold Wolf, a Yale University chaplain known for his civil rights advocacy, who became chair of the organization.[31]

While some of the individuals involved supported Palestinian self-determination before the October 1973 Yom Kippur War—indeed, Breira's founders discussed the issue during the spring and summer prior to it—the joint Egyptian-Syrian surprise attack increased the urgency of the issue. In the aftermath of Israel's monumental 1967 victory, many Jews had seen little need for Israel to make any concessions. While Egypt and Syria's attempt to recapture in 1973 the lands it lost six years prior did not succeed in military terms, the attack shook Israel to its core and indicated to some that territorial withdrawal for peace—an idea elucidated in two United Nations Security Council Resolutions—was in Israel's long-term interests. Peace, according to this logic, would not only require agreements with Arab states but also a resolution to the Palestinian question, which some viewed as the issue at the center of the broader Israeli-Arab conflict.[32]

From its early days, Breira's goals could be divided into two categories. One was to introduce the American Jewish community to Israelis supportive of Israel-Palestinian coexistence. This could be called Breira's "Peace" program. The second was to revitalize American Jewish life and Israel-Diaspora relations, which one could call Breira's "Revitalization" program, and echoed goals of the JLP before it. Within Breira, tension endured between those who prioritized one program over the other. Moreover, even among those who prioritized peace, some felt that Breira first had to gain more "Jewish credibility" by focusing on Jewish revitalization issues in order to "earn" a right to critique Israeli policy.[33]

Yet as Breira matured, its Jewish "Revitalization" program remained vague, while its "Peace" program shifted into sharper focus. In December 1973, Breira spoke publicly of the need for Israel to make territorial concessions and "recognize the legitimacy of the national aspirations of the Palestinians." Originally, Breira spoke only of "introducing" Israeli dovish views not commonly heard in the United States, but the group soon moved toward openly supporting a cohort of Israeli dovish voices that increasingly supported negotiations with the PLO. In late 1974, Arnold Wolf—writing as a member of Breira's advisory committee, as he had not yet been named the group's chair—published a short article in *Sh'ma* titled "Toward Peace with the PLO" outlining the case for negotiations and what a two-state solution would look like. He called on American Jews to promote constructive dialogue between Israel and the Palestinians. Should another war come, Wolf argued, "Israel must have proven . . . that no stone was left unturned in its search for peace. The last, the heaviest, the most unyielding stone is the PLO. American Jews could, if we have the strength, help to raise it while there is still time."[34]

Israeli doves apparently also thought that American Jews could help in this way. Marcia Freedman, an American-Israeli feminist who served as a Knesset member in left-wing parties with Eliav and Aloni in the mid-1970s, later recalled Israeli leftists' feelings regarding the potential of American Jewry. "We all realized . . . that we were a tiny . . . miniscule minority, in the country that was rapidly moving and shifting in the direction counter to where we thought everything should be going," Freedman stated. She and her colleagues, including former IDF general Peled, were convinced that the American Jewish community would be their "savior." They believed that when American Jews started to "understand what they had to understand" and then "put pressure, both economic pressure and political pressure, on the Israeli government we would then have the support that we needed because we didn't have it within Israel. That was the naïve belief at the time."[35]

The initial Breira position of "introducing" the American Jewish community to Israeli dovish views may sound modest, but at the time, even this appeared challenging. Earlier in the seventies, future Breira members faced considerable resistance from mainstream Jewish groups when organizing tours for Israelis. For example, in 1970, when left-wing Knesset member Uri Avnery came to the United States to tour Jewish institutions, the Anti-Defamation League (ADL) sent fliers critical of Avnery to those who had agreed to host him, prompting almost all to cancel. Later that year, Rabbis Michael Robinson and Everett Gendler failed to persuade the Jewish Peace Fellowship to sponsor a national speaking tour for Israeli pacifist Uri Davis. Similarly, when Israeli Arab Fawzi El-Asmar was on his way to North America for a speaking tour, a *Commentary* article by Alan Dershowitz justifying Israel's "preventative detention" of El-Asmar was circulated widely among Jewish groups, leading to many cancellations.[36]

The Israelis whom Breira hosted tended to be less radical, a development aided by the fact that by the mid-1970s a number of former members of the Israeli establishment had begun to support recognition of the Palestinians. This group of individual Israelis could be termed "establishment dissidents," given how their new political perspective pushed them out of Israel's mainstream. Within Breira's first two years, it hosted several of these establishment dissidents, including Knesset members Shulamit Aloni and Meir Pa'il, as well as Mattityahu "Matti" Peled. Unlike Avnery, these Israelis held more conventional understandings of Zionism; Aloni had been in the Labor Party, Pa'il had been an Israel Defense Forces (IDF) colonel, and Peled was a retired IDF general who had served as military governor of Gaza during Israel's four-month occupation of the strip in 1956–1957.[37]

Peled's involvement is particularly notable because of the enduring respect that Israeli prime minister Yitzhak Rabin held for him, which stemmed from their military service together. The two first met when serving in the same Palmach platoon in the 1940s, initiating a friendship that would last fifty years. Later, during the 1967 war, when Rabin was IDF chief of staff, Peled served directly under him in the crucial role of head of the IDF's Supply Division. Peled, a lifelong Zionist, had first advocated for the creation of a Palestinian state only a week after the 1967 war ended, in a meeting of IDF generals, including Rabin. "For the first time in Israel's history, we are face to face with the Palestinians, without other Arab countries dividing us. Now we have a chance to offer the Palestinians a state of their own," Peled declared. For Peled, it had been the Arab states that threatened Israel. Now, in a position of power and with control over lands containing a large Palestinian population, Israel could, for strategic as well as ethical reasons, create a Palestinian state and end the conflict.[38]

Breira frequently drew on these Israeli voices in their publications. In 1975 it issued a booklet titled *Israel and the Palestinians: A Different Israeli View*, with chapters by Peled, Avnery, Shaham, Kenan, and Flapan and an introduction by Samuelson. A lengthy, translated piece by Peled, a "frequent contributor to *Interchange*"—quite possibly its most frequent contributor—appeared as the cover article in the second issue of the journal. *Interchange* also republished newspaper articles detailing new developments and the positions held by this group of Israelis. Breira valued not only the wisdom that these Israelis' experiences brought but also the "Jewish legitimacy" that their affiliations with the IDF and the Israeli government contributed to their case. Breira lacked the time to gain communal credibility by developing a track record on other Jewish issues. Instead, it hoped that it could derive the legitimacy it needed by surrounding itself with Israeli political figures.[39]

Despite—or perhaps because of—the credentials of the Israeli speakers, their remarks often surprised American Jewish audiences while making Breira leaders more confident in their views on the Palestine question. For example, at a Breira-sponsored press conference in the fall of 1974, Aloni, who had recently served as a minister in Yitzhak Rabin's government, raised the possibility of negotiations with the PLO, making her one of the first prominent Israelis to do so. A Breira cosponsored dialogue the next year between Peled and Professor Elias Tuma, a Palestinian American economist, resulted in the two publishing a joint statement in the *New York Review of Books* supporting Israel-PLO negotiations. This came at a time when anti-PLO sentiments were extremely high in Israel and the United States, as Palestinian attacks against Israelis were increasing in number.[40]

Less than a year later, Peled assumed the leadership of a new group, the Israeli Council for Israeli-Palestinian Peace (ICIPP). Its charter called for Israeli territorial withdrawal and the creation of a Palestinian state; Breira soon republished it. Other ICIPP leading members included Pa'il, Avnery, former Finance Ministry director Yaakov Arnon, journalist Amos Kenan, former Knesset member Eliahu Elyasher, former Mapam activist Yossi Amitai, and former Labor Party secretary general Arie "Lova" Eliav. In addition to Peled and Pa'il, Eliav also worked with Breira, embarking on a Breira-sponsored tour in spring 1976.[41]

Most ICIPP figures had been members of the Israeli establishment who shifted their views in the 1970s because they thought that peace with the Palestinians was in Israel's interest. While some commentators and scholars have remarked that Breira moved leftward during its short life, toward advocating negotiations with the PLO, it must be noted that it did so precisely when the Israelis it most admired—the ICIPP's "establishment dissidents"—were doing the same. As late as 1974, Peled "categorically rejected any idea of dealing with the PLO," but he shifted his views significantly over the next year and a half.[42]

Yet to much of the organized American Jewish community, talking with Palestinian leadership made little sense. Many American Jews saw Palestinian nationalism and the refugee issue as fabrications created and maintained by Arab states to harm Israel, a contention made in AIPAC publications that had circulation above 250,000. Moreover, 1974 through 1976 had been marked by heightened condemnation of Israel at the United Nations as its General Assembly increasingly embraced the Palestinian cause. This included not only the 1975 "Zionism Is Racism" resolution but also PLO chairman Yasser Arafat's brandishing of a gun before a 1974 speech for the General Assembly, both of which many American Jews viewed as aggressive and offensive. Palestinian militants' attacks on Israeli civilians during this period only further cemented the view of Palestinians as terrorists bent on destroying the Jewish state.[43]

Yet in the view of the ICIPP, there were nuances to the Palestinian actions that the public did not appreciate, such as which factions carried out the attacks, what specific phrases Arafat used in speeches, and what statements the PLO released. When, for example, the PLO's London representative, Said Hammami, penned articles for the *Times of London* indicating support for a two-state solution in 1973–1974, Uri Avnery interpreted it as a signal of internal changes within the PLO, accurately calculating that Hammami would have only done so with Arafat's approval. This ultimately led Avnery to meet with Hammami in early 1975 in what would be the first time a former Israeli parliamentarian ever met with a PLO official. The ICIPP, founded months after the Avnery-Hammami meeting, would soon build on those conversations, which reflected real changes in the PLO's views on the conflict.[44]

While the American Jewish public at large did not pay much attention to these developments, Breira leaders listened intently to what those in the ICIPP had to say, amplifying these voices to their members. The idea of a Palestinian state alongside Israel always had the appeal of synthesizing the Zionist demand for a Jewish state with the liberal ethical demand of consistency for fulfilling Palestinian national self-determination. It would take one additional step for Breira to advocate for speaking with the much-reviled PLO. In doing so, they would walk in a path just trodden by the ICIPP.

Our Partner for Peace: The ICIPP, Breira, and PLO Moderates

For Breira, 1976 was a pivotal year. On one hand, the group received a major funding boost, as a large grant from the Samuel Rubin Foundation allowed it to ramp up its activities during the second half of the year. On the other hand, 1976 was marked by new controversies. According to some accounts, Breira faced infrequent criticism in the Jewish press until spring of that year, when the organization issued a statement that questioned Israeli appropriation of Arab-owned land in the Galilee and the killing of six Israeli Arab protestors in what later became known as "Land Day." Breira's relatively mild statement, however, received national media attention and led more voices in the American Jewish press to critique Breira for publicly dissenting against Israeli policy. Breira, for its part, began to more openly criticize the Israeli right. In May 1976, *Interchange* published a letter signed by many Breira members in addition to Aviva Cantor, journalist I. F. Stone, academic Leonard Fein, feminist Betty Freidan, and others that urged Jews to "say NO" to Gush Emunim, a religious-nationalist movement that established Jewish settlements in the occupied territories. The letter's signers, who termed themselves "ardent supporters of Israel's existence," would, of course, also invoke Israeli opposition to settlements, noting that "like our brothers and sisters in Israel, we feel that further Jewish settlement in the occupied territories is an obstacle to peace efforts."[45]

But the most consequential moment of that year was linked to moves made by the ICIPP. In mid-1976, the ICIPP took the historic step of meeting with representatives of the PLO to discuss what would later become known as the two-state solution. Over the course of two meetings in Paris, ICIPP leaders spent many hours discussing ideas for peace with PLO moderates—namely, Issam Sartawi and Sabri Jiryis. Born in 1934 in Acre, Sartawi and his family became refugees in 1948 and settled in Iraq. In Baghdad, Sartawi studied medicine, ultimately completing his education in the United States. At the time of the 1967 war, Sartawi worked as a cardiologist in Ohio. However, the Arab defeat led him to abandon his medical career to join the PLO faction Fatah, and before long he found himself fighting in the storied 1968 Battle of Karameh. In Karameh's aftermath,

Sartawi briefly led his own guerilla offshoot within the PLO, the Action Organization for the Liberation of Palestine, which carried out an attack against Israeli civilians in Germany—an act that gave Sartawi credibility in militant circles. In 1970, he was elected to PLO's executive committee, holding a position akin to a cabinet minister.[46]

Despite engaging in violence, Sartawi's faction was among the PLO's most moderate. When the United States put forth its "Rogers Plan" in 1969, which proposed an Israeli-Arab peace settlement based on the pre-1967 armistice lines, Sartawi's group was the only Palestinian faction to support it. Sartawi felt that the reality of the dynamics at play required that the Palestinians compromise with Israel if they hoped to achieve anything. In 1971, he merged his group back into Fatah and became an ally of and advisor to PLO chairman Yasser Arafat. He also served on the Fatah Revolutionary Committee and the Palestine National Council. Yet Sartawi's increasing willingness to make peace with Israel weakened him politically. As he complained to his Israeli negotiating counterpart, Uri Avnery, "When I was a man of war, I advanced to the rank of a cabinet minister. When I became a man of peace, my status diminished, and now, I'm barely a member of the National Council. We people of peace are really stupid." Avnery, himself an outspoken leftist who had once been on the right, replied jokingly, "Yes, we are peace*fool*."[47]

Born in 1938, Sabri Jiryis grew up in a village called Fassouta, which became part of Israel in 1948. An Israeli citizen of Palestinian Christian background, Jiryis earned a degree in law from Hebrew University and in the 1960s became active in al-Ard, an outlawed political movement that demanded an end to Israel's military rule over Arab areas of the country. Facing state harassment, Jiryis left Israel in 1968. Relocating to Beirut, Jiryis joined the PLO and soon headed the Israeli affairs desk at the PLO Research Center, later becoming the center's director. He, too, became an advisor to Arafat. While Jiryis and Sartawi held particularly dovish views by PLO standards, their meeting with Israelis was approved by Arafat, to whom they reported. Correspondingly, though the ICIPP did not enjoy Israeli governmental support, Peled reported on the talks directly to his former military superior, then prime minister Yitzhak Rabin. Though the ICIPP-PLO talks were supposed to be secret, reports were leaked to the media, making headlines in the fall of 1976.[48]

Matti Peled, former Israeli general and head of the Israeli Council for
Israeli-Palestinian Peace, as keynote speaker at Breira's annual conference, 1977.
Photo credit: Bill Aron.

While Breira had initially envisioned itself as simply amplifying pro-
peace Israeli views, it is no surprise that the group gradually shifted from
amplifying to *supporting* both the ICIPP and its platform. Hosting speakers
may have been a worthwhile task for the group, but it needed a concrete
political agenda for a sustaining sense of purpose—and to answer the vexing question of what exactly Breira was "for." As Breira planned its first
major conference, it naturally invited Peled to serve as a keynote speaker
alongside noted American Jewish author and democratic socialist Irving
Howe.[49]

Meanwhile, Sartawi and Jiryis, the daring moderates of the PLO, flew to
the United States in October 1976. Their main purpose was to set up an
office in Washington, but Sartawi's secondary goal was to soften American
Jewish organizations' views of the PLO. Understanding the political weakness of his Israeli allies, Sartawi hoped to mobilize America's Jewish community to help convince Israel to make concessions needed for a peace
agreement. With that aim in mind, Sartawi, working through intermediar-

ies, set up at least three meetings with American Jews—one in Washington, one with a group in New York, and one with former B'nai B'rith leader Philip Klutznick. The meeting with Klutznick was never publicly reported, nor was a secret one in Paris that the PLO duo held with Nahum Goldmann, a former president of the World Zionist Organization who then led the World Jewish Congress. Had news of Klutznick's meeting been leaked, it almost certainly would have prevented him from becoming World Jewish Congress president in 1977 and Jimmy Carter's secretary of commerce in 1980, especially given that Carter had just fired Andrew Young, the first African American United Nations ambassador, for meeting with a PLO member the year prior.[50]

In New York, Sartawi and Jiryis met World Jewish Congress vice president Sam Norich; Peter Weiss, son-in-law of Breira's primary funder Samuel Rubin; George Gruen, a foreign affairs staff member at the American Jewish Committee (AJC); and others. During this time Sartawi expressed the PLO's willingness to accept the two-state solution and asked for American Jews' help in convincing Israel to make concessions. Gruen had received permission to attend from the AJC's executive vice president, and afterward Gruen gave a meeting summary to his boss and to an Israeli diplomat—"I think it was Moshe Arad," he recalled, referring to a future Israeli ambassador to the United States—because Sartawi wanted his support for a two-state solution forwarded to Rabin. Two weeks later, a similar meeting with Sartawi and Jiryis took place in DC, with five American Jews present: Herman Edelsberg, who had recently retired from B'nai B'rith; David Gorin of AJCongress; Olya Margolin of the National Council of Jewish Women; and Breira executive board members Arthur Waskow and Rabbi Max Ticktin, who was also then assistant national director of B'nai B'rith Hillel Foundations. The five attended as individuals rather than representatives of any organization. The conversation was not particularly productive; when the Palestinians asserted their interest in a two-state solution, Edelsberg responded with probing questions that put Sartawi on edge. Though Waskow opined that the PLO's declaration of openness to living with Israel was an unprecedented development, Edelsberg felt that the meeting held only "modest significance . . . inflated all out of proportion to its worth," and Jiryis, at age seventy-eight, had little memory of it.[51]

Like Gruen, Edelsberg had written a memo about his meeting, sending it to B'nai B'rith leaders, to State Department officials, and to Israeli diplomats whom he had considered friends, simply to keep them informed. Soon afterward, reports of both meetings were leaked, with details from the DC meeting first appearing in a November 21, 1976, *Jerusalem Post* article by Wolf Blitzer. Before long, it received coverage in the American Jewish press and the *New York Times*. "I had no doubt it was leaked by someone in the Israel Embassy," wrote Edelsberg in his memoir. Independent of Edelsberg, Gruen also believed that the Israelis had leaked his report. Gruen concluded this because his memo did not list other participants, and only his name appeared in the press. Had the leak came from another source, it likely would have included more of the names. According to Gruen, there was a "campaign by the Israelis to discredit all of the people who went to the Washington meeting. . . . I got flak too."[52]

This "flak" was the swift Jewish organizational response to the news: the AJC, AJCongress, B'nai B'rith, and the National Council of Jewish Women all vocally disavowed the meetings and the very idea of speaking with the PLO, a taboo that would later become strictly illegal for Israelis. AJCongress reprimanded its employee for attending. The Conference of Presidents of Major American Jewish Organizations declared that it "vigorously opposes and deplores any meetings—official or unofficial—with the P.L.O," claiming that "the only purpose and possible result of such meetings is P.L.O. propaganda aimed at providing this terrorist federation with an image of moderation"—an ironic charge given that it had been Jews who leaked and publicized the meetings, while the Palestinians had remained silent about them despite their alleged "propaganda" value.[53]

But as the *New York Times* noted, one Jewish group responded differently—Breira, which supported the idea of meeting with PLO moderates. While Ticktin and Waskow's choice to attend the meeting had been their own, Breira chairman Arnold Wolf's statement in defense of the meeting constituted an official Breira position. Issued in response to the Conference of Presidents' declaration, Wolf's statement specifically cited Israeli "doves" who had called for "continued contact" with senior Palestinians "to pave the way to peace." Besides Wolf's statement, an op-ed by Arthur Waskow in the *New York Times* about the meeting, titled "Talking with the P.L.O.," further

Arthur Waskow, a Breira board member who met with PLO moderates
Sabri Jiryis and Issam Sartawi, speaking on a panel about Jewish identity, Jewish
politics, and Israel at the 1977 Breira conference. Photo credit: Bill Aron.

served to identify him—and Breira—with the PLO in the eyes of many Jewish onlookers.[54]

Other key Breira figures also defended the meeting. While Breira's decision to support PLO meetings could be characterized as a fateful misstep,
given the group's strong embrace of the ICIPP, how could one expect otherwise? To Peled and to Breira, Sartawi and Jiryis were moderate partners
for peace, but to other American Jewish observers, they looked like little
more than Arafat's henchmen. While Breira leaders embraced the ICIPP
because of its "Jewish legitimacy," its credibility did not rub off on Breira.
Though some American Jews might have hesitated to criticize General
Peled for meeting with Sartawi because of Peled's military service, his background did nothing to protect Breira when it echoed Peled's views.

The PLO meeting backlash marked a major increase in criticism of Breira, most notably in a thirty-two-page booklet by Rael Jean Isaac of the right-wing group Americans for a Safe Israel, which was circulated widely and cited by mainstream sources like *Commentary*. Isaac's group represented a small but growing fringe of American Jews who, like their counterparts on the Israeli right such as Gush Emunim, supported settling Jews in the West Bank and Gaza Strip for ideological reasons. These settlements aimed to make Israeli withdrawal from those lands much more difficult, potentially rendering Palestinian statehood impossible.[55]

Knowing that most American Jews did not share their ideology, the Americans for a Safe Israel pamphlet made no mention of the group's support for the settlement project. Its title, "Breira: A Counsel for Judaism," invoked the anti-Zionist American Council for Judaism; similarly, much of its content would make the case that Breira was an anti-Zionist ploy. Isaac placed particular emphasis on Arthur Waskow, one of Breira's more radical members who had made waves for his activities that blended progressive activism with Judaism. This work ranged from Waskow's harsh critiques of America's Vietnam War–era foreign policy to his arrests at civil rights protests and his authorship of the noted "Freedom Seder Hagadah" in 1969, which intertwined the story of the liberation of the Israelites with the U.S. civil rights movement and other modern struggles. Isaac's pamphlet focused on Waskow's radical leftism, not the credentials of the Israelis with similar views, mentioning Waskow's name sixty-five times and casting him as the "organizing genius for the whole network of associations whose personnel was eventually to become important in Breira." In particular, Isaac noted that Waskow had worked with Sharon Rose at JUJ, using the Waskow-Rose connection to tie Breira to MERIP, even though Waskow himself had no involvement in that organization. Despite the fact that Rose never associated with Breira, her name appeared more frequently in the pamphlet than did the name of any single founder or staff member of the group. Isaac also highlighted Ruskay's and Loeb's past work with CONAME to link Breira with Noam Chomsky and critics of Zionism. Breira, Isaac insinuated, was a mere prop for the CONAME and MERIP types who harbored views like those of Sharon Rose. Isaac's arguments were further amplified in an article by Joseph Shattan that appeared in *Commentary* months later.[56]

Appearing subtly in some critiques of Breira—and loudly in others—was the Cold War context. A prime example of the latter came from U.S. congressman Larry McDonald of Atlanta, whose excoriation of Breira appears in the congressional record of February 17, 1977. Breira "pretends to be a Zionist organization but . . . in fact is a support group for the Soviet-supported terrorist P.L.O.," McDonald alleged, remarking that the Breira conference speaker Irving Howe had "previously found virtue in the Vietcong cause." McDonald's statement also singled out Waskow, clearly drawing from Rael Jean Isaac's research. While the politics of Israel lay at the center of the debate over Breira, the politics of American foreign policy also loomed large, helping to account for the great breadth in critiques from both Jewish and non-Jewish platforms.[57]

No Alternative: The End of Breira

Breira did not immediately fold. Its first national conference went on as planned in February 1977, and in summer 1977 it even hired an additional staff member to run West Coast operations. But the PLO episode marked a turning point. Amidst the criticism, some major supporters left the group. For a few months in 1977, it went "silent" in hopes that criticism would subside. B'nai B'rith nearly fired Ticktin and other Hillel rabbis. Some believe that they were saved only by the intervention of former B'nai B'rith head Klutznick, who, unbeknown to most, had also met with Sartawi. Those employed by Jewish organizations felt intimidated. Breira membership ceased growing, and donors fell away. Breira vice president David Tulin, then also chairman of the Philadelphia Zionist Federation, was among those who resigned at this point, publicly citing Breira's reaction to the PLO meeting as the reason but privately reporting that he received pressure from an Israeli consul to denounce the group. The Jewish public's association of Breira with the PLO refused to dissipate. As Breira staff member Dan Gillon wrote in late 1977, Breira's "image problem (particularly with regard to misconceptions about our position on the PLO) is still with us and limits our ability to attract active and public support from many sympathetic elements within the organized Jewish community. . . . Breira has become a divisive public issue."[58]

While most accounts of Breira imply that the attacks against it directly led to its demise, political scientist Matthew Berkman's research shows that the ultimate cause of its dissolution stemmed from its heavy reliance on a single funder, the Samuel Rubin Foundation. As Berkman shows, the pressure from external critiques exacerbated internal conflicts within the group, leading to the ejection of executive director Robert Loeb. Unhappy with how Breira's executive board had treated Loeb, the Rubin Foundation withdrew its large donation, financially crippling the organization as it had prepared to expand. Because of the financial issues, Breira collapsed in winter 1977–1978, though a handful of local chapters continued their activities using the Breira name well into 1978.[59]

Even if the organization had been in a healthier financial state, 1977–1978 would not have been a simple time for Breira, as events in the Middle East disoriented groups across the Jewish political spectrum. First came the Likud party's victory in the May 1977 Israeli elections, elevating to the premiership Menachem Begin, whom many American Labor Zionist sympathizers had long viewed with suspicion. Liberal American Jewish leaders had possessed a certain inherent trust in the Israeli Labor Party because of its many years at the head of Israel's government and because they presumed that it shared their values. While the American Jewish establishment largely went along with the leadership transition, some Zionist notables, such as Nahum Goldmann, Philip Klutznick, and AJCongress president Rabbi Arthur Hertzberg, began dissenting more openly. This was ironic in the case of Hertzberg, since he had recently criticized Breira for doing the same thing.[60]

Within Israel, Likud's victory snapped an important, albeit tenuous, link between the ICIPP and Israel's leadership. Moreover, the rightward shift evident by the 1977 election results diminished any small hope that Israel would start to seriously contemplate granting Palestinian self-determination. Along with Labor's loss to Likud, the two political parties of "establishment dissidents"—Sheli and Ratz—did poorly. Aloni's Ratz went from two seats to one, and Eliav's Sheli Party, also the political home of ICIPP members Pa'il, Peled, and Avnery, won only two seats. Breira had to grapple with the disappointing reality that its allies had minimal support in Israel. At Breira's 1977 summer organizers' institute, for example, a discussion revolved around this question: "Given the poor showing of groups like Sheli in the elections, what is the future of like-minded opposition in Israel?"[61]

In the end, ICIPP members never achieved any significant political power after the group's founding. The group's Palestinian counterparts fared even worse, however. In 1983, Palestinian hardliners assassinated Sartawi in Portugal. That same year, the PLO Research Center that Jiryis then headed was bombed; Jiryis survived, but his wife and coworker, Hani Shaheen, did not.[62]

The year 1977 also marked Egyptian president Anwar Sadat's historic visit to Jerusalem, followed by the 1978 signing of the Camp David Accords and the 1979 Egyptian-Israeli Peace Treaty. These events sowed confusion for the Jewish right and left alike. Israeli-Egyptian peace challenged the right-wing notion that Arabs could never be trusted and that Israel could never withdraw from its 1967 conquests, sentiments that also appeared to represent the stance of much of the American Jewish "center."

Yet while many dovish American Jews, including those in Breira, rejoiced at the peace deal, it also raised troublesome questions for them. Breira had maintained that negotiating with the PLO, and ultimately granting Palestinians statehood, was essential for Israel's security. Camp David seemed to prove that Israel did not, in fact, need to recognize the PLO or give up the West Bank, Jerusalem, the Golan Heights, or Gaza in order to bring an end to hostilities with its greatest military threat, Egypt. Given that Camp David undermined Palestinian national aspirations, should Breira be for or against it? The established Jewish community came out strongly against President Carter's attempts to bring the Palestinians into peace negotiations. Carter's insistence on this would have divided Breira members between those focused on the Palestinian question and those who prioritized Israeli-Egyptian peace, thus challenging the consensus that Breira sought to build. The point is mostly moot, however, considering that national Breira ceased operations prior to the historic agreement, though reports produced in early 1978 by the outgoing executive director and the remaining local chapters indicate its tenuous political position, expressing skepticism that an agreement could be reached without Palestinian involvement.[63]

Conclusion: Historicizing the "Second Generation"

Breira arose within a context of a broader second generation of American Jews sympathetic to the Palestinian plight. A few years before Breira's formation, an array of small local Jewish organizations, some focused on Israel/Palestine, some not, emerged following the 1967 war. Unlike the first generation of American Jews concerned with Palestinian rights, which came of age at a time when most Jewish organizations shut women out of leadership positions and when women had fewer opportunities to travel to the Middle East, this second generation included many women at its forefront, including Aviva Cantor of JLP, Sharon Rose of JUJ and MERIP, and Ellen Siegel, who became involved in Palestine advocacy in the 1970s and later founded Washington Area Jews for an Israeli-Palestinian Peace after witnessing the 1982 Sabra and Shatila massacre. In the specific case of Breira, however, while the group had many women members, some often felt shut out from substantive leadership positions.[64]

Breira, the first national American Jewish organization to openly oppose Israel's occupation of the West Bank and Gaza, was far from the last of its kind. Other groups with similar platforms that emerged after Breira included New Jewish Agenda, founded by Serotta and others in 1980; Americans for Peace Now, established in 1981; and J Street, created in 2007. Like Breira, these groups would often harken to Israeli counterparts, or act as a forum for Israeli dovish views. All have, without a doubt, faced controversy, and often similar forms of critique that aimed to diminish their "Jewishness." In 2016, responding to furor over American Jewish critiques of Israel, former U.S. State Department official and conservative thinker Elliott Abrams wrote an opinion piece asserting that assimilation rather than the occupation was the primary cause of Israel–American Jewish rifts. While this analysis focused on the past, the evidence presented in this chapter shows that at least in the 1970s case of Breira, critiques of Israeli policy owed not to distance between Israel and American Jews but to closeness. Future Breira leaders traveled to Israel in the 1960s and early 1970s not out of antipathy but out of affinity, feelings of strong Jewish identity, or personal interest. It was there, in the land between the river and the sea, that many of them came to the realization that the Jewish state faced deeper dilemmas than they had understood as campers, students, and observers thousands of miles away. They came to these conclusions when they encountered Palestinians living in the territories, where they had often been brought by Israeli friends, or when those friends convinced them through conversations that the occupation was not in Israeli, or Jewish, interest. When these American Jews came back to the United States, they found that dovish views were even less welcomed at home than they had been in Israel. Breira and similar groups sought to bring reputable Israeli doves to speak to broader American Jewish crowds. When those doves mobilized, in the form of the ICIPP, Breira did what it could to support them, but such efforts only prompted more attacks against it, a development apparently aided by the leaks of Israeli officials who were opposed to legitimizing the PLO in any way.[65]

Breira remains an American story. But this chapter makes the case that Breira is not only that; it is also part of Israeli and Palestinian histories, not only because it aimed to influence those two peoples, but also because Israelis and Palestinians influenced it. The Israel-Diaspora relationship is, and always has been, a two-way street. Its history should be written as such.

Conclusion: Diaspora and Dissent

ON OCTOBER 19, 2001, a seventy-eight-year-old Don Peretz received the greatest honor of his career, the Middle East Institute Award, in a televised event. As the mainstream American Jewish community had never celebrated Peretz, it seems appropriate that the honor took place at a meeting of the policy-focused think tank that had published Peretz's earliest research on Israel/Palestine. After being introduced by Assistant Secretary of State William Burns, Peretz thanked the distinguished audience. Toward the end of Peretz's short time at the podium, he quoted a speech that he had heard more than half a century earlier, one that he had carried with him all those years—Judah Magnes's 1947 welcome address to Hebrew University students, which the university president had delivered only weeks before the outbreak of a war that reshaped the trajectories of Jewish and Palestinian histories. Quoting Magnes, Peretz stated:

> What is the duty of the man, more especially of the teacher, who thinks the method of force and violence to be a savage and idolatrous belief? Is there room for that man in our society? Is it his right, or even perhaps his duty, to express an opinion which may differ from the majority decision of official institutions? Is one to sanctify these majority decisions above every other sacred thing?
>
> More than that, is there not laid upon the man the sacred task, despite majority decisions, to warn the people, to teach, to point to its error—nay, perhaps even its iniquity—when it sharpens its swords to the destruction that may overtake the people of the land?

Is there no place in our society for those who dissent from the decisions of the majority and who, conscious of their collective responsibility, obey the command of conscience by lifting their voice, not for murder and destruction, heaven forbid, but for peace and understanding among the peoples?

In his own voice, Peretz noted that "today the Middle East is an even more dangerous place than it was during the time of Magnes . . . a major focus for future wars." Speaking a mere five weeks after the attacks of September 11, Peretz's comment alluded to America's brewing military response to that tragedy.[1]

But his remarks also came amidst renewed crisis in Israel/Palestine, which was then facing its bloodiest period of internal strife since 1948. Frustrated Palestinians had launched the Second Intifada a year prior as peace negotiations faltered. Peretz's lifelong focus, the enduring Palestinian refugee question, had been among the contentious issues that contributed to the breakdown of talks. The ensuing violence left thousands of people dead; one of the highest-casualty terrorist attacks in Jerusalem occurred at Judah Magnes's beloved Hebrew University, where both Peretz and Esther Herlitz, a diplomat who opposed him, had studied.[2]

Peretz did not merely mention Magnes. He had selected a quotation from him about the crisis of dissenters who felt that their society had chosen the wrong path. Is there room, they asked, "for those who dissent from the decisions of the majority and . . . obey the command of conscious by lifting their voice . . . for peace?" Peretz made his speech an ode to Magnes, but he could just as well have been speaking of his own experience.

In working for the American Jewish Committee (AJC), Peretz hoped that his expertise on Palestinian affairs would help the American Jewish community contribute to peace and well-being in the Middle East and ideally avoid the sort of tragedy that reignited in 2000. Instead, in a series of behind-the-scenes events of which Peretz was never fully aware, the AJC dismissed Peretz's work and, before long, parted ways with him as well. While Haym Peretz had dreamed that his son would be lauded as a hero within what he conceived of as the Jewish nation, leaders of that nation more often labeled Don a traitor and undermined his efforts. As with Magnes, who was reviled by many in Mandate Palestine's Jewish community, Peretz witnessed the perils in store for those bearing unwelcomed messages in the transnational Jewish political universe. His marginalization is part of a hidden history of conflict between American Jewish liberalism and Israeli policy—one long lost in sweeping generalizations about relations between these two poles of post-Holocaust Jewish life.

"I'll close with this," Peretz concluded in his televised address. "Do we have any responsibility, not for causing these unfortunate developments, but for attempting to change this situation?" While Peretz addressed a room of Middle East specialists, one could easily imagine him posing the question to fellow American Jews. While at the AJC, and later as part of Breira, Peretz attempted to change the situation for the better but did not succeed. Now, at the very least, it is clearer as to why.[3]

This book ends as it began, recalling the story of Don Peretz. From the 1940s through the 1970s, Peretz had links to nearly every American Jewish effort supportive of Palestinians. In summer 1948, Peretz became involved with a transnational network of dovish figures including Hannah Arendt, Judah Magnes, Hans Kohn, and James Marshall, a group that after Magnes's passing morphed into the Judah L. Magnes Foundation, which funded scholarships for Arab university students in Israel. Peretz then worked for the AJC on its Arab refugee initiative and wrote on Palestinian affairs for William Zukerman's *Jewish Newsletter*. After 1967, he served on the steering committee of the Committee on New Alternatives for the Middle East (CONAME) alongside Noam Chomsky, and then joined Breira's executive committee, acting as a sort of senior scholar-in-residence for the group on Palestinian affairs. Though he never joined the American Council for Judaism ("the Council"), Peretz befriended Rabbi Elmer Berger and Norton Mezvinsky later in life, even writing the foreword for Berger's final book.[4]

Peretz's importance in the history of American Jewish support for Palestinian rights stems not only from his centrality to it but also from the way in which his experience anticipated the trajectory of many younger, like-minded American Jews, including some members of Breira and subsequent pro-peace organizations. Many American Jews of later generations who came to be ardent advocates for Palestinian rights did so after spending time in Israel. They often went because of their Zionist feelings, or at the very least out of a sense of connection to the land and its people premised on their Jewishness. But Peretz went first. Understanding his real-time political evolution not only gives insight into formative moments in the life of the man who wrote the first serious, scholarly study of the Arab refugee issue; it also serves as an unprecedented historical case study of similar processes at work among generations of dovish American Jews. Contemporary activists have antecedents who they did not know existed; here, they, too, have a history, and a Jewish one at that.

It is telling that some young American Jewish activists today searching for role models outside the Zionist orbit have turned to the Bund and Yiddish culture as an alternative. Partly, this attraction is based on the anti-Zionism of the Bund, which, as this book noted, did lead Bundists to support Palestinian rights; however, activists sometimes overlook the extent that Yiddish culture and Zionism overlapped historically. One could envision activists instead looking toward Peretz, Zukerman, the AJC, the Council, the Jewish Liberation Project, or even Breira as forebears to today's Jewish supporters of Palestinian rights. Yet it seems doubtful that they will ever be viewed as quite as compelling as the Yiddishists. The reason for this, one suspects, is the ability of the Yiddish leftist past to provide far more than just a political critique of Israel, offering a more fully articulated Jewish cultural world as well. Jews who harken back to Yiddish socialism appear to be seeking a broader Jewish political-cultural identity to fill a void that they feel exists in contemporary Jewish life in the United States.

It is exactly that perceived void, that longing for a more substantive cultural package and sense of purpose, that has drawn so many American Jews to Zionism, Israel, and Hebrew culture across many decades. This pull persists. Even many Jews who are strongly critical of Israel today engage with its culture quite frequently, whether through its food, books, television shows, through travel, or even by simply following English-language Israeli media such as the *Times of Israel*, *+972 Magazine*, or *Haaretz*.

The research of sociologist Theodore Sasson suggests that growing American Jewish criticism of Israel—a phenomenon that some problematically refer to as American Jewish "distancing" from Israel—has emerged not as a result of greater "distance" from Israel but rather from growing American Jewish proximity to it. A larger proportion of American Jews today have visited Israel than at any time in history, whether on short trips like Birthright or on longer semester or yearlong programs. Through the internet, far greater access to English-language news about Israel and events in the Palestinian territories is available than ever before, and students at many colleges and universities are becoming more conversant in Israeli politics through Israel studies courses than was the case even two decades ago. Brought up in the United States with diasporic ethical sensibilities—left-leaning views inspired by prevailing trends in American political culture as much as by liberal Judaism—many young Jews today find themselves surprised by social and political realities in Israel/Palestine. Beyond Israel's ongoing occupation of the West Bank and its blockade of the Gaza Strip, these realities are also apparent in Israeli mentalities, as reflected by polls showing that Israeli Jews are drifting further and further to the right politically.[5]

Crucially, that surprise and disillusionment often emerge from real, meaningful exposure. Experientially, members of contemporary pro-peace Jewish groups such as J Street, Open Hillel, and IfNotNow would feel they have much more in common with a young Don Peretz than with the typical American Jew of Peretz's generation, who likely donated plenty to Israel but never spent much time there. Peretz and Breira's young leading cohort both felt quite isolated in their day; today, with accessibility to Israel/Palestine and attendant knowledge about the conflict, there are many young American Jewish "Don Peretzes," and many of them are at work in groups that might be considered Breira's successors.[6]

Rather than being acknowledged as proud, well-meaning Jews drawn to examine Israel out of interest in their own Jewish identity, this generation's Breiraniks are dismissed not as "Don Peretzes" but as "Elmer Bergers." Berger, an ideological assimilationist, stood as the most prominent Jewish figure of the era to outspokenly support Palestinian rights without first having sympathized with Zionism or feeling some connection to the land. From Berger onward, Jews supportive of Palestinian rights have been critiqued as overly assimilated and disconnected from Jewish identity. In 2018, Naftali Bennett, then Israel's Diaspora affairs minister and later its prime minister, declared that "Israel and the Diaspora are in the throes of an unprecedented crisis. We're used to being told that it's because of [prayer rules at] the Western Wall, the Palestinian issue and other ideological controversies. It's not correct. There's a terrible problem of assimilation and growing indifference of Jews overseas both to their Jewishness and to Israel. That is the entire story."[7]

Former United States ambassador to Israel Martin Indyk, once an AIPAC staffer, vehemently disagreed, insisting that it was Bennett's "extreme policies" that alienated American Jews from Israel. Critics attributed Indyk's politics not to his expertise but to his "anti-Israel" animus and inherent disloyalty to the Jewish people. Indyk, who grew up in Australia, called his time in Israel during the 1973 war "a defining moment in my life," but that formative experience did little to insulate him from the "anti-Israel" label.[8]

From Bennett all the way back to his predecessors in the 1950s, Israeli officials have, unsurprisingly, been wary of American Jewish support for the Palestinians. Judging by Israeli archival files available from the 1950s and 1960s, however, earlier generations of Israeli officials had much greater tact and nuance in addressing the issue, courting anti-Zionist Jews rather than banning them from the country. During Israel's precarious early years, prior to the christening of the "special relationship" and long before the rise of a powerful, right-wing brand of Christian Zionism, the stakes for the Jewish state in managing Diaspora relations also seemed much higher; America's Jewish community was then even more central to Israel's attempts to marshal support in Washington. Israel had a well-placed fear that the Truman, Eisenhower, or Kennedy administration would pressure the state to allow the return of many Arab refugees, cede land to Arab neighbors, or (in the case of Kennedy) demand serious monitoring of its nuclear program. Perhaps for economic even more than diplomatic reasons, it is unclear how Israel would have survived its first decade without an enthusiastic American Jewry. This applied not only to Zionists but also to the wealthy and well-connected non-Zionists who associated with the AJC. Israeli officials hoped that these non-Zionists would not adopt Don Peretz's sense of urgency about the Arab refugee issue and lose focus on helping the Jewish state.[9]

Yet even after the uncertainty of the 1950s, Israeli officials worked to keep American Jews on their side, including even anti-Zionists of the Council, a faction that shrank further when it was hit by the post-1967 wave of American enthusiasm for the Jewish state. After Fayez Sayegh's successful diplomatic assault at the United Nations—the "Zionism Is Racism" resolution of November 1975—Israel and the Jewish Agency called an emergency conference of worldwide Jewish leaders in Jerusalem. Diaspora leaders arrived with the belief that they would have the chance to give input at what appeared to be a timely opportunity for Israel to reevaluate its political strategies and public relations tactics. Delegates, however, felt disappointed to discover that the "emergency meeting" mostly consisted of orchestrating displays of unity. Instead of partners, the delegates felt more like pawns. As George Gruen, who succeeded Peretz as the AJC's Middle East expert, reflected, "The conference program was structured so as to avoid discussion of any controversial political . . . issues, such as Israel's public stance on the Palestinians . . . or the effect . . . of new Israeli settlements." The program instead consisted of workshops on how diaspora Jews should work to strengthen Jewish education, increase *aliyah*, stimulate economic investment in Israel, and build "public solidarity" for the Jewish state. While no one doubted the value of those objectives, Gruen reported, "some delegates privately shared the view of the Latin American delegate who expressed to the press his disappointment of having travelled thousands of miles merely to endorse resolutions that he said could well have been sent to him by mail." The delegate had "hoped to participate in a basic discussion of the changing international climate facing Israel to which he could contribute the particular insights of a resident of Latin America," according to Gruen, but state officials appeared to be uninterested in the diaspora Jewish leader's insights.[10]

For all of Zionism's rhetoric about global Jewish peoplehood, when it comes to political decision-making in the statehood era, the Jewish state has operated in a remarkably conventional manner. The Jewishness of noncitizens gives them no real political power, and when it comes to major issues like Palestinian affairs, the advice of even well-established diaspora Zionist leaders appears to hold little weight. While some—including Gruen in a later oral history interview—suggested that Breira, which peaked around the same time as the emergency conference in Jerusalem, should have worked on other Jewish issues in order to gain Jewish legitimacy before taking on the Palestinian issue, Gruen's own report shows that greater communal clout likely would have had little influence on Israeli policy.

Israel had no respect for such diasporic dissent, which it viewed as naive at best and dangerous at worst. So Israeli officials apparently leaked the names of Gruen and Breira members who had met secretly with Palestine Liberation Organization (PLO) representatives, seeking to undermine the problematic American Jews just as their predecessors had sought the dismissal of Peretz two decades prior.

If Peretz's story represents the perils of raising the Palestinian question in the American Jewish community, Fayez Sayegh's experience embodies the challenges faced by Palestinians trying to mobilize for their people's cause. Sayegh understood the important distinction between Jews, Zionists, and Israelis; his appreciation for it no doubt only grew through his encounter with Rabbi Elmer Berger. Sayegh also knew that his credibility in American public discourse depended on his ability to distance himself from anti-Jewish individuals and ideas; according even to his staunchest opponents in the 1950s, Sayegh succeeded, studiously avoiding antisemitic rhetoric in his speeches and public appearances.

But Sayegh must have felt that he was playing a game that he could never win. His Arab Information Center faced accusations of antisemitism from the Anti-Defamation League (ADL) even before it opened its doors. The next year, Sayegh met with AJC officials, in part hoping that they could give him a "formula" to help Arabs learn to critique Israel in a way that would not threaten non-Zionist Jews. The Sayegh-AJC meeting, however well intentioned, would not be able to sort out these big questions. Instead, the AJC increasingly began to sense that Sayegh exposed its own fundamental inability to maintain the distinction that it sought to establish between Jews and Zionism. Despite the AJC's rhetoric that separated American Jews from Israel in a political sense, it could not articulate a legitimate way for Arabs to criticize Israel at a time when American Jews were increasingly identifying with the Jewish state. Instead, AJC officials worked with Zionist organizations and other pro-Israel groups, accepting the idea that there was no form of anti-Zionism that was not "bad for the Jews" and ultimately "anti-Semitic in effect."

Sayegh's thankless task as the Arab League's chief spokesman in the United States had been made all the more difficult by others from the Arab world, particularly by Arab diplomats who failed to distance their anti-

Zionism from antisemitism and themselves from antisemites. Arab states would also disappoint Sayegh in a more profound way, which represented, perhaps, how they failed the Palestinian people at large. Writing in his memoirs, Cecil Hourani, a Lebanese-British economist who worked with Sayegh at times over the years, reflected on Sayegh's disappointment from a personal perspective. Noting Sayegh's "encyclopedic knowledge" and "sharp logical mind," Hourani also saw in Sayegh "a streak of intransigence . . . and frustration" that grew "as the faith he had put in . . . Arab regimes to solve the Palestinian question . . . faded away," so much so that bitterness "overshadowed his other more human qualities." As much as the Palestinians' plight can be attributed to Israel, Sayegh's disillusionment is a reminder of the role that Arab states played in it as well.[11]

Despite this bitterness, Sayegh contributed to a new trajectory for critiques of Israel in the 1960s and 1970s with his work tying the Palestinian cause to struggles in the global Third World by equating Zionism with colonialism, racism, and apartheid. Long after Sayegh's death in 1980, the issues that he raised in the 1950s, 1960s, and 1970s remain at the center of heated debates over Israel/Palestine today, seventy-six years after the Palestinians' displacement and fifty-seven years since Israel's capture of the West Bank and Gaza. Palestinians and other activists, including some Jews, work to highlight and address ongoing Palestinian suffering, yet often end up facing the same challenges that their predecessors did decades earlier. Questions over whether anti-Zionism constitutes antisemitism are no more resolved today than they were when Sayegh and the AJC discussed them in the 1950s. If anything, they have only become more contested as many states debate legislation designed to penalize those taking part in some types of pro-Palestine activism. These legislative efforts have unsurprisingly divided the Jewish community, with groups like IfNotNow, J Street, and Jewish Voice for Peace opposing them, and AIPAC, the Zionist Organization of America, and the AJC often supporting them, with encouragement from the Israeli government.

These divisions thus mark a continuation of a long history of debate between Jews not only over Israeli policies but also over how to respond to support for Palestinian rights. While this book has unearthed various episodes of tension and disdain between Israel and American Jews, thus challenging contemporary memories of historical unity, one can also read it as evidence of a greater, and perhaps more enduring, political connectivity between Jews. American Jews did not ignore ongoing debates about the Jewish state's future. From 1948 to the present day, some American Jews, with various stances on Zionism, followed discussions taking place in Israel about the state's Arab policy. While disinterest, silence, or even passive acquiescence could arguably indicate the nonexistence of a global Jewish politics, dissent does the opposite. It indicates participation.

Whether Israelis wish to admit it or not, the Palestinian question has always been their country's most central, if not definitional, dilemma. At the same time, Israel's role in Jewish communities elsewhere in the world has only continued to expand, a development that has meant that as the Palestinian question marches forward unaddressed, the circle of American Jews critiquing Israeli policies has grown larger and larger. Just as previous generations of Jews found a renewed sense of communal purpose in their support for Israel, some American Jews today see their support for Palestinian rights as a meaningful extension of their Jewish identity. Rather than being a countercurrent in American Jewish politics, Palestinian rights advocacy has become a realm of Jewish politics in and of itself. And despite enduring uproars over it, it will define the transnational relationship between Jews even more as time goes on.

NOTES

Introduction

1. Morris Lazaron, *Olive Trees in Storm* (Washington, DC: American Friends of the Middle East, 1955), 40–41.
2. Lazaron, *Olive Trees in Storm*, 40, 107. The Sabra and Shatila massacres occurred after Israel's 1982 invasion of Lebanon and in the context of the Lebanese Civil War. In mid-September 1982, Israeli defense minister Ariel Sharon permitted the Lebanese Christian Phalange militia to enter the Shatila refugee camp and adjacent Sabra neighborhood, which the Israeli army controlled. While Israeli soldiers did not kill any residents themselves, they watched and launched flares as Phalange troops murdered between 500 and 3,500 Palestinian and Lebanese Shia civilians in retaliation for the recent assassination of Bachir Gemayal, Lebanon's Maronite Christian president-elect. See Seth Anziska, "A Preventable Massacre," *New York Times*, September 26, 2012.
3. It is unclear if Lazaron knew of the CIA funding. The return of seventy-five thousand refugees was part of a broader secret Anglo-American proposal to resolve the Arab-Israeli conflict called Operation ALPHA, which was ultimately rejected by both Egypt and Israel. Historian Hugh Wilford writes that though "documentary record is scant . . . clues from a variety of sources" brought together indicate that AFME and its partners mobilized in 1955 to put together a domestic public relations campaign in support of ALPHA. Though Wilford makes no mention of Lazaron's trip, Lazaron was an AFME member and the group published the book just as this "campaign" was in full swing. Wilford considers a similar trip and book by Lazaron's colleague Rabbi Elmer Berger to be part of the campaign and views their organization, the anti-Zionist American Council for Judaism, as central to the public relations push. Hugh Wilford, *America's Great Game: The CIA's Secret Arabists and the Shaping of the Modern Middle East* (New York: Basic Books, 2013), 178–183.

4. Bob Bahr, "Is the Jewish 'Golden Age' Over?," *Atlanta Jewish Times*, July 6, 2022. Stephens's exchange came within the context of a debate with historian Pamela Nadell of American University.

5. Dov Waxman, *Trouble in the Tribe: The American Jewish Conflict over Israel* (Princeton, NJ: Princeton University Press, 2016), 4; Steven T. Rosenthal, *Irreconcilable Differences? The Waning of the American Jewish Love Affair with Israel* (Waltham, MA: Brandeis University Press, 2001); Daniel Gordis, *We Stand Divided: The Rift between American Jews and Israel* (New York: Ecco, 2019).

6. The most cited survey of American Jewish history, Jonathan Sarna's *American Judaism: A History*, for instance, made no mention of the Palestinians in its 2004 first edition, while its 2019 second edition stated that "glimmers of dissent" on Israel/Palestine only went back "as early as 1973." Jonathan Sarna, *American Judaism: A History* (New Haven: Yale University Press, 2019), 377–378, 381. The second most cited survey, Hasia Diner's *The Jews of the United States* (Berkeley: University of California Press, 2004), goes into more depth about the 1970s but does not discuss Jewish support for Palestinian rights that came before that. Books on the non-Zionist AJC such as Zvi Ganin, *An Uneasy Relationship: American Jewish Leadership and Israel, 1948–1957* (Syracuse, NY: Syracuse University Press, 2005), and on the anti-Zionist American Council for Judaism—namely, Thomas Kolsky, *Jews against Zionism: The American Council for Judaism, 1942–1948* (Philadelphia: Temple University Press, 1990)—focus mostly on non-Zionist and anti-Zionist dissent from Jewish nationalism. An exception that does discuss the Palestinians is Jack Ross, *Rabbi Outcast: Elmer Berger and American Jewish Anti-Zionism* (Washington, DC: Potomac Books, 2011).

7. On American Jewish organizations' push for an inclusive America, see Stuart Svonkin, *Jews against Prejudice: American Jews and the Fight for Civil Liberties* (New York: Columbia University Press, 1997).

8. See "Organizations: Dollars for Israel," *Time*, January 21, 1957; David Tal, *The Making of an Alliance: The Origins and Development of the US-Israel Relationship* (Cambridge: Cambridge University Press, 2022); "U.S. Foreign Aid to Israel: Total Aid," Jewish Virtual Library, https://www.jewishvirtuallibrary.org/total-u-s-foreign-aid-to-israel-1949-present, accessed February 7, 2023.

9. Some of these dynamics have been highlighted in recent books on Jews and human rights. See Nathan Kurz, *Jewish Internationalism and Human Rights after the Holocaust* (Cambridge: Cambridge University Press, 2020), and James Loeffler, *Rooted Cosmopolitans: Jews and Human Rights in the Twentieth Century* (New Haven: Yale University Press, 2018).

10. Ganin, *An Uneasy Relationship*. This claim about the AJC's influence does not mean that it had the most members; Hadassah, an "apolitical" women's Zionist organization, for example, was much larger in terms of membership. The Conference of Presidents of Major Jewish Organizations and the American Israel Public Affairs Committee, which later emerged as influential rivals, were only in their infancy by the end of the Eisenhower presidency, while contemporary rivals (the Anti-Defamation League and American Jewish Congress) held less sway in

Washington and focused less on foreign affairs. Charles S. Liebman, *Pressure without Sanction: The Influence of World Jewry on Israeli Policy* (Cranbury, NJ: Associated University Presses, 1977), 118.

11. Lawrence Grossman, "Transformation through Crisis: The American Jewish Committee and the Six-Day War," *American Jewish History* 86, no. 1 (1998); Marianne R. Sanua, *Let Us Prove Strong: The American Jewish Committee, 1945–2006* (Waltham, MA: Brandeis University Press, 2007).

12. Geoffrey P. Levin, "Liberal Whispers and Propaganda Fears: The American Jewish Committee and Israel's Palestinian Minority, 1948–1966," *Israel Studies Review* 33, no. 1 (2018): 81–101; Geoffrey P. Levin, "Arab Students, American Jewish Insecurities, and the End of Pro-Arab Politics in Mainstream America, 1952–1973," *Arab Studies Journal* 25, no. 1 (2017): 30–59.

13. American Jewish anti-Zionists hailed from many quarters of the political spectrum, including the far left, far right, Reform, and Orthodox. On anti-Zionism in Yiddish publications, see Amelia M. Glaser, *Songs in Dark Times: Yiddish Poetry of Struggle from Scottsboro to Palestine* (Cambridge, MA: Harvard University Press, 2020), chapter 2. On anti-Zionism in the AJC, see Ganin, *An Uneasy Relationship*, 10–12. On the Council in general, see Kolsky, *Jews against Zionism*, and Ross, *Rabbi Outcast*, 73.

14. Scholar-activist Naseer Aruri compared Said and Sayegh in a similar manner: "Edward was typically described as 'the conscience of Palestine,' having delivered the kind of eloquent message perhaps unheard since that of the late Fayez Sayegh." Foreword to Nur Masalha, ed., *Catastrophe Remembered: Palestine, Israel and the Internal Refugees* (New York: Zed Books, 2005), xiv. Another comparison between Said and Sayegh appears in As'ad Abu Khalil, "Before Edward Said: A Tribute to Fayez Sayegh," *Al-Akhbar English*, December 9, 2014. On Sayegh's role in the other Palestinian projects, see Jonathan Marc Gribetz, "The PLO's Rabbi: Palestinian Nationalism and Reform Judaism," *Jewish Quarterly Review* 107, no. 1 (2017): 90–112, and Keith P. Feldman, *A Shadow over Palestine: The Imperial Life of Race in America* (Minneapolis: University of Minnesota Press, 2015).

15. Michael E. Staub, *Torn at the Roots: The Crisis of Jewish Liberalism in Postwar America* (New York: Columbia University Press, 2004), 280–308.

16. Avi Shlaim, "The Debate about 1948," *International Journal of Middle East Studies* 27, no. 3 (1995): 287–304; Anita Shapira, "The Debate over the 'New Historians' in Israel," in *Handbook of Israel: Major Debates*, ed. Eliezer Ben-Rafael, Julius H. Schoeps, Yitzhak Sternberg, and Olaf Glöckner (Berlin: de Gruyter Oldenbourg, 2016).

17. Irene Gendzier, *Dying to Forget: Oil, Power, and the Foundations of U.S. Policy in the Middle East* (New York: Columbia University Press, 2015); Neil Caplan, *Operation Alpha and the Failure of Anglo-American Coercive Diplomacy in the Arab-Israeli Conflict, 1954–1956* (London: Routledge, 1997); Hugh Wilford, "American Friends of the Middle East: The CIA, US Citizens, and the Secret Battle for American Public Opinion in the Arab-Israeli Conflict, 1947–1967," *Journal of American Studies* 51, no. 1 (2017): 93–116.

18. It is hard to cite an exact date owing to disagreements as who counts as a Jew, but demographers started making the claim around 2006. "Israel Surpasses United States to Become Most Populous Jewish State," World Jewish Congress, May 2, 2006, https://www.worldjewishcongress.org/en/news/israel-surpasses-united-states-to-become-most-populous-jewish-state.

19. See Natan Aridan, *Advocating for Israel: Diplomats and Lobbyists from Truman to Nixon* (Lanham, MD: Lexington Books, 2017); Shaul Mitelpunkt, *Israel in the American Mind: The Cultural Politics of U.S.-Israel Relations, 1958–1988* (Cambridge: Cambridge University Press, 2018), and other works listed in Geoffrey P. Levin, "Culture, Communities, and Early U.S.-Israel Relations: A State of the Field," *H-Diplo* (2018). On the American Jewish side, I refer especially to the work of Emily Alice Katz, *Bringing Zion Home: Israel in American Jewish Culture, 1948–1967* (Albany: State University of New York Press, 2015). In the realm of Palestinian history, scholars such as Shira Robinson, Leena Dallasheh, Arnon Degani, and Maha Nassar have called new attention to Palestinian citizens of Israel under military rule (1948–1966).

20. Amy Kaplan, *Our American Israel: The Story of an Entangled Alliance* (Cambridge, MA: Harvard University Press, 2018), 2.

21. Weiss notes that the AZC allotted $100,000 in funding for the American Christian Palestine Committee (ACPC) in 1949, equivalent to $1.25 million in 2022 dollars, a reduction of one-third after 1948. While the quasi-state Jewish Agency for Israel only partly funded the AZC, and receiving Jewish Agency funds differs from receiving Israeli funding directly, the link remains important, especially when one considers that Israeli leaders select the Jewish Agency's chairman. Amy Weiss, "Between Cooperation and Competition: The Making of American Jewish Zionist Interfaith Alliances with Liberal and Evangelical Protestants, 1898–1979" (PhD diss., New York University, 2014), 170–171; Caitlin Carenen, *The Fervent Embrace: Liberal Protestants, Evangelicals, and Israel* (New York: New York University Press, 2012); Aridan, *Advocating for Israel*. On *Exodus*, see Mitelpunkt, *Israel in the American Mind*; Tony Shaw and Giora Goodman, *Hollywood and Israel: A History* (New York: Columbia University Press, 2022); M. M. Silver, *Our Exodus: Leon Uris and the Americanization of the Jewish State* (Detroit: Wayne University Press, 2010); and Shalom Goldman, *Starstruck in the Promised Land: How the Arts Shaped American Passions about Israel* (Chapel Hill: University of North Carolina Press, 2019). Goodman first discussed the Israeli state role in the making of the film in Giora Goodman, " 'Operation *Exodus*': Israeli Government Involvement in the Production of Otto Preminger's Film *Exodus* (1960)," *Journal of Israeli History* 33, no. 2 (2014): 209–229.

22. Emma Goldberg, " 'You Never Told Me': Confronting American Jewish Myths about Israel," *+972 Magazine*, June 19, 2018.

Chapter 1. Zionism's Wayward Son

1. Don Peretz to parents, January 9, 1949, Peretz Papers, GPL PDF 5/1; Don Peretz to parents, January 21, 1949, Peretz Papers, GPL PDF 5/3. The unusual notations used for files in the Peretz collection do not correspond with those of any archive but rather refer to how the files are organized in digital format by the author. At the time that the files were consulted in 2017–2018, they were still held by Maya Peretz. They have since been donated to the American Jewish Historical Society, where they will be processed and given a permanent set of box and file numbers, which may not correspond in any way with the author's notation system, particularly as some material has been moved and removed in the interim period. Should any researcher be interested in referencing specific files from the Peretz collection based on this notation system, they may contact the author.

2. Don Peretz to parents, August 18, 1949, Peretz Papers, GPL PDF 12/60; Don Peretz, "Vignettes—Bits and Pieces," in *Paths to the Middle East: Ten Scholars Look Back,* ed. Donald Naff (Albany: State University of New York Press, 1993). The second dissertation, published a few years later, was written by Iraqi-Israeli Rony Gabbay, who earned his doctorate in Geneva in 1959. See Rony E. Gabbay, *A Political Study of the Arab-Jewish Conflict: The Arab Refugee Problem (A Case Study)* (Geneva: Librairie E. Droz, 1959); Shay Hazkani, "Israel's Vanishing Files, Archival Deception and Paper Trails," *MERIP Report* 291 (Summer 2019); and Shay Hazkani, "Catastrophic Thinking: Did Ben-Gurion Try to Rewrite History?," *Haaretz,* May 16, 2013. The quote about Peretz's research referred to his 1955 dissertation and came from Hal Draper, "Israel's Arab Minority: The Great Land Robbery," *New International* 23, no. 1 (Winter 1957): 7–30.

3. As was not uncommon in many Sephardic families in nineteenth-century Palestine, Haym's father, Moshe, spoke Ladino, the Judeo-Spanish language of Sephardic Jewry, and knew Arabic, Hebrew, and Ottoman Turkish. See Peretz, "Vignettes," 231–232. Though he was born in Jerusalem, Egyptian paperwork referred to Haym Peretz as a "Syrian refugee." See Egyptian Passport for Mr. Haim Perez [*sic*], October 21, 1915, Peretz Papers, GPL Photos A2/117. Moshe Peretz's story is independently confirmed here: "Judith Schneidrovitz [in Hebrew]," *Israeli Tombstones* (blog), https://israelitombstones.blogspot.com/2014/05/2.html.

4. In 1916, Haym Peretz offered to say Kaddish upon the death of Szold's mother; she politely declined for feminist reasons. The episode was publicized in the 1940s, and Ruth Bader Ginsburg cited Szold's handling of the situation as inspirational. It is detailed on the Jewish Women's Archive Website and in Peretz Papers, GPL PDF 3; Henrietta Szold to Haym Peretz, July 22, 1942, Peretz Papers, GPL PDF 3/18; Henrietta Szold to Haym Peretz, July 22, 1942, Peretz Papers, GPL PDF 3/18; Haym Peretz to Don Peretz, October 28, 1943, Peretz Papers, GPL PDF 1/33; Haym Peretz CV, Peretz Papers, GPL PDF 1/39.

5. "Translation from the Hebrew, November 7, 1922," Haym Peretz to Don Peretz, July 5, 1947, Peretz Papers, GPL Photo 6/6/2017. The ritual ended up being delayed to another day because of a rash.

6. Don Peretz to Judah Magnes, December 27, 1947, Peretz Papers, GPL PDF 11/11. Peretz's letters imply that he did not consider himself a Zionist before 1946 or after 1948; Peretz, "Vignettes," 232; Aliza Becker's interview with Don Peretz, September 8, 2014 (confirmed by Peretz letters to parents from the 1940s), Veterans History Project Interview with Don Peretz, College Park Aviation Museum, August 6, 2012.

7. Peretz, "Vignettes," 232; Aliza Becker's interview with Don Peretz, September 8, 2014. On Magnes, see David Barak-Gorodetsky, *Judah Magnes: The Prophetic Politics of a Religious Binationalist* (Lincoln: University of Nebraska Press, 2021), and Daniel Kotzin, *Judah L. Magnes: An American Jewish Nonconformist* (Syracuse, NY: Syracuse University Press, 2010).

8. Don Peretz to "Grandma" (Tillie Asiel Lasser), May 1, 1947, Peretz Papers, GPL PDF 6/1.

9. Don Peretz to parents, February 5, 1947, Peretz Papers, GPL PDF 2/42; M. M. Platkin to Don Peretz, September 4, 1947, Peretz Papers, GPL PDF 11/9–10; Don Peretz to parents, May 19, 1947, Peretz Papers, GPL PDF 2/59.

10. Don Peretz to parents, November 30, 1947, Peretz Papers, GPL PDF 2/75. The two massacres listed were among the earliest of the civil war, which lasted from November 1947 to the Arab states' invasion in May 1948. The Haifa Oil Refinery massacre of December 1947 began when an Irgun squad threw bombs into an Arab crowd outside the refinery. After six Arabs died, Arab refinery workers turned on their Jewish coworkers, killing thirty-nine Jews. In response, the Haganah attacked the Arab village of Balad al-Shaykh, executing dozens of civilians in an act of retaliation. See Benny Morris, *Righteous Victims: A History of the Zionist-Arab Conflict, 1881–2001* (New York: Vintage, 2001), 198.

11. Don Peretz to parents, February 14, 1948, Peretz Papers, GPL PDF 8/1–2.

12. Don Peretz to parents, February 14, 1948, Peretz Papers, GPL PDF 8/1–2.

13. Don Peretz, "Arab 'Tried' by Arab Guard," *Palestine Post*, February 17, 1949; Peretz, "Vignettes," 235. Don Peretz to parents, February 21, 1948, Peretz Papers, GPL PDF 8/3–4. "Said Jundi" could be translated as "Mr. Soldier." While Peretz wrote that "Said Jundi" was the man's name, which it could have been, it may also have been that Peretz was confused, which would testify to the limits of his Arabic skills. However, given Peretz's later study of Arabic, and that he recounted in his memoir various other details, including hearing that Jundi has been involved in the assassination of Jordan's King Abdullah, it seems likely that this was indeed the man's name. Other Palestinian Arabs whom he connected with during this era included journalist Abu Said Aburish.

14. Don Peretz to parents, February 28, 1948, Peretz Papers, GPL PDF 8/6; Don Peretz to parents, February 21, 1948, Peretz Papers, GPL PDF 8/4–5. While Arab support for binationalism is commonly believed to have been low, at least one Arab political figure supported binationalism, Jerusalem city councilman Adel Jabre. Jabre reportedly reached out in 1941 to Moshe Shertok and David Ben-Gurion, who rejected the idea. See Mona Hajjar Halaby, "Out of the Public Eye: Adel Jabre's Long Journey from Ottomanism to Binationalism," *Jerusalem Quarterly* 52 (Winter 2013).

15. Don Peretz to parents, February 28, 1948, Peretz Papers, GPL PDF 8/6; Don Peretz to Judah Magnes, December 27, 1947, Peretz Papers, GPL PDF 11/11; Don Peretz to parents, February 21, 1948, Peretz Papers, GPL PDF 8/4–5.

16. Don Peretz to parents, February 28, 1948, Peretz Papers, GPL PDF 8/6; Don Peretz to parents, March 5, 1948, Peretz Papers, GPL PDF 8/8.

17. Don Peretz to parents, March 18, 1948, Peretz Papers, GPL PDF 8/12.

18. Don Peretz to parents, March 28, 1948, Peretz Papers, GPL PDF 8/14; Don Peretz to parents, April 7, 1948, Peretz Papers, GPL PDF 8/17. The Peretz home was on HaYarkon, across the street from the Dan Hotel.

19. Don Peretz to parents, April 19, 1948, Peretz Papers, GPL PDF 8/20–22.

20. Don Peretz to parents, June 16, 1948, Peretz Papers, GPL PDF 8/33.

21. Don Peretz to parents, June 16, 1948, Peretz Papers, GPL PDF 8/33; Don Peretz to parents, June 23, 1948, Peretz Papers, GPL PDF 8/33. The *"Altalena* affair" ended with Begin's Irgun yielding and being absorbed into the Israeli military. On another historic day—June 5, 1967—Peretz was also in Israel, leading his first study-abroad trip for Binghamton University students.

22. Peretz, "Vignettes," 236. Estimates vary. On refugees left outside Israel's borders, Benny Morris cites 700,000 refugees while Shira Robinson cites 750,000. The scholarly consensus seems to be around 750,000 refugees. The 800,000 figure I use includes Palestinians displaced within Israel who were not able to return to their homes. Hillel Cohen put this number at 15 percent of the 156,000 Arabs in Israel (around 23,400), while Nur Masalha refers to nearly a quarter being internally displaced, or 39,000. See Benny Morris, *The Birth of the Palestinian Refugee Problem Revisited* (Cambridge: Cambridge University Press, 2004), 588; Shira Robinson, *Citizen Strangers: Palestinians and the Birth of Israel's Liberal Settler State* (Stanford, CA: Stanford University Press, 2013), 27; Nur Masalha, *The Politics of Denial: Israel and the Palestinian Refugee Problem* (London: Pluto, 2003), 4; Hillel Cohen, *Hanifkadim Hanokhahim: Haplitim Hafalastinayyim Beyisrael Meaz 1948* [The present absentees: the Palestinian refugees in Israel since 1948] (Jerusalem: Centre for the Study of Arab Society in Israel, Van Leer Institute, 2000); Hazkani, "Catastrophic Thinking"; Barak Ravid, "Citing National Security, Israel Likely to Keep Army File on Palestinian Refugees from 1948 Sealed," *Haaretz,* September 20, 2016.

23. Masalha, *Politics of Denial,* 1; Robinson, *Citizen Strangers,* 74–100; Avi Shlaim, *The Iron Wall: Israel and the Arab World* (New York: Norton, 2001), 51; Irene Gendzier, *Dying to Forget: Oil, Power, and the Foundations of U.S. Policy in the Middle East* (New York: Columbia University Press, 2015), 202–204.

24. Nancy Gallagher, *Quakers in the Israeli–Palestinian Conflict: The Dilemmas of NGO Humanitarian Activism* (Cairo: American University in Cairo Press, 2007), 51–52; Asaf Romirowsky and Alexander Joffe, *Religion, Politics, and the Origins of Palestine Refugee Relief* (New York: Palgrave Macmillan, 2013), 5, 42–44. Both books explore Quaker involvement during the same era but take a markedly different stance. Romirowsky and Joffe consider AFSC biased and portray Peretz as a victim of AFSC antisemitism. Had the authors contacted Peretz, they would have

learned of his lifelong admiration for the AFSC. While AFSC took charge of relief in Gaza and the Galilee, LRCS and ICRC aided refugees under UN auspices in Jordan and what became the West Bank, and Lebanon and Syria, respectively. See "U.N. Relief Groups Sign Arab Aid Pacts," *New York Times*, December 18, 1948. On ICRC involvement, see Dominique Junod, *The Imperiled Red Cross and the Palestine-Eretz-Yisrael Conflict 1945–1952: The Influence of Institutional Concerns on a Humanitarian Operation* (London: Kegan Paul International, 1996). No scholarly study on LRCS involvement exists.

25. Peretz, "Vignettes," 236. The AFSC sent most of its volunteers to Gaza. Peretz was certainly the only Jew in the AFSC mission, and very likely the first American Jew to volunteer to help displaced Palestinian Arabs. AFSC, ICRC, and LRCS signed their agreement with the UN on December 18, 1948. The ICRC had been active since the summer in Jerusalem but was traditionally an all-Swiss organization. LRCS tended to rely on local (i.e., Syrian and Lebanese) Red Cross chapters for support. Thus, it is highly unlikely that any other American Jew volunteered for or arrived in one of these Arab countries prior to Don Peretz. Moreover, in a 1949 article, journalist Hal Lehrman described Peretz as the "only American Jew on the Quaker voluntary teams serving in and around Palestine." See Hal Lehrman, "The Arabs of Israel," *Commentary*, December 1949. Don Peretz to parents, January 9, 1949, Peretz Papers, GPL PDF 5/1; Don Peretz to parents, January 21, 1949, Peretz Papers, GPL PDF 5/3. It is likely a sad irony that the "old Arab house in Acre" was the home of people who were made refugees, although this is not mentioned directly in the sources.

26. Don Peretz to parents, February 15, 1949, Peretz Papers, GL PDF 5/5; Don Peretz to Simon Segal, June 21, 1949, Peretz Papers, GL A13/41–42.

27. Don Peretz to parents, February 15, 1949, Peretz Papers, GPL PDF 5/5; Don Peretz to Simon Segal, March 2, 1949, Peretz Papers, GPL A13/38–40. On Israeli policy toward Arab refugees trying to return, see Robinson, *Citizen Strangers*.

28. Don Peretz to his parents, September 5, 1949, Peretz Papers, GPL PDF 12/73; Morris, *Palestinian Refugee Problem*, 510.

29. Don Peretz to his mother, July 11, 1949, Peretz Papers, GPL PDF 12/63.

30. Ibid.; Don Peretz to his parents, March 20, 1949, Peretz Papers, GPL PDF 12/72; Don Peretz to his parents, August 18, 1949, Peretz Papers, GPL PDF 12/60. One villager remembered Peretz when he returned fifty years later and gave him a gift for helping her brother down from a fig tree; Veterans History Project Interview with Don Peretz, College Park Aviation Museum, August 6, 2012.

31. Peretz, "Vignettes," 237–239; Don Peretz to his parents, September 5, 1949, Peretz Papers, GPL PDF 12/73; personal correspondence between Don and Heidy Peretz, Peretz Papers. The couple divorced in 1955, with distance compounding other issues, including problems related to a tragic event referenced in vague terms. According to Ancestry.com records, Heidy was born Erika Sulamith Babette Mayer in Stolp, Germany, in 1924; immigrated to Jacksonville, Florida, via Panama in 1940; and passed away in 1989 as Heidy Maynard. Heidy and Don had no children together. Don later remarried twice. Don's third wife, Maya, re-

called that he regretted how his lack of maturity contributed to the end of his marriage with Heidy.

32. Peretz, "Vignettes," 239–240. Peretz's letters confirm and add detail to these stories, such as Peretz's meeting with the Mufti, which Peretz claimed was distorted by the newspapers *Morgen Journal* and *Maariv*. See letters to parents, February 1, 1953, and November 19, 1953, Peretz Papers, GPL PDF 7/30–35.

33. Peretz, "Vignettes," 239–240.

34. A contemporaneous assessment of Peretz's language skill comes from Hannah Arendt: "Don Peretz's Hebrew seems shaky," she wrote to Judah Magnes in September 1948. Peretz had been asked to translate Ihud material for her. The Judah L. Magnes Foundation Papers, American Jewish Archives 389; Peretz, "Vignettes," 240–241; Don Peretz, *Israel and the Palestine Arabs* (Washington, DC: The Middle East Institute, 1958).

35. Peretz, *Israel and the Palestine Arabs*, ix.

36. Peretz, *Israel and the Palestine Arabs*, 6. The "New Historians" refers to a loosely defined cohort of Israeli scholars, particularly Benny Morris, Avi Shlaim, and Ilan Pappé, who, on the basis of recently released historical archives, published books in the 1980s that challenged traditional Israeli historical views of the state's early years, the 1948 war, and Israel's role in the Palestinian refugee crisis, which included expelling civilians. The findings caused considerable scandal in Israel at the time but have since become broadly accepted within academia. See Avi Shlaim, "The Debate about 1948," *International Journal of Middle East Studies* 27, no. 3 (1995): 287–304.

37. Peretz, *Israel and the Palestine Arabs*, 4–5, 45; Adi Yafeh to Simon Siegal [sic], March 17, 1958, File: Don Peretz, Box 129, Folder 7, Record Group 347.17.12—Records of the American Jewish Committee, Alphabetical Files (GEN-12), YIVO Archives, New York; Yaakov Morris to Don Peretz, February 20, 1958, File: Don Peretz, Box 129, Folder 7, Record Group 347.17.12—Records of the American Jewish Committee, Alphabetical Files (GEN-12), YIVO Archives, New York.

38. Peretz, *Israel and the Palestine Arabs*, 45.

39. Joseph Schechtman, *The Arab Refugee Problem* (New York: Philosophical Library, 1952). On Schechtman, see Mark Mazower, *No Enchanted Palace: The End of Empire and the Ideological Origins of the United Nations* (Princeton, NJ: Princeton University Press, 2013), chapter 3; Nur Masalha, "From Propaganda to Scholarship: Dr Joseph Schechtman and the Origins of Israeli Polemics on the Palestinian Refugees," *Holy Land Studies* 2, no. 2 (2004): 188–197; Antonio Ferrara, "Eugene Kulischer, Joseph Schechtman and the Historiography of European Forced Migrations," *Journal of Contemporary History* 46, no. 4 (2011): 715–40; and books by Rafael Medoff such as *Zionism and the Arabs: An American Jewish Dilemma, 1898–1948* (Westport, CT: Praeger, 1997), 118, 151.

40. Joseph Schechtman, *European Population Transfers, 1939–1945* (New York: Oxford University Press, 1946); Medoff, *Zionism and the Arabs*, 149–151; Masalha, "From Propaganda to Scholarship," 188–197.

41. Walid Khalidi, "The Fall of Haifa," *Middle East Forum*, December 1959; also published in 1952 was Fayez Sayegh's *The Palestine Refugees* (Washington, DC: Amara, 1952), which, at sixty-one pages, could be considered a book or a booklet. It was a response to a proposal that pro-Israel American Christian leaders submitted to the UN, titled *The Arab Refugee Problem: How It Can Be Solved*. Letter from Harold E. Beckman to Milton Weill, forwarded to Simon Segal, File: Don Peretz, Box 129, Folder 7, Record Group 347.17.12—Records of the American Jewish Committee, Alphabetical Files (GEN-12), YIVO Archives, New York.

42. "Israel and the Arab Refugees: A Survey of the Problem and Its Solution," Israeli Office of Information, 1949; "Israel and the Arab Refugees," American Zionist Council, 1951; Ethel C. Phillips to John Slawson, "Meeting with Mr. Avraham Harman," November 17, 1953, American Jewish Committee Archives Online (henceforth AJCAO); Mizra Khan, "The Arab Refugees: A Study in Frustration," *Midstream: A Jewish Quarterly Review*, Spring 1956. The pseudonym "Mizra Khan" was used to write at least three pro-Israel articles in the 1950s. In June 1956, the Israeli Consulate in Los Angeles ordered three hundred reprints of the article. Netanel Lorch to Reuven Dafni, "Re: Midstream Magazine, Spring Edition," June 26, 1956, MFA 13/813, Israel State Archives.

43. Zvi Ganin, *An Uneasy Relationship: American Jewish Leadership and Israel, 1948–1957* (Syracuse, NY: Syracuse University Press, 2005), chapter 1.

44. Thomas Kolsky, *Jews against Zionism: The American Council for Judaism, 1942–1948* (Philadelphia: Temple University Press, 1990), 41; James Loeffler, *Rooted Cosmopolitans: Jews and Human Rights in the Twentieth Century* (New Haven: Yale University Press, 2018), 85–189; Natan Aridan, *Advocating for Israel: Diplomats and Lobbyists from Truman to Nixon* (Lanham, MD: Lexington Books, 2017); Ariel Feldstein, *Ben-Gurion, Zionism and American Jewry: 1948–1963* (London: Routledge, 2006); Ganin, *An Uneasy Relationship*, 154–155, 169; AJC Executive Board Meeting Minutes May 8–9, 1954, AJCAO; Ganin, *An Uneasy Relationship*, 195–196; Loeffler, *Rooted Cosmopolitans*, 173, 245. In the context of peacemaking, Blaustein discussed refugee compensation in 1954 with Egyptian official Mahmoud Riad.

45. Glenn Feldman, *Politics, Society, and the Klan in Alabama, 1915–1949* (Tuscaloosa: University of Alabama Press, 1999), 56; "Irving Engel Dead at 87," JTA, December 5, 1978.

46. On rising Christian interest in the Arab refugee issue, see Amy Weiss, "Between Cooperation and Competition: The Making of American Jewish Zionist Interfaith Alliances with Liberal and Evangelical Protestants, 1898–1979" (PhD diss., New York University, 2014); on American Jewish concerns regarding Arab propaganda, see Geoffrey P. Levin, "Arab Students, American Jewish Insecurities, and the End of Pro-Arab Politics in Mainstream America, 1952–1973," *Arab Studies Journal* 25, no. 1 (2017): 30–59; AJC Administrative Board Meeting Minutes, January 3, 1956, AJCAO. In an internal memo, Israeli officials called Rifkind a "friend" within the AJC.

47. AJC Administrative Board Meeting Minutes, June 5, 1956, AJCAO.

48. A full list is included in "In Vigilant Brotherhood: The American Jewish Committee's Relationship with Palestine and Israel," 1964, AJCAO, written by Peretz's successor George Gruen; "Christian Communities in Israel: A Fact Sheet," May 1957, AJCAO; "Arab Propaganda in the United States," April 1955, AJCAO. "American Jews and Israel Membership Information Program: AJC Workbook for Discussion Leaders," September 1958, AJC FAD-2 RG 347.7.2, YIVO.

49. "The Arab Refugee Dilemma: A Fact Sheet from The American Jewish Committee," September 10, 1956, AJCAO. Also present in MFA 8/151, Israel State Archives. A small number of Palestinians were allowed back into the country right after the war for family reunification purposes. See "Nabila El-Ahmed and Nadia Abu-Zahra, Unfulfilled Promise: Palestinian Family Reunification and the Right of Return," *Journal of Palestine Studies* 45, no. 3 (2016): 24–39. According to Peretz's close friend Philip Mattar, who knew Peretz during the last several decades of Peretz's life, Peretz felt that the Arab refugee issue and question of reparations for Middle Eastern Jews needed to be addressed simultaneously. Phone call with Philip Mattar, April 15, 2020.

50. "Memorandum on Conference with Secretary of State Dulles," August 9, 1956, AJCAO and Engel at YIVO, 43:3. Remarks by Secretary of State John Foster Dulles, August 21, 1955, *Department of State Bulletin*, vol. 33, July–September 1955, 378–380.

51. Pinhas Eliav to Yohanan Maroz, "Steps to Middle East Peace of the American Jewish Committee," October 11, 1956, Israel State Archives, MFA 151/8 (GPL Photo 222 2/8/16).

52. Ibid.

53. Esther Herlitz to Yohanan Maroz and others, September 12, 1956, Israel State Archives, MFA 151/8 (GPL Photo 231 2/8/16). A reference in Peretz's letters indicate that he and Herlitz may have met in 1947, when he and other Americans at Hebrew University had dinner with all twenty-seven students in the diplomacy school that Herlitz was then part of. Peretz taught at Dropsie contemporaneously with Noam Chomsky's father, William Chomsky, and Benjamin Netanyahu's father, Benzion Netanyahu. I have encountered no evidence that Peretz knew either William Chomsky or Benjamin Netanyahu personally. Peretz CV, Peretz PDF 4/1.

54. "Address of Irving M. Engel, the American Jewish Committee Executive Board Dinner, October 13, 1956," Israel State Archives, MFA 151/8. I am deeply grateful to Nathan Kurz for first making me aware of MFA 151/8 and sending me a PDF with part of its contents, which I was able to view in full myself shortly before the closing of the Israel State Archives' reading room in 2016; "AJC Leader Proposed Interfaith Body to Aid Arab Refugee Youth," *The American Israelite*, October 18, 1956.

55. Esther Herlitz to Yohanan Maroz and others, "The American Jewish Committee and the Arab Refugees," October 26, 1956, Israel State Archives, MFA 151/8 (GPL Photo 198). I have not yet found additional documentation in AJC archives to further verify many of the most colorful claims made within these Israeli memos, though the *National Jewish Post* provides evidence of Blaustein's role. See

Charles Roth, "AJCommittee Defers Decision on Plan for Arab Refugee Aid," *National Jewish Post*, October 19, 1956.

56. Roth, "AJCommittee Defers Decision." It is implied that Blaustein and Eban spoke in late September about Ben-Gurion's rhetoric; I have been unable to locate any sort of transcript. David Ben-Gurion to Jacob Blaustein, October 2, 1956, AJC YIVO Subject Files, Box 315, Folder 8, 55607.

57. AJC Administrative Board Meeting Minutes, June 5, 1956, AJCAO.

58. Ibid.

59. Ibid. It is more in line with Lawrence Grossman's assertion that Slawson played a key role in shifting the AJC toward Israel. In any case, characterizing the views of Slawson—who led the AJC's professional staff for a quarter century (1943–1967)—and other AJC leaders clearly requires greater nuance. See Lawrence Grossman, "Transformation through Crisis: The American Jewish Committee and the Six Day War," *American Jewish History* 86, no. 1 (1998): 27–54; Roth, "AJCommittee Defers Decision."

60. Don Peretz to John Slawson, 22 October 1956, File: Don Peretz, Box 129, Folder 7, Record Group 347.17.12—Records of the American Jewish Committee, Alphabetical Files (GEN-12), YIVO Archives, New York. Emphasis mine.

61. Ibid.

62. Ibid.

63. Irving Engel to Hans Kohn, January 7, 1957, Hans Kohn Collection, Leo Baeck Institute (LBI). Adi Gordon also references these documents, but without the broader context of the AJC refugee initiative. Hans Kohn to Irving Engel, January 8, 1957, Hans Kohn Collection, LBI. Hans Kohn to Frank Sulzberger, January 15, 1957, Hans Kohn Collection, LBI.

64. Hans Kohn to AJC, April 1957, Hans Kohn Collection, LBI. Both Brian Smollett and Adi Gordon note these letters and Kohn's resignation from the AJC over Israel issues but do not explore the full context of the Arab refugee initiative. See Brian Smollett, "The Rise and Fall of a Jewish Vision in the Life and Thought of Hans Kohn," in *Reappraisals and New Studies of the Modern Jewish Experience*, ed. Brian Smollett and Christian Wiese (Leiden: Brill, 2014), 282; Adi Gordon, *Toward Nationalism's End: An Intellectual Biography of Hans Kohn* (Waltham, MA: Brandeis University Press, 2017), 242. Hans Kohn to Louis Lempel, April 7, 1957, American Jewish Archives 157-6-4.

65. Pinhas Eliav to Yohanan Maroz and Esther Herlitz, "The AJC's Stance on Israel," October 24, 1956, Israel State Archives, MFA 151/8. An obituary for Haym appears in the *New York Times* on December 6, 1956. In his later years, Haym had risen to the position of United Jewish Appeal Director for the Bronx. His obituary appeared in Israel as his father, brother, and six sisters still lived there with their families; Haym had returned to his birth country at least twice, once for an extended period in 1933–1934 and once to visit Don in 1949. Peretz Papers, GPL PDF 12/54; Esther Herlitz to Yohanan Maroz and others, "The American Jewish Committee and the Arab Refugees," October 26, 1956, Israel State Archives, MFA 151/8 (GPL Photo 198).

66. Esther Herlitz to Yohanan Maroz and others, January 18, 1957, Israel State Archives, MFA 151; Peretz, "Vignettes," 243.

67. Peretz, "Vignettes," 244–247. Norman Thomas's papers show that the trip made him discouraged about the prospects for peace; Norman Thomas Papers, January 1958, New York Public Library. Though not apparent in most of his writings, Peretz was a longtime socialist. Peretz's wife, Maya, mentioned his enduring love of Norman Thomas; after every presidential election, when asked whom he voted for, Peretz replied, "I wrote in Norman Thomas."

68. Yaakov Morris to Don Peretz, February 20, 1958, File: Don Peretz, Box 129, Folder 7, Record Group 347.17.12—Records of the American Jewish Committee, Alphabetical Files (GEN-12), YIVO Archives, New York; also found in Peretz's papers. Benny Morris's book, which maintained that Zionist and Israeli soldiers forced some Palestinians out of their homes, launched a major debate in Israel, leading Morris to become perhaps the best known of the "New Historians" revising narratives surrounding Israel's birth. See Benny Morris, *The Birth of the Palestinian Refugee Problem, 1947–1949* (Cambridge: Cambridge University Press, 1988).

69. Adi Yafeh to Simon Siegal [*sic*], March 17, 1958, File: Don Peretz, Box 129, Folder 7, Record Group 347.17.12—Records of the American Jewish Committee, Alphabetical Files (GEN-12), YIVO Archives, New York.

70. Eliezer Whartman to George Kellman, undated, likely September or October 1957, File: Don Peretz, Box 129, Folder 7, Record Group 347.17.12—Records of the American Jewish Committee, Alphabetical Files (GEN-12), YIVO Archives, New York.

71. Peretz, "Vignettes," 247–248.

72. Lucy Dawidowicz, "The American Jew: A Zionist Analysis, Ben Halpern," *Commentary*, April 1958; Peretz was involved with this Institute for Mediterranean Affairs (IMA) proposal, as was "Peter Bergson" (former Herut MK Hillel Kook), but the leading force behind it appears to have been former Herut MK Shmuel "Samuel" Merlin, then based in America along with Bergson. The IMA proposal accepted the right of refugee return and anticipated 200,000 would move to Israel. Merlin and Kook worked to gain support for it in Israel and America, including through the AJC, but to no avail. The only book to discuss it is Joseph Agassi, *Liberal Nationalism for Israel: Towards an Israeli National Identity* (New York: Gefen, 1999), though recent work by Becky Kook has as well. See American Jewish Yearbooks, 1957–1959; "Interview with George E. Gruen," The AJC Oral History Project at the New York Public Library; Grossman, "Transformation through Crisis," 37. Ignoring Peretz, Grossman called Gruen the AJC's first Middle East staff member, which is inaccurate.

73. Esther Herlitz to Yohanan Maroz and others, "The American Jewish Committee and the Arab Refugees," October 26, 1956, Israel State Archives, MFA 151/8 (GPL Photo 198).

74. Derek Penslar, "Solidarity as an Emotion: American Jews and Israel in 1948," *Modern American History* 5, no. 1 (2022): 41–45.

75. Peretz, *Israel and the Palestine Arabs*, 45.

Chapter 2. A Yiddishist's Dissent

Epigraph 1: William Zukerman, "Israel and the Arab Refugees," *Jewish Newsletter*, September 22, 1950.
Epigraph 2: Y. Harry Levin to Abe Harman, April 11, 1951, William Zukerman file: 100, Israel State Archive, MFA 112/16.

1. In legal documents, Zukerman lists his birthplace as Brest-Litovsk (now Brest, Belarus), while family sources maintain that he was born near Bialystok (in Poland) and that his father was born in a town he called Tishkevurud (Juszkowy Grod, Poland). All these locations were in the Grodno Governate. Passport applications of William Zukerman, 1919 and 1921, accessed through Ancestry.com; George Zukerman memoir (unpublished), chapter "Willie the Zuk"; Max Zukerman, *Autobiographical Sketches* (unpublished), and material provided by relative Zalman Usishkin on December 28, 2017; Mark Mazower, *What You Did Not Tell: A Russian Past and the Journey Home* (New York: Other Books, 2017), 21; Hasia Diner, *The Jews of the United States* (Berkeley: University of California Press, 2004).

2. Max Zukerman, *Autobiographical Sketches*, 213, and material provided by relative Zalman Usishkin. According to the memoir provided to me by George Zukerman, William's son, the information about Zukerman's journey to Chicago is based on contemporaneous notes that William took on scraps of paper during the trip. George Zukerman memoir, chapter "Willie the Zuk."

3. George Zukerman memoir, chapter "Willie the Zuk." On the *Forward*'s history, see "Records of the Forward Association," Center for Jewish History, https://archives.cjh.org/repositories/7/resources/3530, accessed February 22, 2023.

4. Zeltzer was his second wife. He had married Becky Goodman in New York in 1918, but they divorced a year later after Zukerman left her for Zeltzer, whom he married only in 1925. Their sons were musicologist Joseph Kerman (1924–2014), born Joseph Zukerman, and bassoonist George Benedict "Dick" Zukerman (1927–2023), who was named after George Washington and Benedict Spinoza; George Zukerman memoir, chapter "Willie the Zuk"; Max Zukerman, *Autobiographical Sketches*, and material provided by Zalman Usishkin on December 28, 2017; author's phone interview with George Zukerman, December 21, 2017.

5. On the history of the Yiddish press, see Ayelet Brinn, "Miss Amerike: The Yiddish Press's Encounter with the United States, 1885–1924" (PhD diss., University of Pennsylvania, 2019).

6. "William Zukerman, Editor of Anti-Zionist Publication, Dies in New York," JTA, October 9, 1961; author's phone interview with George Zukerman, December 21, 2017. George Zukerman memoir, chapter "Willie the Zuk"; Max Zukerman, *Autobiographical Sketches*. On Zukerman's friendship with Emma Goldman and the Mazowers, see Mazower, *What You Did Not Tell*, 259–269. On Birobidzhan and Zukerman's public advocacy on behalf of the project, which lasted from at least 1931 to 1934, see Henry Felix Srebrnik, *Dreams of Nationhood: American Jewish Communist and the Soviet Birobidzhan Project, 1924–1951* (Brighton, MA: Academic Studies Press, 2010), 11, 29–30. A deeper analysis of Zukerman's thought will

appear in Marjorie Feld's forthcoming book on American Jewish anti-Zionism. Feld cites a 1948 letter from Zukerman to Henry Hurwitz in which he wrote that his "attitude toward pro-Sovietism and Zionism" had "changed considerably."

7. William Zukerman, "The Menace of Jewish Fascism," *The Nation*, April 25, 1934; William Zukerman, "The Palestine Boom and the Passing of the Zionist Dream," *Harper's*, May 1933; William Zukerman, "The Passing of Political Zionism," *Current History*, December 1929; William Zukerman, "The Jewish Problem: Greatest Bubble of Our Age," *Antioch Review*, Autumn 1942; William Zukerman, *The Jew in Revolt: The Modern Jew in the World Crisis* (London: Martin Secker & Warburg, 1937). Marjorie Feld notes that Zukerman wrote for the Labor Zionist *Jewish Frontier* in 1942.

8. According to historian Eric Goldstein, the circulation of the Yiddish press began to decline each year after 1920, and even more rapidly after 1931 (going down tens of thousands each year). Regarding the masthead, see *Jewish Newsletter* publications from 1948 to 1961.

9. When Zukerman announced that a new Israeli correspondent named Jacob Becht would be writing for the *Newsletter* in 1954, Israeli officials were anxious to determine his identity; Shimson Arad to Abe Harman, "Jewish Newsletter," April 22, 1954, William Zukerman file: 4, Israel State Archive, MFA 112/16. Initially all board members were Jewish but later several prominent non-Jews were added. Other names on the board included University of California provost Monroe Deutsch, Quaker educator William Hubben, and disillusioned former AJC member Herman Gray. On the AJC's view of Zukerman, see YIVO, 347.17.12, Box 10; Abe Harman to Shimson Arad, May 13, 1954, William Zukerman file: 1, Israel State Archive, MFA 112/16. Zukerman told Hertz he was one of the three largest donors. See Zukerman to Hertz, December 10, 1954, File 3 Box 1, William Zukerman Papers, YIVO. Only about a quarter of *Newsletter* revenue ($23,005) came from subscriptions in 1953–1954, whereas 70 percent came from donations, with a third of that coming from the three biggest donors. See Fiscal Statement of Friends of the Jewish Newsletter for year ending September 30, 1954, Folder 4, Box 1 of William Zukerman Papers. On circulation, see Zukerman to Lessing Rosenwald, November 12, 1954, Folder 14, Box 2, William Zukerman Papers, YIVO. Zukerman says there were only about two thousand paid subscriptions. See list of "Friends of the Jewish Newsletter, Inc." in Folder 14, Box 2, William Zukerman Papers, YIVO. A May 1957 financial summary shows that Rosenwald was by far the largest donor (40 percent of all donations) followed by Aaron Straus of Baltimore, Walter Neustadt of Oklahoma, Council member Henry Loeb of New York, John Hertz of New York, and Modie Spiegel of Chicago. See Financial Summary, Folder 6, Box 1, William Zukerman Papers, YIVO.

10. "William Zukerman, Editor of Anti-Zionist Publication, Dies in New York," JTA, October 9, 1961; Michael Kaplan and Jack Ross, "Before Mondoweiss: Jewish Anti-Nationalism in the Wake of the Holocaust," *Tikkun*, January 29, 2015. They used the term "anti-Zionist" to laud, not defame, Zukerman; *Jewish Newsletter*, December 24, 1948. "Disappointment at UN," *Jewish Newsletter*, March 11, 1949;

Jewish Newsletter, February 4, 1949; *Jewish Newsletter*, March 18, 1949; *Jewish Newsletter*, May 13, 1949. See *Jewish Newsletter*, 1948–1949; "The Editor's Chair," *National Jewish Post*, November 25, 1949.

11. *Jewish Newsletter*, June 24, 1949; *Jewish Newsletter*, July 22, 1949.

12. *Jewish Newsletter*, October 14, 1949. This is also quoted in Marc Ellis, *Toward a Jewish Theology of Liberation* (Waco, TX: Baylor University Press, 2004), 79, and Ellis is cited in Michael R. Fischbach, *Records of Dispossession: Palestinian Refugee Property and the Arab-Israeli Conflict* (New York: Columbia University Press, 2003), 74. This story should not necessarily lead one to think that the Yiddish press was more open-minded than the English Jewish press; in 1948, Zukerman heavily criticized the Yiddish press as less open and inferior to English-language papers, which he viewed as the Jewish press of the future. See "William Zukerman Folio" provided by George Zukerman.

13. B. Hoffman, "Israel Passes a Discriminatory Law," *Jewish Labor Bund Bulletin* 5, no. 15–17 (March/April 1952).

14. "Arab Refugees," *Jewish Labor Bund Bulletin* 1, no. 9 (August/September 1948). It is important to emphasize that this book involved no primary source research in Yiddish, with the exception of the material related to the Free Jewish Club. More research is needed to make definitive statements on how American Yiddishists viewed the Palestinian question after 1948. On debates on Israel/Palestine before 1948, including after the 1929 Hebron massacre, see Amelia M. Glaser, *Songs in Dark Times: Yiddish Poetry of Struggle from Scottsboro to Palestine* (Cambridge, MA: Harvard University Press, 2020). Adi Mahalel touches on debates on Israel/Palestine among American Yiddishist in Adi Mahalel, "Yiddish, Israel, and the Palestinians: Yosl Birshteyn's 'Between the Olive Trees,' " *Israel Studies Review* 30, no. 2 (Winter 2015): 71–91.

15. Dorothy M. Zellner, "What We Did: How the Jewish Communist Left Failed the Palestinian Cause," *Jewish Currents*, May 12, 2021. The article notes that one writer, A. B. Magil, dissented and expressed sympathy with the Palestinians. Zellner acknowledges that her study draws only from English-language publications. *Jewish Life*, now known as *Jewish Currents*, was published monthly in English by the Yiddish language daily *Morgen Freiheit*. "Jewish-Arab Relations," *Jewish Labor Bund Bulletin* 5, no. 13–14 (January/February 1952). The Bund's enduring international nature makes it challenging to fit into a book on American Jewish politics. The Bund's Third World Congress in 1955 called on Israel to "recognize the moral rights of the Arab refugees to repatriation and compensation." *Jewish Labor Bund 1897–1957* (New York: International Jewish Labor Bund, 1958). On the Bund's position toward Israel overall on this period, see David Slucki, *The International Jewish Labor Bund after 1945: Toward a Global History* (New Brunswick, NJ: Rutgers University Press, 2012), 210. In 1953–1954, American Bundists also harshly criticized Israel over the Qibya massacre, as did noted Yiddish writer Yankev Glatshyen in his poem "Kibiya," which Mahalel translated for *In geveb*. See Mahalel, "Yiddish, Israel, and the Palestinians," 85.

16. *Jewish Newsletter*, October 21, 1949. A microform in the Jewish Labor Committee Record at Tamiment Library has five pages in Yiddish on the Free Jewish Club, which lists Zukerman and thirteen other names as founders.

17. The Yiddish flyer is from the Jewish Labor Committee Records at Tamiment Library on the Free Jewish Club. I thank Marjorie Feld for providing an English-language version of this for me, which was translated by Ri Turner along with the booklet "A Ruf Tsu Der Yidisher Efntlekhkeyt: N. Free Jewish Club (New York)," 1950, digitized by the Yiddish Book Center (https://www.yiddishbookcenter.org/collections/yiddish-books/spb-nybc212482/a-ruf-tsu-der-yidisher-efntlekhkeyt).

18. *Jewish Newsletter*, February 11, 1950; "The Editor's Chair," *National Jewish Post*, November 25, 1949.

19. *Jewish Newsletter*, June 23, 1950; *Jewish Newsletter*, September 22, 1950; *Jewish Newsletter*, July 16, 1956. On the September 3, 1956, the newsletter ran a "special supplement" on the refugee issue. Note that this is also around the same time that the AJC perceived that the Arab refugee issue was becoming increasingly prominent in American public discourse. Correspondence between William Zukerman and Lessing Rosenwald, William Zukerman Papers, YIVO, Box 2, Folder 5. Zukerman publicly noted he was not a Council member in 1951 and never had any real role in the Council (*Council News*, March 1951, 22). Morris and Hilda Lazaron played notable roles in both groups. In later years, Rosenwald become a significant donor to the *Newsletter*. See also Jack Ross, *Rabbi Outcast: Elmer Berger and American Jewish Anti-Zionism* (Washington, DC: Potomac Books, 2011), for Zukerman's relationship with Elmer Berger. For more on the Council, see chapter 5.

20. Michael Kaplan and Jack Ross, "Before Mondoweiss: Jewish Anti-Nationalism in the Wake of the Holocaust," *Tikkun*, January 29, 2015; "Philadelphia's 'Jewish Exponent' to Celebrate Its 75th Anniversary," JTA, March 30, 1962; "About Us," *The Jewish Advocate*, https://www.thejewishadvocate.com/about-us/, accessed February 22, 2023. I looked at these two papers because they are easily accessible; it is likely that other, smaller mainstream Jewish presses also carried Zukerman's work during this period. William Zukerman, "Fighting Back," December 30, 1949; William Zukerman, "To Be or Not to Be for the ZOA?," *The Jewish Advocate*, June 14, 1951; William Zukerman, "UN Mulls Arab Refugee problem," *The Jewish Advocate*, November 16, 1950. The latter article contained little that Zionists could find controversial.

21. Harman went on to serve as Israel's consul general in New York City (1953–1955) and its third ambassador to the United States (1959–1968). He later served as the president of Hebrew University in Jerusalem (1968–1983). Harman's daughter is former Meretz Knesset member Naomi Chazan, who led the New Israel Fund and is subject to frequent criticism of the Israeli right. Don Peretz hinted that it was Harman who, criticizing his work, told him, "Mr. Peretz, there's nothing here but facts! You haven't shown what we're trying to do in this country!" Don Peretz, "Vignettes—Bits and Pieces," in *Paths to the Middle East: Ten Scholars Look Back*, ed. Donald Naff (Albany: State University of New York Press, 1993), 241;

Y. H. Levin to Abe Harman, "Re: Wm Zukerman," December 8, 1950, William Zukerman file: 162, Israel State Archive, MFA 112/16.

22. Abe Harman to Harry Levin, "Re: Wm Zukerman," December 12, 1950, William Zukerman file: 159, Israel State Archive, MFA 112/16; Y. H. Levin to A. Harman," December 29, 1950, William Zukerman file: 156, Israel State Archive, MFA 112/16; various correspondence, February–March 1951, William Zukerman file: 106–154, Israel State Archive, MFA 112/16.

23. Y. Harry Levin to Abe Harman, April 11, 1951, William Zukerman file: 100, Israel State Archive, MFA 112/16. Emphasis is mine.

24. Michael Arnon to Abe Harman, September 25, 1951, William Zukerman file: 56, Israel State Archive, MFA 112/16; Eva N. Ballo to Abe Harman, "Re Jewish Newsletter," July 23, 1951, William Zukerman file, Israel State Archive, MFA 112/16.

25. "William Zukerman and His Journalistic Work in the Last Two-Three Years," September 25, 1951, William Zukerman file, Israel State Archive, MFA 112/16; letter from National Office of the American Council for Judaism to One Hundred Select Members, September 21, 1951, in Box 90, Folder 7 of the American Council for Judaism Records at the Wisconsin Historical Society.

26. Rita Grossman to Louis Lipsky and Jerome Unger, September 27, 1951, William Zukerman file: 60, Israel State Archive, MFA 112/16.

27. Y. Levin to A. Harman, December 6, 1951, William Zukerman file: 54, Israel State Archive, MFA 112/16; Y. Levin to A. Harman, February 8, 1952, William Zukerman file: 53, Israel State Archive, MFA 112/16. Levin wrote that letter once he learned that an editor at the *Christian Science Monitor* had commissioned a piece on Israel's controversial Nationality Law (1952) after reading Zukerman's critique of it. Y. Harry Levin to A. Harman, August 27, 1952, William Zukerman file: 46, Israel State Archive, MFA 112/16; Judd Teller to Y. Harry Levin, August 27, 1952, William Zukerman file: 48, Israel State Archive, MFA 112/16.

28. A. Harman to Michael Arnon, October 3, 1951, William Zukerman file, Israel State Archive, MFA 112/16; A. Harman to Michael Arnon, October 3, 1951, "William Zukerman," Israel State Archive, MFA 112/16. Arnon worked at the embassy in Washington. It is worth noting that Harman was born in the United Kingdom himself.

29. Letter from William Zukerman to Elmer Berger, November 20, 1952, in Box 130, Folder 1 of the American Council for Judaism Records at the Wisconsin Historical Society. Of these, the Jewish World News Service was of particular importance as it brought Zukerman's work to smaller Jewish newspapers throughout the country. Zukerman's *Morning Journal* dismissal was unrelated to Israel issues and came as retaliation for his criticism of the Yiddish press in 1948. See "William Zukerman Folio" provided by George Zukerman.

30. Letter from William Zukerman to Elmer Berger, November 20, 1952, in Box 130, Folder 1 of the American Council for Judaism Records at the Wisconsin Historical Society; Arthur Lourie to Bernard G. Richards, December 8, 1952, "William Zukerman," Israel State Archive, MFA 112/16, 29.

31. Alternatively, it is possible that Israeli officials created a second file on Zukerman, though I have found no evidence to indicate this. Interestingly, Zukerman appears to have met Harman in 1954, shortly before new letters stopped being added to the file. Zukerman sometimes corresponded with Israeli officials to get a quote or see their reaction to his work. The diplomats found this annoying. Knowing how Harman felt about Zukerman, one of Harman's colleagues penciled in jokingly "Your pal!" at the top of a letter discussing "the burden of corresponding with W. Zukerman." David Marmor to Abe Harman, October 3, 1952, "William Zukerman," Israel State Archive, 29. Harry Steinberg to Jerome Unger, November 16, 1959, MFA 10–383, A.Z.C. II, Israel State Archives; William Zukerman, "Arab Refugees—a Moral Problem," *Jewish Newsletter*, December 1, 1958. The *Menorah Journal* might challenge Zukerman's claims of being the "only" such publication, given that it occasionally published lengthy pieces criticizing Israeli policies toward the Arabs, including a notable 1954 article by Henry Hurwitz in response to the Qibya massacre. See Marjorie Feld's forthcoming book on American Jewish anti-Zionism.

32. Zukerman, "Arab Refugees—a Moral Problem."

33. *Jewish Newsletter*, February 9, 1959. Correspondence between Chofshi and Peretz from the 1940s appears in Peretz's papers, in which Chofshi attempted to get Peretz to join his pacifist group. On the "New Historians," see chapter 1, note 36. Zukerman's unpublished book manuscript is located in William Zukerman Files, American Jewish Archives, Collection 326, Box 1, Folder 4.

34. Natan Aridan, *Advocating for Israel: Diplomats and Lobbyists from Truman to Nixon* (Lanham, MD: Lexington Books, 2017).

35. Louis Lipsky, *Memoir in Profile* (Philadelphia: Jewish Publication Society, 1976), 630.

36. Some would call Herlitz Israel's second female ambassador given that Golda Meir served as Israel's minister plenipotentiary to Moscow from 1948 to 1949, in effect functioning as an ambassador even though she lacked that title. The appendix of Aridan's *Advocating for Israel* offers the career background of these figures; Jonathan Beck, "Nation's 'Cultural Prowess' Hailed at Israel Prize Ceremony," *Times of Israel*, April 23, 2015; Moshe Sharett to William Zukerman, November 4, 1952, Box 130, Folder 1 of the American Council for Judaism Records at the Wisconsin Historical Society.

37. Peretz Papers, GPL Photos, 7. The anthology is William Zukerman, *Voice of Dissent: Jewish Problems, 1948–1961* (New York: Bookman Associates, 1964). The Center for Jewish History holds Kohn's bound volume of the *Jewish Newsletter*, with an inscription from July 1958: "To Dr. Hans Kohn, with profound gratitude for your interest, friendship, and guidance, which have made possible this volume—William Zukerman." Hans Kohn's name was never on the *Jewish Newsletter*'s masthead, but he served as "honorary chair" of Friends of the Jewish Newsletter, the publication's fundraising arm. In the 1970s, Peretz became a member of CONAME and Breira. On these groups, see chapters 5 and 6.

Chapter 3. An American Light unto the Jewish Nation

1. Elias N. Koussa to James Marshall, June 17, 1957, American Jewish Archives (henceforth AJA), Collection 157, Box 49, Folder 1 [92]. Gal Amir and Na'ama Ben Ze'ev, "Lawyers in Transition—Palestinian Arab Lawyers in the First Decade of the Jewish State," *Continuity and Change* 35, no. 3 (2020): 371–392. According to Sabri Jiryis, by the early 1960s, Koussa was one of only two Arab Palestinian lawyers in Israel who had remained active since before 1948, the other being Hanna Nakkrah, for whom Jiryis worked. Author's interview with Sabri Jiryis, November 22, 2016.

2. Shira Robinson, *Citizen Strangers: Palestinians and the Birth of Israel's Liberal Settler State* (Stanford, CA: Stanford University Press, 2013). Geoffrey P. Levin, "Liberal Whispers and Propaganda Fears: The American Jewish Committee and Israel's Palestinian Minority, 1948–1966," *Israel Studies Review* 33, no. 1 (2018): 81–101. Upon Louis Marshall's death, for example, the Jewish Telegraphic Agency simply referred to him as "leader of American Jewry," and even his Zionist rivals compared him to Moses. See Louis Marshall, "Leader of American Jewry, Dies in Zurich; World Jewry Mourn," JTA, September 12, 1929. Louis Marshall and Magnes had been married to sisters Florence and Bea Lowenstein, respectively.

3. Notes from the AJC Delegation's Trip to Israel, June 24, 1957, American Jewish Committee Archives Online (henceforth AJCAO).

4. On the AJC, see Naomi W. Cohen, *Not Free to Desist: The American Jewish Committee, 1906–1966* (Philadelphia: Jewish Publication Society of America, 1972), and Marianne R. Sanua, *Let Us Prove Strong: The American Jewish Committee, 1945–2006* (Waltham, MA: Brandeis University Press, 2007).

5. Cohen, *Not Free to Desist.* Also on the relationship between Central European and Eastern European Jews and their integration, see Eric Goldstein, "The Great Wave: Eastern European Jewish Immigration to the United States, 1880–1924," in *The Columbia History of Jews and Judaism in America*, ed. Marc Lee Raphael (New York: Columbia University Press, 2008), chapter 3.

6. The platform appears in Michael Meyer, *Response to Modernity: A History of the Reform Movement in Judaism* (Detroit: Wayne State University Press, 1988), 387–388.

7. On the earlier roots of this, see Naomi W. Cohen, *Encounter with Emancipation: The German Jews in the United States, 1830–1914* (Philadelphia: Jewish Publication Society, 1984).

8. "American Jews and Israel," December 17, 1953, AJCAO. Zvi Ganin, *An Uneasy Relationship: American Jewish Leadership and Israel, 1948–1957* (Syracuse, NY: Syracuse University Press, 2005), 8, 36; Charles S. Liebman, *Pressure without Sanction: The Influence of World Jewry on Israeli Policy* (Cranbury, NJ: Associated University Presses, 1977), 118–123.

9. Henry Sloane Coffin, "Perils to America in the New Jewish State," *Christianity and Crisis*, February 21, 1948. Quoted from Hertzel Fishman, *American Protestantism and a Jewish State* (Detroit: Wayne State University Press, 1973), 141; "Zi-

onists Jeopardize Status of U.S. Jews, Dorothy Thompson Tells Council for Judaism," JTA, November 2, 1949. Years later, U.S. senator Ralph Flanders, Republican of Vermont, stated that "unless Jews make concessions to the Arabs 'such a wave of anti-Semitism as the Jewish race has never faced will sweep, not only this country, but the world.' . . . Israel is becoming a 'loaded time bomb' . . . bent on 'ingathering of the Jews from all over the earth.' " "Sen. Flanders 'Warns' Jews in Violent Anti-Israel Speech in Senate," JTA, July 30, 1958.

10. Stuart Svonkin, *Jews against Prejudice: American Jews and the Fight for Civil Liberties* (New York: Columbia University Press, 1997).

11. "Meeting of Committee on Israel and AJC Policy," July 11, 1949, AJCAO. The committee was renamed the Impact of Israel Committee. "Impact of Israel Committee Meeting Minutes," March 16, 1950, AJCAO; Marc Vosk to Louis Bennett, Richard Rothschild, John Slawson, and Simon Sigel, "Palestine Poll," August 8, 1948, AJCAO. In contrast, 93 percent of Jews supported the Jewish side, and less than 1 percent supported the Arabs.

12. Liebman, *Pressure without Sanction*, 120–123; *Fortune*'s list of corporate size began in 1955, at which time Blaustein's American Oil Company (AMOCO) was ranked eleventh in terms of revenue and tenth in terms of profit. See "Fortune 500: A Database of 50 Years of FORTUNE's List of America's Largest Corporations," https://money.cnn.com/magazines/fortune/fortune500_archive/full/1955/1.html, accessed February 22, 2023.

13. Liebman, *Pressure without Sanction*, 120–123. Regarding 1967, see Lawrence Grossman, "Transformation through Crisis: The American Jewish Committee and the Six Day War," *American Jewish History* 86, no. 1 (1998): 53. On struggles between the AJC and other major American Jewish groups on the question of Zionism in the 1940s, see Melvin I. Urofsky, *We Are One! American Jewry and Israel* (Garden City, NY: Doubleday, 1978). Ganin, *An Uneasy Relationship*, 26–48; Charles S. Liebman, "Diaspora Influence on Israel: Ben-Gurion-Blaustein 'Exchange' and Its Aftermath," *Jewish Social Studies* 36. no. 3/4 (1974): 271–280.

14. Nathan Kurz uses this term to characterize the AJC and similar Western European groups. See Nathan Kurz, *Jewish Internationalism and Human Rights after the Holocaust* (Cambridge: Cambridge University Press, 2020).

15. Samuel Moyn, *The Last Utopia: Human Rights in History* (Cambridge, MA: Harvard University Press, 2010), 124; James Loeffler, " 'The Conscience of America': Human Rights, Jewish Politics, and American Foreign Policy at the United Nations San Francisco Conference, 1945," *Journal of American History* 100 (2013): 401–428; James Loeffler, "The Particularist Pursuit of American Universalism: The American Jewish Committee's 1944 'Declaration on Human Rights," *Journal of Contemporary History* 50, no. 2 (2015): 274–295.

16. Ganin, *An Uneasy Relationship*, 6, 182–220. "Report from Israel," December 1948, AJCAO. "Executive Committee Meeting Minutes," May 7–8, 1949, AJCAO. On Blaustein's relationship with Israel, see also Ariel L. Feldestein, *Ben-Gurion, Zionism, and American Jewry 1948–1963* (New York: Routledge, 2006). On

Blaustein and human rights, see James Loeffler, *Rooted Cosmopolitans: Jews and Human Rights in the Twentieth Century* (New Haven: Yale University Press, 2018).

17. Homer Bigart, "Military Checks Irk Israel Arabs: They Complain of Restriction on Movement—Concede Economic Gain," *New York Times*, May 28, 1956; Dana A. Schmidt, "Israeli Arabs' Life Held on Upswing," *New York Times*, August 13, 1953; Dana A. Schmidt, "Israeli Arabs Push Plea for New Deal," *New York Times*, August 17, 1953; "Communist Deputy Charges Atrocities against Arabs in Israel," JTA, November 15, 1951; Kathleen Teltsch, "U.N. Inquiry Asked in Israeli 'Abuses': Spokesman for Arab Refugees Charges Tel Aviv Mistreats Land's Moslem Minority," *New York Times*, November 26, 1954; "Arab Charges Denied: Israel Says Local Self-Rule Is Being Rapidly Extended," *New York Times*, July 30, 1953. Doug Rossinow, " 'The Edge of the Abyss': The Origins of the Israel Lobby, 1949–1954," *Modern American History* 1, no. 1 (2018): 30.

18. Judd L. Teller, "Israel Faces Its Arab Minority Problem: The Native within the Gates," *Commentary*, December 1951, 551–557. Prior to Teller's piece, *Commentary* also published two pieces by Hal Lehrman on the topic in 1948–1949 that were also nuanced but slightly more sympathetic to Israel.

19. Don Peretz, "The Arab Minority of Israel," *Middle East Journal* 8, no. 2 (1954): 139–154. It was the first article ever published in an American academic journal on the topic.

20. On the Suez Crisis and America's response, see Peter L. Hahn, *Caught in the Middle East: U.S. Policy toward the Arab-Israeli Conflict, 1945–1961* (Chapel Hill: University of North Carolina Press, 2004).

21. "48 Arabs Killed; Israel Penitent," *New York Times*, December 13, 1956. For an in-depth discussion of the Kafr Qasim massacre, see Shira Robinson, "Local Struggle, National Struggle: Palestinian Responses to Kafr Qasim and Its Aftermath, 1956–66," *International Journal of Middle East Studies* 35, no. 3 (2003): 393–416. See "Special Report from Israel: Israel and Her Arab Minority," December 24, 1956, AJCAO.

22. Abe Harman to Rose Halperin, November 24, 1953, and other files in "Teller Judd—Director of the Department of Journalism in the Jewish Agency, 1952–1954," Israel State Archives. Teller began working for the Jewish Agency in 1952, but still criticized Israel's nationality law. Rossinow, " 'The Edge of the Abyss,'" 23–43. AZC leading figure Jerome Unger noted that the AJC had been helpful to Israel "in terms of the incident around Kibya." See "Statement on Israel and the Near East," January 29–31, 1954, AJCAO. David A. Sawyer to Manhaim S. Shapiro, "American Council for Judaism Annual Meeting," March 29, 1954, AJCAO.

23. Don Peretz to John Slawson and Simon Segal, December 24, 1956, AJC FAD-2 RG 347.7.1, Box 52, Folder December–July 1956, YIVO. Memo on January 1957 AJC Meeting with Raymond Hare, Donald Bergus, and Maurice Rice of U.S. State Department, AJC Alphabetical Files RG 347.17.12, Box 43, File 3, YIVO. The AJC spent considerable effort aiding Middle Eastern and North African Jews. See Nathan Kurz, " 'A Sphere above the Nations?' The Rise and Fall of International Jewish Human Rights Politics, 1945–1975" (PhD diss., Yale University, 2015),

chapters 3 and 4. Letter from Simon Segal to John Slawson, "Topics for Discussion in Connection with the Proposed AJC Trip to Israel," May 1, 1957, AJCAO.

24. "American Jews and Israel," December 17, 1953, AJCAO; "Arab Propaganda in the United States," April 1955, AJCAO; Memorandum from Dr. Morris N. Kertzer to Mr. Edwin J. Lukas, "Interreligious Activities on Israel," March 9, 1956, 15–16, AJCAO; Memorandum II from S. Andhil Fineberg to Area Directors, "The Controversy over Israel," March 16, 1956, AJCAO.

25. Fayez Sayegh, *The Arab-Israeli Conflict* (New York: Arab Information Center, 1956), 53.

26. Fayez Sayegh, *Arab Property in Israeli-Controlled Territories* (New York: Arab Information Center, 1956); Timothy Gloege, *Guaranteed Pure: The Moody Bible Institute, Business, and the Making of Modern Evangelicalism* (Durham: University of North Carolina Press, 2015); Don Peretz, "Syrian Antisemitic Propaganda," *Jewish Newsletter*, February 27, 1956. Author's phone interview with Don Peretz on July 26, 2015. Peretz did not name Sayegh and Draper directly but said he had no objection to pro-Arab pieces citing his research if they did so accurately, and he clearly respected Sayegh's opinion, having said Sayegh gave "the best presentation of the Arab case that I have ever heard," after Peretz invited him to speak at Columbia. Peretz to Sayegh, November 28, 1955, Box 208, Folder 15, Fayez A. Sayegh Collection, University of Utah Marriott Library (henceforth FAS-Utah). Draper in 1956 referred to Peretz's dissertation as "the most authoritative work on the subject in English," and in 1957 said that the dissertation, then still unpublished, had "no near rival as the authoritative and scholarly work on the subjects covered." See Hal Draper, "Israel's Arab Minority: The Beginning of a Tragedy," *New International* 22, no. 2 (Summer 1956): 86–106, and Hal Draper, "Israel's Arab Minority: The Great Land Robbery," *New International* 23, no. 1 (Winter 1957): 7–30.

27. "Memorandum from S. Andhil Fineberg to CRC and Select Lists," June 21, 1956, AJCAO; "The Middle East Ferment: A Fact Sheet," April 1956, AJCAO; "Christian Communities in Israel: A Fact Sheet," May 1957, AJCAO; "Arab Propaganda in the United States," April 1955, AJCAO. "American Jews and Israel Membership Information Program: AJC Workbook for Discussion Leaders," September 1958, AJC FAD-2 RG 347.7.2, YIVO.

28. Notes from June 20, 1957, of the AJC Delegation's Trip to Israel, AJCAO; Minutes of Second Meeting of Ben-Gurion with the Delegation of the American Jewish Committee June 24, 1957, MFA/151/8, Israel State Archives (henceforth ISA). Others in the meeting included senior Israeli foreign ministry officials Yaakov Herzog and Adi Yaffe along with Martin Gang, Zacheria Shuster, future AJC president Frank Greenman, and Mrs. Greenman. Future Israeli president Yizhack Navon attended an earlier AJC-Ben-Gurion meeting. Israeli officials had a complicated relationship with Hakim. Ben-Gurion's advisor on Arab affairs, Uri Lubrani, characterized their relationship as friendly but said the government felt that his political rhetoric was inconsistent. He also stated that Hakim smuggled foreign currency into the country, and that Israeli officials wanted him to know

that they knew he was breaking the law, presumably to have some leverage over him. Author's interview with Uri Lubrani in Tel Aviv, June 15, 2016. Marshall notes on meeting at Quaker House, AJA 157-49-1. Marshall's notes show that they also met with a wide array of Israeli officials, including a number of ministers and Herut opposition figure Menachem Begin, among others.

29. Minutes of Second Meeting of Ben-Gurion with the Delegation of the American Jewish Committee June 24, 1957, MFA/151/8, ISA.

30. Notes from June 20, 1957, of the AJC Delegation's Trip to Israel, AJCAO; Minutes of Second Meeting of Ben-Gurion with the Delegation of the American Jewish Committee June 24, 1957, MFA/151/8, ISA, 8; Minutes of First Meeting of Ben-Gurion with the Delegation of the American Jewish Committee June 18, 1957, MFA/151/8, ISA, 17. In his notes on the meeting, James Marshall softened Ben-Gurion's claim, summarizing the prime minister's words as "the Mufti was with Hitler."

31. Notes from June 20, 1957, of the AJC Delegation's Trip to Israel, AJCAO; Minutes of Second Meeting of Ben-Gurion with the Delegation of the American Jewish Committee June 24, 1957, MFA/151/8.

32. "AJC President Reports in New York on His Talk with Vatican," JTA, July 12, 1957; Natan Aridan has stated that there is "no documentary evidence to support their claim." Natan Aridan, *Advocating for Israel: Diplomats and Lobbyists from Truman to Nixon* (Lanham, MD: Lexington Books, 2017), 166–167. Ben-Gurion Diary Entry for June 24, 1957, via the Ben-Gurion Digital Archive. The Hebrew word translated as "complaint" can also be translated as "objection" or "claim." Two former Israeli advisors on Arab affairs from the era said they remembered no such American Jewish role, though it should be noted that Ben-Gurion advisor Uri Lubrani was then aged ninety and Eshkol advisor Shmuel Toledano was then aged ninety-five. Author's interview with Uri Lubrani in Tel Aviv, June 15, 2016, and author's interview with Shmuel Toledano in Jerusalem, June 22, 2016; Sabri Jiryis, *The Arabs in Israel* (New York: Monthly Press Review, 1976), 35.

33. James Marshall, "The Workshop of Israel," *Menorah Journal*, April 1928. M. M. Silver, *Louis Marshall and the Rise of Jewish Ethnicity in America* (Syracuse, NY: Syracuse University Press, 2013), 518. Louis Marshall and Weizmann were reportedly more concerned with the Yishuv's precarious economic state.

34. On the complicated history of the phrase "for a people without a land, a land without a people," see Adam M. Garfinkle, "On the Origin, Meaning, Use and Abuse of a Phrase," *Middle Eastern Studies* 27, no. 4 (1991): 539–559; Marshall wrote in 1957 that he never considered himself a Zionist. James Marshall to Donald Burgus, May 23, 1957, AJA 157-6-5; James Marshall, "Home Rule in Palestine," *New Palestine*, January 1930.

35. Marshall to Magnes, September 10, 1947, AJA 157-21-9.

36. Marshall to Magnes, February 27, 1947, AJA 157-21-9; Marshall to Magnes, September 9, 1948, AJA 157-21-9; Arendt to Marshall, August 4, 1948, AJA 157-21-9; Letters to James Marshall, 1945–1947, AJA 157, Box 6, Folder 5; The Judah L. Magnes Foundation Papers, AJA 389, Box 1, Folder 2. Letter from Ernst Simon to

James Marshall, October 2, 1952, AJA 389, Box 1, Folder 2; Letter from James Marshall to Rabbi Benjamin, April 17, 1957, AJA 389, Box 1, Folder 2; *Ner* issues with Koussa's writings include October 1952, November 1952, January 1953, and many others. Hans Kohn suggested the idea of the foundation. See Hans Kohn to James Marshall, November 21, 1948, AJA 389-1-4. Others involved in the Foundation included Elliot Cohen of *Commentary*, Nelson Glueck of Hebrew Union College, Rabbi Leo Baeck, Edward Greenbaum, and Eric Warburg.

37. Glenn Fowler, "James Marshall, Lawyer, Is Dead; Ex-Member of Board of Education," *New York Times*, August 13, 1986; James Marshall Papers, Biographical Sketch, American Jewish Archives, http://collections.americanjewisharchives. org/ms/ms0157/ms0157.html.

38. James Marshall, "Israel: 1950 to 1976," AJA 157, Box 51, Folder 10.

39. Zachariah Shuster to James Marshall, September 6, 1957, AJA 157, Box 6, Folder 5.

40. James Marshall, "Memorandum for the AJC with Reference to Israeli Arabs," September 18, 1957, AJA 157, Box 49, Folder 1.

41. Ibid.

42. Ibid.

43. Ibid.

44. Ibid. "Human relations" or "intergroup relations" refers to an approach focused on diminishing societal prejudice through education, media, and intercommunal communication, differing from a human rights approach emphasizing governmental reform and legal guarantees. In their fight against antisemitism at home, human relations had become the AJC's preferred tool. See Svonkin, *Jews against Prejudice*. For more on the human rights versus human relations distinction within this context, see Levin, "Liberal Whispers."

45. Internal AJC Correspondence, AJC FAD-2 RG 347.17.12, Box 42, Folder 12, YIVO; James Marshall to Irving Engel, September 3, 1957, AJA 157-49-1. "I am glad to say that Don Peretz . . . had approved it," gave suggestions, and recommended publication, Marshall told Engel, mentioning that he had sent it to *New York Times* journalist Lester Markel; Zachariah Shuster to James Marshall, September 6, 1957, AJA 157, Box 6, Folder 5.

46. Letter from Shmuel Divon to James Marshall, GL17044/8, ISA; Comments on Marshall Memorandum, GL17044/8, ISA.

47. *Jewish Newsletter*, July 8, 1957; *Jewish Newsletter*, July 22, 1957. Quotes from the Yiddish press are based on the *Jewish Newsletter*'s translations from the June 5 issue of *Yiddisher Kempfer* and June 29 and July 2 issues of *Journal-Tog*.

48. *Jewish Newsletter*, July 22, 1957.

49. Minutes from AJC Executive Board Meeting, October 26–27, 1957, AJCAO; Review of Minutes from Administrative Board Meetings, AJC, October 1957–July 1958, AJCAO.

50. Sami Hadawi, *Israel and the Arab Minority* (New York: Arab Information Center, 1959), 40.

51. Grossman, "Transformation through Crisis," 40; Aridan, *Advocating for Israel*, 167; Loffler, *Rooted Cosmopolitans*, 245–246; Deborah E. Lipstadt, *The Eichmann Trial* (New York: Schocken Books, 2011), 32–36; "Report by Maximo Yagupsky on Recent Activities of the Israel Office," March 1962, AJC FAD-1 RG 347.7.1, Box 34, YIVO.

52. "AJC Office in Israel: Statement of Objectives, 1966," AJC FAD-1 RG 347.7.1, Box 34, YIVO; "Committee on Israel Meeting, February 5, 1962," AJCAO; "Committee on Israel Meeting, May 4, 1962," AJCAO; Letter from Maximo Yagupsky to Irving Engel, December 3, 1963, AJC FAD-1 347.7.1, Box 34, YIVO; "In Vigilant Brotherhood: The American Jewish Committee's Relationship to Palestine and Israel," 1964, AJCAO.

53. "AJC Office in Israel: Statement of Objectives, 1966," AJC FAD-1 RG 347.7.1, Box 34, YIVO; "Committee on Israel Meeting, February 5, 1962," AJCAO; "Committee on Israel Meeting, May 4, 1962," AJCAO; Letter from Maximo Yagupsky to Irving Engel, December 3, 1963, AJC FAD-1 347.7.1, Box 34, YIVO; "In Vigilant Brotherhood: The American Jewish Committee's Relationship to Palestine and Israel," 1964, AJCAO.

54. "American Jewish Group Teaches Israelis to Be Tolerant of Minority," *Trenton Times*, April 26, 1966.

55. Ibid. Yagupsky appears not to have condemned Israel's suppression of the Arab political movement al-Ard. On al-Ard, see Leena Dallasheh, "Political Mobilization of Palestinians in Israel: The al-Ard Movement," in *Displaced at Home: Ethnicity and Gender among Palestinians in Israel*, ed. Rhoda Ann Kanaaneh and Isis Nusair (Albany: State University of New York Press, 2010), 21–38. As Shira Robinson writes, "In the view of the Israeli consensus, the massacre in Kafr Qasim . . . was committed by an unusually barbaric group composed largely of uneducated Moroccan immigrants and (other) 'Arab-haters' who did not reflect the general population of citizen-soldiers or the ethos and conduct of the army," when in actuality only "a few of the accused border patrol guards were in fact Moroccan or of 'Mizrahi' background. Mainstream liberal Ashkenazi discourse in Israel has tended historically to attribute anti-Arab racism and brutality to Arab Jews, thereby deflecting attention from the participation of European Jews." See Robinson, "Local Struggle," 396, 411.

56. Svonkin, *Jews against Prejudice*; Jiryis, *The Arabs in Israel*.

57. Kurz, " 'A Sphere above the Nations?,' " chapters 3 and 4.

Chapter 4. "Such Distinctions Cannot Be Maintained"

Epigraph 1: S. Andhil Fineberg to Harry Winton, July 13, 1956, Box 143, Folder 5, AJC Gen-12, YIVO.

Epigraph 2: "Zionist and Pro-Israel Activities in the United States: A Fact Sheet from the American Jewish Committee," Box 315, Folder 1, AJC Gen-10, YIVO.

1. Richard Pearson, "Fayez Sayegh, Leader of Arab Groups in U.S., U.N., Dies in New York City," *Washington Post*, December 14, 1980; Salman Abu Sitta, *Mapping My Return: A Palestinian Memoir* (Cairo: American University of Cairo Press, 2016), 329; Keith P. Feldman, *A Shadow over Palestine: The Imperial Life of Race in America* (Minneapolis: University of Minnesota Press, 2015), 23; Fayez A. Sayegh, "Zionism: 'A Form of Racism and Racial Discrimination'—Four Statements Made at the U.N. General Assembly," https://www.ameu.org/Resources-(1)/Zionism-A-Form-of-Racism-2.aspx, accessed February 22, 2023. The date of the resolution's passage—November 10, 1975—was also Sayegh's daughter Reema's birthday. It was not odd for Palestinians like Sayegh to work as diplomats for Kuwait, as "Gulf regimes were so sensitive to Arab public opinion at the time, that they employed and utilized Palestinian scholars and diplomats. Gulf regimes also lacked a native diplomatic service, and often relied on Lebanese and Palestinian academics." See As'ad Abu Khalil, "Before Edward Said: A Tribute to Fayez Sayegh," *Al-Akhbar English*, December 9, 2014.
2. "The resolution's 72 supporters included the 19 members of the Arab League, 12 Communist states, 21 black African states . . . four Latin American countries . . . and three European states. . . . The 35 nos included five from Africa, one from Asia (Fiji), ten from Latin America, and 18 from the 'Western European and other' (U.S., Canada, Australia, New Zealand) category. Abstentions included 12 black African, eight Asian, 11 Latin American" countries, and Greece. Sidney Liskofsky, "UN Resolution on Zionism," *American Jewish Year Book* 77 (1977): 101–102. Lawrence Grossman, "Transformation through Crisis: The American Jewish Committee and the Six Day War," *American Jewish History* 86, no. 1 (1998): 53; the American Jewish Committee, Statement on the United Nations adopted by the National Executive Council on November 1, 1975, American Jewish Committee Archives Online (henceforth AJCAO); Norman G. Finkelstein, *Beyond Chutzpah: On the Misuse of Anti-Semitism and the Abuse of History* (Berkeley: University of California Press, 2005).
3. Arnold Forster and Benjamin Epstein, *The New Anti-Semitism* (New York: McGraw-Hill, 1974); Daniel J. Schroeter, " 'Islamic Anti-Semitism' in Historical Discourse," *American Historical Review* 123, no. 4 (2018): 1172–1189. See Matthew Berkman, "Coercive Consensus: Jewish Federations, Ethnic Representation, and the Roots of American Pro-Israel Politics" (PhD Diss., University of Pennsylvania, 2018). Berkman shows that NCRAC's entrance into political lobbying for Israel began around 1956 in the context of concerns about antisemitism and "Arab propaganda." Berkman also notes the AJC's shift in the 1950s.
4. "Dr. Sayegh 'Faces the Nation,' " *The Caravan*, May 2, 1957; Sam Salem, "Fayez A. Sayegh: Missionary of Arabism in America," *The Caravan*, February 19, 1959, FAS-Utah. Members of American Jewish groups called Sayegh the Arabs' "most competent speaker and propagandist" in AJC Alphabetical Files (GEN-12), Box 143, Folder 5, YIVO. Don Peretz and anti-Zionist leader Rabbi Elmer Berger made similar remarks. Don Peretz to Fayez Sayegh, November 28, 1955, Box 208, Folder 15, FAS-Utah; Elmer Berger, *Memoirs of an Anti-Zionist Jew* (Beirut: Institute

for Palestine Studies, 1978). Other superlatives on Sayegh's effectiveness came from AFME leaders and Arab American newspaper editors. See Garland Hopkins's blurb on the back cover of Fayez A. Sayegh, *Arab Unity: Hope and Fulfillment* (New York: Devin-Adair, 1958), and George S. Debs, "Hail Doctor," *The Caravan*, May 3, 1956, FAS-Utah. See testimonials in Salem, "Fayez A. Sayegh." Salem, an Arab American, is quoted in the text.

5. The AJC and ADL, two of the "Big Three" Jewish defense agencies, raised money together through the Joint Defense Appeal. See Stuart Svonkin, *Jews against Prejudice: American Jews and the Fight for Civil Liberties* (New York: Columbia University Press, 1997), 3, 23.

6. Jacob Blaustein to David Ben-Gurion, "Personal," September 30, 1956, AJC YIVO Subject Files, Box 315, Folder 8. Blaustein also raised the issue with Abba Eban and Reuven Shiloah; Jacob Blaustein to Ethel Phillips, July 12, 1956, AJC YIVO Subject Files, Box 315, Folder 8 [55593]. John Slawson, "Zionist and Pro-Israel Activities in the United States," AJC Executive Board Meeting in Chicago, October 27, 1957.

7. Hugh Wilford, "American Friends of the Middle East: The CIA, US Citizens, and the Secret Battle for American Public Opinion in the Arab-Israeli Conflict, 1947–1967," *Journal of American Studies* 51, no. 1 (2017): 93–116.

8. S. Andhil Fineberg to Harry Winton, July 13, 1956, Box 143, Folder 5, AJC Gen-12, YIVO [55435]. "Anti-Semitism by Detour" by Earl Raab—San Francisco JCRC in Harry Winton (AJC) to S. Andhil Fineberg, "The Arab Boys—Speech of Dr. Sayegh at Commonwealth Club," July 3, 1956, Box 143, Folder 5, AJC Gen-12, YIVO. On page 212, Berkman also notes the AJC's 1958 vote to table the "Fact Sheet" on Zionism; Berkman, "Coercive Consensus," 212.

9. As Rafael Medoff has noted, there was a secret reason why some of the leaders had defended WNYC: "At that moment Arab representatives—including one of those whose speeches were broadcast on WNYC—were conducting secret negotiations with several prominent American Jews about the future of Palestine; the Arabs asked their Jewish interlocutors to help insure that the WNYC official who supervised the broadcast not be fired as a result of the affair." These requests, in this author's view at least, should not be read as negating the sincerity in Wise's or Goldstein's view about anti-Zionism. See Rafael Medoff and Raymond A. Smith, *Jewish Americans and Political Participation: A Reference Handbook* (Santa Barbara, CA: ABC-CLIO, 2002), 126–127, 274–275, and Geoffrey P. Levin, "Before the New Antisemitism: Arab Critics of Zionism and American Jewish Politics, 1917–1974," *American Jewish History* 105, no. 1/2 (2021): 103–126. Audio of the 1937 event is available at the Ameen Rihani Organization's website, http://ameenrihani.org/index.php?page=multimedia. See also Hani J. Bawardi, *The Making of Arab Americans: From Syrian Nationalism to U.S. Citizenship* (Austin: University of Texas Press, 2014), 198, 333, and Stuart E. Knee, *The Concept of Zionist Dissent in the American Mind 1917–1941* (New York: Robert Speller and Sons, 1979), 221. "Wise and Silver to Answer Arabs on Station WNYC," *Jewish Post of*

Indianapolis, June 18, 1937. "Anti-Jewish Bias on WNYC Is Denied," *New York Times,* June 16, 1937.

10. *American Jewish Year Book* 48 (1946–1947): 244; Levin, "Before the New Anti-semitism," 112–113; Eliahu Epstein, "Middle Eastern Munich," *The Nation,* February 9, 1946; Aaron Berman, *Nazism, the Jews, and American Zionism, 1933–1948* (Detroit: Wayne State University Press, 1990).

11. For example, one attack against the IAAA came from the fact that Fuad Shatara, leader of the Arab National League, had spoken at a pro-Nazi German National Bund event in the 1930s. The accusation against Shatara was true—but he had died in 1942, three years before the IAAA was even created. IAAA leaders included Khalil Totah, Habib Katibah, Ismail Khalidi, Faris Malouf, and Philip Hitii. See Levin, "Before the New Antisemitism," 115. People involved in running the Arab Office included future PLO leader Ahmad Shukeiri; Cecil Hourani, a Lebanese British economist and brother of historian Albert Hourani; Ismail Khalidi, father of Palestinian historian Rashid Khalidi and later a UN official; and Anwar Nashashibi. On the Arab Office and allegations against it, see Rory Miller, "More Sinned Against Than Sinning? The Case of the Arab Office, Washington, 1945–1948," *Diplomacy and Statecraft* 15 (2004): 316, and Michael R. Fischbach, "Palestinian Offices in the United States: Microcosms of the Palestinian Experience," *Journal of Palestinian Studies* 48, no. 1 (August 2018): 104–119. On the IAAA and allegations against it, see Bawardi, *The Making of Arab Americans.* On the Non-Sectarian Anti-Nazi League, see Richard A. Hawkins, "The Internal Politics of the Non-Sectarian Anti-Nazi League to Champion Human Rights, 1933–1939," *Management & Organizational History* 5, no. 2 (2013): 251–278. The apparent first national ADL criticism of pro-Arab voices was "Organized Arab Propaganda in the United States," *The Facts: Reported Monthly by the National Fact-Finding Department of the Anti-Defamation League,* June 1946, followed by "Anti-Semitism and the Palestine Issue—Part I," *The Facts: Reported Monthly by the National Fact-Finding Department of the Anti-Defamation League,* May 1948, and "Anti-Semitism and the Palestine Issue—Part II," *The Facts: Reported Monthly by the National Fact-Finding Department of the Anti-Defamation League,* June 1948.

12. Hugh Wilford, "American Friends of the Middle East: The CIA, US Citizens, and the Secret Battle for American Public Opinion in the Arab-Israeli Conflict, 1947–1967," *Journal of American Studies* 51, no. 1 (2017): 100–103; Wilford, *America's Great Game: The CIA's Secret Arabists and the Shaping of the Modern Middle East* (New York: Basic Books, 2013), 89–116.

13. Historians debate whether it is fair to term AFME a "CIA front organization," a question that remained obscured by a lack of declassified CIA material. On one hand, the importance of CIA funding to AFME operations is hard to dispute. No one put this more bluntly than Elmer Berger, who himself was on the AFME's payroll, when he wrote in his 1978 memoir that "by now . . . everyone knows it was conceived and financed by the CIA." On the other hand, the terms could wrongly imply that AFME members were simply tools of the state. On the contrary, AFME leaders undeniably believed in what they were doing. As historian

Karine Walther put it, "The CIA's financial support clearly facilitated the AFME's ability to perpetuate their views, but it was not responsible for initiating them," while scholar Hugh Wilford, who uses the term "CIA front" as a convenient shorthand, notes that it would be best to characterize AFME as one of several "state-private networks" funded by the CIA because its leaders' goals and those of the CIA overlapped. Wilford, "American Friends," 100–103; Wilford, *America's Great Game,* 89–93; Karine Walther, "Dorothy Thompson and American Zionism," *Diplomatic History* 46, no. 2 (2022): 263–291; Berger, *Memoirs of an Anti-Zionist Jew,* 103.

14. Walther, "Dorothy Thompson," 263–291; Geoffrey P. Levin, "Arab Students, American Jewish Insecurities, and the End of Pro-Arab Politics in Mainstream America, 1952–1973," *Arab Studies Journal* 25, no. 1 (2017): 30–59.

15. Wilford, "American Friends," 100–103.

16. OAS Files, Box 229, Folder 15, FAS-Utah; Caitlin Carenen, *The Fervent Embrace: Liberal Protestants, Evangelicals, and Israel* (New York: New York University Press, 2012), 102; Amy Weiss, "Between Cooperation and Competition: The Making of American Jewish Zionist Interfaith Alliances with Liberal and Evangelical Protestants, 1898–1979" (PhD diss., New York University, 2014); Fayez Sayegh, *The Palestine Refugees* (Washington, DC: Amara, 1952).

17. Sayegh's brother Yusif noted Fayez's youthful religiosity, a background that came in handy in political rhetoric; Sayegh even quoted Jesus Christ in his critique of the Eisenhower Doctrine. Rosemary Sayigh, ed., *Yusif Sayigh: Arab Economist and Palestinian Patriot* (Oxford: Oxford University Press, 2014), 133. Fayez A. Sayegh's curriculum vitae, circa 1960, Box 239, Folder 3, FAS-Utah. Adel Beshara documents Sayegh's relationship with the Syrian Social Nationalist Party and his painful ejection from it in 1947. The break came because of Sayegh's insistence on including existential themes in party publications and his butting heads with party leader Antoun Saadeh after Saadeh's exile. According to Beshara, the young Sayegh had been considered a possible future leader of the pan-Syrian party. During this period, in the 1940s, it should be noted that Sayegh made at least one speech containing antisemitic generalizations about the "Jewish psyche." See Adel Beshara, *Fayez Sayegh—The Party Years 1938–1947* (London: Black House, 2019), and Carl C. Yonker, *The Rise and Fall of Greater Syria: A Political History of the Syrian Social Nationalist Party* (Berlin: de Gruyter, 2021).

18. Fayez A. Sayegh's curriculum vitae, circa 1960, Box 239, Folder 3, FAS-Utah; Sayigh, *Yusif Sayigh.* The Legation became upgraded to an embassy only in 1953; Fayez Sayegh to Elmer Berger, November 6, 1954, Box 239, Folder 8, FAS-Utah; Berger, *Memoirs of an Anti-Zionist Jew,* 28–30.

19. Gideon Tadmor to Michael Arnon, "Fayez Sayagh at AFME Headquarters," November 19, 1959, AFME III, ISA. Sayegh acknowledges AFME's support in the book itself. See Sayegh, *Arab Unity;* Fayez Sayegh to David Heinlein, October 11, 1959, Box 239, Folder 1, FAS-Utah; Fischbach, "Palestinian Offices," 104–118.

20. Fayez Sayegh to Garland Evans Hopkins, February 5, 1954, Box 233, Folder 2, FAS-Utah. See also Fischbach, "Palestinian Offices," 104–118. Arlene Briem, "Dr.

Sayegh's Final Lecture before His Return to the Arab World," *The Caravan*, January 8, 1959, Box 193, Folder 3, FAS-Utah.

21. "Kamil Rahim, 68, Arabs' Observer," *New York Times*, February 17, 1966; Fayez A. Sayegh's curriculum vitae, circa 1960, Box 239, Folder 3, FAS-Utah.

22. "Index—Lectures, Televisions, and Radio Appearances," FAS-Utah, Box 208, Folder 1; "Cross-Country Lecture Tour, 7–23 April 1956," FAS-Utah, Box 233, Folder 2; Flyer for March 4, 1956, debate between Fayez Sayegh and Basil Herman of Israel's UN Delegation, FAS-Utah, Box 404, Folder 4. Fayez Sayegh to Elmer Berger, January 17, 1955, FAS-Utah, Box 238, Folder 8. George Debs, "Is He Coming Back?," *The Caravan*, June 18, 1959, Box 193, Folder 3, FAS-Utah; Ali Othman to Fayez Sayegh, FAS-Utah, Box 233, Folder 2.

23. Salem, "Fayez A. Sayegh." Salem quotes Dr. John C. Campbell from the *New York Herald Tribune*. Wallace's 1957 interview of Sayegh "was his first serious encounter with a spokesman for the Palestinian cause and it left an enduring impression. . . . Wallace was so impressed and stimulated by Sayegh that he invited him home to dinner the following week, a social courtesy he seldom extended to guests on the program. The two men talked for several hours that night, first over dinner, then over coffee; or to be more accurate, Wallace listened as Sayegh elaborated on the tragic dilemma of the Middle East from a Palestinian point of view." Jason Maoz, "Mike Wallace's Fateful Encounter," *Jewish Press*, August 7, 2002; "Reflections from Mike Wallace," *Jewish Community Voice*, April 18, 2012.

24. Wilford, *America's Great Game*; Salim Yaqub, *Containing Arab Nationalism: The Eisenhower Doctrine and the Middle East* (Chapel Hill: University of North Carolina Press, 2004), 26–29.

25. Wilford, "American Friends," 93–116.

26. Wilford, *America's Great Game*, 147–177; Wilford, "American Friends," 16; AFME Press Release, December 6, 1955, ISA files on AFME, November 1955–1956, 326.

27. Mitchell G. Bard, "Opinion Toward the Sinai Crisis," Jewish Virtual Library, accessed October 6, 2016, http://www.jewishvirtuallibrary.org/jsource/US-Israel/po1956.html.

28. Wilford, *America's Great Game*, 185; Wilford, "American Friends," 105. Levin, "Arab Students."

29. "Arab Propaganda in the United States," AJC Fact-Finding Division, April 1955, AJCAO.

30. "Background Memorandum for Executive Board Meeting: The Middle East Crisis and Its Impact on American Jews," AJC, May 7–8, 1955, AJCAO. "The Controversy over Israel—Memorandum II: From S. Andhil Fineberg to Area Directors," AJC Community Affairs Department, March 16, 1956, AJCAO. "Hopkins Charged with Injecting Anti-Semitism in Middle East Issue," JTA, October 12, 1955.

31. On AJCongress's response, see American Jewish Congress, *The Arab Campaign against American Jews* (New York: International Press, 1956); Irving Spiegel, "Dulles Accused by Jewish Group: American Congress Charges Apathy to Arab Campaign of Discrimination," *New York Times*, April 15, 1956.

32. "The Middle East Ferment: A Fact Sheet," April 1956, AJCAO; "Fact Sheet on the Middle East (title to be determined)," undated, AJCAO.

33. Arnold Forster and Benjamin R. Epstein, *Cross-Currents* (Garden City, NY: Doubleday, 1956), 305–309. The book was published on March 14, 1956; "Dr. Sayegh Mentioned in Interview with Authors of 'Cross-Currents,' " March 14, 1956, Box 60, Folder 1, FAS-Utah; Basil Herman to H. Y. Levin, December 21, 1955, ISA files on AFME, November 1955–1956, 309. Forster opposed starting any campaign before *Cross-Currents* was published, out of concern that it would diminish book sales.

34. According to the 1951 *American Jewish Yearbook*, Smith's publication had a circulation of twenty thousand, a number roughly on par with AJC membership. Smith's obituary called him "proud of being a purveyor of antisemitism and other forms of religious and racial bigotry." See Albin Krebs, "Gerald L. K. Smith Dead; Anti-Communist Crusader," *New York Times*, April 16, 1976. Freedman's anti-Jewish speeches are sometimes available on YouTube, posted by his contemporary supporters, but are sometimes removed because of their content; Svonkin, *Jews against Prejudice*, 9–10. In the late 1950s, antisemitism in America by rightwing fringe elements became even more threatening because of a series of bombing attempts at Jewish communal buildings, mostly in the South. Some bombs went off, and though no Jews died, the events did instill fear. See Clive Webb, "Counterblast: How the Atlanta Temple Bombing Strengthened the Civil Rights Cause," *Southern Spaces*, June 22, 2009.

35. Forster and Epstein, *Cross-Currents*, 301–305.

36. Ibid., 311, 322.

37. Ibid., 328.

38. "Jewish Congress Urges U.S. to Demand Recall of Syrian Ambassador," JTA, July 12, 1956. The antisemitic publication *Common Sense*, for example, reprinted an article that Sayegh had written for the publication *American Mercury*. Sayegh wrote a letter of protest to the *Mercury* editor; Fayez Sayegh to William Lavarre, March 12, 1958, Box 285, Folder 7, FAS-Utah. *Tension, Terror and Blood in the Holy Land*, distributed by the Syrian Consulate General, and *Zionist Espionage in Egypt*, circulated by Egyptian officials, are two that contain antisemitic content.

39. "Arab Information Center, New York: Resume of Report of Survey, 1955," Box 233, Folder 2, FAS-Utah; Don Peretz to Simon Segal, "Interview with Dr. Fayez Sayegh Concerning Arab Anti-Semitism in U.S.," March 22, 1956, AJC Alphabetical Files (GEN-12), Box 143, Folder 5, YIVO.

40. *Jewish Newsletter*, June 13, 1955; William Zukerman wrote to Morris Lazaron that "D.P." was "Mr. Don Peretz, a promising young man who has made a special study of the Arab refugee issue." William Zukerman to Morris Lazaron, June 17, 1955, AJA 71, Box 12, Folder 2.

41. "Preliminary Report on Neo-Fascist and Hate Groups," U.S. House Committee on Un-American Activities, December 17, 1954, http://debs.indstate.edu/u588n4_1954.pdf.

42. *Jewish Newsletter*, June 13, 1955. Other instances of Arab interactions with antisemitic groups, beginning in the 1930s, are discussed in Levin, "Before the New Antisemitism."

43. Fayez Sayegh to Kamil Abdul Rabim, November 15, 1955, FAS-Utah; "From Within," *The Caravan*, September 24, 1959, Box 193, Folder 3, FAS-Utah; "Arab Information Center, New York: Resume of Report of Survey, 1955," Box 233, Folder 2, FAS-Utah.

44. Garland Hopkins to Morris Lazaron, June 29, 1955, AJA-13-3; Daniel Rickenbacher, "Arab States, Arab Interest Groups and Anti-Zionist Movements in Western Europe and the US" (PhD diss., University of Zurich, 2017), 315.

45. Don Peretz to Simon Segal, "Interview with Dr. Fayez Sayegh Concerning Arab Anti-Semitism in U.S.," March 22, 1956, AJC Alphabetical Files (GEN-12), Box 143, Folder 5, YIVO.

46. Transcript of April 27, 1956, interview of Fayez Sayegh on *Tex and Jinx* reproduced by *The Caravan*, AJC Alphabetical Files (GEN-12), Box 143, Folder 5, YIVO; Fayez A. Sayegh to Ambassador Kamil Abdul Rahim, "Interoffice Memorandum," June 6, 1956, Box 60, Folder 1, FAS-Utah. Bill Debs, "Anti-Defamation League Defames Arabs," *The Caravan*, May 3, 1956, Box 193, Folder 1, FAS-Utah; Salem, "Fayez A. Sayegh." Salem claimed that Sayegh's response made "New York City's Zionists . . . shudder."

47. Transcript of April 27, 1956, interview of Fayez Sayegh on *Tex and Jinx* reproduced by *The Caravan*, AJC Alphabetical Files (GEN-12), Box 143, Folder 5, YIVO.

48. Fayez A. Sayegh to Ambassador Kamil Abdul Rahim, "Interoffice Memorandum," June 8, 1956, Box 60, Folder 1, FAS-Utah. I am near certain, on the basis of correspondence found in Sayegh's papers and in AJC files, that the unnamed messenger from the AJC was Don Peretz, who had invited Sayegh to speak at Columbia in 1955 and had a cordial relationship with him. Don Peretz to "Fayez," November 28, 1955, Box 208, Folder 15, FAS-Utah.

49. Samuel Halperin, *The Political World of American Zionism* (Detroit: Wayne State University Press, 1961), 113–153; for an example of the ADL's tactics during this era, see Forster and Epstein, *Cross-Currents*.

50. Svonkin, *Jews against Prejudice*, 7; "Community Program for Dealing with the Domestic Impact of the Middle East Crisis," April 1956, AJCAO.

51. "Minutes of Meeting with Dr. Fayez Sayegh at Delmonico Hotel, Tuesday, June 26, 1956," AJC Alphabetical Files (GEN-12), Box 143, Folder 5, YIVO. The Delmonico is now the Trump Park Avenue.

52. S. Andhil Fineberg to Allie Bernheim, May 2, 1956, AJC YIVO Subject Files, Box 315, Folder 8 [55494]; Ethel Phillips to Jacob Blaustein, July 3, 1956, AJC YIVO Subject Files, Box 315, Folder 8; Jacob Blaustein to Ethel Phillips, July 12, 1956, AJC YIVO Subject Files, Box 315, Folder 8; G. Snyder, secretary, to John Slawson, August 2, 1956, AJC YIVO Subject Files, Box 315, Folder 8.

53. Jacob Blaustein to David Ben-Gurion, "Personal," September 30, 1956, AJC YIVO Subject Files, Box 315, Folder 8. "Lists of Richest Men Are Many and Varied," *New York Times*, October 28, 1957.

54. Jacob Blaustein to David Ben-Gurion, "Personal," September 30, 1956, AJC YIVO Subject Files, Box 315, Folder 8. Ben-Gurion did reply to Blaustein, but not to his letter, only to the complaints forwarded orally by Eban. Letters between Blaustein and Ben-Gurion crossed paths in the mail, and the AJC felt that the response provided by Ben-Gurion was insufficient. In December, the AJC requested that Blaustein ask again; Ethel Phillips to Jacob Blaustein, December 6, 1956, AJC YIVO Subject Files, Box 315, Folder 8; David Ben-Gurion to Jacob Blaustein, October 2, 1956, AJC YIVO Subject Files, Box 315, Folder 8. Geoffrey P. Levin, "Liberal Whispers and Propaganda Fears: The American Jewish Committee and Israel's Palestinian Minority, 1948–1966," *Israel Studies Review* 33, no. 1 (2018): 81–101.

55. Jonathan Marc Gribetz, "The PLO's Rabbi: Palestinian Nationalism and Reform Judaism," *Jewish Quarterly Review* 107, no. 1 (2017): 90–112; Judge Charles Breitel, "Report to the Administrative Board," March 4, 1958, Box 315, Folder 1, AJC Gen-10, YIVO; "Background Memorandum for Executive Board Meeting—Zionist and Pro-Israel Activities in the United States: Their Implications for American Jews," October 27, 1957, AJC FAD-1 347.7.1, Box 51, Folder December–October 1957, YIVO. AJC Administrative Board Meeting Minutes, March 2, 1958, AJCAO.

56. Judge Charles Breitel, "Report to the Administrative Board," March 4, 1958, Box 315, Folder 1, AJC Gen-10, YIVO; "Background Memorandum for Executive Board Meeting—Zionist and Pro-Israel Activities in the United States: Their Implications for American Jews," October 27, 1957, AJC FAD-1 347.7.1, Box 51, Folder October–December 1957, YIVO; AJC Administrative Board Meeting Minutes, March 2, 1958, AJCAO; AJC Administrative Board Meeting Minutes, December 3, 1957, AJCAO. Also noted in Berkman, "Coercive Consensus," 212.

57. Svonkin, *Jews against Prejudice*, 152. Fineberg won the award in 1950. Other writers who won the anti-racism, pro-diversity book award during that decade included Dr. Martin Luther King Jr. and Langston Hughes; Anisfield-Wolf Book Awards, https://www.anisfield-wolf.org/winners/?sort=ASC.

58. Drew Himmelstein, "Earl Raab, Iconic Figure in Jewish Community, Dies at 96," *Jewish News of Northern California*, October 30, 2015; "Anti-Semitism by Detour" by Earl Raab—San Francisco JCRC in Harry Winton (AJC) to S. Andhil Fineberg, "The Arab Boys—Speech of Dr. Sayegh at Commonwealth Club," July 3, 1956, Box 143, Folder 5, AJC Gen-12, YIVO. Salem, "Fayez A. Sayegh."

59. "Anti-Semitism by Detour" by Earl Raab—San Francisco JCRC in Harry Winton (AJC) to S. Andhil Fineberg, "The Arab Boys—Speech of Dr. Sayegh at Commonwealth Club," July 3, 1956, Box 143, Folder 5, AJC Gen-12, YIVO [55435]. Underlined in the original.

60. S. Andhil Fineberg to Harry Winton, July 13, 1956, Box 143, Folder 5, AJC Gen-12, YIVO [55435]; Isaiah Terman (AJC) to Dick Abel (ADL) and S. Andhil Fienberg, July 5, 1956, Box 143, Folder 5, AJC Gen-12.

61. S. Andhil Fineberg to John Slawson, "Proposed Trip to Israel," May 27, 1957, Folder 1a, Box 51, AJC FAD-1, YIVO. Doug Rossinow, " 'The Edge of the Abyss': The Origins of the Israel Lobby, 1949–1954," *Modern American History* 1, no. 1

(2018): 23–43. See also John Slawson's October 1957 AJC Executive Board Speech on the AJC's resistance to such efforts, which Rossinow's article implies did not exist. "Fayez Sayegh," AJC Alphabetical Files (GEN-12), Box 143, Folder 5, YIVO.

62. According to Fineberg, the committee was to be run by a twenty-seven-year-old former refugee from Nazi Germany, Rabbi Henry Siegman; over six decades later, however, Siegman denies hearing about such a committee, though he was employed by the AZC to work on university-related issues, which led to him founding American Association for Middle East Studies. Phone interview with Henry Siegman, November 8, 2022; see also Zachary Lockman, *Field Notes: The Making of Middle East Studies in the United States* (Stanford, CA: Stanford University Press, 2015). Andhil Fineberg to Samuel Lubin, December 23, 1957, Box 51, Folder 4, AJC FAD-1, YIVO; "Fayez Sayegh," AJC Alphabetical Files (GEN-12), Box 143, Folder 5, YIVO; Salem, "Fayez A. Sayegh"; Levin, "Arab Students," 42.

63. Richard Maass to Ethel Phillips, February 2, 1958, Box 315, AJC Gen-10, YIVO.

64. Breitel, "Report to the Administrative Board." According to Esther Herlitz (page 72), Breitel was also the person who slowed the passage of the 1956 refugee initiative in committee.

65. Ibid.; emphasis his. Richard Maass to Ethel Phillips, February 2, 1958, Box 315, AJC Gen-10, YIVO.

66. AJC Administrative Board Meeting Minutes, March 4, 1958, AJCAO.

67. Pinhas Eliav to Yohanan Maroz, "Steps to Middle East Peace of the American Jewish Committee," October 11, 1956, Israel State Archives, MFA 151/8.

68. S. Andhil Fineberg to Area Directors, January 2, 1958, "Third Memorandum on Israel's Tenth Anniversary Celebration," AJCAO; S. Andhil Fineberg to Norman Stack, January 2, 1958, "In Reply to Your Memo on AJC's Participation in Israel's Tenth Anniversary Celebration," AJCAO.

69. Levin, "Before the New Antisemitism."

70. Michelle Mart, *Eye on Israel: How America Came to View Israel as an Ally* (Albany: State University of New York Press, 2006), ix, 57; Amy Kaplan, *Our American Israel: The Story of an Entangled Alliance* (Cambridge, MA: Harvard University Press, 2018), 59–60.

71. Yaqub, *Containing Arab Nationalism*, 237–238; Wilford, "American Friends."

72. "President Nasser Receives Dr. Sayegh," *The Caravan*, June 4, 1959, Box 193, Folder 3, FAS-Utah; "Statement by Dr. Fayez A. Sayegh, President, Palestine Arab Congress: Beirut, July 17, 1959," *The Caravan*, August 13, 1959, Box 193, Folder 3, FAS-Utah; "Photographs: End of First Arab League Period, Decorated by the Lebanese Government, 1958–1960," Box 213, Folder 7, FAS-Utah; Nameeda Kantawy, "Warm Welcome in Lebanon for Dr. Fayez A. Sayegh," *The Caravan*, April 30, 1959, Box 193, Folder 3, FAS-Utah. Debs, "Is He Coming Back?" (see note 22 above); "A Letter from Doctor Sayegh," *The Caravan*, September 24, 1959, Box 193, Folder 3, FAS-Utah; Correspondence with AFME, Box 239, Folder 2, FAS-Utah. "Protest Removal of Dr. Sayegh," *The Caravan*, July 2, 1959, Box 193, Folder 3, FAS-Utah. "From Within," *The Caravan*, September 24, 1959, Box 193, Folder 3, FAS-Utah.

73. Rickenbacher, "Arab States," 318–319; S. Andhil Finberg to the Executive Director of the JCRC of Minneapolis, Jerome Unger, and Isaiah Kenen, "Fayez Sayegh," AJC Alphabetical Files (GEN-12), Box 143, Folder 5, YIVO.

74. The Student Nonviolent Coordinating Committee renounced nonviolence in the mid-1960s and switched its name to the Student National Coordinating Committee. Pamela Pennock, *The Rise of the Arab American Left: Activists, Allies, and Their Fight against Imperialism and Racism, 1960s–1980s* (Chapel Hill: University of North Carolina Press, 2017), 85, 254; Stokely Carmichael and Ekwueme Michael Thelwell, *Ready for Revolution: The Life and Struggles of Stokely Carmichael (Kwame Ture)* (New York: Scribner, 2003), 558–561.

75. "Anti-Semitic Attack in Organ of Extremist Negro Organization Evokes Jewish Protests," JTA, August 16, 1967. As Melani McAlister notes, many have tended to entirely conflate "black anti-Semitism" with Black support for Palestine: "While it is clear that the two issues—domestic relationships, on the one hand, and representations of Israel and the Arab Middle East, on the other—are related, too often the assumption has been that African American views of the Middle East must reflect black-Jewish relations in the United States and must be, to the degree that these views are critical of Israel or express affiliation with Arabs, an expression of black anti-Semitism." See Melani McAlister, *Epic Encounters: Culture, Media, and U.S. Interest in the Middle East since 1945* (Oakland: University of California Press, 2005), 112–114.

76. "Anti-Semitic Attack"; Pennock, *Rise of the Arab American Left*, 85, 254.

77. "Anti-Semitic Attack"; Pennock, *Rise of the Arab American Left*, 85, 254; McAlister, *Epic Encounters*, 112–114.

78. Michael R. Fischbach, *Black Power and Palestine* (Stanford, CA: Stanford University Press, 2018), 39. SNCC later acknowledged that sources for the article had come from material obtained from Arab embassies; the ADL identified both Sayegh's pamphlet and a piece by Izzat Tannous of the PLO's New York office as SNCC's sources.

79. Grossman, "Transformation through Crisis"; Matthew Frye Jacobson, *Roots Too: White Ethnic Revival in Post–Civil Rights America* (Cambridge, MA: Harvard University Press, 2006).

80. Feldman, *A Shadow over Palestine*, 23; Gribetz, "The PLO's Rabbi," 109. Scholars have only in the last decade begun to acknowledge Sayegh's profound role in shaping discourse about Palestine. Lori Allen states that "Fayez Sayegh had pinpointed the powerful role of colonial knowledge in maintaining colonial power over Palestine and Palestinians well before Edward Said's interventions in *Orientalism*, and well before postcolonial theory made the interrogation of representation and discourse a typical feature of critique." See Lori Allen, "Subaltern Critique and the History of Palestine," in *A Time for Critique*, ed. Didier Fassin and Bernard E. Harcourt (New York: Columbia University Press, 2019), 157. Nina Fisher claims that "Sayegh was almost singlehandedly responsible for introducing the apartheid analogy at the United Nations." See Nina Fischer, "Palestinian

Non-violent Resistance and the Apartheid Analogy," *Interventions* 23, no. 8 (2021): 1124–1139,

81. Sayegh did, however, speak at the 1968 OAS conference along with keynote speaker Stokely Carmichael, former SNCC chair.

82. Gil Troy, *Moynihan's Moment: America's Fight against Zionism as Racism* (Oxford: Oxford University Press, 2012); *Saturday Night Live* transcript, November 15, 1975: "Weekend Update with Chevy Chase." Chase "reported" to viewers that "the United Nations General Assembly passed a resolution equating Zionism with racism. Black entertainer Sammy Davis, Jr., a convert to Judaism, was quoted as saying: What a breakthrough! Now, finally, I can hate myself!" Available at SNL Transcripts Tonight, https://snltranscripts.jt.org/75/75eupdate.phtml.

83. "A Letter from an American Rabbi to an Arab Ambassador," *New York Times*, November 23, 1975, advertisement on page 205. According to Berger's friend, Berger and Sayegh drafted the ad together and it had originally been titled "Zionism Is Racism." Interview with former Council and AJAZ staff member Professor Norton Mezvinsky in New York, August 12, 2016.

Chapter 5. Anti-Zionists for Israel

Epigraph 1: Avraham Harman to the Israeli Foreign Ministry's American Department in Jerusalem, copy to R. Shiloah and H. Levine in Washington, January 25, 1954, "Lazaron, Rabbi Morris," Israel State Archive (henceforth ISA), MFA 109/37 [36].

Epigraph 2: Elmer Berger to Fayez Sayegh, March 13, 1952, Box 293, Folder 5, Fayez A. Sayegh Collection, University of Utah Marriott Library (henceforth FAS-Utah).

1. Albin Krebs, "U.S. Jews Split on Mideast War; Some See Response in Nation as 'Hysteria,' " *New York Times*, July 16, 1967; Elmer Berger, *Memoirs of an Anti-Zionist Jew* (Beirut: Institute for Palestine Studies, 1978), 108–130; see speech and letters from Council president Richard Korn in Box 6, Folder 2 of Collection 17 at the American Jewish Archives; Marcia Friedman, "Council for Judaism Lives, Reincarnation Letter Errs," *Jewish Post and Opinion of Indianapolis*, January 28, 1977. A critic of Breira termed it a "reincarnation" of the Council. As of 2023, the Council still exists, maintaining a website and an e-newsletter, though it appears to have few active members.

2. This basic misunderstanding about the organization's later decades has been somewhat corrected by two recent works, but there remains no scholarly history of the Council after 1948. Jonathan Marc Gribetz, "The PLO's Rabbi: Palestinian Nationalism and Reform Judaism," *Jewish Quarterly Review* 107, no. 1 (2017): 90–112, explores Berger's impact on PLO discourse; Jack Ross, *Rabbi Outcast: Elmer Berger and American Jewish Anti-Zionism* (Washington, DC: Potomac Books, 2011), a thorough though nonacademic biography, depicts Berger as a tragic hero. Thomas Kolsky, *Jews against Zionism: The American Council for Judaism, 1942–1948*

(Philadelphia: Temple University Press, 1990). Anthologies include Adam Shatz, *Prophets Outcast: A Century of Dissident Jewish Writing about Zionism and Israel* (New York: Nation Books, 2004); Judith Butler, *Parting Ways: Jewishness and the Critique of Zionism* (New York: Columbia University Press, 2013). Overviews of American Jewish history and Reform Judaism neglect or are dismissive of the post-1948 Council; see Michael Meyer, *Response to Modernity: A History of the Reform Movement in Judaism* (Detroit: Wayne State University Press, 1988); Hasia Diner, *The Jews of the United States, 1654 to 2000* (Berkeley: University of California Press, 2004); Jonathan Sarna, *American Judaism: A History* (New Haven: Yale University Press, 2019); "Organizations: Who Is a Jew?," *Time*, May 19, 1961.

3. Gribetz, "The PLO's Rabbi," 97; Meyer, *Response to Modernity*, 244–295, 326–334, 387–388; Kolsky, *Jews against Zionism*, 24–34, 42.

4. Kolsky, *Jews against Zionism*, 42, 46–62. Council headquarters later moved to New York City.

5. Ibid., 59–60, 66.

6. *American Jewish Year Book* 48 (1946–1947): 244. According to the Roper poll, 9.4 percent were undecided. "The vast majority of the Council membership was concentrated far away from the East Coast." Kolsky, *Jews against Zionism*, 82–86. On resignation from the Council, see the unpublished work by Jason Lustig, "Resigning to Change: The Foundation and Transformation of the American Council for Judaism" (MA thesis, Brandeis University, 2009). The thesis focuses mostly on the 1940s.

7. Elmer Berger, *The Jewish Dilemma* (New York: Devin-Adair, 1945), 3–7, 29; Elmer Berger, *A Partisan History of Judaism* (New York: Devin-Adair, 1951), 131–133. Both Devin-Adair and Henry Regnery, which published Alfred Lilienthal's book, were known as conservative publishing outfits. Devin-Adair also published Fayez Sayegh's 1958 book.

8. Berger, *A Partisan History of Judaism*, 131–133.

9. Ibid., 136–140; Alfred H. Lilienthal, *What Price Israel* (Chicago: Henry Regnery, 1953). Lilienthal served as counsel to the Council's Washington chapter; he had no role in national Council leadership, though he had become well-known for his role in espousing anti-Zionist views owing to a piece that he wrote for *Reader's Digest* in 1949. One of America's most important pro-Palestine Arab American activists, Abdeen Jabara, cited *What Price Israel* as waking him up to critiques of Zionism. Email from Abdeen Jabara to author, September 20, 2018.

10. Rafael Medoff, *Zionism and the Arabs: An American Jewish Dilemma, 1898–1948* (Westport, CT: Praeger, 1997); Elmer Berger to I. Edward Tonkon, June 16, 1948, American Council for Judaism Records at the Wisconsin Historical Society (henceforth Council-Wisc); Mark Glickman, "One Voice against Many: A Biographical Study of Elmer Berger, 1948–1968" (rabbinical diss., Hebrew Union College, 1990), 91. "Religious Bodies Confer on Refugee Appeal by Council," *Council News*, June 1949. For a fuller account of the Council's 1949 refugee letters, see folder "Arab Refugee Problem—1949, 1951," Box 24, Folder 11, Council-Wisc. See *Council News* issues from the era. After initially criticizing Rosenwald's

letter in the harshest of terms, the Synagogue Council for America soon felt obligated to issue its own sympathetic letter of support for the refugees; Elmer Berger to Sidney Wallach, March 3, 1949, Box 24, Folder 11, Council-Wisc; Thomas McMaron to Lessing Rosenwald, March 22, 1949, Box 24, Folder 11, Council-Wisc; Elmer Berger to Kim Roosevelt, March 25, 1949, Box 24, Folder 11, Council-Wisc; Elmer Berger to Forrest L. Knapp, March 25, 1949, Box 24, Folder 11, Council-Wisc.

11. Kolsky, *Jews against Zionism*, 138–139; Hugh Wilford, "American Friends of the Middle East: The CIA, US Citizens, and the Secret Battle for American Public Opinion in the Arab-Israeli Conflict, 1947–1967," *Journal of American Studies* 51, no. 1 (2017): 93–116; Hugh Wilford, *America's Great Game: The CIA's Secret Arabists and the Shaping of the Modern Middle East* (New York: Basic Books, 2013), 87–93. Kim Roosevelt, a grandson of President Theodore Roosevelt, is best known for his role in the CIA-backed coup against Iranian prime minister Mohammad Mosaddegh. Lazaron does not appear to have been on the CIA's payroll, but his 1953 trip to the Middle East was sponsored by AFME. Caitlin Carenen, *The Fervent Embrace: Liberal Protestants, Evangelicals, and Israel* (New York: New York University Press, 2012), 102; Elmer Berger to Fayez Sayegh, March 13, 1952, Box 293, Folder 5, FAS-Utah; Fayez Sayegh to Elmer Berger, March 14, 1952, Box 293, Folder 5, FAS-Utah.

12. Berger, *Memoirs of an Anti-Zionist Jew*, 28–30. Interview with former Council and AJAZ staff member Professor Norton Mezvinsky in New York, August 12, 2016. An emerging personal friendship is evident in their correspondence from the 1950s. Henry Hurwitz to Fayez Sayegh, December 2, 1954, Box 239, Folder 8, FAS-Utah. It was ultimately not published because Sayegh wanted it printed in full form, whereas *Menorah Journal* editor Henry Hurwitz, an idiosyncratic editor and growing critic of Israel, wanted to publish it serialized; Elmer Berger to Fayez Sayegh, October 15, 1954, Box 239, Folder 8, FAS-Utah.

13. Berger, *Memoirs of an Anti-Zionist Jew*, 28–30; Fayez Sayegh to Elmer Berger, November 6, 1954, Box 239, Folder 8, FAS-Utah; Berger, *Memoirs of an Anti-Zionist Jew*, 28–30.

14. Wilford, *America's Great Game*, 184–185; Glickman, "One Voice," 112. Not all AFME funding came from the CIA. Most did, though some came from oil companies and individual donors; Elmer Berger, *Who Knows Better Must Say So!* (New York: American Council for Judaism, 1955), 43–46. In letter, Berger in Damascus to Rosenwald and Coleman, May 14, 1955. Ihud member Ernst Simon discussed Berger's Middle East trip in a December 16, 1955, *Haaretz* article. Simon, a dovish figure who had met with Berger, harshly criticized the Council director. A. E. Simon, "Anti-Zionism Jeopardizes Peace," ISA MFA 8246/1 [ISA LA ACJ1 (25)].

15. Berger, *Who Knows Better*, 43–46; Glickman, "One Voice," 113–117. Glickman's unpublished 1990 study involved archival work and interviews with Berger, then in his early eighties.

16. "Council for Judaism Attacks Rabbis for Ignoring 'Plight of Arabs,'" JTA, May 11, 1953.

17. Morris S. Lazaron, *Olive Trees in Storm* (Washington, DC: American Friends of the Middle East, 1955), 44, 81–90, 207; Alfred Lilienthal, *There Goes the Middle East* (New York: Devin-Adair, 1957); Garland Evans Hopkins to Alfred Lilienthal, March 2, 1954, "Alfred Lilienthal," ISA MFA 3/110. Hopkins felt Lilienthal was being ungrateful for publicly criticizing AFME and not acknowledging the full amount (over $2,500 in cash plus bulk book purchases) that the group gave him.

18. Wilford, *America's Great Game*, 184–185; Douglas Little, *American Orientalism: The United States and the Middle East since 1945* (Chapel Hill: University of North Carolina Press, 2002), 80–87.

19. Proposal, Lessing J. Rosenwald to Harry S. Truman, December 4, 1945. Truman Papers, President's Secretary's Files, Palestine-1945–1947, Harry S. Truman Library and Museum files online. "Council for Judaism Opens Three-Day Parley Today; Rosenwald Attacks Zionist Fund Raising," JTA, April 12, 1951.

20. Reverend Edward Elson even baptized Eisenhower in 1953. According to Wilford, Elson shared his antipathy toward Zionism with his congregants and wrote to Eisenhower and Dulles on the topic, telling Eisenhower to resist "minority" pressure to pander to Israel. See Wilford, *America's Great Game*, 179–180, and Wolfgang Saxon, "Edward L. R. Elson Dies at 86; Influential Cleric in Washington," *New York Times*, August 28, 1993; "Second Annual Report," AFME, 1952–1953, Berman Jewish Policy Archive; Isaac Alteras, *Eisenhower and Israel: U.S.-Israeli Relations, 1953–1960* (Gainesville: University Press of Florida, 1993), 35. The quote also indicates Israel's lack of knowledge about AFME-CIA ties. David Tal, *The Making of an Alliance: The Origins and Development of the US-Israel Relationship* (Cambridge: Cambridge University Press, 2022), 57, 87. The report Tal cites about Dulles was written by Esther Herlitz. Given that it is unclear how Herlitz would have learned this information, the credibility of the source may be somewhat questionable, though Tal may have reason to support its validity.

21. Tal, *The Making of an Alliance*, 78; Wilford, *America's Great Game*, 177–178; Isaac Alteras, "Eisenhower, American Jewry, and Israel," *American Jewish Archives* 37, no. 2 (1985): 257.

22. Wilford, *America's Great Game*, 177–178; Alteras, "Eisenhower, American Jewry, and Israel," 257.

23. Wilford, *America's Great Game*, 177–178; "Council for Judaism Leaders Meet with Assistant Secretary Byroade," JTA, December 3, 1953.

24. Berger, *Memoirs of an Anti-Zionist Jew*, 42–43. The Kibya incident, also known as the Qibya massacre, resulted in sixty-seven Palestinian civilian deaths at the hands of Israeli forces. For more on that raid and others, see Avi Shlaim, *The Iron Wall: Israel and the Arab World* (New York: Norton, 2001), 91. "Byroade Inferentially Blames Israel for Middle East Tension," JTA, April 12, 1954. The Deir Yassin massacre of April 9, 1948, was carried out by the right-wing Zionist militias Lehi and the Irgun in an Arab village near Jerusalem that soon became part of Israel. Over one hundred Palestinian Arab were killed, most of them civilians. Irene Gendzier, *Dying to Forget: Oil, Power, and the Foundations of U.S. Policy in the*

Middle East (New York: Columbia University Press, 2015), 121. "1949–1955 Ministerial Committee on Foreign Affairs and Security," ISA P8/762.

25. "1949–1955 Ministerial Committee on Foreign Affairs and Security," ISA P8/762; "Byroade Inferentially Blames Israel"; "Israel Assails Byroade's Statement; Says He Hinders Peace," JTA, May 2, 1954; Ross, *Rabbi Outcast*, 109; "Council for Judaism Lauds Byroade View on Israel As State," JTA, April 14, 1954.

26. On Zionist criticism of the Council, see Kolsky, *Jews against Zionism*, and Matthew Berkman, "Coercive Consensus: Jewish Federations, Ethnic Representation, and the Roots of American Pro-Israel Politics" (PhD diss., University of Pennsylvania, 2018).

27. Abe Harman to the Israeli Foreign Ministry's American Department in Jerusalem, October 27, 1953, "Lazaron, Rabbi Morris," ISA MFA 109/37 (51); Abe Harman to the Israeli Foreign Ministry's American Department in Jerusalem, January 25, 1954, "Lazaron, Rabbi Morris," ISA MFA 109/37 (36). Yaakov Herzog was the brother of Chaim Herzog, Israel's president during the 1980s and uncle of current Israeli president Isaac Herzog and of Israeli ambassador to the United States Michael Herzog. Yaakov's father, also named Isaac Herzog, served as the first Askhenazi Chief Rabbi of Israeli and Chief Rabbi of Ireland.

28. Abe Harman to the Israeli Foreign Ministry's American Department in Jerusalem, October 27, 1953, "Lazaron, Rabbi Morris," ISA MFA 109/37 (51); Abe Harman to the Israeli Foreign Ministry's American Department in Jerusalem, January 25, 1954, "Lazaron, Rabbi Morris," ISA MFA 109/37 (36). Harman mused that perhaps Lazaron and his wife had divorced. Actually, Lazaron became a widower with the death of his first wife, Pauline Horkheimer Lazaron, sister of Virginia Horkheimer Silver of Wheeling, West Virginia. Abba Hillel Silver had succeeded Lazaron as rabbi at a congregation in Wheeling in 1915.

29. Abe Harman to the Israeli Foreign Ministry's American Department in Jerusalem, October 27, 1953, "Lazaron, Rabbi Morris," ISA MFA 109/37 (51); Abe Harman to the Israeli Foreign Ministry's American Department in Jerusalem, January 25, 1954, "Lazaron, Rabbi Morris," ISA MFA 109/37 (36).

30. "Lessing Rosenwald Tells Israelis He Is Anti-Zionist, Not Anti-Israel," JTA, January 15, 1957; Abe Harman to the Israeli Foreign Ministry's American Department in Jerusalem, October 27, 1953, "Lazaron, Rabbi Morris," ISA MFA 109/37 (51); Lucy S. Dawidowicz to Milton Himmelfarb, "Lessing J. Rosenwald's Report on His Visit to Israel," February 14, 1957, AJCAO. Rosenwald had also served as an AJC executive board member until at least 1949.

31. "Lessing Rosenwald Tells Israelis"; Abe Harman to the Israeli Foreign Ministry's American Department in Jerusalem, October 27, 1953, "Lazaron, Rabbi Morris," ISA MFA 109/37 (51); Lucy S. Dawidowicz to Milton Himmelfarb, "Lessing J. Rosenwald's Report on His Visit to Israel," February 14, 1957, AJCAO; "Zionists' Foe Pays a Visit to Israel," *New York Times*, January 21, 1957.

32. "Zionists' Foe Pays a Visit to Israel."

33. "The Editor's Chair . . .," *National Jewish Post*, March 15, 1957. The *New York Times* also reported on Rosenwald's talk. Kohn felt, probably accurately, that the *Times*

report did too much to emphasize Rosenwald's enduring opposition to Zionism over his surprising praise of Israel, which the Jewish press highlighted. See "Council Hard Put to Find Fault, Not Lessing," *National Jewish Post*, April 12, 1957; "Critic Unswayed by Visit to Israel," *New York Times*, February 14, 1957. Lucy S. Dawidowicz to Milton Himmelfarb, "Lessing J. Rosenwald's Report on His Visit to Israel," February 14, 1957, AJCAO.

34. Lucy S. Dawidowicz to Milton Himmelfarb, "Lessing J. Rosenwald's Report on His Visit to Israel," February 14, 1957, AJCAO; Berger, *Who Knows Better*, 43–46. In letter, Berger in Damascus to Rosenwald and Coleman, May 14, 1955; Dawidowicz reviewed Berger's next book later in 1957. See Lucy S. Dawidowicz, "Judaism or Jewish Nationalism: The Alternative to Zionism, by Elmer Berger," *Commentary*, October 1957.

35. Zvi Ganin, *An Uneasy Relationship: American Jewish Leadership and Israel, 1948–1957* (Syracuse, NY: Syracuse University Press, 2005), 133–134.

36. Theodore Kollek to Lessing Rosenwald, October 2, 1964, Folder: Public Inquiries from the Teddy Kollek Period—Rosenwald, Lessing, Elmer Berger, ISA GL 68/11887 (15); Lessing Rosenwald to Theodore Kollek, October 7, 1964, Folder: Public Inquiries from the Teddy Kollek Period—Rosenwald, Lessing, Elmer Berger, ISA GL 68/11887 (12); Lessing Rosenwald to Theodore Kollek, November 13, 1963, Folder: Public Inquiries from the Teddy Kollek Period—Rosenwald, Lessing, Elmer Berger, ISA GL 68/11887 (19); Theodore Kollek to Lessing Rosenwald, October 31, 1963, Folder: Public Inquiries from the Teddy Kollek Period—Rosenwald, Lessing, Elmer Berger, ISA GL 68/11887 (23).

37. On the "New Historians," see chapter 1, note 36. Lessing Rosenwald to David Ben-Gurion, July 23, 1961, Folder: Public Inquiries from the Teddy Kollek Period—Rosenwald, Lessing, Elmer Berger, ISA GL 68/11887 (42); Elmer Berger to David Ben-Gurion, July 1, 1961, Folder: Public Inquiries from the Teddy Kollek Period—Rosenwald, Lessing, Elmer Berger, ISA GL 68/11887 (53); Erskine B. Childers, "The Other Exodus," *The Spectator*, May 12, 1961; Theodore Kollek to Lessing Rosenwald, July 17, 1961, Folder: Public Inquiries from the Teddy Kollek Period—Rosenwald, Lessing, Elmer Berger, ISA GL 68/11887 (59–61).

38. On Berger's impact on the PLO, see Gribetz, "The PLO's Rabbi," which inspires this section heading; ABB [likely Albert Belton] to Sal, "Supplying own publications to Arab Offices in NYC, and in Boston, Mass.," July 31, 1961, AJA 17, Box 2, Folder 3 (24); Saadat Hassan to Elmer Berger, June 28, 1965, AJA 17-6-2. Geoffrey Moorehouse, "The Rabbi with More Friends in Islam," *The Guardian*, February 16, 1970; "Rabbi Berger, Anti-Zionist," *Vrije Volk*, March 21, 1968 [ISA LA ACJ1 (34)]; Glickman, "One Voice," 125, 132; Bill Gottlieb to Al Laurence [of the Betty Furness Program], Station WNTA-TV, AJA 17, Box 2, Folder 3 (1).

39. Glickman, "One Voice," 132–135; from a February 1959 letter from Berger to Hays Solis-Cohen, and quoted from a May 1965 letter from Berger to Coleman. H. L. Kahn, "Israel's Ties with American Jews," *Chicago Tribune*, January 25, 1965. "Council for Judaism Announces $5,000 Contribution for Arab Refugees," JTA, December 5, 1962.

40. Ross, *Rabbi Outcast*, 146; Krebs, "U.S. Jews Split on Mideast War"; "Jewish Group Hit over View on Israel War," *New York Post*, July 19, 1967 [ISA-LA]; "Five Prominent Jews Repudiate Position of American Council for Judaism," JTA, July 19, 1967.

41. William Schack, "Neiman-Marcus of Texas," *Commentary*, September 1957, 212–222; Ralph Blumenthal, "Dallas Comes to Terms with the Day That Defined It," *New York Times*, November 20, 2003.

42. Krebs, "U.S. Jews Split on Mideast War"; "Jewish Group Hit over View"; "Five Prominent Jews Repudiate Position of American Council for Judaism," JTA, July 19, 1967; Eric Pace, "John L. Loeb Sr. Dies at 94; Investor and Philanthropist," *New York Times*, December 9, 1996. Loeb's brother Henry had served as the Council's vice president, which is perhaps why John did not denounce it. Henry Loeb was also a significant donor to Zukerman's *Jewish Newsletter*.

43. Berger, *Memoirs of an Anti-Zionist Jew*, 108–130; Ross, *Rabbi Outcast*, 146.

44. These pet projects included Berger's work with Thomas Mallison on research projects negating "Jewish peoplehood" as a concept in international law. Ross, *Rabbi Outcast*, 140. "A Statement by Norton Mezvinsky," May 27, 1968, AJA 17, Box 9, Folder 7; Glickman, "One Voice," 120–140; "National Executive Committee Meeting, June 30, 1968," AJA 17, Box 6, Folder 2 (9).

45. Salim Yaqub, *Containing Arab Nationalism: The Eisenhower Doctrine and the Middle East* (Chapel Hill: University of North Carolina Press, 2004); Warren Bass, *Support Any Friend: Kennedy's Middle East and the Making of the U.S.-Israel Alliance* (Oxford: Oxford University Press, 2003).

46. Author's interview with former Council and AJAZ staff member Professor Norton Mezvinsky in New York, August 12, 2016; see also Ross, *Rabbi Outcast*, 132–175; Seth Farber, *Radicals, Rabbis and Peacemakers: Conversations with Jewish Critics of Israel* (Monroe, ME: Common Courage, 2005). Mezvinsky's best-known family member is nephew Marc Mezvinsky, husband of Chelsea Clinton. Marc's parents served in the United States House of Representatives. Incidentally, among Mezvinsky's PhD classmates in U.S. history at Wisconsin was future rabbi Arthur Waskow, who at the time had a much weaker sense of Jewish identity and ridiculed Mezvinsky for his religiousness, according to conversations with both men.

47. Author's interview with former Council and AJAZ staff member Professor Norton Mezvinsky in New York, August 12, 2016.

48. Resignation Statement of Norton Mezvinsky, May 1968, AJA 17, Box 9, Folder 7. While it is hard to assess the validity of Mezvinsky's claim of racism, it should be pointed out that at least two Council figures—Stanley Marcus and Morris Lazaron—advocated for the rights of African Americans earlier in life.

49. This included Moshe Menuhin, who rallied support for Berger during the 1967–1968 controversy in the Council, encouraged him to form a new group, but then left that as well. On Menuhin and the Council, see Moshe Menuhin, *Jewish Critics of Zionism: A Testamentary Essay, with the Stifling and Smearing of a Dissenter* (New York: League of Arab States, Arab Information Center, 1974), and Berger, *Memoirs of an Anti-Zionist Jew*. Ross, *Rabbi Outcast*, 147.

50. "Rabbi Berger, Anti-Zionist," *Vrije Volk*, March 21, 1968 [ISA LA ACJ1 (35)].

51. Ross, *Rabbi Outcast*, 154; interview with former Council and AJAZ staff member Professor Norton Mezvinsky in New York, August 12, 2016.

52. Mouin Rabbani, "Reflections on a Lifetime of Engagement with Zionism, the Palestine Question, and American Empire: An Interview with Noam Chomsky," *Journal of Palestine Studies* 41, no. 3 (2012): 92–120.

53. Ibid.

54. Author's email correspondence with Noam Chomsky, May 29, 2022.

55. "CONAME," Box 9, Folder 15, Allan Solomonow Papers, University of Pennsylvania Archives (henceforth Solomonow Papers); Berta Langston Letter, February 5, 1972, Box 9, Folder 22, Solomonow Papers; CONAME Letterhead, Solomonow Papers; see Doug Rossinow, "The 1900-Year Crisis: Arthur Waskow, the Question of Israel/Palestine, and the Effort to Form a Jewish Religious Left in America, 1969–1974," in *The Religious Left in Modern America: Doorkeepers of a Radical Faith*, ed. Leilah Danielson, Marian Mollin, and Doug Rossinow (Cham: Palgrave Macmillan, 2018), 233–254; Robert Loeb Oral History Transcript, AJPA Interview, November 28, 2014; Rael Jean Isaac, *Breira: A Counsel for Judaism* (New York: Americans for a Safe Israel, 1976).

56. Author's interview with former Council and AJAZ staff member Professor Norton Mezvinsky in New York, August 12, 2016. Berger sent much of AJAZ's archival material to be held at the Institute for Palestine Studies in Beirut, though microform of that material is available at the American Jewish Archives in Cincinnati. Author's interview with Uri Davis in Ramallah, November 27, 2016; author's email correspondence with Noam Chomsky, November 30, 2017; Uri Davis, *Crossing the Border: An Autobiography of an Anti-Zionist Palestinian Jew* (London: Books & Books, 1995).

57. Fouzi El-Asmar, *To Be an Arab in Israel* (Beirut: Institute for Palestine Studies, 1978); interview with Mezvinsky, 2016; author's email correspondence with Noam Chomsky, November 30, 2017.

58. Isadore Zack to Moshe Ofer, February 19, 1970, Folder 4, Box 16, Solomonow Papers. In 1985, the Anti-Defamation League prepared a thick dossier on Chomsky to send to attorney and pro-Israel speaker Alan Dershowitz, to help the latter prepare for a debate with the esteemed linguist. The action, however, upset one ADL employee enough that she or he leaked a copy of the dossier to Chomsky, who later copied and sent it to his friend Allan Solomonow. Email correspondence with Noam Chomsky, February 13, 2018.

59. Matthew Frye Jacobson, *Roots Too: White Ethnic Revival in Post–Civil Rights America* (Cambridge, MA: Harvard University Press, 2006).

Chapter 6. Zionists for Palestine

1. Author's interview with Sabri Jiryis, November 22, 2016, in Fassuta, Israel; Herman Edelsberg, *Not for Myself Alone: Memoir of a Lawyer Who Fought for Human Rights* (Berkeley, CA: Interstellar Media, 1988), 205; Arthur Waskow Oral History

Transcript, AJPA interview, November 24, 2014; Arthur I. Waskow, "Talking with the P.L.O.," *New York Times*, December 16, 1976; AJC Oral History Interview with George Gruen, tape 1, 52–62. Both Gruen and Edelsberg concluded that Israel leaked their memos. The meeting was organized with the help of a woman named Rosalie Riechman (later Pressman); "Memo Released on Meeting between Jews and Representatives of PLO," JTA, December 1, 1976.

2. "Memo Released on Meeting"; Michael E. Staub, *Torn at the Roots: The Crisis of Jewish Liberalism in Postwar America* (New York: Columbia University Press, 2004), 300–304.

3. Staub, *Torn at the Roots*, 281.

4. Staub, *Torn at the Roots*, chapter 8; Jack Wertheimer, "Breaking the Taboo: Critics of Israel and the American Jewish Establishment," in *Envisioning Israel: The Changing Ideals and Images of North American Jews*, ed. Allon Gal (Detroit: Wayne State University Press, 1996), 406; Steven T. Rosenthal, *Irreconcilable Differences? The Waning of the American Jewish Love Affair with Israel* (Waltham, MA: Brandeis University Press, 2001); Dov Waxman, *Trouble in the Tribe: The American Jewish Conflict over Israel* (Princeton, NJ: Princeton University Press, 2016). One possible exception may be Marla Brettschneider, *Cornerstones of Peace: Jewish Identity Politics and Democratic Theory* (New Brunswick, NJ: Rutgers University Press, 1996), a political theory book that draws in part from material then held by Breira's Gerry Serotta. Matthew Berkman's dissertation and forthcoming book also make use of Breira archives.

5. Breira Report, November 1976, Yoav Peled Papers, Folder 1. Robert Gordis was the grandfather of author Daniel Gordis, who surprisingly did not mention Breira in his book on Israel–American Jewish ties. Daniel Gordis, *We Stand Divided: The Rift between American Jews and Israel* (New York: Ecco, 2019).

6. Breira Report, November 1976, Yoav Peled's box of Yozma/Breira files, currently being processed by the American Jewish Historical Society, Folder 1. Though I group them together, there were political differences and personal tensions between these members of the Israeli left, as noted in various interviews and memoirs. For issues within the Israeli Council for Israeli-Palestinian Peace, see Uri Avnery, *My Friend, the Enemy* (Westport, CT: Lawrence Hill, 1986); for tensions between Freedman and Aloni, whom Freedman saw as reluctant to publicly embrace Palestinian rights, see Marcia Freedman, *Exile in the Promised Land: A Memoir* (Ann Arbor, MI: Firebrand Books, 1990).

7. American Jewish Peace Archives director Aliza Becker kindly made available to me over two dozen transcripts from oral history interviews that she conducted from 2013 through 2018. In addition, I spoke or corresponded with Noam Chomsky, Arthur Waskow, Don Peretz, Sam Norich, Norton Mezvinsky, John Ruskay, Steven Zipperstein, Yoav Peled, Uri Davis, Uri Avnery, Aviva Cantor, Irene Gendzier, Ellen Siegel, and Sabri Jiryis.

8. Markus Krah, "Clinging to Borders and Boundaries? The (Sorry) State of Transnational American Jewish Studies," *American Jewish History* 101, no. 4 (2017): 519–533.

9. Staub, *Torn at the Roots*, chapter 6. Michael Staub, ed., *The Jewish 1960s: An American Sourcebook* (Waltham, MA: Brandeis University Press, 2004), 229–250. On the Havurah movement, see Riv-Ellen Prell, *Prayer and Community: The Havurah in American Judaism* (Detroit: Wayne State University Press, 1989).

10. Michael R. Fischbach, "The New Left and the Arab-Israeli Conflict in the United States," *Journal of Palestine Studies* 49, no. 3 (Spring 2020); Michael R. Fischbach, *The Movement and the Middle East: How the Arab-Israeli Conflict Divided the American Left* (Stanford, CA: Stanford University Press, 2020); oral history interview transcript of Aviva Cantor, American Jewish Peace Archive, November 26, 2018.

11. Arthur Waskow, *The Bush Is Burning! Radical Judaism Faces the Pharaohs of the Modern Superstate* (New York: Macmillan, 1971), 67–73; Staub, *Torn at the Roots*, 205; oral history interview transcript of Aviva Cantor, American Jewish Peace Archive, November 26, 2018.

12. Arthur Waskow, *The Bush Is Burning! Radical Judaism Faces the Pharaohs of the Modern Superstate* (New York: Macmillan, 1971), 67–73; Staub, *Torn at the Roots*, 205; oral history interview transcript of Aviva Cantor, American Jewish Peace Archive, November 26, 2018.

13. Waskow, *The Bush Is Burning!*, 67–73. Rose's piece was first published in *Win*, June 15, 1970, then republished in Waskow's book and anonymously in an Atlanta-based alternative newspaper as "A Nice Jewish Girl," *The Great Speckled Bird*, October 26, 1970. All the versions are different. This material is quoted from the Waskow book. Michael R. Fischbach, "How a Middle Eastern Experience Helped Lead to the Formation of MERIP," *Review of Middle East Studies* 55 (2022): 230–240.

14. Waskow, *The Bush Is Burning!*, 67–73.

15. Fischbach, "Middle Eastern Experience," 230–240.

16. Staub, *Torn at the Roots*, 186; Fischbach, *The Movement and the Middle East*, 185. The article, which Sharon Rose wrote with Cathy Tackey, was published in October 1970 in the journal *off our backs*. For more on Palestine debates in the women's movement, see Fischbach, *The Movement and the Middle East*, chapter 12. Though individual feminists, including some Jews, would voice support for the Palestinians from the 1960s onward, 1975 would mark a major expansion of the issue's role in the global women's movement when a resolution on it was passed at the World Conference on Women in Mexico City. The resolution upset some prominent feminist leaders such as Betty Friedan, who recalled it in her memoir. See Betty Friedan, "Scary Doings in Mexico City," in *It Changed My Life: Writings on the Women's Movement* (Cambridge, MA: Harvard University Press, 1998). Months later Friedan signed onto a Breira statement opposing Israeli settlement growth.

17. Staub, *The Jewish 1960s*, 230; oral history interview transcript of Aviva Cantor, American Jewish Peace Archive, November 26, 2018.

18. Staub, *The Jewish 1960s*, 230; oral history interview transcript of Aviva Cantor, American Jewish Peace Archive, November 26, 2018.

19. *Arab-Israeli Debate: Towards a Socialist Solution* (New York: Times Change Press, 1970), 16; review of *Jewish Liberation Journal* issues from its full run, 1969–1972; Amos Kenan, "New Left Go Home," *Jewish Liberation Journal* 1, no. 2 (June 1969).

20. Staub, *The Jewish 1960s*; Radical Zionist Alliance, "Zionist Platform," 1971.

21. Staub, *The Jewish 1960s*, 230. Oral history interview transcript of Aviva Cantor, American Jewish Peace Archive, November 26, 2018.

22. Staub, *Torn at the Roots*, 291–292; Breira Report, November 1976, Yoav Peled Papers, Folder 1; Breira Report, June 1977, Yoav Peled Papers, Folder 1; cities included Berkeley, Boston, Chicago, Los Angeles (formerly Yozma), New Haven, New York, Philadelphia, St. Louis, San Francisco, and Washington, DC (formerly Tzedek Tzedek), and had nascent chapters in Cincinnati, Cleveland, Minneapolis, Seattle, Denver, and Brooklyn.

23. "Jewish Youths Protest Civilian Settlements in West Bank and Gaza Strip," JTA, December 21, 1972. In more recent years, Lustick has again caused controversy for publicly giving up on his longtime support for the two-state solution, declaring that it is no longer viable and arguing that people must come to terms with the "one-state reality." See Ian Lustick, *Paradigm Lost: From Two-State Solution to One-State Reality* (Philadelphia: University of Pennsylvania Press, 2019).

24. Ian Lustick Oral History Transcript, AJPA Interview, September 15, 2014.

25. Arthur Waskow, Oral History Transcript, AJPA Interview, November 24, 2014; Waskow, *The Bush Is Burning!*; "The Liberation of Palestine and Israel," *New York Review of Books*, July 1, 1971. The ad was put together by Waskow and Paul Jacobs. Other signatories included Benjamin Spock, Todd Gitlin, and Abbie Hoffman. For a full analysis of Waskow's thought at the time of the statement, see Doug Rossinow, "The 1900-Year Crisis: Arthur Waskow, the Question of Israel/Palestine, and the Effort to Form a Jewish Religious Left in America, 1969–1974," in *The Religious Left in Modern America: Doorkeepers of a Radical Faith*, ed. Leilah Danielson, Marian Mollin, and Doug Rossinow (London: Palgrave Macmillan, 2018), 233–254.

26. Robert Skeist Oral History Transcript, AJPA Interview, September 12, 2014; Skeist said the article was titled "Coming Out Jewish." Chutzpah document from 1980s found in the Yoav Peled Papers, Folder 1. Chutzpah was founded in 1971 as a multi-issue Jewish left-wing organization; though its interests included Israel/Palestine, it did not join Breira. *New Outlook* was an Israeli journal that supported Arab-Jewish rapprochement.

27. Author's correspondence with Steven Zipperstein, June 25, 2018; Yozma letterhead listing executive committee members, Yoav Peled Papers, Folder 9; Joel Beinin, "Remembering Reuven Kaminer, the Godfather of Israel's Radical Left," +972 *Magazine*, November 2, 2020; author's interview with Yoav Peled in Tel Aviv, May 22, 2018; Breira Summer Organizer's Institute—Summary of Working Session YP 1; Yoav Peled Papers, Folder 7. Peled received the staff position only in summer 1977.

28. Aliza Becker's interview with Gerry Serotta, September 21, 2014; John Ruskay, "John Ruskay Looks Back," *New York Jewish Week*, December 10, 2013; Allan Solomonow

Papers, University of Pennsylvania Archives (henceforth Solomonow Papers); William Novak, "The Breira Story," *Genesis 2* (March–April 1977).

29. Ruskay, "John Ruskay Looks Back"; Solomonow Papers; Robert Loeb Oral History Transcript, AJPA Interview, November 28, 2014; Rael Jean Isaac, *Breira: A Counsel for Judaism* (New York: Americans for a Safe Israel, 1976).

30. Breira Report, November 1976, Yoav Peled Papers, Folder 1; Arthur Samuelson Oral History Transcript, AJPA Interview, July 8, 2015.

31. Intergenerational dialogue, AJPA Interviews, December 21, 2015; Breira Preliminary Program Proposal (Preliminary Draft): September 1974–August 1975. Breira Records 1970–1979, American Jewish Historical Society (henceforth Breira Records); Novak, "The Breira Story." Wolf later became a friend of Barack Obama's when the rabbi's synagogue was across the street from the home of the future president in Chicago. On Brickner, see Doug Rossinow, "Rabbi Balfour Brickner, Interreligious Dialogue, and the Ironies of Liberal Zionism in America," *Journal of American Studies* 57, no. 1 (2022).

32. Avi Shlaim, *The Iron Wall: Israel and the Arab World* (New York: Norton, 2001); Lior Lehrs, *Unofficial Peace Diplomacy: Private Peace Entrepreneurs in Conflict Resolution Processes* (Manchester: Manchester University Press, 2022), chapter 5.

33. Breira Funding Proposal 1976, Submitted January 1976, Breira Records; Breira Preliminary Program Proposal (Preliminary Draft): September 1974–August 1975, Breira Records; Novak, "The Breira Story."

34. Staub, *Torn at the Roots*, 281; Arnold Jacob Wolf, "Toward Peace with the PLO," *Sh'ma*, December 13, 1974, also published in *Fellowship* next to a similar Breira statement that explained the group's decisions not to join the Jewish community's "rally against terror" anti-PLO demonstration, endorsed by many Breira figures. See "Our Anxieties Should Not Blind Us," *Fellowship* 4, no. 11 (December 1974) in Yoav Peled Papers, Folder 1. The *Fellowship* issue also contained pieces by John Ruskay, Fawaz Turki, and Edward Said.

35. Oral History Profile: Marcia Freedman, American Jewish Peace Archive. Yoav Peled felt his father, Matti, had similar sentiments and goals regarding his American Jewish engagement; author's interview with Yoav Peled in Tel Aviv, May 22, 2018.

36. Oral History Profile: Rabbi Max Ticktin, American Jewish Peace Archive; Abraham H. Foxman to ADL Regional Offices, "Uri Avnery" September 18, 1970, Breira Records; Rabbi Judah Cahn to Allen Brick, October 30, 1970, Breira Records; Waskow, *The Bush Is Burning!*, 72–73; author interview with Uri Avnery, May 27, 2018; Uri Davis, *Crossing the Border: An Autobiography of an Anti-Zionist Palestinian Jew* (London: Books & Books, 1995), 107; oral history interview transcript of Rabbi Everett Gendler, American Jewish Peace Archive, July 29, 2014; Alan Dershowitz, "Terrorism and Preventative Detention: The Case of Israel," *Commentary*, December 1970; Fawzi El-Asmar, *To Be an Arab in Israel* (Beirut: Institute for Palestine Studies, 1978); Davis, *Crossing the Border*, 111.

37. Breira Funding Proposal 1976, Submitted January 1976, Breira Records; Itamar Rabinovich, *Yitzhak Rabin: Soldier, Leader, Statesman* (New Haven: Yale University Press, 2017), 42.

38. Miko Peled, *The General's Son: Journal of an Israeli in Palestine* (Charlottesville, VA: Just World Books, 2016), 41, 59.

39. "Special Supplement," *Interchange* 1, no. 5 (January 1976), Yoav Peled Papers; Mattitiyahu Peled, "Why the Interim Accords Are Bad for Israel and Why the Doves Voted for Them Anyway," *Interchange* 1, no. 2 (October 1975). Other Israelis whose writings were published or republished in *Interchange* included Boaz Evron, Yitzhak Rabin, Zvi Yaron, Shimon Shamir, Nahum Barnea, Yoav Peled, Abba Eban, Ehud Ben-Ezer, Yehoshaphat Harkabi, Bernard Avishai, and Raul Teitlbaum. On multiple occasions, articles were drawn from the Israeli monthly magazine *Emda*, as well as from Israeli newspapers such as *Ma'ariv*. *Interchange* appears to have been published from September 1975 through September 1977 and dealt with an array of Jewish issues. "Special Supplement," *Interchange* 1, no. 5 (January 1976), Yoav Peled Papers.

40. Breira Annual Report (1974–1975), Robert Loeb, Executive Director, Breira Records; Mattitiyahu Peled and Elias H. Tuma, "Israel and the PLO: A Way Out of the Impasse," *New York Review of Books*, May 15, 1975; Paul Chamberlain, *The Global Offensive: The United States, the Palestine Liberation Organization, and the Making of the Post–Cold War Order* (Oxford: Oxford University Press, 2012), chapter 5.

41. Avnery, *My Friend, the Enemy*, 72–96; Lehrs, *Unofficial Peace Diplomacy*, chapter 5.

42. *Interchange* 1, no. 7 (March 1976), Yoav Peled Papers; Avnery, *My Friend, the Enemy*, 72–74, 94–96, 119; *New Outlook* staff David Shaham and Simha Flapan were also on the ICIPP at different moments; Arie Eliav, "The Times They Are A'Changing," *New Outlook*, June 1976, Breira Records; Eliav also spoke in New York to a group called the Socialist Zionist Union, "Socialist Zionist Union," Yoav Peled Papers, Folder 1. Mitchell Cohen was among its active members. Avnery is an outlier, having supported two states much earlier. Eliav outlined his views in his 1973 book *Land of the Hart*, which Breira sold at a special rate to members; "Breira Co-Sponsoring Tour for Eliav," *Interchange* 1, no. 6 (February 1976), Yoav Peled Papers.

43. Staub, *Torn at the Roots*, 285; Chamberlain, *The Global Offensive*, chapter 7.

44. Avnery, *My Friend, the Enemy*, 35–51; Lehrs, *Unofficial Peace Diplomacy*, 213–219.

45. Berkman, "Coercive Consensus," 375; Staub, *Torn at the Roots*, 295–298.

46. Lehrs, *Unofficial Peace Diplomacy*, chapter 5; Avnery, *My Friend, the Enemy*, 94, 130–134.

47. Lehrs, *Unofficial Peace Diplomacy*, chapter 5; Avnery, *My Friend, the Enemy*, 119–136.

48. Author's Zoom interview with Sabri Jiryis, January 27, 2022; Lehrs, *Unofficial Peace Diplomacy*, chapter 5; Avnery, *My Friend, the Enemy*, 119–136.

49. National Membership Conference—"New Perspectives: Israel and the Diaspora" and Keynote Speeches by Prof. Howe and Matti Peled, Box 5, Folder 17, Breira Records, American Jewish Historical Society; Breira Report, November 1976, Yoav Peled Papers, Folder 1.

50. Avnery, *My Friend, the Enemy*, 144–151; Klutznick tacitly acknowledged such a meeting took place when confronted by Arthur Waskow in letters now held in the Waskow collection at the American Jewish Historical Society. No information about the meeting can be found in Klutznick's papers, but these details have been confirmed in interviews with Jiryis, Waskow, and Sam Norich; oral history interview transcript of Rabbi Arthur Waskow, American Jewish Peace Archive, November 24, 2014; phone interview with Sam Norich, December 3, 2018. Norich helped arrange Klutznick's meeting in New York; Zoom interview with Sabri Jiryis, January 27, 2022. Jiryis did not recall the date of the meeting with Goldmann, which had not previously been disclosed to academics or the media. On Young, see Salim Yaqub, "Our Declaration of Independence: African Americans, Arab Americans, and the Arab-Israeli Conflict, 1967–1979," *Mashriq & Mahjar* 3, no. 1 (2015): 18–46.

51. Sartawi/Jiryis Meeting Attendance sign-in sheet, Solomonow Papers; Sartawi/Jiryis Meeting Notes, Solomonow Papers; Sartawi/Jiryis Meeting Potential Invitees, in Box 17, Folder 31, Solomonow Papers. Other names signed in included Leo and Judith A. Disendruck (WZC/AZYF), Melvin Merians (AJC), Martin Popper (NLG), Morton Stavis, Robert Boehm, Norton Mezvinsky, Rev. Charles Angell, and one illegible signature. Gruen's memo noted only seven Jews and two Christians; "Changing Views within the PLO Regarding Israel?," Solomonow Papers (full draft noting multiple meetings at the same house); "Changing Views within the PLO Regarding Israel," November 2, 1976, draft with date, Box 16, Folder 9, Solomonow Papers; "Memo Released on Meeting"; AJC Oral History Interview with George Gruen, conducted by Jill Levine on June 13, 1980, at New York Public Library, tape 1, 52–62; Ticktin also worked for B'nai B'rith Hillel Foundations. See Bernard Gwertzman, "American Jewish Leaders Are Split over Issue of Meeting with P.L.O.," *New York Times*, December 30, 1976; author's interview with Sabri Jiryis, November 22, 2016, in Fassuta, Israel; Edelsberg, *Not for Myself Alone*, 205. According to Edelsberg, Sartawi said that the New York meeting went better than the DC one.

52. Wolf Blitzer, "Group of Jews Meet with PLO Men in U.S.," *Jerusalem Post*, November 21, 1976; Staub, *Torn at the Root*, 299; "Memo Released on Meeting"; Edelsberg, *Not for Myself Alone*, 205. AJC Oral History Interview with George Gruen, tape 1, 52–62.

53. Gwertzman, "American Jewish Leaders"; "B'nai B'rith Denies Role in PLO Meeting; AJCongress Staff Member Who Attended Is Given Reprimand," JTA, December 2, 1976; Waskow, "Talking with the P.L.O."; Joel Greenberg, "Israeli Parliament Lifts a Ban on P.L.O. Contacts," *New York Times*, January 20, 1993. According to Avnery, the 1986 law banning contact with the PLO came in response to his 1983 meeting with Arafat. Prior to that, it had been illegal to meet with enemy agents unless there were "valid reasons" and "no intent to hurt the security of the state." Avnery, *My Friend, the Enemy*, 40.

54. Gwertzman, "American Jewish Leaders"; "B'nai B'rith Denies Role"; Waskow, "Talking with the P.L.O."

55. Staub, *Torn at the Roots*, 300–302.
56. Joseph Shattan, "Why Breira?," *Commentary*, April 1977, 60–66; Isaac, *Breira: A Counsel for Judaism*, 6; Staub, *Torn at the Roots*, 300; David Szyoni, "What Happened When the P.L.O. Came to Town," *Interchange* 2, no. 5 (January 1977).
57. McDonald was one of the staunchest anti-communist voices in Congress in the 1970s, and ironically would be the only congressman known to be killed by the Soviets when the Korean Air Lines flight he was on was accidentally shot down in 1983. Larry McDonald, "The P.L.O.'s Terrorist Support Network in the United States," Extension of Remarks, U.S. Congressional Record, February 17, 1977 (vol. 123), 4710, https://www.congress.gov/bound-congressional-record/1977/02/17/extensions-of-remarks-section.
58. Novak, "The Breira Story," 25; Breira Summer Organizer's Institute—Summary of Working Session YP 1. Breira leaders noted in late summer 1977 that they had "been silent since May 17." Arthur Waskow Oral History Transcript, AJPA interview, November 24, 2014. For threats against Hillel staff jobs, see Wertheimer, "Breaking the Taboo," 407; Berkman, "Coercive Consensus," 373–380.
59. The most detailed account of Breira's financial woes is in Berkman, "Coercive Consensus," 373–380. This acts as an important corrective to inaccurate reports in much of the secondary literature, which appear to indicate that Breira simply folded to direct external pressure; Breira Report—March 1978 (Produced by the Washington Chapter), Yoav Peled Papers, Folder 3; North Bay Chapter Meeting Agenda, January 27, 1978, in Bay Area Breira Files, Yoav Peled Papers, Folder 6. DC, Boston, and California chapters endured the longest. Matti Peled continued to appear at West Coast Breira events in 1978.
60. Novak, "The Breira Story," 24.
61. Breira Summer Organizer's Institute—Summary of Working Session, Yoav Peled Papers, Folder 1; Avnery, *My Friend, the Enemy*.
62. Avnery, *My Friend, the Enemy*. On the 1983 bombing of the PLO Research Center, see the forthcoming book on the PLO Research Center by Jonathan Gribetz. Jiryis heard that the bombing was carried out on the orders of Elie Hobeika, a right-wing Lebanese commander and then ally of Israeli forces who was directly involved in the Sabra and Shatila massacre. Jiryis agrees with the common belief that Sartawi was killed by the Abu Nidal Organization, but while Avnery claims it was because of Sartawi's politics, Jiryis said it was because Sartawi planned to kill the radical Abu Nidal. Author's Zoom interview with Sabri Jiryis, January 27, 2022.
63. Robert S. Perlzweig to East Bay Jewish Community, JCRC for Alameda and Contra Costa Counties, September 20, 1977, Yoav Peled Papers, Folder 6; see Seth Anziska, *Preventing Palestine: A Political History from Camp David to Oslo* (Princeton, NJ: Princeton University Press, 2018); Breira Report—March 1978 (Produced by the Washington Chapter), Yoav Peled Papers, Folder 3; "Policy Statement" in Bay Area Breira Files, Yoav Peled Papers, Folder 6; "Breira Policy Statement," LA files, YP 7; Dan Gillon to board members, January 17, 1978, Yoav Peled Papers, Folder 8.

64. Fischbach, *The Movement and the Middle East*, 48; Rex Wingerter, "Personality: Ellen Siegel," *Washington Report on Middle East Affairs*, September 17, 1984. See "Women in Breira," posted by AmericanJewishPeaceArchive, October 3, 2016, YouTube video, https://youtu.be/oGnosIfh_Yg.

65. Elliott Abrams, "If American Jews and Israel Are Drifting Apart, What's the Reason?," *Mosaic*, April 4, 2016.

Conclusion

1. Don Peretz, *Israel and the Palestine Arabs* (Washington, DC: The Middle East Institute, 1958); Don Peretz, "The Arab Minority of Israel," *Middle East Journal* 8, no. 2 (1954): 139–154. The latter is Peretz's first scholarly article and the first article ever published in an American academic journal on the topic. Don Peretz's address to the Middle East Institute, televised on C-SPAN, October 19, 2001, https://www.c-span.org/video/?166788-3/middle-east-challenges&start=598.

2. Esther Herlitz studied at the Hebrew University Secondary School.

3. Don Peretz's address to the Middle East Institute.

4. Elmer Berger, *Peace for Palestine: First Lost Opportunity* (Gainesville: University Press of Florida, 1993). Other efforts in which Peretz was involved in the 1950s included heading a group called American Friends of Ihud and working with former Herut Knesset members Shmuel Merlin and Hillel Kook/Peter Bergson on an Institute for Mediterranean Affairs plan to solve the Palestinian refugee issue.

5. Theodore Sasson, *The New American Zionism* (New York: New York University Press, 2013); Carrie Keller-Lynn, "Jewish Israeli Voters Have Moved Significantly Rightward in Recent Years, Data Shows," *Times of Israel*, August 29, 2022, https://www.timesofisrael.com/israeli-jewish-voters-moved-significantly-rightward-in-recent-years-data-shows/.

6. Sasson, *The New American Zionism*; Dov Waxman, *Trouble in the Tribe: The American Jewish Conflict over Israel* (Princeton, NJ: Princeton University Press, 2016). Other such groups include Jewish Voice for Peace, Encounter, and Extend.

7. Andrew Silow-Carroll, "Naftali Bennett Blames Western Assimilation for Crisis in Israel-Diaspora Relations," JTA, December 10, 2018.

8. Ibid. Isi Leibler, "From Pro-Israel to Anti-Israel Apologist," *Jerusalem Post*, April 29, 2010; Nathan Guttman, "Mideast Mediator Martin Indyk Draws Ire from Both Sides of Israeli Spectrum," *Forward*, August 2, 2013.

9. One could argue that today Israel is less reliant on American Jewry in part because of the strength of Christian Zionism.

10. George E. Gruen, "Group Solidarity and Dissent in Israel-Diaspora Relations," AJC Task Force on Israel-American Jewry Interaction, 1976, Allan Solomonow Papers, University of Pennsylvania Archives.

11. Cecil Hourani, *An Unfinished Odyssey: Lebanon and Beyond* (London: Weidenfeld and Nicolson, 1984), 77.

ACKNOWLEDGMENTS

WRITING A BOOK IS A SOLITARY PROCESS. Yet, if you are fortunate, it can also involve stimulating intellectual interaction with friends, colleagues, and mentors alike. Over the course of nearly a decade of working on this project, which began with dissertation research at New York University and ended with manuscript revisions at Harvard University and Emory University, I have been privileged to have learned from a wide array of colleagues and teachers who have helped me make this book what it is.

First, I thank my colleagues at Emory University's Middle Eastern and South Asian Studies Department (MESAS) and the Tam Institute for Jewish Studies who make Emory such an enriching academic home. In MESAS, I particularly acknowledge members of my reading group—Craig Perry, Devin Stewart, Roxani Margariti, and Scott Kugle—who gave insightful feedback on much of this book, as well as colleagues Harshita Kamath, Carrie Wickham, Courtney Freer, Ofra Yeglin, and Kevin Corrigan. At the Tam Institute, I thank Eric Goldstein, Kate Rosenblatt, Miriam Udell, and Ellie Schainker. I also benefited from the aid of Juana McGhee, Paul Entis, Brent Buckley, Malory Mibab, Eric Weeks, and Jody Baily. I also want to note the role of my students in my thinking about this project, especially those in my first teaching of Israel/Palestine in World Politics.

While Emory is my current academic home, most of the research for this book was conducted while I was a graduate student at New York University. The members of my dissertation committee, Ron Zweig, Hasia Diner,

Zachary Lockman, Jonathan Gribetz, Salim Yaqub, and, originally, the late Marilyn Young, each helped guide me through this process in their own different ways.

From the very beginning, Ron was a strong advocate for my project, and I appreciate the trust he put in me to create something important out of a topic that others had overlooked. Moreover, the broader academic environment that Ron fostered at the Taub Center for Israel Studies did much to influence my intellectual trajectory and shape the questions that I sought to answer in this book and beyond.

As my project shifted toward the realm of American Jewish history, Hasia Diner seamlessly became an enthusiastic mentor. My seminar paper for her Jews and the History of American Diversity course marked the first time I explored many of the themes that ultimately became central to this book. Hasia's contrarian spirit has informed the way I approach American Jewish history, and I thank her for her contribution to my development as a scholar.

I feel fortunate that Zachary Lockman played a role in this process ever since I enrolled in his Literature of the Field course, which helped me ground my research in Middle Eastern history. Marilyn was my history department advisor when I first came to NYU, and she served on my committee until her untimely passing in 2017. She was an incredibly kind and encouraging human being. It is an honor to be counted among Marilyn's students.

Jonathan Gribetz has been an important mentor and role model as a historian of Jewish-Arab relations. I also thank Salim Yaqub for his guidance. As he is one of the foremost experts on U.S.–Middle East relations during the 1950s and 1970s, Salim's role is a source of pride.

I am especially grateful to three individuals—Nathan Kurz, Aliza Becker, and Maya Peretz—who played essential roles in shaping the direction of this book. From the day I met Nathan Kurz, he exemplified the role of collaborative scholar, offering research leads and archival material. Nathan was the first to review the earliest drafts of parts of this book and has no doubt left his mark on the final product.

Aliza Becker's American Jewish Peace Archive will be a treasure to scholars for years to come. I feel lucky to be among the first historians to review transcripts of Aliza's interviews with the founding members of Breira and similar groups. I thank Aliza for kindly sharing them with me, as they proved essential to the writing of the book's final chapter.

This would be a different book if not for the late Maya Peretz. I first encountered Maya when trying to arrange a meeting with her husband, Don, an effort that began a bit too late. After Don's passing in 2017, Maya kindly gave me access to his files, which included the amazing collection of material from the 1940s and 1950s that inspired this book's first chapter. It saddens me that she did not live to see this book in print given her excitement over the first draft. As a child Holocaust survivor saved by a Ukrainian peasant who pretended to be her mother, Maya had her own incredible life story. She and Don witnessed two very different pivotal events in modern Jewish history yet came away with similar conclusions about the need to remember the humanity of all peoples. I thank Maya for her role in this book and for her friendship.

I only had the fortune of speaking with Don and Maya thanks to Paul Scham, an introduction that, in turn, was made by Yael Aronoff. From my time as her student at Michigan State University, Yael's guidance profoundly influenced the trajectory of my career, and I am grateful for it. I also thank other early mentors from Michigan State and Johns Hopkins University—namely, Ken Waltzer, David Unger, John Harper, Ken Moss, and Bob Freedman.

NYU's Skirball Department of Hebrew and Judaic Studies, Department of History, and the Taub Center for Israel Studies were wonderful academic homes for six years. As Taub Center administrator, Shayne Figueroa did a remarkable job of smoothing out the rough edges of the PhD student experience. To take a line from the countless emails I have sent her over the years, "Thanks, Shayne!" I also thank administrators Yarmine Fernandez, Ryan Grubbs, Kirsten Howe, Maddy Goico, and Tali Gluch, as well as faculty members Gennady Estraikh, Annette Yoshiko-Reed, Benny Hary, Itamar Rabinovich, and especially Marion Kaplan. Finally, I thank the many friends and colleagues whom I met in the department, including Sandy Fox, Dotan Greenvald, Donna Herzog, Amy Weiss, Jehad Abusalim, Hannah Zaves-Greene, Shayna Weiss, Brett Levi, Judah Bernstein, Kimmi Cheng, Roni Masel, Gavin Beinart-Smollan, Tova Benjamin, Shay Hazkani,

Hillel Gruenberg, Ilan Benattar, Hadas Binyamini, and David Weinfeld. At NYU's history department, I appreciated the work of administrator Chelsea Rhodes and the supportive friendships of Gaurav Churiwala Garg, Sara Kozameh, Brittany Edmoundson, Timo McGregor, Rosie Johnston, Cayetana Adrianzen Ponce, Troy Vettese, Aviv Derri, and the rest of my doctoral cohort.

As an Alan M. Stroock fellow at Harvard University, I was grateful for the mentorship of Derek Penslar, who fostered a rich intellectual community, and the support of administrators Rachel Rockenmacher and Sandy Cantave. I also appreciated the intellectual comradery of the Starr fellows' cohort—Orit Rozin, Paul Nahme, Hadar Feldman-Samet, Josh Meyers, Francesca Bregoli, and Josh Teplitsky.

This research was possible only because of funds generously provided by an array of academic organizations and institutions. At Harvard, I benefited from the Alan M. Stroock fellowship fund. New York University supported my research through the MacCracken Fellowship, Global Research Initiative Fellowships in Washington, DC, and Tel Aviv, and various sources within the Department of History, the Skirball Department, the Graduate School of Arts and Sciences, and the Taub Center for Israel Studies. The AICE Schusterman Israel Scholar Award provided important funding and access to a broader scholarly network in Israel studies. The Katherine W. Davis Fellowship for Peace supported a helpful summer of language training at Middlebury College's School of Hebrew.

I appreciate the support of the Israel Institute in the form of an Israel Institute Doctoral Fellowship and through a workshop run by Erika Falk. I am also profoundly grateful for the funding provided by the Memorial Foundation for Jewish Culture, the Feinstein Center for American Jewish History at Temple University, the Association for Israel Studies, the American Academy for Jewish Research, and the National Endowment for the Humanities. I feel especially fortunate for receiving the Association for Jewish Studies (AJS) Dissertation Completion Fellowship, with funding provided by the Legacy Heritage Fund. More recently I benefited from the support of a Scholarly Writing and Publishing Fund Grant from Emory's Center for Faculty Development and Excellence (CFDE), and the Tam Institute's Evans Directorship Endowment Fund and Judaica Book Fund.

Archives are central to the writing of history, including this book. I great-ly appreciate the support provided by the many archives that I visited. Chief among them is the Center for Jewish History (CJH), which funded a year of my research through a Graduate Research Fellowship. The Center's staff throughout the years, including Malgo Duverger, Ilya Slavutskiy, Michelle McCarthy, J.D. Arden, Chris Barthel, Zachary Loeb, Melanie Meyers, Tam-ar Zeffren, and Tyi-Kimya Marx, has proved very helpful, as have staff of its partner archives, YIVO, the Leo Baeck Institute, the American Sephardi Federation, and the American Jewish Historical Society.

My research at the Jacob Rader Marcus Center of the American Jewish Archives in Cincinnati was made possible by the Marcus Center's Ameri-can Council for Judaism Fellowship. I appreciate the support of the ar-chives' staff, including Gary Zola, Dana Herman, and Kevin Proffitt, who made it an enjoyable and productive stay. I similarly thank archivists Betsey Welland, Judy Jarrow, and Gregory Thompson of the University of Utah archives, a trip generously supported by a Friends of the J. Willard Marriott Library Research Grant. I thank Michael Koncewicz of Tamiment Library and Robert F. Wagner Labor Archives.

I also thank the many staff members who aided my research at the New York Public Library, the American Jewish Committee archives, the Colum-bia University archives, the Yale University archives, the Northwestern University archives, the University of Chicago archives, the Wisconsin His-torical Society, the Berman Jewish Policy Archive, the Israel State Archives, the Central Zionist Archives, the National Library in Jerusalem, the Pin-chas Lavon Institute for Labor Research Archives, the Yad Yaari Research and Documentation Center, the Ben-Gurion archives, the University of Pennsylvania archives, the National Archives, the Johns Hopkins Univer-sity archives, and the New York University archives and library.

At conferences, seminars, and through various conversations and corre-spondences, I benefited from hearing the thoughts of James Loeffler, Mel-ani McAlister, Philip Mattar, Lila Corwin Berman, Jonathan Judaken, Susannah Heschel, Michael Fischbach, Liora Halperin, Rashid Khalidi, Deborah Dash Moore, Riv-Ellen Prell, Fred Lazin, Ian Lustick, Hugh Wil-ford, Rebecca Kobrin, Anita Norich, Hillel Cohen, Arie Dubnov, Mira Sucharov, Sherene Seikaly, Robert Johnston, Avinoam Patt, Phil Hollander,

Jonathan Sarna, Tony Michels, Pamela Pennock, Hani Bawardi, Yuval Ben-Bassat, Abigail Jacobson, Ofer Shiff, Zohar Segev, James Stocker, Noam Pianko, Shaul Kelner, Yisrael Ne'eman, Ken Stein, Carl Yonker, Natan Aridan, Avi Shilon, Michael Brenner, Barry Trachtenberg, David Biale, and Shaul Magid. Of particular note are Marjorie Feld and Matt Berkman, who have been important and generous interlocutors as we have researched related topics, including at times the same colorful cast of characters.

A number of other people read all or most of my manuscript in virtual reading groups and offered helpful comments. I thank Ayelet Brinn, Ashley Walters, Geraldine Gudefin, Michael Rom, Ofer Dynes, Will Pimlott, and Rebekka Grossmann. I give special thanks to those who read late drafts of chapters with a remarkable turnaround time, giving generous and insightful feedback—Hilary Falb Kalisman, Nimrod Ben Zeev, Adam Rasgon, Shay Hazkani, Amy Weiss, Karine Walther, and my longtime friend and collaborator Liz Imber.

I also thank those whom I interviewed or corresponded with, including Ellen Siegel, Uri Avnery, Noam Chomsky, Uri Davis, Elaine Hagopian, Abdeen Jabara, Sabri Jiryis, Don Peretz, Uri Lubrani, Norton Mezvinsky, Atallah Mansour, Sam Norich, Sammy Smooha, Shmuel Toledano, John Ruskay, Arthur Waskow, Aviva Cantor, Irene Gendzier, Mark Mazower, Zalman Usishkin, and Steve Zipperstein. Sabri in particular I thank for his willingness to endure my periodic questions over the course of years. I am also very grateful to Deb Peretz, George Zukerman, Yoav Peled, Reema Sayegh, Yezid Sayigh, and members of the Marshall-Scholle family for sharing memories, thoughts, photos, or other material that helped make this book what it is.

At Yale University Press, I thank Adina Berk, Eva Skewes, Ash Lago, Ann-Marie Imbornoni, and the rest of their team for helping make this book a reality. I also appreciated the insightful feedback of the anonymous reviewers. For research assistance, I thank Layla Wofsy and Natalia Dubno Shevin, who read over the entire manuscript. I also thank Katie Van Heest for editing services, Ryan Davis for copyediting, and Amanda Wilson for indexing.

I also appreciate the personal and scholarly relationships forged over the years with Lior Lehrs, David Barak-Gorodetsky, Bryan Roby, Mostafa Hussein, Caroline Kahlenberg, Anastasiia Strakhova, Netta Cohen, Rebecca

Stoil, Matthew Brittingham, Michael Samuel, Shari Rabin, Tal Elmaliach, Rafi Stern, Ben Steiner, Sa'ed Atshan, Charles Chavis, Amy Milligan, Aaron Welt, Jason Lustig, Sara Halpern, Tarek Tutunji, Yoni Abramson, Tristan Klingelhöfer, and Seth Anziska.

The many friendships that precede graduate school have helped me make it through this long process: Yoni Solomon, Brian Palmiter, Henry Anreder, Josh Zelmar, Maria Bianchi, Kelly Millet, Kelly Harro, Aaron Magid, Nat Sufrin, Ari Gore, and Aaron Gore. I thank them all. Yoni deserves special credit for proofreading on a transpacific flight, as does Henry for hearing more about Don Peretz than any normal person should wish to know. Brian has been a source of intellectual stimulation since college days. I also thank all of my Bologna friends, especially Bobby Strauss and Corey Cox for housing during my DC research trips. I also appreciate the support of my extended family, especially Barbara Schwartz, Jamie Spitz, Cindy Simon, and their respective families. I am especially grateful to the Mir-Halabi family—Adva, Dudi, Debby, Ronen, and the rest—for providing me with a real home and warm *mishpacha* during my research in Israel.

I have much to thank the Kurland family for and do not even know where to begin. I suppose I should start by acknowledging the literal refuge that Susan and Larry provided at the beginning of the pandemic, which ended up being where I revised much of this book. I thank Larry for his insightful feedback on several chapters, Susan for countless meals, and both of them for their help with Gabby and for all of the other support that they have provided Jenny and me.

Finally, I thank my sister Melanie and my parents, Mark and Jan Levin. They have encouraged me in so many ways, and their unceasing support has sustained me for decades. During my years traveling around the world for research, they provided me with an anchor and a home. I thank my dad for reviewing much of what I have written over the years, including the final book manuscript in less than a week, and my mom for her loving support and for always being available for a phone call. Their love of books and of history has done much to influence my own trajectory as a historian, as a teacher, and now as an author.

Jenny, you have been my caring partner from dissertation to book, from Brooklyn to Atlanta, and from well-rested young person to exhausted parent.

We made it through so much while I worked on this project—a pandemic, several moves, bringing a new child into the world, and so much more, none of which has been easy to juggle. I could not put into words my appreciation for your support. To baby Gabby, I wish against all evidence to the contrary that you will someday live in a world with fewer agonizing ethical dilemmas. But if the world's moral quandaries stubbornly endure, I hope this book provides you with some small bit of guidance from those who grappled with tough questions in generations past. With love, I dedicate this book to both of you.

INDEX

Page numbers in **bold** indicate illustrations.

1947 United Nations Partition Plan, 12, 23, 97, 115

1948 war, 9, 56, 83, 181

1949 Israeli election, 63

1950 Blaustein–Ben-Gurion "exchange of views," 8, 135–36

1952 Nationality Law, Israel's, 64, 101–2

1957 memorandum, J. Marshall's, 95–101

1967 war: American Jewish sentiment after, 174; Berger on Israel's "aggression" in, 153; conflating anti-Zionism with antisemitism after, 110, 144; Israeli territorial gains from, 10, 188, 194; left-wing condemnation of Israel after, 179, 189–90, 192, 215

1970s Israeli left-wing politics, 188, 194–216

1977 Breira conference, 207, **207**, 212

1977 Israeli election, 213–14

1979 Egyptian-Israeli Peace Treaty, 214

2021 Gaza crisis, 3

2022 AJC Global Forum, 2–3

Aaronsohn, Aaron, 20

abduction by Arab militia, Peretz's, 24–25

Abram, Morris B., 147–48

Abrams, Elliott, 215

Absentees' Property Law of 1950, Israel's, 89, 93

Acre, 29, 92–93

Action Organization for the Liberation of Palestine, 206

AFME. *See* American Friends of the Middle East (AFME)

AFME-Council Network, 162–64

AJC. *See* American Jewish Committee (AJC)

Aloni, Shulamit, 188, 202, 203, 213

ALPHA, Operation, 12, 121, 145, 163, 227n3

Altalena, 27, 233n21

American Anglo-Jewish press, 37, 54, 68–70, 205, 209

American Christians: AJC's concerns about, 41, 92, 112; at AUB, 33; on Palestinian refugee issue, 158

American Civil Liberties Union (ACLU), 34, 62

American Council for Judaism (the Council): AFME and, 162–64; AJC's criticism of, 137; anti-Zionist ideology of, 9, 152–55, 174; Berger at, 15–16, 153, 155, 174–76; formation and demise of, 9, 153–56, 179, 184–85, 222; Harman on, 152, 168–69, 177; influence in Washington of, 165–67; on Israeli-Palestinian conflict, 153; *Jewish Newsletter* and, 67; L. Rosenwald and, 16, 155, 176; membership, 263n1; Mezvinsky and, 153–54, 177–79; Slawson and Peretz on, 46–47; Truman's message to, 163; Zionist groups on, 167

American Council for Judaism Philanthropic Fund, 174

American Friends of Hebrew University, 79, 175

American Friends of Ihud, 278n4

American Friends of the Middle East (AFME): AJC on, 90, 123–24; on Arab collaboration with known antisemites, 130–31; Berger and, 158–59, **159**; CIA-backed, 2, 112, 116, 159, 227n3, 255–56n13, 265n14; the Council and, 162–64; expenditures, 39; Lazaron and, 159; Sayegh and, 117, 146, 159; undertakings, 116–22

American Friends Service Committee (AFSC): director, 93; grant to CONAME, 182; Peretz and, 18–19, 22, 29–32, **30**, 234n25; refugee relief by, 29–32, 233–34nn24–25; volunteers, **30**

American Israel Public Affairs Committee (AIPAC), 7, 74–75, 140, 204, 225, 228–29n10

American Israelite, 44

American Jewish activists today, 220

American Jewish Alternatives to Zionism (AJAZ), 154, 180

American Jewish anti-Zionism, 8–9, 156, 178, 184, 229n13

American Jewish Committee (AJC): 1957 visit to Israel, 15, 79, 92–95, 249–50n28; 2022 Global Forum, 2–3; ADL and, 111; on AFME, 90, 123–24; Arab minority concerns, 86 90, 107–8; "Arab Propaganda in the United States," 90, 122–23; AZC committee involving, 140–41; Ben-Gurion meeting with, 93–95; under Blaustein, 7–8, **8**, 37–38, 84, **85**, 86; on the Center, 123; on the Council, 137; "dual loyalty" anxiety of, 7–8, 112, 124, 137, 142, 145; under Engel, **8**, 38–39, 43–44, 143; "fact sheets," 92, 109, 124, 141; history of, 80; human relations approach, 100, 251n44; human rights and, 85–86; involvement in Arab affairs in Israel, 86–90, 107–8; Israel and, 7, 15, 38, 53, 80–90, 144; Israel on, 42–43; Israel trip, 92–100; Israeli diplomats on, 56; J. Marshall and, 9, 79, 142; on L. Rosenwald's report of his 1957 Israel trip, 170–71; in the late 1950s, 100–103, 143–44, 148, 251n44; leadership, **8**; "The Middle East Ferment," 92, 124; motivations and scope of, 79–90, 133–34, 144; non-Zionist ideology of, 7, 38, 80–86, 113, 148–49; objectivity and neutrality of, 143; office in Tel Aviv, 15, 79, 103–6; Palestinian refugee initiative, 39–49, 53–54; Peretz and, 19, 40–42, 49–53, 142, 218–19; on PLO meeting, 209; pro-Arab "propaganda" concerns and response of, 90–92, 122–24, 133–42; on pro-Palestinian activism, 225; Sayegh meeting, 133–34, 224; on SNCC, 147–48; on UNGA 3379, 110

American Jewish community. *See* American Jewry; American Jews

American Jewish Congress (AJCongress), 113–14, 124, 133, 209

American Jewish liberalism and Israeli policy, 213, 219

American Jewish press, 37, 54, 68–70, 205, 209

American Jewish Yearbook, 53

American Jewry: "Arab Propaganda Network" and, 90–92, 122–24; Israel and, 2–3, 5, 12, 76, 84, 143–44, 220; Israeli diplomats and, 5, 12, 37, 53–54, 76, 84; on Jewish statehood, 114, 156, 222. *See also* American Jews

American Jews: on Berger's criticism of Israel in Six-Day War, 153; in Israel, 194–98, 220–21; Israeli narrative's effect on, 37–38, 83–84; on Palestinian nationalism and the refugee issue, 39, 204, 226; on Sartawi and Jiryis, 210; Zionism and, 75, 114, 156, 179, 194

American Nationalist, 126

American press on the Arab minority issue, 86–90

American Protestants on Jewish nationalism, 82–83

American University of Beirut (AUB), 33, 117, 146

American Zionist Council (AZC): anti-Zukerman campaign of, 68–70; Campus Coordinating Committee spearheaded by, 140–41; on Council criticism of Berger's July 1967 *NYT* interview, 175–76; Jewish Agency-backed, 14; pamphlets, 37; on Peretz, 52

American Zionist Emergency Council (AZEC), 36

American Zionists, Israeli diplomats' relationship with, 68–69, 74

"Americanization" of Jews and Israel, 144

Americans for a Safe Israel (AFSI), 186, 211

Americans for Peace Now, 215

Americans for Progressive Israel (API), 190

Amitai, Yossi, 203

Ammot, 104

AMOCO, 84, 85, 247n12

Anglo-Jewish press, 37, 54, 68–70, 205, 209

Anisfield-Wolf Book Award, 137

anti-Communism, 83

Anti-Defamation League (ADL): AJC parting ways with, 111; antisemitic accusations of pro-Arab groups by, 114–15, 125–33, 224; against Chomsky, 183–84, 270n58; *Cross-Currents,* 125–27; against left-wing Israelis, 201; "the new anti-Semitism" term coined by, 110; pro-Arab "propaganda" concerns and response of, 111, 124–27; public relations campaigns, 83; on *SNCC Newsletter,* 148

anti-PLO sentiments, 203, 274n34

antisemites, Arab collaboration with known, 128–30

"anti-Semites, professional," 125

antisemitic periodicals and organizations, 128–29

antisemitism: ADL's allegations of pro-Arab, 114–15, 125–33, 224; in America in the late 1950s, 258n34; anti-Zionism and, 10, 81–84, 110, 113–14, 144, 225; white Christian, 90–91, 112

anti-Zionism: American Jewish, 8–9, 156, 178, 184, 229n13; antisemitism and, 10, 81–84, 110, 113–14, 144, 225; Arab, 15, 23; Berger's, 151, 153, 155, 173–74, 180; Orthodox Jewish, 229n13; Reform Jewish, 154, 229n13; Zionists and non-Zionists countering, 144

anti-Zionist Jews, 90
anti-Zionist legislation, 113
anti-Zionists of the Jewish Labor Bund,
    37–38, 59–60, 65, 220, 242n15
Arab anti-Zionism, 15, 23
Arab civil rights, J. Marshall's interest
    in, 97–98
Arab collaboration with known
    antisemites, 128–30
Arab fears of Israeli expansionism, 166
Arab flight, 41
Arab League, 90, 118
Arab League's Arab Information Center
    in New York City (the Center): ADL
    on, 111, 132, 224; AJC on, 123; *Cross-
    Currents* on, 125–27; expenditures,
    39; Fayez Sayegh at, 91, 118–19;
    opening of, 12, 118; pro-Arab
    publications by, 91, 102–3; Sayegh
    on, 145–46
Arab Legion, 27
Arab majority in Palestine, 23, 96
Arab militia's abduction of Peretz, 24–25
Arab minority: AJC's concern with,
    86–90, 107–8; under military rule,
    4, 15, 78, 92–95, 104, 191; *NYT* on,
    86–87; rights, 92–95
Arab minority issue: American press
    on, 86–90; for Israel, 107; J.
    Marshall on, 39, 98; Koussa on, 78;
    Lazaron on, 162; Maximo
    Yagupsky's AJC work to address,
    103–6; Peretz on, 47–48, 90, 91;
    Sayegh on, 91
"Arab Minority of Israel, The" (Peretz),
    278n1
Arab National League, 113
Arab Office, 114–15, 255n11
"Arab Plight in the Holy Land, The"
    (Sayegh), 91
"Arab Propaganda and Antisemitism"
    (Peretz), 129
"Arab Propaganda in the United States"
    (AJC), 90, 122–23

"Arab propaganda network," 90–91
Arab property, mass confiscation of,
    89, 93
*Arab Property in Israeli-Controlled
    Territories* (Sayegh), 91
Arab public advocacy, 15, 88, 111–12,
    122–27
"Arab Refugee Dilemma, The" (Peretz),
    41
Arab refugee initiative, AJC's, 39–49,
    53–54
Arab refugee issue. *See* Palestinian
    refugee issue
Arab Refugee Problem, The
    (Schechtman), 35, 37
Arab refugees. *See* Palestinian refugees
"Arab Refugees: Facts and Figures"
    (Schechtman), 36–37
Arab States Delegations Office. *See*
    Arab League's Arab Information
    Center in New York City (the
    Center)
Arab states' invasion, May 1948,
    232n10
Arab student convention, 117
Arab Unity: Hope and Fulfillment
    (Sayegh), 118
Arabic-Hebrew dictionary, 96–97
*Arab-Israeli Debate: Toward a Socialist
    Solution* (Times Change Press), 193
"Arabists," 115
Arab-Jewish rapprochement, 25–26,
    273n26
Arabs: Berger and, 180; depiction of,
    144
Arabs in Israel, The (Jiryis), 182–83
Arafat, Yasser, 173, 204
al-Ard, 206, 252n55
Arendt, Hannah, 97, 219
Arnon, Yaakov, 203, 244n28
Ashkenazi Jewry, 60, 105
El-Asmar, Fouzi, 182–83, 201
assimilation, problem of Jewish,
    221–22

Association of Jewish Community
    Relations Workers, 137–38
Avnery, Uri, 188, 201–4, 206, 213,
    275n42, 276n53
Avnery-Hammami meeting, 204

Balad al-Shaykh massacre, 23, 232n10
Baldwin, Roger, 34, 62
Begin, Menachem, 11, 27, 213, 249–
    50n28
Ben Yehuda Street explosions, 25
Bendor, S., 167
Ben-Gurion, David: AJC officials'
    meeting with, 93–95; Blaustein and,
    84, **85**, 135–36, 171–72; on
    Eisenhower, 163; L. Rosenwald and,
    170, 172; quote on *Tex and Jinx*, 132,
    135; on Zionism, 94–95
Ben-Horin, Eliahu, 35–36
Bennett, Naftali, 221–22
Berger, Elmer: 1955 Middle East trip by,
    160–61; 1971 Arab Middle East tour
    by, 182; AFME and, 158–59, **159**;
    AJAZ and, 180; anti-Zionism of, 151,
    153, 155, 173–74, 180; Arabs and,
    180; Byroade and, 165–67; CJP and,
    115; the Council and, 15–16, 153, 155,
    174–76; as a "first generation"
    advocate for Palestinians, 9, 221;
    Institute for Palestine Studies and,
    182; on Israel, 174; *The Jewish
    Dilemma*, 156; on Judaism as a
    religion, 156; July 1967 *NYT*
    interview with, 16, 174–76;
    Mezvinsky and, 177–78, 180; on
    Palestinian refugee camps, 161; on
    the Palestinian refugee issue, 158–
    61, 173; *A Partisan History of
    Judaism*, 157; PLO and, 173; Sayegh
    and, 118, 152, 158–60, 173, 224; on
    UNGA 3379, 151; on Zionism, 157,
    161; Zukerman in a letter to, 71–72
Bernadotte, Folke, 29
Bernstein, Vic, 68

Binationalism, 22, 25, 181, 191, 196,
    232n14
Biran, Avraham, 138
Bishop Isidorus of the Greek Orthodox
    Church, 93
al-Bitar, Salah al-Din, 51
Black Power movement, 148, 149, 179
Black-Jewish relations, 146–48,
    262n75
Blaustein, Jacob: as AJC president, 7–8,
    8, 37–38, 84, **85**, 86; on the AJC's
    refugee initiative, 44–46; Ben-
    Gurion and, 84, **85**, 135–36, 171–72;
    Israeli officials and, 86, 135; non-
    Zionist, 155; on repatriation and
    resettlement, 38
Blitzer, Wolf, 16, 209
B'nai B'rith, 113–14, 140, 209
Bober, Arie, 181
Borowitz, Eugene, 188
"Breira: A Counsel for Judaism"
    (Americans for a Safe Israel), 211
Breira: A Project of Concern in
    Diaspora-Israel Relations: 1977
    conference, 207, **207**, 212; American
    Jewish press's critique of, 205;
    founders, membership, and
    initiatives, 182, 188, 195; ideology
    and goals of, 187–89, 198–200;
    *Interchange: A Monthly Review of
    Issues Facing Israel and the Diaspora*,
    188, 198, 202, 205, 275n39; *Israel
    and the Palestinians: A Different
    Israeli View*, 202; Israeli left-wing
    figures hosted by, 188, 202–3;
    members' formative visits and
    connections to Israel, 194–99, 219–
    20; Peretz and, 195, 218, 245n37;
    -PLO meeting, 16, 186, 189, 204,
    208–11; rise and fall of, 10–11, 15–16,
    186–87, 194, 199, 211–14, 277n59;
    scholars' characterization of, 187–
    88; two-state solution proposed by,
    10–11, 200–201

Breitel, Charles, 141–42, 261n64
Brickner, Balfour, 199
Briem, Arlene, 146
British forces, withdrawal of, 28
British Jewry, 57
British Mandate of Palestine, 22, 35,
    96, 117
Britton, Frank, 126
Bund, Jewish Labor, 37–38, 59–60, 95,
    220, 242n15
Burns, William, 217
Byroade, Henry, 165–67

Camp David Accords, 11, 214
Campus Coordinating Committee,
    140–41
Cantor, Aviva: on Gush Emunim, 205;
    Israel Horizons and, 190; JLP and,
    190, 192–93; Lilith and, 192;
    "Radical Zionist" views of, 190
Caplan, Louis, 8, 141
Caravan, 146
Carmichael, Stokely, 180
Carnegie Endowment for Peace, 45
Carter, Jimmy, 209, 214
Catholic Near East Welfare Association,
    158
Central Conference of American
    Rabbis (CCAR), 155
Central Intelligence Agency (CIA):
    officials, 12–13, 115, 121; -funded
    AFME, 2, 112, 116, 159, 227n3, 255–
    56n13, 265n14
Chanin, Nathan, 62
Childers, Erskine B., 172
Chofshi, Natan, 73, 245n33
Chomsky, Noam: American Jewish
    groups against, 183–84, 270n58;
    background, career, and views
    of, 180–83; CONAME and, 154,
    180–82, 198, 211; Israeli and
    Palestinian activists and, 183;
    "Nationalism and Conflict in
    Palestine," 181; New York Review of

Books ad involving, 196–97; Peace in
    the Middle East, 181
"Christian Communities in Israel"
    (Peretz), 41, 50, 92
Christian groups. See American
    Friends of the Middle East (AFME)
Christian Zionism, 222
Christianity and Crisis, 82
"Christianization" of Jews and Israel,
    144
Chutzpah, 197, 273n26
CIA-funded AFME, 2, 112, 116, 159,
    227n3, 255–56n13, 265n14
clericalism, 63
Coffin, Henry Sloane, 82–83
Cohen, Eliot, 87
Cold War, 13, 121, 149, 212
Coleman, Clarence, 161, 176
Columbia University, Peretz at,
    32–35
Columbus Platform, 155
Commentary, 87–88, 175, 201, 211
Committee for Justice and Peace in the
    Holy Land (CJP), 115–16, 159
Committee on New Alternatives in the
    Middle East (CONAME), 154, 180–
    82, 198, 211, 219, 245n37
Conference of Presidents of Major
    American Jewish Organizations, 7,
    140, 142, 188, 209, 228–29n10
Cronbach, Abraham, 62
Cross-Currents (Epstein and Forster),
    125–27

Davis, Uri, 182–83, 201
Dawidowicz, Lucy, 171
Dayan, Moshe, 147
Defender, 125, 126
Deir Yassin Massacre, 28, 266–67n24
Dershowitz, Alan, 201, 270n58
"Development of Israeli Left Attitudes
    Towards the Palestinian Question"
    (Samuelson), 198
Diamond, Stanley, 182

Diaspora-Israel relations, 2–3, 5, 13, 86, 200, 216, 222

Dingol, S., 102

diplomatic pressure, Israeli, 37, 53–54

diplomats. *See* Israeli diplomats

discrimination, Maximo Yagupsky on, 105–6

dissenters, crisis of, 217–18

Divon, Shmuel, 101

Documents from Israel, 1967–73: Readings for a Critique of Zionism (Davis and Mezvinsky), 183

Donovan, John, 24, 27

Draper, Hal, 91, 249n26

"dual loyalty" anxiety, AJC's, 7–8, 112, 124, 137, 142, 145

Dulles, John Foster: L. Rosenwald and, **164**, 165; on Nasser, 121; on the Palestinian refugee issue, 41–42; on the Truman administration, 164

Eban, Abba, 36, 46, 118, 135

Edelsberg, Herman, 186, 208–9

Egypt: 1973 Yom Kippur War and, 200; Camp David Accords with, 11, 214; Operation Alpha and, 12, 145; U.S. and, 120–22

Egyptian embassy, 90

Egyptian Jewry, plight of, 49

Egyptian-American relationship, 121–22

Egyptian-Israeli Peace Treaty, 1979, 214

Egypt's Liberation, 122

Ehrmann, Herbert, 89, 93

Eisenhower, Dwight, 12, 38, 163, 165

Eisenhower administration, 145, 164–65, 222

"Eisenhower Doctrine," 145

Elath, Eliahu, 36, 71

Eliav, Arie "Lova," 188, 203, 213

Eliav, Pinhas, 42–43, 49, 76, 142–43

Elson, Edward, 266n20

Elyasher, Eliahu, 203

Engel, Irving M.: 1957 Israeli visit by, 79, 92–95, 136; as AJC president, **8**, 38–39, 43–44, 143

Epstein, Benjamin: on the Center, 111, 132; *Cross-Currents*, 125–27

Epstein, Eliahu, 114

Eshkol, Levi, **75**

"establishment dissidents," 202, 203, 213

ethnic revivalism, 153

ethno-national particularism, 17

European Jewry, Nazi genocide of, 85

Exodus (Uris), 144

Exponent, 67–68, 70

Face the Nation, 111, 119

"fact sheets," AJC's, 92, 109, 124, 141

Fatah, 193, 205

Federation of Jewish Philanthropies of New York, 46

Fein, Leonard, 205

Fineberg, Solomon Andhil: Campus Coordinating Committee and, 140–41; career, publications, and views of, 137–38, 140, 142, 260n57; on Sayegh, 109, 112, 139–40, 146

"first generation" of American Jews concerned with Palestinian rights, 9–10, 220–21

Flanders, Ralph, 246–47n9

Flapan, Simcha, 188, 202

Forster, Arnold, 111, 125–28, 132, 258n33

Forverts, 58–59

Free Jewish Club, 65–66

"Free Officers" Revolt of 1952, 120

Freedman, Benjamin, 125

Freedman, Marcia, 188, 201

Freedom House, 178

"Freedom Seder Hagadah" (Waskow), 211

Freeman, Charles, **30**

Freidan, Betty, 205, 272n16

Fromm, Erich, 61

Galilee, the: AFSC relief in, 29–32, 233–34n24; refugees in, **32**

Gaza Strip: AFSC refugee relief in, 29–32, 233–34nn24–25; Israel's 1956–57 occupation of, 202; Israel's post-1967 occupation of, 10, 180, 194

Gendler, Everett, 182, 201

Gendzier, Irene, 182, 198

General Jewish Labor Bund in Russia, 59–60

Georgetown University, Sayegh at, 117

Gildersleeve, Virginia, 117

Gillon, Dan, 198, 212

Ginsburg, Faye, 195, 198

Golan Heights, 153, 214

Goldberg, B. Z., 102

Goldman, Emma, 59

Goldman, Nahum, 155, 208, 213, 276n50

Goldstein, Herman, 114

Gordis, Robert, 188

Gorin, David, 186, 208

Gottlieb, Bill, 173

Government Yearbook of Israel 1953–1954, 132, 135–36

Grossman, Rita, 70

Gruen, George, 53, 208–9, 223–24

Gush Emunim, 205, 211

Haaretz, 34, 220

Hadassah, 20, 228–29n10

Hadassah Magazine, 188

Hadawi, Sami, 102–3

Haganah, 23, 26, 232n10

Haifa Oil Refinery massacre, 23, 232n10

Hakim, George, 93, 249–50n28

Haliq, Omar, 126

Halpern, Ben, 53

Hammami, Said, 204

Hardman, J. B. S., 61

Harman, Avraham "Abe": anti-Zukerman campaign of, 15, 56, 67–74, 245n31; career of, **75**, 243–44n21;

on the Council, 152, 168–69, 177; Lazaron and, 167–68

Hart, Merwin K., 125

hasbara, Israel's attempts to improve its, 35–38

HaShomer HaTzair (Socialist-Zionist youth movement), 22, 181, 195

Hassan, Abdul H., 129–31

Hassouna, Abdul Khalek, 118, 122, 134

Havurah movement, 189, 195

Hebrew Immigrant Aid Society (HIAS), 58

Hebrew University of Jerusalem, 22, 24, 79, 93, 97, 183, 218, 278n2

Held, Adolph, 62

Heller, James, 155

Herald Tribune, 70, 120

Herlitz, Esther: on the AJC's refugee initiative, 43–45; career of, 76, 218, 245n36; with Moshe Sharett, **45**

Herman, Basil, 125

Hertz, John, 62, 241n9

Hertzberg, Arthur, 213

Herzl, Theodore, 68

Herzog, Yaakov, 167, 267n27

Hillel, 67, 140, 195, 208, 212, 276n51, 277n56

Hitler, Adolf, 94, 114–15

Hocking, William Ernest, 117

Hoffman, Benzion "Zivion," 64–65

Hoffman, Isidor, 22

Holyland Emergency Liaison Program, 115–16

Hoover, Herbert, 36

Hopkins, Garland Evans, 124–25, 254n4

Hotel Delmonico, 134, 259n51

Hourani, Cecil, 225

Howe, Irving, 207, 212

human relations approach, AJC's, 100, 251n44

human rights, AJC as a champion of, 85–86

Hurewitz, J. C., 32

Hussein, King of Jordan, 51, 173
al-Husseini, Amin, 33, 94, 113–15, 235n32, 250n30

ICIPP-PLO talks, 16, 205–6
IfNotNow, 221, 225, 235n34, 265n14, 278n4
Ihud, 22, 79, 97
Impact of Israel on American Jews, The (Zukerman), 73
Indyk, Martin, 222
Inselbuch, Samson, 113–14
Institute for Arab American Affairs (IAAA), 114–15, 255n11
Institute for Mediterranean Affairs (IMA), 53, 239n72
Institute for Palestine Studies, 182
Institute for Policy Studies, 195, 196
Interchange: A Monthly Review of Issues Facing Israel and the Diaspora (Breira), 188, 198, 202, 205, 275n39
interfaith citizens' initiative, 44
International Committee of the Red Cross (ICRC), 29, 234n25
International Jewish Labor Bund, 65, 242n15
International League for the Rights of Man, 34
Iraq, Palestinian Arab resettlement in, 36
Irgun and Lehi militias, 23, 28
Isaac, Rael Jean, 211–12
Israel: 1948 creation of, 1, 117; 1949 election in, 63; 1952 Nationality Law in, 64, 101–2; 1953 Land Acquisition Law in, 89, 93; 1977 election in, 213–14; "active defense" policies of, 42; AJC and, 7, 15, 38, 53, 80–90, 144; AJC's 1957 visit to, 15, 79, 92–95, 249–50n28; American cultural identification with and support for, 144, 145, 148, 153–54; American Jewish press on, 37, 54, 68–70; American Jewry and, 2–3, 5, 12, 76,

84, 143–44, 220; American Jews in, 194–98, 220–21; "Americanization," "Christianization," and "masculinization" of, 144; America's Middle East strategy and, 145; Arab minority issue for, 107; Arab-owned land appropriation laws of, 89, 93; Berger on, 174; Breira members' formative visits and connections to, 194–99, 219; Eisenhower administration and, 164–65; MERIP on, 192; military rule in, 15, 92, 94–95, 104, 206; Palestinian refugee issue for, 106–7; repatriation resistance by, 28–29, 37, 42, 54; Truman administration and, 163, 165; UN condemnation of, 204
Israel and the Arab Minority (Hadawi), 102–3
Israel and the Palestine Arabs (Peretz), 34–35
Israel and the Palestinians: A Different Israeli View (Breira), 202
Israel Defense Forces (IDF), 26, 188, 202
"Israel Faces Its Arab Minority: The Native within the Gates" (Teller), 87–88
Israel Horizons, 190
Israel State Archives (ISA), 11, 69, 171
Israel-American Christian relations, 14
Israel-Diaspora relations, 2–3, 5, 13, 86, 200, 216, 222
Israeli Council for Israeli-Palestinian Peace (ICIPP): Breira and, 210, 216; Jiryis meeting with, 205, 206; leadership, membership, and views of, 203, 213, 275n42; -PLO talks, 16, 205–6; Sartawi meetings with, 205, 206
Israeli diplomats: on the AJC, 56; American Jewry and, 5, 12, 37, 53–54, 76, 84; American Zionists and, 68–69, 74; anti-Zukerman

Israeli diplomats: (*continued*)
campaign of, 15, 56, 67–76, 245n31;
Lazaron and, 167–68; on Peretz, 43;
against Zukerman, 15, 56, 67–76,
245n31
Israeli expansionism, Arab fears of, 166
Israeli Government's Transfer
Committee, 36
Israeli immigration policy, 4
Israeli Jews, political leanings of, 221
Israeli Labor Party, 11, 213
Israeli League for Human and Civil
Rights, 183
Israeli leftists, 188, 194–216
Israeli left-wing politics, 1970s, 188,
194–216
Israeli military forces, Palestinian Arab
expulsion and governance by, 28, 31,
78
Israeli military government
restrictions, 4, 78, 92–95
Israeli narrative, 37–38
Israeli rhetoric on mass American
Jewish Immigration to Israel, 82
Israeli-Arab armistice agreements, 32
Israeli-Palestinian conflict, the Council
on issues related to, 153
Israeli-PLO negotiations, 200, 203

J Street, 215, 221, 225
Jacobs, Paul, 182, 196
Jerusalem Post, 16, 25, 209
Jewish advocacy groups. *See* American
Jewish Committee (AJC); Anti-
Defamation League (ADL)
Jewish Advocate, 67–68, 70
Jewish Agency, 26, 36–37, 96, 223,
230n21
Jewish anti-Zionism, 8–9, 156, 178,
184, 229n13
Jewish Chronicle, 57, 71
Jewish Community Relations Council
(JCRC), San Francisco's, 138–39
Jewish Daily Forward, 58

Jewish Dilemma, The (Berger), 156
Jewish Exponent, 67–68, 70
Jewish Frontier, 71, 196, 241n7
Jewish identity, 2–4, 6, 85, 173, 210,
215, 221, 226
Jewish integration, 156
Jewish Labor Bund, 37–38, 59–60, 65,
220, 242n15
Jewish Labor Bund Bulletin, 65
Jewish Labor Committee, 62
Jewish Liberation Journal, 192, 193
Jewish Liberation Project (JLP), 190,
192–94
Jewish Morning Journal, 59, 72, 244n29
Jewish nationalism, 3–4, 7, 81–83, 155,
162
Jewish Newsletter: on AJC's meeting
with Ben-Gurion, 101; board
members, 61–62, 241n9;
characterization of, 62–63; Lazaron
and, 62, 161–62; on the Palestinian
refugee issue, 72–73, 243n19; Peretz
and, 47, 52, 55, 62, 72, 129, 219; Y.
H. Levin on, 70–71; Zukerman's
founding of, 14–15, 56–57, 61–63
Jewish Peace Fellowship, 22, 201
Jewish press, 37, 54, 68–70, 205, 209
Jewish refugees from Arab countries,
30, 41
Jewish statehood: American Jews on,
114, 156, 222; implications of, 82
Jewish Telegraphic Agency (JTA), 62–
63, 166, 175, 195–96, 246n2
Jewish Voice for Peace, 225
Jewish Welfare Board, 59
Jewish World News Service, 72,
244n29
Jewish-Black relations, 146–48, 262n75
Jewish-Christian relations in the
United States, AJC's views of, 39,
92
Jews, "Americanization,"
"Christianization," and
"masculinization" of, 144

Jews against Zionism (Kolsky), 154
Jews for Urban Justice (JUJ), 190, 192, 196, 211, 215
Jiryis, Sabri: *The Arabs in Israel*, 182–83; background, career, and views of, 206; Breira meeting with, 186; ICIPP meeting with, 205, 206; on the July 1957 reform, 95; Mezvinsky and, 182
Johnson, Lyndon, **75**, 175, 177
Johnson administration, 185
Jordan: civil war in, 191; refugee relief in, 233–34n24
Journal-Tog, 102
Judah L. Magnes Foundation, 97, 219, 250–51n36
Judaism: liberal, 221; as a religion, not as a nationality or race, 155, 156
July 1957 reform, 95
Jundi, Said, 25, 232n13
June 1967 war. *See* 1967 war

Kafr Qasim massacre, 88–90, 252n55
Kallen, Horace, 62
Kaminer, Reuven, 197
Karameh, 1968 Battle of, 205
Kassis, Masad, 41
Kazin, Alfred, 61
Kenan, Amos, 188, 193, 202, 203
Kennedy, John F., **8**, 175
Kennedy administration, 222
kibbutz experiences by American Jews, 181, 188, 191, 197, 198
Kibya incident, 89, 126, 166, 242n15, 266–67n24
Klopfer, Donald, 174–75
Klutznick, Philip, 208, 212, 213, 276n50
Knesset, 76, 166–67, 188, 202
Kohn, Hans, 48–49, 62, 76, 97, 218, 245n37
Kohn, Leo, 167
Kohn, Moshe, 170–71
Kolack, Sol, 125

Kollek, Theodore, 171–73, 176
Kolsky, Thomas, 154
Korn, Richard, 174
Koussa, Elias, 78–79, 87, 97, 246n1
Ku Klux Klan, 38–39, 147
Kuwait, 110, 149, 253n1

Labor Zionism, 60, 181
Land Acquisition Law of 1953, Israel's, 89, 93
"Land Day," 205
Langston, Berta, 181–82
Lasser, Josephine, 20
Lazaron, Morris: 1953 Middle East trip by, 1–2, 161–62, 265n11; AFME and, 159; anti-Zionist views of, 2, 168; on the Arab minority issue, 162; CJP and, 115; Harman and, 167–68; Israeli diplomats and, 167–68; *Jewish Newsletter* and, 62, 161–62; *Olive Trees in Storm*, 162; on the Palestinian refugee issue, 1–2, 161–62; on the Shatila refugee camp, 1, 161–62
League of Red Cross Societies (LRCS), 29, 234n25
Lebanon: Palestinian refugees in, 31; refugee relief in, 233–34n24
left-wing Jewish organizations and publications, 189–93
left-wing politics, 1970s Israeli, 188, 194–216
Legation of Lebanon in Washington, 118
Leon, Dan, 196
Levin, Yehuda Harry, 56, 67–74
Levison, George, 158–59
liberal Christian groups, AJC and ADL and, 83
liberal Judaism, 221
"liberalizing" of Israel through education, 103–7
"Liberation of Palestine and Israel, The" ad, 196–97

Likud party, 11, 213
Lilienthal, Alfred, 157, 162, 264n9,
266n17
Lilith, 192
Lipsky, Louis, 70, 74–75
Loeb, Robert, 176, 182, 195, 198, 211,
213
Louchheim, Joseph, 174–75
Lourie, Arthur, 72
Lowenberg, Helmuth, 42, 86, 88–89
Lukas, Edwin, 134
Lurie, Jesse Zel, 188
Lustick, Ian, 195–96, 273n23

Maass, Richard, 141–42
MacDonald, Dwight, 61
Madole, James H., 125, 129–30
Magnes, Judah: binationalist beliefs of,
22, 23, 96–97; J. Marshall and, 39,
79, 95, 96–97, 246n2; Peretz on,
25, 27, 217–18
Malik, Charles, 118
Mandate Palestine, 22, 35, 96, 117
Marcus, Stanley, 174–75
Margolin, Olya, 186, 208
Margoshes, Samuel, 63–64
Maroz, Yohanan, 76
Marshall, James: 1927 Palestine visit
by, 95–96; 1957 Israeli visit by, 79,
92–95, 249–50n28; 1957
memorandum by, 95–101; AJC and,
9, 79, 142; on the Arab minority
issue, 39, 98; career of, 97–98;
Magnes and, 39, 79, 95, 96–97,
246n2
Marshall, Louis, 79, 95, 246n2, 250n33
"masculinization" of Jews and Israel,
144
Matzpen, 182
Mazower, Max, 59
McCarthyism, 83, 184
McDonald, Larry, 212, 277n57
Meir, Golda, 42, 51, 76, **85**, 245n36
Melman, Seymour, 182

"Menace of Jewish Fascism, The"
(Zukerman), 60
Menorah Journal, 96, 160, 245n31
Meyerson, Golda. *See* Meir, Golda
Mezvinsky, Norton: background and
academic career of, 177–78,
269n46; Berger and, 177–78, 180;
the Council and, 153–54, 177–79;
Documents from Israel, 183; Middle
Eastern travel and relationships
formed by, 182–83
Middle East: American foreign policy
toward, 2, 145; bloody crises in, 88–
90
"Middle East Ferment, The," 92, 124
Middle East Institute Award, Peretz's,
217
Middle East Journal, 34, 87–88
Middle East Research and Information
Project (MERIP), 192
Middle East Today, The (Peretz), 77
Middle Eastern Jewry, 37
Middle Eastern oil, 164
military government restrictions,
Israeli, 4, 78, 92–95
military rule, 15, 92, 94–95, 104, 191
militias, Irgun and Lehi, 23, 28
Mizrahi Jews, 105
Moked left-wing political party, 198
monoculture, American, 83
Moody Monthly, 91
Morgan, Rita, 31
Morgen Freiheit, 59
Morgen Zshurnal, Der, 59, 72, 244n29
Morris, Yaakov, 51
Mosler, John, 175
Moynihan, Daniel Patrick, 110
Mufti. *See* al-Husseini, Amin
Muslim Brotherhood, 33

NAACP, 97
Nasser, Gamal Abdel: American foreign
policy establishment on, 120–22,
145; Berger's visit with, 173; Dulles

on, 121; Egypt and, 88, 120; Peretz's
visit with, 51; Sayegh's visit with,
145
Nation, 114
National Communal Relations
Advisory Council (NCRAC), 110,
140, 253n3
National Council of Jewish Women,
113, 140
National Jewish Post, 46, 66–67, 170–71
National Renaissance Party (NRP), 129,
147
nationalism: Jewish, 3–4, 7, 82–83;
Palestinian Arab, 34–35, 160, 185,
204; wartime, 26
"Nationalism and Conflict in Palestine"
(Chomsky), 181
Nazareth, AJC delegation's 1957 trip to,
92–93
Nazism, 36, 60
Nelson, Louis, 61
neo-Nazi organizations, 129
Ner, 79, 97
Netanyahu, Benjamin, 76
Neusner, Jacob, 188
"new anti-Semitism, the" term, 110
"New Historians," 34, 73, 172, 234n36,
239n68
New International, 91
New Jewish Agenda, 215
"New Left Go Home" (Kenan), 193
New Left/Leftists, 10, 154, 180–81, 189–
93, 197
New Outlook, 197, 198
New Palestine, 96
New York Herald Tribune, 70, 120
New York Review of Books, 196–97, 203
New York Times: on the Arab minority,
86–87; Berger's July 1967 interview
with, 16, 174–76; Berger's support
of UNGA 3379 in, 151; on PLO
meeting, 209; "U.S. Jews Split on
Mideast War: Some See Response in
Nation as 'Hysteria,' " 174–76

Night Beat, 119–20, 131–31
Nixon, Richard, 185
nongovernmental organizations
involved in refugee relief, 29–32,
233–34nn24–25
Non-Sectarian Anti-Nazi League, 115
nonsectarian leftist organizations, 154
Non-Zionism, AJC on, 7, 38, 80–86,
113, 148–49
Non-Zionist American Jews, Israeli
diplomats and, 37, 53–54
Norich, Sam, 208
North African Jewry, 39
Novak, William, 199

Office of Strategic Services (OSS), 115
Olive Trees in Storm (Lazaron), 162
Open Hillel, 221
Operation Alpha, 12, 121, 145, 163,
227n3
Organization of Arab Students in the
United States (OAS), 117, 122
"Oriental Jews," 105
Orthodox Jewish anti-Zionism, 229n13

Pa'il, Meir, 188, 198, 202, 203, 213
Painter, Levinus, 29, **30**
Palestine: Arab majority in, 23, 96; civil
war in, 23, 232n10; J. Marshall's
1927 visit to, 95–96; Jewish
settlement in, 155
Palestine Arab Congress, 145
Palestine Conciliation Commission, 31
Palestine Liberation Organization
(PLO): Berger and, 173; Breira
meeting with, 16, 186, 189, 204,
208–11; ICIPP talks with, 16, 205–6;
Research Center, 10, 149, 206, 214,
277n62; Sayegh and, 109
Palestine National Council, 206
Palestine Post explosions, 25. *See also*
Jerusalem Post
Palestine Week rally at George
Washington University, 180

Palestinian Arab nationalism, 34–35, 160, 185, 204

Palestinian Arab resettlement in Iraq, 36

Palestinian Arabs in Israel. *See* Arab minority

Palestinian militants' attacks on Israeli citizens, 204

Palestinian national movement, 185

Palestinian national self-determination, 194, 196, 204, 213

Palestinian refugee camp visits, Berger's, 161

Palestinian refugee issue: American Jews on, 204; Berger on, 158–61, 173; Dulles on, 41–42; for Israel, 106–7; *Jewish Labor Bund Bulletin* on, 65; *Jewish Newsletter* on, 72–73, 243n19; L. Rosenwald on, 158; Lazaron on, 1–2, 161–62; Peretz on, 18–19, 33–38, 76–77, 237n49; Schechtman on, 35–38; Zukerman on, 9, 56, 64, 67, 72–73

Palestinian refugees: displacement of, 28, 31; in Lebanon, 31; in northern Israel, 29; number of, 69; relief for, 29; return to Israel of, 2, 28; at Shatila refugee camp, 1; suffering of, 1–2

Palestinian Refugees, The (Sayegh), 117

Palestinian rights: American Jewish support for, 9–10, 180, 220–21, 226, 228n6; "second generation" of American Jews concerned with, 10–11, 189–216

Palestinian statehood: Breira's push for, 187; ICIPP's push for, 203

Panken, Jacob, 61

Partisan History of Judaism, A (Berger), 157

partition vote, UN's November 1947, 23

Peace in the Middle East (Chomsky), 181

Peled, Mattityahu "Matti": hosted by Breira, 188, 202, **207**; ICIPP and, 203, 213; IDF and, 202; *Interchange* and, 202; Rabin and, 202; on Sartawi and Jiryis, 210; shifting views of, 203

Peled, Yoav, 195, 197

Peretz, Don: in the 1950s, **40**; about, 9; as the AJC's Middle East consultant, 19, 40–42, 49–53, 218–19; as an AFSC relief worker, 18–19, 22, 29–32, **30**, 233–34nn24–25; Arab militia's abduction of, 24–25; on the Arab minority issue, 47–48, 90, 91; "The Arab Minority of Israel," 278n1; "Arab Propaganda and Antisemitism," 129; "The Arab Refugee Dilemma," 41; AZC on, 52; binationalism and, 23, 26; at Binghamton University-SUNY, 76–77; Breira and, 195, 218, 245n37; as a child, **21**; "Christian Communities in Israel," 41, 50, 92; CONAME and, 182, 198, 219, 245n37; as a doctoral student, 32–35; *Israel and the Palestine Arabs*, 34–35; Israeli diplomats on, 43; *Jewish Newsletter* and, 47, 52, 55, 62, 72, 129, 219; on Magnes, 25, 27, 217–18; Middle East Institute Award received by, 217; *Middle East Journal* article by, 34, 87–88; *The Middle East Today*, 77; on objectivity, 46–48; pacifism of, 22, 24; on Palestinian life, 30–31; on the Palestinian refugee issue, 18–19, 33–38, 76–77, 237n49; "The Plight of the Jews in Egypt," 41; on Sayegh, 131, 249n26; Slawson and, 44, 50; "Steps to Middle East Peace," 41–43; on Zionism, 23–28, 232n6

Peretz, Haym, 20–21, **21**, 49, 218, 231n4, 238n65

Peretz, Heidy Mayer, 33, 234–35n31

"Perils to America in the New Jewish State" (Coffin), 82

Pinski, David, 64

Pittsburgh Platform of 1885, American
     Reform rabbis', 81, 155
"Plight of the Jews in Egypt, The"
     (Peretz), 41
PLO Research Center, 10, 149, 206,
     214, 277n62
"population transfer," 35–36
Prinz, Joachim, 188, 199
pro-Arab public relations efforts, 15, 88,
     111–12, 116–22, 143
"professional anti-Semites," 125
pro-Palestine anti-Zionism with
     antisemitism, conflating, 110,
     144
pro-Palestine stance, Black Power
     movement's, 180
pro-Palestinian activism, 189–92
"prophetic Judaism," 156
Proskauer, Joseph, 38, 82
Protestant "Arabists," 115, 148, 159

Qibya massacre, 89, 126, 166, 242n15,
     266–67n24
Quaker-affiliated AFSE. *See* American
     Friends Service Committee (AFSC)

Raab, Earl, 138–39
Rabbinical Council of America (RCA),
     113–14
Rabin, Yitzhak, 202, 203, 206, 208
"Radical Jews," 190
Radical Zionist Alliance, 193–94
"Radical Zionists," 190, 192–93
Rahim, Kamil Abdul, 119, 125–27, 131,
     133, 146
Ratz Party, 213
Red Scare, 83
Reform Jewish anti-Zionism, 81, 154–
     55, 184, 229n13
refugee relief, 29–32, 233–34nn24–25
refugee return, Israeli government
     on, 37
refugees left outside Israel's borders,
     28, 233n22

repatriation of refugees: American
     pressure for partial, 42; Blaustein
     on, 38; Israel's opposition to, 28–29,
     37, 42, 54; Peretz on, 37;
     Schechtman on, 35–38
Reploge, Ruth, **30**
resettlement, 38, 43
"Resettlement Prospects for Arab
     Refugees" (Schechtman), 36–37
Resolution 3379, UNGA's, 109–10,
     149–51, 204, 223, 253nn1–2
Revisionist Zionism, 35, 60
Riegelman, Harold, 39
Riesman, David, 61
Rifkind, Simon, 39
right-wing Christian antisemites, 90–
     91, 112
Robinson, Michael, 201
"Rogers Plan," 206
Roosevelt, Theodore, 115
Roosevelt Jr., Kermit "Kim," 115–16,
     121, 158–60, 265n11
Rose, Sharon: JUJ and, 190, 211;
     MERIP and, 192; *New York Review of
     Books* ad involving, 196–97;
     "Radical Jewish" anti-Zionist
     ideology and political trajectory of,
     190–91
Rosenberg, Ethel and Julius, 83, 138
Rosenberg trial, 83, 184
Rosenwald, Lessing: 1957 Israel trip
     and report by, 169–73; anti-Zionist
     stance of, 153; Ben-Gurion and, 170,
     172; on Byroade speeches, 167; the
     Council and, 16, 155, 176; Dulles
     and, **164**, 165; Eisenhower and, 165;
     Harman on, 152; as *Jewish Newsletter
     donor*, 62, 241n9; Kollek and, 171–
     72; on Palestinian refugee issue,
     158
Rosenwald, William, 169
Rothschild Jr., Walter N., 174–75
Ruskay, John, 182, 195, 196, 198,
     199, 211

Sabra and Shatila massacre, 215, 227n2
Sadat, Anwar, 214
Said, Edward, 10, 183
Samuel Rubin Foundation, 205, 213
Samuelson, Arthur, 195, 198, 202
Sartawi, Issam: assassination of, 214, 277n62; background, career, and views of, 205–6; Breira meeting with, 186, 208; ICIPP meetings with, 205, 206
Saturday Night Live, 150, 263n82
Sayegh, Fayez: 1956 booklet by, 91; about, 9–10, 117; AFME's support of, 117, 146, 159; AJC meeting with, 133–34, 224; on the AJC refugee initiative, 45; on Arab collaboration with known antisemites, 130; Arab League and, 111; on Arab minority issue, 91; "The Arab Plight in the Holy Land," 91; *Arab Property in Israeli-Controlled Territories*, 91; *Arab Unity: Hope and Fulfillment*, 118; at AUB, 117; Berger and, 118, 152, 158–60, 173, 224; career of, 145–46, 149; at the Center, 91, 118–19; on the Center, 145–46; with family, **119**, **150**; Fineberg on, 109, 112, 139–40, 146; at Georgetown University, 117; *The Palestinian Refugees*, 117; Peretz on, 131, 249n26; PLO and, 109; Raab's analysis of a speech by, 138–39; as a speaker for the Arab cause, 111, 119–20, 253–54n4; on *Tex and Jinx*, 132; UNGA 3379 and, 149–51, 223; on Zionism, 10, 149–50, 225; *Zionist Colonialism in Palestine*, 149
Sayigh, Yusif, 118, **119**, 256n17
Schechtman, Joseph: *The Arab Refugee Problem*, 35, 37; "Arab Refugees: Facts and Figures," 36–37; on Palestinian refugee issue, 35–38; "Resettlement Prospects for Arab Refugees," 36–37
Schiff, Jacob, 175

Second Intifada, 218
Second World Conference on Palestine, 191
Segal, Simon, 30, 51, 83, 93, 134
Sekaly, Rushdie, 32
Sephardic Jewry, 9, 20, 231n3
Serotta, Gerold, 195, 197–98, 215
Shaare Tzedek hospital, 174
Shahak, Israel, 182–83
Shaham, David, 188, 197, 202
Shaheen, Hani, 214
Sharett, Moshe: on Byroade speeches, 167; with Esther Herlitz, **45**; as Israeli foreign minister, 28–29, 36; letter to William Zukerman, 76
Shatila refugee camp, Lazaron's 1953 visit to, 1, 161–62
Shattan, Joseph, 211
Sheli Party, 213
Shertok, Moshe. *See* Sharett, Moshe
Sh'ma, 188, 200
Siach, 197
Siegel, Ellen, 215
Siegman, Henry, 261n62
Silver, Abba Hillel, 168, 267n28
Sinai Peninsula invasion and capture, Israel's, 48, 88, 153
Singer, Richard, 62
Six-Day War. *See* 1967 war
Skeist, Robert, 197
Slawson, John, **8**; 1957 Israeli visit by, 92–95; at AJC-Sayegh meeting, 133, 134; October 1957 speech by, 112, 137, 141; Peretz and, 44, 50; pro-Israeli orientation of, 46–47, 238n59
Smith, Gerald L. K., 125, 139, 258n34
SNCC Newsletter, 146–49
Solomonow, Allan, 182, 198, 270n58
Soviet Jewry movement, 178
Soviet Union, secular nationalist Arab regimes and, 149, 177
Spectator, 172
Stephens, Bret, 2–3

"Steps to Middle East Peace" (Peretz), 41–43
Stone, I. F., 205
Stroock, Alan, 103, 134
Student National Coordinating Committee (SNCC), 146–49, 262n74
Student Nonviolent Coordinating Committee (SNCC), 146–49, 262n74
Students for a Democratic Society (SDS), 192
Suez War, 49, 88, 145
Sulzberger, Arthur Ochs, 174
Sussman, Leonard, 178
Synagogue Council of America, 188
Syria: 1973 Yom Kippur War and, 200; persecution of Jews in, 50–51; refugee relief in, 233–34n24
Syrian Consulate General, 91
Syrian Social Nationalist Party, 117, 256n17
Szold, Henrietta, 20, 22, 231n4

Taft, Robert, 163
"Talking with the P.L.O." (Waskow), 209–10
Tarshiha, displacement of residents of, 31
Tel Aviv, AJC office in, 15, 79, 103–6
Teller, Judd, 87–88, 89, 248n22
Tex and Jinx, 111, 132, 135–37
Tfutsot Israel, 104
Third Arab Students Convention, 160
"Third World Round-Up—The Palestinian Problem" (SNCC), 146–47
Thomas, Norman, 51, 61–62, 239n67
Thompson, Dorothy, 82–83, 116, 117, 122, 159, 163
Tiberias, 10, 117, 150
Ticktin, Max, 186, 208, 209, 276n51
Time, 154–55
Times Change Press, 193

Times of London, 204
Tog, Der, 59, 63–64
"Toward Peace with the PLO" (Wolf), 200
travel restrictions for Palestinian Arabs, 4, 78, 92–95
Trenton Times article on AJC's work in Israel, 104–5
Truman, Harry, 12, 38, 163
Truman administration, 121, 159, 163–65, 222
Tulin, David, 199, 212
Tuma, Elias, 203
two-state solution, 10–11, 196, 200–201, 204, 205, 208, 273n23
Tzedek Tzedek, 195, 273n22

UN Partition Plan, 1947. See 1947 United Nations Partition Plan
UNESCO, 97
UNGA 3379, 109–10, 149–51, 204, 223, 253nn1–2
Unger, Jerome, 68–70
United Jewish Appeal (UJA), 141, 169
United Nations General Assembly (UNGA): Arafat's 1974 speech before, 204; Resolution 3379, 109–10, 149–51, 204, 223, 253nn1–2
United Nations Relief and Works Agency for Palestine Refugees in the Near East (UNRWA), 29
Uris, Leon, 144
U.S. House Committee on Un-American Activities, 83, 129, 184
"U.S. Jews Split on Mideast War: Some See Response in Nation as 'Hysteria' " (NYT), 174–76
U.S.-Egyptian ties, 120–22
U.S.-Israel relations, 14, 153–54, 177

Vietnam, 179, 181, 187, 211

Wallace, Mike, 120, 130–31, 257n23
Warburg, Felix, 175

wartime nationalism, 26

Washington Area Jews for an Israeli-Palestinian Peace, 215

Waskow, Arthur: at the 1977 Breira Conference, **210**; activism of, 196, 211; "Freedom Seder Hagadah," 211; PLO meeting including, 186, 208; "Talking with the P.L.O.," 209–10; Tzedek Tzedek and, 195

Weill, Milton, 134

Weiss, Peter, 208

Weizmann, Chaim, 96, 250n33

West Bank: Israel's post-1967 occupation of, 10, 180, 194; refugee relief in, 233–34n24

Whartman, Eliezer, 52

white Christian antisemites, 90–91, 112

"white ethnic revival," 185

Willen, Joseph, 46

Win, 190

Winrod, Gerald, 125, 126

Wise, Stephen, 21, 63, 114

WNYC radio town hall event, 113–14, 254n9

Wolf, Arnold, 196, 200–201, 209, 274n31

women in Jewish organizations, 215

women's movement, 192, 272n16

Workman's Circle, 62

World Jewish Congress, 114, 208

World Zionist Organization, 208

Yafeh, Adi, 51–52

Yagupsky, Maximo, 103–6, 252n55

Yaish Breira, 195

Yiddish press, 58–59, 64–65, 101–2, 241n8, 242n12

Yiddisher Kempfer, 101–2

Yiddishists, 220

Yom Kippur War, 200

Young Americans for Progressive Israel (YAPI), 192

Yozma, 195, 197

Zeineddine, Farid, 128

Zeltzer, Frieda, 59, 240n3

Zionism: about, 13; American Jewish, 75, 114, 156, 179, 194; Ben-Gurion on, 94–95; Berger on, 157, 161; Christian, 222; D. Thompson on, 116; Labor, 60, 181; Peretz on, 23–28, 232n6; Reform Jews on, 155; Revisionist, 60; Sayegh on, 10, 149–50, 225; Stephens on, 2–3; UNGA 3379 on, 109–10, 149–51; Zukerman on, 60–61

"Zionism is Racism" resolution, UN, 109–10, 149–51, 204, 223, 253nn1–2

Zionist Colonialism in Palestine (Sayegh), 149

Zionist Organization of America (ZOA), 74, 96, 225

Zipperstein, Steven, 195, 197

Zoll, Allen, 126

Zuckoff, Aviva. *See* Cantor, Aviva

Zukerman, William: on the AJC's Ben-Gurion meeting, 101–2; background and journalistic career of, 58–67, **62**, 240n1; death of, 76–77; Free Jewish Club and, 65–66; *The Impact of Israel on American Jews*, 73; Israeli diplomats' campaign against, 15, 56, 67–76, 245n31; *Jewish Newsletter* and, 14–15, 56–57, 61–63; in a letter to Berger, 71–72; "The Menace of Jewish Fascism," 60; on the Palestinian refugee issue, 9, 56, 64, 67, 72–73; Sharett in a letter to, 76; on Zionism, 60–61; Zionist critiques of, 66–70